TEWA TALES

TEWA TALES

Elsie Clews Parsons

With a New Foreword by Barbara A. Babcock

The University of Arizona Press / Tucson & London

The University of Arizona Press
Copyright © 1994
The Arizona Board of Regents
All rights reserved

Published by arrangement with the American Folklore Society
Tewa Tales was originally published in 1926 as volume 19 of the Memoirs of the American Folk-Lore Society.
Reprint copy of this book was provided by the Folklore Archives of the Department of Folklore and Folklife, University of Pennsylvania.

99 98 97 96 95 94   6 5 4 3 2 1

Library of Congress Cataloging-in-Publication Data

Parsons, Elsie Worthington Clews, 1875–1941.
    Tewa tales / Elsie Clews Parsons : with a new foreword by Barbara
A. Babcock.
        p.   cm.
    Originally published: New York : American Folk-Lore Society, 1926.
    "Originally published in 1926 as volume 19 of the Memoirs of the
American Folk-Lore Society"—T.p. verso.
    Includes bibliographical references.
    ISBN 0-8165-1452-6
    1. Tewa Indians—Legends.   2. Tewa Indians—Religion and
mythology.   I. Title.
E99.T35P37   1994   93-46970
398.2'089'974—dc20   CIP

British Cataloguing-in-Publication Data
A catalogue record for this book is available from the British Library.

CONTENTS

FOREWORD

Like many visitors to New Mexico, Elsie Clews Parsons first encountered the world of the Pueblo in the Tewa villages north of Santa Fe.[1] En route to the Grand Canyon in 1910 to meet her husband, Herbert, then a congressman and member of the House Committee on Public Lands, Parsons decided to visit the "cliff houses of New Mexico." She ended up exploring and excavating ruins on Clara True's ranch with a Tewa guide from Santa Clara Pueblo. As a result of that first experience, Parsons predicted:

> If ever I come to work seriously in this country, I suspect that it will not be as an archaeologist, but as a student of the culture of today. It is interesting to reconstruct the culture of the ancient town builders, but it is still more interesting to study the minds and ways of their descendents.[2]

In 1912 and 1913 she made extended ethnographic reconnaissance trips on horseback among the Rio Grande Pueblos, and in August 1915, at the age of forty-one, she began doing fieldwork in Zuni. That year she published the first of many essays in the *American Anthropologist* and presented her first paper on Zuni at the 19th Congress of Americanists, "Zuni Conception and Pregnancy Beliefs." This essay was the beginning of ninety published books, essays, notes, and reviews that culminated in *Pueblo Indian Religion* (2 vols., 1939). All were based on her field research among the Pueblos of Arizona and New Mexico between 1915 and 1927.

Feminist, sociologist, anthropologist, folklorist, wife, mother, socialite, and field-worker, Elsie Clews Parsons (1874–1941) is, in her own words, "perhaps unclassifiable." Franz Boas said that both her life and her work were "characterized by a strenuous revolt against convention" (1942:480).[3] Parsons was a regular contributor to *The Masses* and *The New Republic*, and in 1915, the same year that she began doing Pueblo ethnography, she also published twenty-seven notes, articles, and reviews on such feminist and pacifist subjects as "Marriage and the Will to Power" and "Anti-suffragists and the War," as well as *Social Freedom*, her fifth volume of feminist sociology.[4]

The following year, Parsons published no less than seven articles on Zuni, more than twice that number on feminist and pacifist issues, and her sixth and last feminist monograph, *Social Rule*. It was this pattern of scholarly productivity that led Pliny Earle Goddard to tease her that year about doing "research in the summer" and writing "propaganda in the winter." Alfred Kroeber joked about her "provocative books" and addressed her as "Dear Propagandist," but in response to one of her first essays on Zuni, he lamented: "I wish we could write *our* anthropology as well as you do."[5] Robert Lowie similarly taunted her, and finally in 1916 she wrote to him: "You, Kroeber, and Hocart make the life of a psychologist not worth living. I see plainly I shall have to keep to the straight and narrow path of kinship nomenclature and folktale collecting" (quoted in Hare 1985:135–39). As of 1920 her published scholarship consisted almost entirely of Pueblo ethnography and Afro-American folktales.

There is no doubt that Franz Boas and his male colleagues in anthropology influenced not only the shape and substance of Parsons' research but her discursive practices as well. Her unpublished works, however, reveal other important influences. World War I crushed Parsons' radical hopes for progress and reform and created ruptures within her family and her intellectual circle. Even after her husband enlisted and her friends deserted the cause, she persisted in her pacifism. Increasingly, however, her essays against the war were rejected. Between 1914 and 1921 no less than forty-five manuscripts dealing with feminist and pacifist subjects were "declined."[6] During the same time, all the fieldwork-based essays she submitted to folklore and anthropological journals were accepted for publication. In 1917 she wrote to Kroeber, "Life for a militant pacifist has been rather trying these past months and if I hadn't my Zuni notes to write up and no end of Negro folk tales to edit—I'd be worse off than I am" (quoted in Hare 1985:138).

Finally, personal factors influenced her turn to anthropological fieldwork in 1915. Several years before, Elsie had not only lost a child but had discovered a serious affair on her husband's part. Prior to beginning her field research, her response had been to take an increasing number of trips with other men. "The only alternative," she wrote to Herbert, "was staying home with you depressed and so repressed that I know that at any moment I might be very disagreeable in all sorts of unreasonable ways" (quoted in Hare 1985:126).

Already estranged, the war left them little common ground. Anthropology—with its combination of adventure, hard work, and a sense of mission—engaged Elsie emotionally as well as intellectually and physically, resolved a midlife crisis, and offered a legitimate escape. As Desley Deacon (1992:14) has also observed, "During those years, fieldwork provided the distance, the stimulus, the intellectual and physical rigor, and the supportive professional ties she needed to escape from the more conventional aspects of her life, helping her to rebuild her intellectual and personal life along what she considered more rational and ethical lines."

Between 1915 and 1927, Parsons frequently escaped to the Southwest, savoring both the beauty of the landscape and the alternative existence that anthropological research offered. "This cave room faced south," she wrote of one of the sites she visited, "and that night I looked out from its frame on the moonlit talus below and the pines beyond and thought that whether Indian or White one was fortunate indeed to live for a time in a world of such beauty."[7] Her mother, however, regarded the Southwestern transformation that began on this first night of camping in Pueblo cliff dwellings as "scandalous." Daughter Lissa described how her mother would return to New York "looking perfectly dreadful, a bandanna around her hair, and her disreputable saddlebags full of manuscripts" (quoted in Rosenberg 1982:168). Parsons' field notes, letters, and both published and unpublished essays all attest that she loved both the open spaces of the Southwest and the experience of being on "the edge of adventure."[8]

Parsons established unusually close friendships with her Pueblo hosts and hostesses, had her hair washed at Hopi in 1920, and cherished the gift of an Indian name (Yuyuhunnoma) and identity (1920:179 –80). In her obituary essay, Gladys Reichard recalled that

> [Parsons'] success with natives, hosts of whom count themselves her
> friends, was due to an innate simplicity. She used to say that her idea
> of complete comfort was to have *at the same time* a cigarette, a cup of
> coffee, and an open fire. And characteristically she added quietly,
> "You know it is very hard to get all three together. It is easier among
> Indians than among ourselves." (Reichard 1943:48)

When back on the East Coast, she corresponded with and sent gifts to her Pueblo friends, as well as reimbursing those who continued to do research for her. And, much to her mother's and daughter's dismay, even in New York City she persisted in adopting an early version of the "Santa Fe Style." In an interview in 1986, archaeologist Dorothy Keur recalled, "I still can see her coming to the seminars at Columbia, being driven by her chauffeur, getting out with a long fur coat and Indian beaded moccasins on her feet. She was a great character, really."[9]

In addition to sharing both domestic and discursive space with her Pueblo collaborators, Parsons also shared significant periods of fieldwork and publications with anthropologists Alfred Kroeber, Franz Boas, Esther Goldfrank, and Ralph Beals, and corresponded and shared materials with many others, notably Ruth Bunzel, Gladys Reichard, and Leslie White. Even when they were not literally co-authors, these other voices, Anglo and Indian, speak in the intertextuality of her prose, which she herself described as a mosaic (Reichard 1943:47). Parsons' style of writing, with page after page consisting largely of notes and countless references to other texts, including her own publications, reflects not only the thoroughness of her scholarship and her desire to leave as complete a record as possible for later scholars but also her belief that anthropology—especially Southwestern studies—should be a collaborative, comparative, and cooperative enterprise. It also revealed a belief, echoing the Pueblo worldview she studied, that everything she wrote about was connected to everything else she had written. As she self-critically observed many years later in the American Anthropological Association presidential address that she did not live to present, "I am scrambling a good many things together that you would expect me to keep separate" (1942:339).[10]

Because of her desire to encourage and coordinate as well as do research among Southwestern Native Americans, Parsons, with her New York anthropological colleagues, organized the Southwest Society in 1918. As she wrote to Clark Wissler at the beginning of that year,

> Research in the Southwest is being done in a desultory, individualistic fashion, although the workers in that field or certain of them are convinced that what is most needed is intensive, comparative study. Such study will be possible only through some plan of cooperative work and a general research program. (Quoted in Deacon 1992:28)

Eleven months later, Parsons' plan was formally realized, as described in the following minutes:

> The Southwest Society was organized on November 25th at a lunch club made up of members of the American Museum of Natural History, the Museum of the American Indian, and Columbia University. Dr. Goddard was chosen temporary chairman, and Dr. Parsons temporary Secretary-Treasurer. Dr. Boas, Dr. Hodge and Dr. Parsons were appointed a committee to draw up a Constitution. (Quoted in Zumwalt 1992:270–71)

In the constitution that Parson published in 1919, the stated purpose of the society was "to promote inquiries into the culture of the peoples of the Southwest through field-work undertaken independently or, whenever possible, in cooperation with other institutions; and to arrange for the publication of the material collected" (quoted in Zumwalt 1992:271). Over the next thirty years, Parsons put thousands of dollars into the society's treasury to underwrite the fieldwork and publications of numerous anthropologists, notably Boas and his female students. Without her considerable support, neither the American Folklore Society nor the *Journal of American Folklore* would have survived the 1930s.

After working in the Western Pueblos herself for seven years, Parsons turned her attention to the communities of the Rio Grande Tewa in November 1923. In the preface to *The Social Organization of the Tewa* (1929:7), she described her reasons for doing so:

Of all the more visited Pueblo peoples the Tewa have been the least systematically described. . . . As no publication was in prospect and no material available even in manuscript, and as we had reached a point in our general survey of the social organization of the Pueblo Indians where more knowledge of the Tewa was indispensable for coordination and interpretation, I undertook in November, 1923, the unwelcome task of duplicating research among a people who are past masters in the art of defeating inquiry.

She also described her method of working during the three years when she collected the narratives published in *Tewa Tales* (1926a): [11]

Imitating the secretiveness observed in all the Rio Grande pueblos, I settled in Alcalde, the Mexican town two or three miles north of San Juan, and, here, thanks to my helpful and understanding hosts of San Gabriel ranch, I secured informants from San Juan, Santa Clara, and San Ildefonso. My informants worked singly or in couples, niece and uncle, sister and brother, mother and daughter, one interpreting for the other. (1929:7)

In her first letter to Herbert from Alcalde, she was rather more candid:

A dude ranch indeed, and I stick to it. My informants are brought out from the pueblo, two and one-half miles away, and this week I have cleaned out one woman and last night started with her as interpreter for her uncle, one of the ceremonialists of this town. He told two beautiful tales, one my pet White Buffalo or Escape up the Tree. These from San Juan. Today I hope to get somebody from Santa Clara. It is a good technique, I think, to work like this away from the towns. [12]

The following year, she published three essays based on this initial Tewa research: "Tewa Kin, Clan and Moiety" (1924a), "The Religion of the Pueblo Indians" (1924b), and "Tewa Mothers and Children" (1924c). The first two follow her agenda of making comparisons throughout the Pueblos in terms of religion and social and ceremonial organization. Leslie Spier described "Tewa Kin" as a landmark, "the first definitive statement of a basic plan, the alignment of elements between polar extremes of west and east" (1943:247–48).

"Tewa Mothers and Children" is the last of a series of essays on the Pueblo construction of gender and maternity that Parsons wrote during her first decade of research. Beginning at Zuni, Parsons established close relationships with women and collected material on mothers and children and on the pragmatic and symbolic aspects of reproduction. [13] In addition to these essays, which deal explicitly with mothers and children (collected in Babcock, ed. 1991), Parsons gave specific attention to female sexuality, reproduction, and sex roles in each of her Pueblo monographs. No less than thirty pages of *The Social Organization of the Tewa* (1929) is devoted to these concerns. Similarly, in her collections of Pueblo folktales she focuses on courtship and marriage customs, as in the introduction to *Tewa Tales* (1926a), where she compares the Tewa of the Rio Grande and the Hopi-Tewa of First Mesa, among whom she had worked in 1920 and 1921 (1926a: 2–3).

While this "maternalist" preoccupation with other ways of being female is explicitly expressed only in the notes to her later ethnological writings, Parsons never forgot that she was both a woman and a feminist. Her gender and her politics shaped not only the substance but also the style of her anthropology, influencing what she studied, whom she talked to, and how she wrote about it in both published and unpublished contexts. For example, in discussing the influence of the anthropologist's interests on the nature of the tales told by Pueblo narrators, Parsons recalled that "wedding minutiae would get into almost every tale of the First Mesa narrator who knew I was interested in Hopi weddings" (1937:109).

All the Hopi-Tewa tales in Part II of this volume were told by another First Mesa narrator, "a Tewa Bear clansman married at Sichumovi" (1926a: 6).[14] The narratives show "a surprising range of variation," however, depending on when they were collected by Parsons or recorded by Ruth Bunzel several years later. Although these Tewa migrants had lived hundreds of miles from the Rio Grande for over a century when Parsons collected their stories in 1920, "their language," she wrote, "is still Tanoan; the scene of many of their folk-tales is laid, not at one or another of the ruins of the surrounding country, like the scene of Hopi tales, but at *kunlyukyut'ee*, which is also a place name in several tales told by the Tewa of New Mexico" (1926b:209). In *Tewa Tales* she identified *kunlyukyut'ee* as "the underworld place where the Tewa lived before the emergence" (1926a:7).

While Parsons does not focus on the context and circumstances of storytelling in the way that more recent folk narrative scholarship has, it is nonetheless significant in this period of collecting that she remarks on the ways that the collector, her interests, and her relationship with the narrator influenced the stories her narrators told. Still, her primary concern in this and other folktale collections was with the stories themselves, for she did not hesitate to collect stories wherever she could and did not seem concerned that many of these tales are not told in the landscape and community of which they are a part. At the same time, she was, as her introduction to *Tewa Tales* indicates, sensitive to the importance of localization within the stories themselves and to the seasonal prohibition against telling stories in the summer, when "the snakes are stirring" (1926a:8).

Parsons did, however, comment at length on the variation created by the individual storyteller (1926a:5) and insisted on including all the variants, much to the dismay of her publisher. *Tewa Tales* consists of more than a hundred tales and variants collected from seven Rio Grande Tewa informants, in addition to the Hopi-Tewa man. Most of these texts were recorded from a San Juan uncle and niece, and a Santa Clara brother and sister. A few were provided by two San Ildefonso informants and another from San Juan. She does not, however, indicate a particular informant for the fragments from Tesuque published here as variants, and stories she collected later at Nambe were published as an appendix to *The Social Organization of the Tewa*. None of the informants is identified except by number, "names being withheld in consideration of the story tellers" she tells us in a note, because "storytelling is not always a harmless pastime in the Southwest" (1926a:6). Here, of course, she is referring to the patterns of secrecy that have developed among the Rio Grande pueblos and the widespread prohibition against "spilling the beans" to outsiders. Her awareness that her informants might be punished for sharing their culture with her led her to modify her fieldwork methods and to maintain anonymity in publication but not to give up the anthropological enterprise, for, as Rosemary Zumwalt has observed, "Parsons' tenacity in gathering the esoteric secrets of the Pueblo Indians and her insistence on publishing sensitive material were linked to her idea of science. For her, only a complete account would provide the substance for future study" (1992:256).[15] When she collected these Pueblo stories, her unrealized goal was nothing less than a complete comparative concordance for Southwestern mythology, which she refers to at the end of the introduction.

The principal narrator of Tewa tales, and presumably the source for much of the other Tewa material she published, was "Informant 1 of San Juan." The first ten stories and more than a third of the total in this volume were collected from him with the assistance of his niece. In her introduction Parsons describes them as follows:

> My San Juan informants were uncle and niece. The woman interpreted for the man, who was also the source of all the stories she told independently. . . . The San Juan uncle, a man of about sixty, and a member of the hierarchy, was a highly accomplished narrator, the most accomplished I happen to have met in any pueblo. Not merely was his memory excellent and his general intelligence high, but he was an artist, truly a great artist, with feeling for values, humorous and dramatic, yet using with fidelity as well as with resourcefulness the patterns of his narrative art and of his daily life. (1926:5–6)

Both the last sentence and a similar description of this informant in the preface to *The Social Organization of the Tewa* reveal the extent to which Parsons and other Boasians regarded and relied on folktales as a native commentary on native life. As she remarks of Hopi studies in the introduction to *A Pueblo Indian Journal* (1925:6), the chronicle of Hopi-Tewa life kept by her Sichumovi informant, "In all this volume of record, for all the towns, there is one striking gap: there is little or no record of the life of the people from within, so to speak. For such, ethnologists have come to rely largely upon texts of folk-tales and narratives of daily or ceremonial life."

One has only to look at any of Parsons' publications to realize the extent to which Pueblo stories provided primary or corroborating data. Both the text and notes of *The Social Organization of the Tewa*, for example, are filled with references to Tewa folktales, and frequently entire texts are reprinted, as in her 1927 essay on witchcraft. Unfortunately, the reverse is not the case, since the stories in *Tewa Tales* were recorded and published at the beginning of her fieldwork and she regarded them as the database for subsequent discussions of Tewa culture. "Emergence myth and pre-historic migration myth are *their history*," she wrote (1926a:2).

The organization of the stories in this volume as Part I, "Tewa of New Mexico," and Part II, "Tewa of Arizona," and then within each of these divisions into "Emergence and Migration Tales," and "Animal," and "Novelistic Tales" does not reflect indigenous categories so much as Parsons' interest in diffusion and acculturation. Stories, she said elsewhere, were "great travellers," and in "passing from people to people changes [were] made" in the tales that might cast light on the "differences in life between the two peoples" (quoted in Zumwalt 1992:197). For example, the "passing out" of corn grinding in the New Mexico pueblos and the "few references to grinding" in the New Mexico tales was, she suggested, "an instance, perhaps, of how quickly a change in the daily life may be expressed in the folktale" (1926a:3). She was particularly interested in the impact of Spanish culture on the Pueblo and in the fact that "in their folk-tales as in their ritual and daily life the Pueblos have drawn much from their Mexican neighbors" (1926a:3). This influence is reflected in the separation Parsons maintains in this collection between myth and tale because, as she notes elsewhere, "in Pueblo Indian opinion, there is no distinction" (1925:31). Whether marked as Mexican or not, Parsons regarded most animal and novelistic tales as being of Spanish provenience, and she focuses here as elsewhere on "tale stratigraphy" and "enigmas of acculturation."[16] Unlike many of her fellow anthropologists—who were preoccupied then as now with issues of cultural integrity, authenticity, and originality—Parsons had a "passion for cultural overlays" and embraced hybridity (quoted in Zumwalt 1992:210). As Kroeber revealingly observed when he wrote to her in the fall of 1923, "You . . . are enough of an individualist to be at bottom a bit anticultural, and when two civilizations get tangled and fuse their patterns perceptibly, it gives you a bit of satisfaction at the break-up of the patterns, as I feel shock" (quoted in Zumwalt 1992:210).

In many ways, Parsons wrote her own best introduction to this and to her other collections of Native American and Afro-American folktales in a talk she delivered at the Hampton Institute. She argued that it is important to collect tales because "knowledge of old stories contributes to knowledge of civilization and to the history of the human mind"; because tales reveal the life of the people and indigenous "ways of thinking and feeling"; because in the absence of writing, tales are history; because they provide a record of language and dialects; and because storytelling was an art that contributes to the enrichment of American culture (quoted in Zumwalt 1992:205). Here, just as surely as in her feminist sociology, she was arguing for social equality, for "she was recording the voices of those who had for so long gone unheeded" and was according "the tellers of tales . . . the respect due to a creator of something beautiful" (Zumwalt 1992:206). What she said about Joel Chandler Harris (1919:493) applies equally to Parsons herself: "Arrogance or condescension stand in the way of story telling. . . . It takes something of an artist to listen to a folk-tale as well as to tell it, and between artists theories of social inequality do not obtrude."

Barbara A. Babcock
Regents Professor and Director
Comparative Cultural and Literary Studies
University of Arizona

NOTES

1. This foreword is based on my previous research and publications concerning Parsons, especially Babcock 1988 and 1991.

2. Parsons made this remark in her unpublished account of visiting New Mexico and the Pueblo people for the first time. "The Accident of the Forester" is the first chapter of "In the Southwest," a collection of personal essays about her Southwest fieldwork that she never published and that I am editing for publication. This manuscript is with Parsons' papers in the American Philosophical Society Library in Philadelphia.

3. For discussions of Parsons' life and work, ranging from obituaries and short biographical dictionary entries to full-length biographies, see Babcock 1987, 1988, 1991; Boas 1942a, 1942b; Bunzel 1960; Deacon 1992; Friedlander 1988; Hare 1985; Hieb 1986; Kroeber 1943; Lamphere 1989; Lurie 1966, 1968; Reichard 1943; Rosenberg 1982; Spier 1943; White 1973; and Zumwalt 1992.

4. In addition to the unpublished manuscripts listed in the bibliography, see Parsons 1906, 1913a, 1913b, 1916.

5. A. Kroeber to E. Parsons Jan. 13, 1916. Letters cited in this manner refer to correspondence in the Elsie Clews Parsons papers in the American Philosophical Society Library (hereafter abbreviated APS) and are cited with its permission.

6. Among Parsons' papers at APS is an index card file of all the essays she submitted for publication between 1914 and 1921. For each entry there is a "date" and a "fate" column. For more on Parsons' turn to anthropology, and the mistaken characterization of her work as, for example, "before and after Boas" and "feminism vs. science," see Babcock 1988, 1991.

7. "In the Southwest," APS.

8. Parsons used this phrase in a letter to her son John describing a horseback trip, similar to those in the Southwest, that she made in Haiti in 1912; ECP to John E. Parsons, Feb. 29, 1912.

9. Interview with Dorothy Keur by Jennifer Fox for Daughters of the Desert

research project, funded by the Wenner-Gren Foundation and archived at the Arizona State Museum, University of Arizona.

10. For more on the polyphonic pastiche of Parsons' texts, her shifting and reflexive subject position, and her questioning of ethnographic authority, see Babcock 1988, 1991. For a discussion of issues of gender and ethnographic authority, see Gordon 1986.

11. In addition to the Tewa Pueblos, Parsons collected and published folktales from all the pueblos she worked in. At the same time, she continued to collect and publish Afro-American folklore. For a discussion of Parsons' folklore scholarship, see Zumwalt 1992, chap. 9.

12. ECP to H. Parsons, Nov. 17, 1923.

13. For further discussion of Parsons and the Pueblo construction of gender, see Babcock 1991.

14. This is Crow-wing, who kept the journal that Parsons edited and published in 1925. In her introduction she described him as "enough of a traveller and observer of disparate cultures to understand the interests of the ethnologist, enough of an Indian to respect the town life and to acquire and cherish knowledge of ceremony. In other words he belongs to that choice class of informants, middle-aged men for the most part, who are 'Americanized' sufficiently for ethnological work, and who appreciate, without disclaiming, their own culture" (1925:7).

15. For more on the consequences of Parsons' Pueblo research and publications, particularly the controversy, pain, and unhappiness caused by her studies of Jemez and Taos, see Zumwalt 1992, chap. 11.

16. For more recent discussion of the Tewa of Arizona and New Mexico and of the issue of acculturation by anthropologists who are themselves Tewa, see Dozier 1966 and 1970, and Ortiz 1969 and 1979.

BIBLIOGRAPHY

Babcock, Barbara A.
    1987   Taking Liberties, Writing from the Margins, and Doing It with a Difference. *Journal of American Folklore* 100:398, 390–411.
    1988   "Not Yet Classified, Perhaps Not Classifiable": Elsie Clews Parsons, Feminist/Anthropologist. Paper presented at the American Anthropological Association Meetings, November 16.
    1991   Elsie Clews Parsons and the Pueblo Construction of Gender. Introduction to Babcock, ed. 1991:1–23.

Babcock, Barbara A., ed.
    1991   *Pueblo Mothers and Children: Essays by Elsie Clews Parsons, 1915–1924.* Santa Fe: Ancient City Press.

Babcock, Barbara, and Nancy J. Parezo
    1988   *Daughters of the Desert: Women Anthropologists and the Native American Southwest, 1880–1980.* Albuquerque: University of New Mexico Press.

Boas, Franz
    1942A   Elsie Clews Parsons. *Scientific Monthly* 54:480–82.
    1942b   Elsie Clews Parsons. *Science* 95 (no. 2456): 89–90.

Bunzel, Ruth L.
  1960   Elsie Clews Parsons, 1875–1941. In Margaret Mead and Ruth Bunzel, eds., *The Golden Age of American Anthropology*, 546–47. New York: George Braziller.

Deacon, Desley
  1992   The Republic of the Spirit: Fieldwork in Elsie Clews Parsons' Turn to Anthropology. *Frontiers* 12 (3):12–38.

Dorson, Richard M.
  1974   Elsie Clews Parsons: Feminist and Folklorist. *Folklore Feminists Communications* 2 (4):22–25.

Dozier, Edward
  1966   *Hano: A Tewa Community in Arizona*. New York: Holt, Rinehart and Winston.
  1970   *The Pueblo Indians of North America*. New York: Holt, Rinehart and Winston.

Friedlander, Judith
  1988   Elsie Clews Parsons. In Ute Gacs, Aisha Khan, Jerrie McIntyre, and Ruth Weinberg, eds., *Women Anthropologists: A Biographical Dictionary*, 282–90. New York: Greenwood Press.

Gordon, Deborah
  1986   Among Women: Gender and Ethnographic Authority in the Southwest, 1930–1980. Paper prepared for the Daughters of the Desert Symposium, Wenner-Gren Foundation, March 12–23, Tucson, Ariz.

Hare, Peter H.
  1985   *A Woman's Quest for Science: Portrait of Anthropologist Elsie Clews Parsons*. Buffalo, N.Y.: Prometheus Books.

Hieb, Louis
  1986   Elsie Clews Parsons in the Southwest. Paper prepared for the Daughters of the Desert Symposium, Wenner-Gren Foundation, March 12–23, Tucson, Ariz.

Kroeber, Alfred L.
  1943   Elsie Clews Parsons. *American Anthropologist* 45:252–55.

Lamphere, Louise
  1989   Feminist Anthropology: The Legacy of Elsie Clews Parsons. *American Ethnologist* 16:518–33.

Lurie, Nancy
  1966   Women in Early American Anthropology. In June Helm, ed., *Pioneers of American Anthropology*, 29–81. Seattle: University of Washington Press.
  1968   Elsie Clews Parsons. *International Encyclopedia of the Social Sciences* 11:426–28.

Ortiz, Alfonso
  1969   *The Tewa World: Space, Time, Being, and Becoming in a Pueblo Society*. Chicago: University of Chicago Press.

Ortiz, Alfonso, ed.
  1979   *Handbook of North American Indians*. Vol. 9: *Southwest*. Washington, D.C.: Smithsonian Institution Press.

Parsons, Elsie Clews
    n.d.   Correspondence. American Philosophical Society.
    n.d.   Journal of a Feminist. Manuscript. American Philosophical Society.
    n.d.   In the Southwest. Manuscript. American Philosophical Society. (Being
              edited for publication by Barbara A. Babcock; forthcoming from the
              University of New Mexico Press)
    n.d.   The World Changes. Unpublished fragment. American Philosophical
              Society.
    1906   *The Family.* New York: G. P. Putnam's Sons.
    1913a   *The Old-Fashioned Woman: Primitive Fancies About the Sex.* New York:
              G. P. Putnam's Sons.
    1913b   *Religious Chastity: An Ethnological Study.* New York: Macaulay Co. (Pub-
              lished under the pseudonym John Main)
    1916   *Social Rule.* New York: G. P. Putnam's Sons.
    1919   Joel Chandler Harris and Negro Folklore. *The Dial* 66:491–93.
    1920   A Hopi Ceremonial. *Century* 101:177–80.
    1924a   Tewa Kin, Clan and Moiety. *American Anthropologist* 26:333–39.
    1924b   The Religion of the Pueblo Indians. *Proceedings of the Twenty-first Interna-
              tional Congress of Americanists,* 140–48.
    1924c   Tewa Mothers and Children. *Man* 112:148–51. (Reprinted in Babcock,
              ed. 1991:132–40)
    1925   *A Pueblo Indian Journal, 1920–1921.* Introduction and notes by Elsie
              Clews Parsons. Memoirs of the American Anthropological Association,
              no. 32. Menasha, Wis.: American Anthropological Association.
    1926a   *Tewa Tales.* Memoirs of the American Folklore Society, no. 19. New
              York: G. E. Stechert and Co.
    1926b   The Ceremonial Calendar of the Tewa of Arizona. *American Anthropolo-
              gist* 28:209–29.
    1926c   Cérémonial Tewa au Nouveau Méxique et en Arizona. *Journal de la
              Société des Américanistes de Paris* 18:9–14.
    1927   Witchcraft Among the Pueblos: Indian or Spanish? *Man* 27:106–12,
              125–28.
    1929   *The Social Organization of the Tewa in New Mexico.* Memoirs of the Ameri-
              can Anthropological Association, no. 36. Menasha, Wis.: American
              Anthropological Association.
    1937   *Review of Zuni Mythology,* by Ruth Benedict, and *Zuni Texts,* by Ruth
              Bunzel. *Journal of American Folklore* 50:107–9.
    1939   *Pueblo Indian Religion.* 2 vols. Chicago: University of Chicago Press.
    1942   Anthropology and Prediction. *American Anthropologist* 44:337–44.
Reichard, Gladys
    1943   Elsie Clews Parsons. *Journal of American Folklore* 56:45–48.
Rosenberg, Rosalind
    1982   *Beyond Separate Spheres: Intellectual Roots of Modern Feminism.* New Haven:
              Yale University Press.
Spier, Leslie
    1943   Elsie Clews Parsons. *American Anthropologist* 45:244–51.

White, Leslie
1973   Elsie Clews Parsons. In Edward T. James, ed., *Dictionary of American Biography*, Supplement 3 (1941–45), 581–82. New York: Charles Scribner's Sons.
Zumwalt, Rosemary Levy
1992   *Wealth and Rebellion: Elsie Clews Parsons, Anthropologist and Folklorist.* Urbana: University of Illinois Press.

TEWA TALES

INTRODUCTION

Over two hundred years ago there was a Tewa migration from New Mexico into Arizona, and on First Mesa, a new Tewa town was built, Hano, or, as its inhabitants prefer to call it, Tewa. The Tewa of today say that their forebears were invited over by the Hopi to serve as a bulwark against raiding hostile tribes. [1] That this is more than legend, or, rather, is legend which is acted upon, appears strikingly in a note entered in the journal kept for me by a Tewa of First Mesa during the year 1920-21. [2] After writing that meetings are being held in order to fill an office within the Snake clan, the incumbent having gone blind, the journalist states that Tewa men have been sent for to attend the meetings because they are the "watchers", i.e. guards, or, in New Mexican phrase, war captains, for the Snake clan. "If anything goes wrong with the Snake clan people, the Tewa people have to settle it. " Therefore the Tewa go to the meeting and listen. "At last we Tewa people say that we want to have the same man keep on till the end of his life because he is the only good man, even if he is blind. " The day following the meeting the journalist records : " All the Hopi men are very glad that we did not put anybody else in the place. ... If danger comes, we Tewa people have to go first. We are watchers for the Snake clan. And if ever the Snake clan people do wrong, we make them behave. " This predication by the Tewa of warrior–police function in relation to the Hopi Snake clan is the more striking when we recall that the Snake clan or rather society was formerly, there is little doubt, a war society. Tewa warriors were advance guard for Hopi warriors.

The ceremonial relations in general between Tewa and Hopi are fairly close. There is an independent Tewa ceremonial organization which preserves pre-migration Tewa features, although showing

---

1. See pp. 175-177.
2. Parsons 6 : 116.

Hopi influence; but Tewa individuals may belong to Hopi ceremonies and Tewa men married into Walpi or Sichumovi frequent Hopi kivas. Tewa men and women are bilingual; but Tewa is not spoken by the Hopi, for a very good reason, say the Tewa. Did they not bury their language, when they first came, in a deep hole, with spittle and prayer feathers? Once when I was telling a San Juan man of how the Hopi had found Tewa too difficult ever to learn, although Hopi and Tewa houses were within a stone's throw and Hopi and Tewa intermingled constantly, this Tewa of New Mexico gave the same explanation of this linguistic oddity.

How their departed tribesmen had protected their language was known to the New Mexican Tewa, but other experiences of those who had left them were not known. There is no migration tale about them, nor can they themselves give any account of from what Tewa pueblo they split off or what was the cause. (The Hopi invitation was not, we may be sure, the motivating cause.) And, as we shall see, the migration tale told as an alternative to the tale of the Hopi invitation and described as of equal validity is quite classifiable with their other myths. Nor can they give account of changes in their customs since their arrival on First Mesa. These lacks or obscurities in tradition go to support other evidences that in what we call history the Pueblo Indians are very little interested; emergence myth and pre-historic migration myth are *their history*, fully satisfying their sense of the historic.

Something of what has happened to the Tewa emigrants, however, during the past two centuries may be learned from a comparison of the following folk tales from the two divisions of the tribe, as well as what during that period has been happening in the life of the home-staying Tewa. Take courtship and wedding customs. In the joint tales courtship is a simple affair, the meeting is very casual, the boy looks in through the window (Arizona), [1] or there is play in the field, or converse at the spring, and either the boy returns with the girl or girls [2] to their house to spend the night, or the girl takes a basket of meal to his house. There is probably little doubt that such suit by the girl was an ancient Pueblo practice. Today there is much visiting by relatives whose formal consent to the marriage is in order, both in New Mexico and Arizona; but this does not come into the New Mexico tales at all (I take it that this family consultation has been derived from the Spanish-speaking neighbors), whereas

1. There is no mention of this practice at all in the New Mexico tales.
2. In view of the strict monogamy of the Pueblos this pattern of marrying two sisters which runs throughout Pueblo tales is a curiosity such as it would not be in Navaho tales, where marriage with two sisters is one of the favored forms of marriage. See Robbins, Harrington, Freire-Marreco, 86.

in the Arizona tales not only is the family council alluded to, but a very elaborate wedding ceremonial will be described at length, a ceremonial which we recognize as Hopi. The Tewa of First Mesa do in fact follow the wedding ceremonial of their neighbors.

In wedding ceremonial on First Mesa, corn grinding figures conspicuously, as well as in the daily life. This is so, too, in the Arizona tales. Now in the New Mexican pueblos grinding is passing out — corn is taken to the mill or ground in a coffee mill — the metates are being removed from the floors, and the daily life of woman is thereby transformed. In the New Mexican tales there are few references to grinding, an instance here, perhaps, of how quickly a change in the daily life may be expressed in the folk tale.

In the Arizona tales racing figures conspicuously, as it does in the life of First Mesa. Racing of the relay type occurs among the Northern Tewa, but only once a year; in the tales there is no reference to racing. First Mesa racing is engaged in by the kachina, and in the tales the kachina race, too. The kachina cult is highly developed on First Mesa, and the kachina figure in the tales. They figure far less in the New Mexican tales, just as the kachina cult among the Northern Tewa is very meagre. At San Juan there is said to be but one kachina dance during the year. Inferably in respect to the kachina cult as in that of racing, the First Mesa tales express Hopi influence.

Of the eighteen Arizona tales nine, in whole or in part (Tales 5, 10, 16, 19, 21, 24, 27, 28, 30) are paralleled in the New Mexican tales. But a still larger measure of parallelism will appear if we consider such characteristic incidents or features as : the helpfulness of Spider old woman and her possession of medicine; the test or trial by smoking; the outcast situation of the boy of the story; creating life magically under a blanket; showing the boy about game animals by marking their tracks; the magically rapid growth of the story child; Coyote beguiling girls into marriage; the girl rejecting her suitors, in one case, — a very striking little parallel here between the Santa Clara tale and the First Mesa tale, — because of the jar included in the gifts of courtship : all these incidents or features are constructive elements in the tales, and having these elements in common gives the tales a family resemblance independently of specific plot.

The incident of rejecting suitors is one of those baffling tale elements in Pueblo folklore which is both Indian and Spanish. In their folk tales as in their ritual and daily life the Pueblos have drawn much from their Mexican neighbors. The Pueblo novelistic type of tale, distinctive in Indian folklore, has certainly been influenced by, it may have developed from, the Hispanic or European type of "fairy tale". In most cases the content of this Pueblo type is wholly Pueblo or Indian, but now and again, indubitable incidents from Spanish folklore are introduced, and there are many Spanish tales transposed bodily into Pueblo setting. This transposition has occurred, as might be expected, at different periods, that is, there is an older stratum of acculturated tale and a more recent. Of course it must be borne in mind that in such tale stratigraphy the reckoning may be far from chronological, depending not merely on the date when the Spanish tale was taken over, but on the integrity of the native culture. A Spanish tale might be introduced today into Zuñi folklore and have the same acultural cast, or very nearly, as one introduced one hundred years, even two hundred years, ago, shall we say, into the folklore of one of the Eastern pueblos. This might be true likewise of Spanish tales introduced today on First Mesa. And yet all the Spanish tales recorded in Part II, Tales 21 (False Message), 24, 25, 27, 28 are, I think, of the older stratum; they are tales that were carried from New Mexico.

In Part I, the older Spanish tale stratum is represented, I sugges , among the novelistic tales, by tales 35-37, 39 ; among the animal tales, by tales 61-69, although some of these may well have been acquired comparatively recently. Indubitably recently acquired tales are tales 38, 40-44. Tale 38, the familiar Spanish tale of Missing Tongues, and the variant in tale 39 afford an interesting illustration of the difference between the recently acquired tale and the tale acquired long enough ago to be well worked into the native lore. Tale 42, The Three Bears, is, I think, of recent borrowing, but the narrator, an artist and imbued with the native culture, seems to me to have already fitted the tale in to his Pueblo culture with the admonition, " Whenever you see a bear, do not kill it. " I confess the speculation is finely drawn.

In many cases tales from the older or more thoroughly acculturated stratum are enigmatic, so thoroughly blended are the two cultural elements, Pueblo and Spanish, that analysis is extremely difficult, if not impossible. As usual in such cases of blending, only through a richer material of variants can analysis proceed, each new variant supplying, so to speak, a bit of connective tissue. The following collection of tales is distinctly valuable, I think, from this point of view. In particular I have in mind the elusive folklore about the so-called Pueblo culture-hero, Poshaiyanki (Zuñi-Laguna) or Poseyemu (Tewa), who has been more or less identifiable with Montezuma or Jesus or the war gods. In old Mexico, God the father and God the son were identified with Sun and Morning Star. In Pueblo myth there are traces of a like identification, through the war god or gods, the two little boys, Ahayuta achi of Zuñi, the Towae of the Tewa. These two were conceived magically, begotten by Sun whom they journey to search for in the sky. Cast away, unfathered, and at first abused of boys and men, these two in the end triumph and put to shame their persecutors. These two, or the one they vaguely merge into, are identified with Morning Star. That Jesus was identified with these little boys when he was first heard about from the Franciscan Friars I long since surmised. Now the Tewan tale of Poseyemu as recorded at San Juan supplies evidence of that identification, at least a few links of evidence. Poseyemu was begot by World Man, magically by piñon. He was treated badly by his people, even after he was recognized by his father, World Man, given a name and finely arrayed. However, with Pontius Pilate, his enemies say, " We did not find anything bad in him. " He predicts coming events, and then he leaves his people, " that Montezuma, " as he is now called, going to the South and saying that some time he will come back to restore his people to their own.

That the tale of Escape up the Tree was European we have had little or no doubt since its Negro-Indian distribution from the Southeast to the Northwest was worked out. [1] However the long, very Indian-seeming story as it is told at Zuñi is so different in its elaboration from the story told by several other tribes that links between are most welcome. Such a link is the San Juan version. But what of The Woman Stealer of Santa Clara (Pt. I, Tale 34) and of First Mesa (Pt. II, Tale 10)? Are we to see in it a variant of Escape up the Tree, or the original Pueblo tale which made it easy to take over the Spanish tale? In the first hypothesis, to which I incline, the Santa Clara-First Mesa tale belongs to an earlier stratification, a more thorough adaptation, and the Zuñi-San Juan tale is later or less adapted.

In Pueblo witchcraft belief and throughout Pueblo folk tales is expressed the idea that the animals or birds have but to take off their skin to become human. This belief seems as native as any I know. And yet it is also a belief of European witch-lore, occurring also in European folk tales. In these Tewan tales it is interesting to find the incident occurring in the European tales of The Duck Girls and The King's Son Becomes a Deer, as well as in the Pueblo tale of The Witch Wife, if that tale is of Pueblo origin. The witch meetings sound strangely European.

In contrast to those enigmas of acculturation there are in the collection Amazon tales of women going to war, which have very obviously separate sources, and show no acculturation at all. They are a good instance of how the same general idea may be expressed so dissimilarly that there is no suspicion of common origin.

In the collection, variation of still another type may be noted, that of the individual story-teller. My San Juan informants were uncle and niece. [2] The woman interpreted for the man, who was also the

1. Parsons 1.
2. They will be referred to as Informant 1 of San Juan and Informant 2 of San

source of all the stories she told independently. Therefore where the same story was told by both, the differences may be fairly put down to individual variation.

The San Juan uncle, a man of about sixty, and a member of the hierarchy, was a highly accomplished narrator, the most accomplished I happen to have met in any pueblo. Not merely was his memory excellent and his general intelligence high, but he was an artist, truly a great artist, with feeling for values, humorous and dramatic, yet using with fidelity as well as with resourcefulness the patterns of his narrative art and of his daily life. His sister's daughter, a woman of forty, was a good interpreter, knowing enough English for clear and full statement, and yet not too much to mislead her into paraphrasing and dressing up, vernacularly. The Santa Clara narrators were a middle-aged brother and sister,[1] both more Americanized than the San Juan narrators and consequently more reticent in ritualistic references, but they were passable story-tellers, the brother at least, and to him in particular are due the more recently borrowed Spanish tales, heard by him in Tesuque. My own Tesuque informant, a man whose daughter interpreted for him, was not a competent narrator, so that with two exceptions, his brief tales are grouped as fragments or variants. The narrators from San Ildefonso were by far the least satisfactory. The man was unscrupulous and lazy, the woman, for whom a young daughter interpreted very badly, was extremely timid; so that the San Ildefonso contribution is scanty and incoherent. I include it merely for the sake of minor points of comparison. The First Mesa tales (*pe'yuh*) were told in English by a Tewa Bear clansman married at Sichumovi. Some of them he heard from his mother at Hano[2] or Tewa. His mother was a good story-teller, he says, but as a rule the men are far better narrators, he thinks, than the women. As at Zuñi and at Jemez, men get practice telling the tales in the kiva. In narrating in English the Tewan was quite carefully translating, as he related, sentence by sentence; the repetitious character of the narrative is in evidence. His narrative style is very similar, as far as I can appreciate, to the style of the New Mexican narrators, and similar, I may add, to Zuñi narrative.[3] All of which differs from the more prolix style of Keresan narrative,

Juan. The other informants will be similarly referred to Informant 3 of Santa Clara, etc., names being withheld in consideration of the story tellers; story telling is not always a harmless pastime in the Southwest.

1. Referred to as Informant 3 of Santa Clara and Informant 4 of Santa Clara.

2. The place name Hano is used only by the Hopi; the Tewa themselves refer to their town as Tewa and they consider the term Hano derogatory.

3. The Hopi tales recorded in English by Voth are in some cases synopses rather than close renderings of the originals and the native style in narrative is necessarily lost.

as Dr. Boas has recorded it in text, although a part of this difference, not all, I think, may be accounted for by the inevitable difference between narrative in Indian with literal translation and narrative in English.

Since writing the foregoing both Miss Bunzel and I have recorded additional tales or variants from the same First Mesa narrator. Comparison of the variants, making due allowance for the difference in audience, Miss Bunzel having had a comparatively slight acquaintance with the narrator, shows a surprising range of variation in the same narrator. Compare, for example, Tales 8 and 9, in both of which the maiden leaves home in temper, but the cause of her outbreak is different enough to make of the matter two quite independent tales which in their second parts, however, merge into the same tale with differences which are merely variants. Possibly the narrator would assert that Tales 8 and 9 are throughout two entirely different tales and always told as such. Nevertheless I would surmise from the whole evidence that the narrator feels free to combine and recombine tale parts or incidents.

Properly told, a Tewa tale opens by naming the tale personages and stating where they were living. This is characteristically Pueblo. An expression for long ago and far away [*owewehembayo* (N. M.), *oweheyamba* (A.)] may be used. There is no closing phrase, unless the phrase *hawage upo* or *hǫ heinamu* (N. M.), translated " thus it happened " or *naheimoʻtʻopitai* (A.), translated, " thus far I know, " may be so considered. At San Juan, a forcible expiration is the customary conclusion — *huʻ*! with the right hand held palm upward to the mouth and motioned in the direction of the listeners. The expression is also used, " I throw it to you, " or " I pass it on to you, *huʻ*! " which is, I take it, the regular implication of *huʻ*!, i. e., it is the Pueblo breath rite to convey quality or vitality. On First Mesa on concluding a tale the narrator might stretch his arms out or up and say, " May my melons grow so large, my corn so high ! " [1] This is not done by the Northern Tewa.

In the New Mexican tales a large number of places are referred to in localization, including ruins; actual place names are used in the Arizona tales, but generally the localization is at Kuṇluokyuteʼ e, described as the underworld place where the Tewa lived before the emergence. This place word appears in the New Mexican tales as Kuṇochuteʼ e which is translated as Green Corn kiva. Sometimes the name is used alone as in the Arizona tales, sometimes with another place name. In the names of tale personages there is less resemblance in the two groups of tales. The Corn girls figure in both ; but Oli-

[1]. This is Zuñi usage. We may compare the Apache tale ending, " Many my jucca fruits lie. " (Goddard).

vella Flower boy, counterpart of White or Yellow corn girl, does not appear in the Arizona tales, nor do the names for the older generation, Uroto sendo, Prayer-stick old man, or Kontsibu kwiyo, Shrivelled corn old woman. The war spirits or Towae of the Northern Tewa, on First Mesa are called Eweļę, but in both groups their soubriquet, variously translated Ash boy, Poker boy, Fire making boy, is the same — Pategee, Potekeęnu. In both groups Coyote keeps a similar tale-appellation which is translated on First Mesa as Water-drag man, and was explained as a reference to Coyote pawing at a spring. It may be, I surmise, a reference to him as a water or rain caller. [1] When he calls in the day time it is for rain, they say on First Mesa, at night he calls out to give notice of sickness or disease or enemies.

The Northern Tewa entertain the same reluctance against telling stories in summer as the people of Taos and of Zuñi. " The snakes will bite you, " they say at Zuñi and at San Juan. Were a story asked for, at San Juan, somebody might say, " No, the snakes are stirring. "

Since Dr. Ruth Benedict is about to publish a concordance of Pueblo Indian folk tales it has seemed unnecessary to give general bibliographical references for the tales in the following collection. The bibliographical note is only for particular points of comparison.

---

1. Cp. pp. 15, 20, 21.

PART I.
TEWA OF NEW MEXICO.
EMERGENCE AND MIGRATION TALES.

I. THE EMERGENCE. [1]

There was a big lake, Ohange pokwinge, Sand Lake. [2] There were lots of people in there. They stayed underneath the water. Then they were talking about it, how to go up from the water, how to get ready to go up. And so our mother was born, Kutsæbukwi payokaga, [3] corn white our summer mother. In four days after our mother was born, our ice mother, Kutsæbukwi oyikaga, was born. Where she was born there was a little green grass (*tatsauwe behge* [4], *ta*, grass, *tsauwe*, green-blue). And so they said, those people, " This is our mother, summer one, " said the people. When our corn white mother, ice mother, was born there was just the same round place. So the people said, " This is our mother, winter mother. "

Then those people said they would get a man. They said, " You are a man and a woman. " [5] Then the man said, " I am not a man, I am not a woman. " Then they asked him again if he would not be a man and woman. And he repeated he was not a man and a woman. They asked him three times. " You ought to be a man and a woman. " He said he was not. The fourth time they spoke, they said, " You have to be a man and a woman. " So he said, " All right. Yes, I am a man and a woman for all the people who are in here. " [6] At that time while they were under the water they did not

1. Informant I of San Juan.
2. At Montevista, said the narrator. Visitors from Taos would throw bread into this lake, which had never been visited by informant. *Okọnge*, a Santa Clara man called the lake of emergence, which he also placed near Taos.
3. Corn, white, *bu'u*, " large low roundish place " (Harrington, 50), *kwi*, woman, *paye*, summer, *kaga* (?).
4. *Be'e*, small low roundish place ; *ge*, locative (Harrington, 50).
5. This puzzling phrase appears to be synonymous in Tewa usage for ceremonial potency, also for personal courage and adequacy. There is no implication of hermaphroditism. Cp pp. 10, 23, 26, 38.
6. Note the characteristic Pueblo implication of the compulsive nature of the fourth request.

know where was north (*pimpiye*), west (*tsampiye*), south (*akompiye*), east (*tampiye*), zenith (*opamakore*), nadir (*nạsogenoye*). [1] So they told this man he was to go up. They did not know where north was. Then they let him go up. Then he went up northwards. " Wonder if you are going to have good fortune, " they said. " If you find anything good, you must come and let us know it. " Then he came back all ragged and brown. They said, " What did you see where you were ? " He said he did not see anything except the ground, near the big hills. They said to him, " You must think like a man and a woman. Now you must go westward. " Then he came back. So again when he came they asked what he had seen. He had seen everything all dry, nothing but ground. Now he was to go southward. He went, he came back. They asked him again. In just the same words he answered. Then they said to go out eastwards. When he came back, they asked him again, and in the same words he answered. They said, " You have to be a man and a woman, now you are going up above. " He went up. So they said to him, " You did not see anything when you went, now you belong to Kanyotsanyotse. You have to go out from here. Wonder if anybody will love you. " So he went out and to a big court. And then he came to a certain place. They opened to go down. He was in the upper story with a man. And under them were different kinds of animals (*tsiwi*), mountain lion (*kạ*), bear (*ke*), *koho* (*kuyo*, wolf) [2], fox (*de*), *mosa*, different kinds of cat, *tamagin* (dragon flies), also bees (*worobe*), the big and the little ones. Then they told the man to go in. Then he saw those things and when he saw those things, he got scared. They said, " We are your friends. " He was afraid and pushed the other one. Those animals jumped up on him and scratched him all over. They were supernatural (*pinan*). Then he stood up a sound man again. Then they sat him down. They gave him arrow points and buckskin to hang over the right shoulder, red feathers for his hair, moccasins, leggings and shirt of buckskin. They told him, " These are what you are to use. " They put black dirt (*poshụ*) [3] all over his face. They put downy feathers all over his hair. They told him to take his bow and arrows. " Now you are ready. We love you. " So he went out from there. He went back to the lake. He came near the lake and he began to dance and to sing and to call, U....u ! They heard it, they said, " That's good ! That's good ! " They said, " Maybe somebody loves us. " He came in and they saw him. He

1. Note the characteristic Pueblo circuit. Cp. Harrington, 42.
2. Harrington, 43.
3. " The black and sparkling fine sand seen on water-washed sand surfaces along the banks and islets of the Rio Grande. " (Harrington, 582). It is used not only as a ritual face adornment, but in offerings, together with meal or pollen, to Lightning and to the Horned water serpent.

was Kanyotsanyotse. [1] That was the first one (i. e. he was the original Kanyotsanyotse). [2]

And those *na imbi kwiyo kǫtsæbukwi pàyokaga oyikaga* (Corn Mothers), they stayed in the same place where they were born. Then he (Kanyotsanyotse) said, " I need a woman. " There were lots of men. He was walking around where they were sitting and he caught hold of one and stood him up and he got *kǫtsæbukwi* and gave it to the man he caught. So he took the Mother and gave it to him. " You are Poætoyo ; [3] you have to care for all these people in the summer time. You are their father and mother. " Then he said, " Yes. " " You are the father and you are the mother, " they said to him. So Kanyotsanyotse said to the man, " You are the father and you are the mother. If any little boy or any man or woman talks about you, do not get mad with your children. You have to treat them well, even if they speak against you. " Then he was looking for another mother. He was looking and looking around when he saw another man. He caught him. He gave *na imbi kwiyo kǫtsæ bukwi oyikaga* to the man and said, " You are the father and you are the mother. If any man or woman speaks against you, do not get mad. You have to treat your children well " (as Winter chief). So those were the old ones, *pat'owa sendo.* [4] Then they said, " Yes ; now we have found a mother and a father, " they said. " So we have to walk up from here, " they said. So they stood up in the north. They said, " Here is not the place. " They stood up in the west. They said, " Here is not the place. " They stood up in the south. They said, " Here is not the place. " They stood up in the east. They said, " Here is not the place. " Then they were singing *poæka.* [5] Then they went northwards and they came out from there.

1. His full name is Kanyotsanyotse tetseenubu'ta^a (bird, yellow, boy, " round place where they stand up "). Harrington translates *but'a* as big rcund circle. It is applied to an October dance and tò a circular constellation (Harrington, 50). So we may translate Tetseenubu'ta^a as yellow bird circle boy. As for Kanyotsanyotse, it was translated by an Arizona Tewa as White wildcat man, *yo* being a song syllable. In the Arizona songs Wildcat and the other animals, Mountain lion, Bear, Badger, Wolf, Snake, are referred to in the color circuit of yellow, blue, red, white, dark, and all colors.

2. Represented in San Juan today by the Hunt chief, Pįkæsendo.

3. The Tewa have a moiety organization, being divided into Summer People and Winter People. There are two Town chiefs. The Chief of the Summer People (Summer chief, Summer Man) is called Poætoyo (poingtoyo), and as Town chief he is in charge of all the people from March to November. The chief of the Winter People (Winter chief, Winter Man), *oyike*, is in charge as Town chief from November to March.

4. " Fish people old men " is the accepted translation, but the clue to the meaning of this term is lacking.

5. Water runs song. It is sung to ask the Mother " to give good times, " in the seasonal transfer ceremonies of Winter chief and Summer chief.

While they were under the lake they had made two T'owa'e. [1]
So they said, "Those two little boys have to think like a man and a
woman. " From the Lake they went up and said, " Whatever you
see you must come and let us know. " So they came in and let them
know. So they questioned them. They said, " Yes, we went up and
we did not see any hills. " Then they told them again and so they
said to them, " You belong to our father and mother, " said they to
them. Then they were getting ready what they would need when
they went up from the Lake. They were thinking about how they
could live in this world. They went out again. As they were walking
they saw *węke*. The younger one was ahead of the elder. [2] The elder
said, " Wait for me, *tiupare*. " [3] He waited, they changed places.
The younger said, " Wait for me, *tiupare*. " Then they came to the Lake.
They said, " We are *tiunpare*. " So they went on. Then they told them,
" You have to go out from here and go to the north, the west,
the south, the east, and bring back a true account of what you see. "
So they went out. They stood up. Then they said to them, " Try it,
tiupare. " So he took out his arrows. Then he said, " If I shoot it
this way, if the arrow does not come back, that way is the north. "
Then it went and did not come back. They said, " Now we know
where the north is. " They gave the name " north. " " Now, *tiupare*, try with the arrow again. " He shot and the arrow did not come
back. They named it " west. " " Try with the arrow again, *tiupare*.
If the arrow does not come back, that is south. " He shot and the
arrow did not come back. That was south. He shot again and the
arrow did not come back. That was east. " Shoot the arrow up and
if it does not come back that will be *opamakore* (sky). " [4] He shot it,
it did not come back. So he said, " Try, *tiupare*. Shoot up the arrow
and if it comes down on the ground and into the ground that will
belong to the nadir. " He shot up the arrow. It came down and went
into the ground. That was the nadir (*nansogenoge*). [5] Then they went
in. Then they asked them, " How did you fare ? " They said, " We
fared well. We know where north is, and west, south, east, above and
below. " So they said, " That is all right. Thank you. Now we know
you have placed the steps (directions). " Then they said, " You have
left out one word yet (you have omitted one thing). You have to

1. Literally, people small. These correspond to the " two little war gods " of
Zuñi. As appears later the T'owa'e of the Tewa are in a set of six or rather twelve,
according to the color-directions.
2. The relative positions were shown on the fingers, by placing the index finger
of the left hand ahead of the index finger of the right hand.
3. Younger older (brother or sister). This compound term is applied to a ceremonial colleague.
4. See Harrington, 24, 42, giving *opamakowa, world sky.*
5. *Nan*, earth ; *soge*, to sit ; *nuge*, below, Harrington, 42.

get them all together, two by two, blue, yellow, red, white and *nokuṇwi* and *tsǽge* (all colored) (six T'owa'e). " Those are Indians, what they need they are to mind them (guards for them). [1] They still use them. They belong to the *akonotuyu* [2] of Taos, Picuris, San Juan, Santa Clara, San Ildefonso, Nambe, Cochiti. So they were all two by two. They said, " Now you have to think like a woman. You have to put up the big hills now to the north. " So they took a little mud and they threw it this way (indicating the directions) and there were the hills. Then they said, " When we work *pinan*, the sky will get dark, there will be white ones, like a flower, (clouds), [3] there will be a rainbow and lightning (*tsiguwenu*) and the sound of rain falling, and fog. "

They came out from that Lake. They could not walk. Poǽtoyo kicked a ball [4] and it could not go. So he said, " Oyike, now you try, *tiupare.* I wonder could you do it ? " He threw it. It ran and it made a noise. Where it stopped was hoarfrost (*oyegebeye*). It made the ground hard. [5]

Then they were going along walking and walking. And some got head-ache and some, stomach-ache. And they said they needed something again. " That is why we have head-ache and stomach-ache. " And so they said, " Maybe those mothers we. are carrying are not good mothers. " So they went back again. Then Kanyotsanyotse said, " Whatever does she (*payokaga*) need ? " He opened her stomach and she had pointed things and stones in her stomach. [6] He took all these bad things out and put in good things. [7] Then they moved on again. They still had head-ache and stomach-ache. They still needed something. So they came back again. They needed Pu'fona. [8] They made four Pu'fona, and went out again. The Pu'fona gave them medicine.

1. Meaning that the six or rather twelve T'owa'e were manlike, and were to safeguard the people in what they needed and, through their ceremonies, got.

2. Outside chiefs i. e. war chiefs or captains.

3. Or possibly sheet lightning, which is referred to at Jemez as flower-like.

4. Cp. the Laguna account of how they come up from the Under World playing kick-stick. (Boas, 1).

5. This seems to be a version of the general Pueblo theory that at the time of the Emergence the earth was soft and not viable. Since writing the foregoing a Tesuque informant states that, "When the people were coming the earth was soft. They left prints in the stones. They were moving slowly. Then Oyike with his kickstick, (*w'ebi*) made the earth hard. "

6. Implying the usual theory of sickness caused by such intrusive things, which are considered to be sent into the body by witches. Cp. Dumarest, 154.

7. Presumably seeds. Elsewhere corn ear fetiches are hollowed and seed filled. In the Santa Clara tale (see p. 115) where Arrow-point Wind boy is subjected to similar treatment, the good things are pink quartz and turquoise, the bad things removed are cactus spines.

8. Doctors or members of the curing society.

They came to a big river. There was Magpie (kwǽǽ). He put his tail across the river and on it the T'owa'e passed over. The two old ones, the caciques (Summer Chief and Winter Chief), came on the other side. Then Magpie's tail turned over in the middle of the river and the people fell down into the water. [1] Those old mothers (caciques) said, " You have to turn into fish. Who is not lazy will catch the fish and eat the fish. " Some were left on one side, some on the other side. They were calling to one another. They threw stones and sticks at one another. Then those who stayed on the other side said, " That is what you need. You are Navaho, Ute, Apache, Kaiowa, Comanche. " So when they called their names, they said, " You belong to them. " They have their own languages. They could not talk to each other. So the caciques told them, " You do not need to build houses. You can build houses of deer hide and buffalo hide. When you have babies you have to use deer meat. That is what you will use, " they said to them. " If you come and try and fight with our people, it will run blood. " That is why when the Comanche and Kaiowa fought with our people only one or two of our men were killed. Our father and our mother said, " You are my own fighting people. Our houses are adobe houses. " Thus they said to them, " Sometimes you will come to our places, when you need meal and corn. " [2] So they went out walking to the north, west, south, east. " There you are going to be with all your children. " [3]

Those Akọgee [4] were walking along, they were very sorrowful. " We need something, " they said, so they went back again, those older ones, into the Lake. Then they brought those Kossa. [5] They were making fun, those Kossa. And the people began to laugh and grow glad again.

The Summer Mother got the western hills and the Winter Mother got the eastern hills. So the Winter Mother comes up in the east and

1. This incident was given by a Santa Clara man. " When they came out from the Lake, they reached a river. They tried hard to cross it. Put across was the tail feather of Magpie. They crossed on the feather which broke. Some were on the other side, the others stayed on their side. " Cp. Harrington, 214.

2. Cp. Robbins, Harrington, Freire-Marreco, 97.

3. From a like account given by a San Juan woman of the origin of the fighting people (*hǽming t'owa*) I infer that this part of the myth at least is non esoteric. " After they came up from Ohange pokwinge, their leader was Tsew"ǽ, Eagle tail feather, (presumably a reference to the forelock feather worn by Kanyotsanyotse) they came to a river. Those who did not cross became the Pueblo peoples, some of those who crossed fell in and became fish, those who got across became the fighting peoples, Pima, Apache, Navaho, Kaiowa, Ute. "

4. Another term for T'owa'e or Akonotoyo, outside chief. A " little yard dog " is called *akọge.*

5. Clown society. In this account there is no reference to the Kwirano, the other clown group. There is but one Kwirano at San Juan and none at Santa Clara.

the Summer Mother in the west with their Oxuwah. [1] Those people, their children, were coming along the hills. The Winter Man was coming with his children on the hills. The last ones were coming on, back on the hills. " When they were going to have *oxuwahi* [2] Posew'a [3] would call from one side to the other side. So they came together in Tekeowinge. [4] That is the way it happened, how they came up from that Lake. *Hu'* !

2. MIGRATION [5] : THE BOY WHO BROKE HIS FAST. [6]

Oweweham'baiyo lived at Uwįpinge [7] all the people (*t'ǽkitowa.*) [8] The people had moved along Pingkwaiye [9] (Sangre de Cristo Mountains) and along Tsąmpiripingkwaiye, the west side range (Jemez Mountains). The eastern mountains belonged to the Winter People and the western mountains belonged to the Summer People. Those on the Eastern Mountains, the Winter People, were eating deer, elk (the meat of wild animals); and the Summer People were eating jucca fruit (*pahbe*), *mantsanitabe* (? apples), berries (*puhpahbe*), [10] *okumbe*, [11] prickly pear (*sǫbe*) [12] — all different kinds of fruit. The Winter People's leader was Oyi'ke, the Summer People's leader was Poǽtoyo. As they were walking divided, [13] some on the west side liked the east side and walked over, some on the east side liked the west side and walked over. All came down there to Uwįpinge. So when they were all down together, they talked about where they were going to make a place to live. So they said, " From here we ought to find a place to live, wherever we like. " Some said, " We like Oke'anyebu'. " So they said, " Then you will be Oke' (San Juan)". Others said, " We

1. Cloud People, i.e. kachina. Ordinarily they are orientated according to the six color directions. Cp. p. 30, n: 1.
2. Cloud People, moving, i.e. kachina dance.
3. The Tewa folk-tale name for Coyote.
4. See below, n.7.
5. Informant I of San Juan.
6. Cp. Harrington, 208.
7. Called more commonly Tekeowinge (*tekeuwinge*, cottonwood bird pueblo place, Harrington, 336). It was called *ongwįpinge* (*ongwi*, pueblo ; *pįnge*, in the middle of) Harrington was told, because it was " centrally situated among the pueblos. " So it is, but other ruins, as Harrington pointed out to his informants, are also central. The fact is that in Tewa myth this was where all the Tewa first lived together after the Emergence and before they separated.
8. Translated " all the Indians. "
9. " Moutain heights. " Probably this should be Tampije'i'ipįng, eastern mountains, as Harrington writes (Harrington, 104).
10. See Robbins, Harrington, Freire-Marreco, 116.
11. Possibly " turtle plant, " a fern. (Robbins, Harrington, Freire-Marreco, 53, 59).
12. Robbins, Harrington, Freire-Marreco, 62.
13. Cp. Harrington, 344.

like to be on the other side of the river. " So they gave them a name, Kahpo, Leaf water (Santa Clara). So others said, " We like that place, on the other side of the river. " So they gave them the name Pow'oge (San Ildefonso). Others said, " We like the same river, clear up there, Kibu' (gopher place). " — " Well, you have the name Nambe'. " ¹ Others said, " We like way up there, Tatunge, dry ones. " ² — " You have the name T'et'suge. " The people from down there, they always like to drink water. " So you have the name Posuwege ³ (Pojoaque). " These six have just one language.

We used to live at Okeowingeanyebu'. ⁴ So they said, " Here we do not have a good life. Let us go over to Okeowinge powongwi kǫochute'. At Okeowinge powongwi kǫochute' at that time it was new.

(Follows the story why they moved.) At that time they would keep the boys ⁵ *pinangkwa* ⁶ and those T'owa'e they would take care of the boys. They kept them in the house for twelve days. They kept them in there for rain, to have good rains. And one of those boys, he was waiting until those who were taking care of them fell asleep. It was the business of the guards to give them rain water. ⁷ The guards saw a boy going up, and they went after him, they ran after him. He ran over to a lake, and they ran after him, but they did not catch him; and he jumped into the water and he drank all he needed, and he got full of water; and they brought him back and took him back to Sibo'pene ⁸ (where they were in). And all the water he drank came up from his mouth and all those in there turned ed into frogs (*pembowin*). Then they said, " We do not have good times here. " So then they went to where we live now. They all moved. Only Tesuque did not move. *Hǫheinamu* (thus it happened). *Hu'* !

3. THE MASK THAT STUCK : ⁹ DOWN RIVER TO THE SNAKES.¹⁰

At Pow'oge (San Ildefonso), long ago, when the Kwǽko (Mexicans) first came, when their godfathers took them to the priest, they

---

1. This is indirect corroboration of Harrington's surmise that the name Nambe means a small round mound of earth (Harrington 381).

2. Cp. Harrington, 387.

3. Drink water place. See Harrington, 334 (*po*, water; *sǫngwǽ*, to drink; *ge*, down at).

4. See Harrington, 207.

5. Boys of fourteen or fifteen, only boys with a good heart, and only in time of drought.

6. Magic(?) working. See p. 19, n. 5.

7. Cp. the Hopi rain-water drinking girls in the Lalakunti ceremony.

8. Possibly the Keresan term Sipap for the underworld.

9. A story is told at Zuñi of the Sumaikoli mask sticking to the face of the imper-

See note 10 p. 17.

had a great big *oxuwahhe* (kachina dance). At that time there were few Mexicans, so the *oxuwahhe* was in the day time. Those making *oxuwahhe* were always guarded. When the impersonator went out to urinate, somebody went with him. They kept them in four days. They gave them only green corn (*tsihku*) and corn bread (*kupawa*) without salt, and no meat, three times a day. One of those boys said he wanted to urinate, and so they took him out. He had been three days in. The boy said to the guard, " You stand here and I will go on the other side and urinate. " Now this boy had a friend (*k'ema*), and he went in there. He said to her, " I am the chief of the Oxuwah. You will see me tomorrow. I am going to come in the day time. " Then he said, " Tomorrow when I come, I will jump into one corner of a ruined house and you stay there and I will move my mask and take it off and you will see I am not lying. " Next day the Oxuwah were coming, and she saw them and went into the ruin. And they were waiting for this Oxuwah toyo (chief), for he always went first. Then they saw that girl and she came out and went into town. Those Kossa talked to those Oxuwah and told them to go home. [1] That Oxuwah chief did not go out, and the next one took them out. They went into the house and found that Oxuwah chief walking up and down. The Kossa caught him and tried to take off the mask (*tsemu*) and it stuck to him. They could not take it off. He just walked up and down, and could not take it off. So they called there all the men they knew. " Because this boy talked with a girl that is why it is like this. " That boy was the son of Poӕtoyo (Summer chief). They told the old ones to bring prayer-feathers for all the Oxuwah, so they would help them. Then if they loved that boy he could go straight into the big lake. Their Outside chief (*akonotoya*) took the boy to Blue water old man [2] (*potsa'we seno*). They did not love him, so they would not take him in. They found another lake, Yellow water old man (*potseyi seno*), but he did not love him, he would not take him in. They found another lake, Red water old man (*popi seno*). He did not love him, he would not take him in.

sonator who had broken the continence taboo. On First Mesa there is a story that once during the performance of the long form of the Powamu ceremony in which a girl and two boys in masks (those of any kachina) are represented by each kiva, a girl and boy from Chief kiva " tried at being sweethearts " on their way up from Kowaiwaimowe (the kachina house, i.e. shrine), and that on their return, when they undertook to remove their masks, these stuck to them. Now they tell the young people not to think of love-making at this time lest their masks stick to them. This is the only occasion, by the way, that females on First Mesa wear masks.

10. Informant I of San Juan.

1. Implicit here is the usual relationship of guardianship held by the clowns (Kossa) towards the kachina.

2. Cp. Harrington, 263. The tale appears to answer in the affirmative his query as to whether or not Blue water man is a mythic being.

They came to a big river (*pokege*). [1] All their feathers were gone, they had put them in all the lakes. So they let him go. They said, " If you find those who love you, they will take you. " Then he went through the woods. The woods whipped him and tore his clothes. He came to Spider old woman's house. She said to him, " You are the son of Summer chief. You showed yourself to your girl. Now you have gone to every lake and there is no door for you. You thought you were playing, but this was not play. " " That is what happened to me, " he said. " If you ask your Mother to help you, maybe she will help you. " Then he walked on, and came to the house of Tarantula (K'etopuye). [2] So Tarantula said to him, " You are Summer chief's son. You have walked all round and nobody has loved you, and I do not know whether to love you or not. You believed in nothing. " But that Tarantula did love him, and made a box and put him in the box, and put in some seeds of corn, and made a piece of mud and put seeds of corn in this piece of mud. " This is the one to tell (direct) you. When it is October [3] the leaves will turn yellow. " So Tarantula smeared the box all over on the outside with gum, put the boy inside and took it to the river, and shoved the box into the water and said, " You will come to a waterfall, it will turn you four times, four times you will go down again, to the end of the river. Then kick open the box and come out. " As he went, in time the corn leaves began to turn yellow. So he kicked open the box and came out and came to where lived two Yellow snake girls (Pænyotseyianyo) who were a kind of *pinandi*. [4] And they loved him. And they said, " Now you are going to your home, but you are going as a kind of priest ('ow'a). When you come to be priest in your home, if no words come out from your mouth for twelve days, you will be a good man. " So those Yellow snake girls went with him to his house and left him there. (This boy was married and had one son). People said, " A new priest has come. " (They used to live near Santa Fé.) His wife was living yet, and his father. It was within one day of the twelve days. They had told him not to speak, so he had not told who he was. They were calling the priests to Santa Fé. When the priest went they would send a boy with him. They chose his son to go with him. He knew that was his son. So they were going; it was very far. And the boy was walking. So the priest said to the boy, in Mexican, " Come on, my son, get on the back of my horse, we will both ride. " " I am a good walker, " said the boy. " You are my son, " the priest said in Indian, " come and sit on my

1. River bank (Harrington, 85).
2. Henderson and Harrington, 60.
3. *Poyeripo.* Cp. Harrington, 66.
4. See p. 19, n. 5.

horse. " The boy got scared. " *Harạhi* ! this priest knows how to talk Indian. " He got on the horse's back. " I am your father, " he said. " Did you ever hear your grandfather and mother say how one year Summer chief's son came out Oxuwah ? " " That one who made up as Oxuwah, that was my father, " said the boy and began to cry. " I am that one, " he said. " Do not talk, my son, to anybody, even to your grandfather or mother or *tiu* (younger brother or sister), just sit by and you will know it. " (Those Yellow snake girls had said he was not to talk for twelve days. He had only one day left and he talked to his son. They had said if he talked within twelve days, two days later they would kill him.) The boy said, " I wonder why this priest talks to me in Indian? I wonder if it is the truth ? " The next day they came back to San Ildefonso. (They always get the house ready for the priest.) The boy when he came into the house thought, " I guess I better let my grandfather hear about it. " — " Did you come, son, with the priest ? " — " Yes ! " — " Did that priest give you enough to eat, take good care of you ? " — " Yes. That priest could talk Indian. " At those words the priest fell sick. The boy said, " That priest said he was my father. " When they went to see the priest he was dying, those two Yellow snake girls had bitten him. So he died. There was just one day left for him not to talk, and he talked, and died. That is the way it happened at San Ildefonso.

4. OLIVELLA FLOWER ESCAPES. [1]

At Okeowinge kọochute'e, [2] were living Olivella Flower [3] and Yellow corn girl. Olivella Flower would go hunting every day and bring a deer. He is a good boy, he never thinks of anything bad. He gives meat to every one, he leaves out nobody. To Spider old woman (*awạkwiyo*), to Buffalo and Deer, Olivella Flower took downy feathers (*be*), [4] to all these he took them, to ask them to help him, to do whatever he wants. He asks them every morning for help. So they help him. He kills one or two deer every day. Then those *pinạndi* [5] got angry with him. So they called everybody. They

---

1. Informant 1, of San Juan.
2. San Juan pueblo green corn kiva.
3. Tinihipowi.
4. Literally, stick; but it is the term used for prayer-feathers.
5. Magic(?) having. *Pinạn* has the general meaning of magical or supernatural. A study of its applications would amount to a summary of the Tewa theory of magic in behaviour and results. Through *pinạn* inaudibility and invisibility (pp. 27, 67) are achieved ; through *pinạn*, people are put to sleep (p. 120), made fly (pp. 26, 37), transported over a distance (pp. 42, 167), transformed into animals (pp. 20-21, 32), cured, killed (pp. 45, 19), and revived (pp. 36, 56, 63); through *pinạn* the hidden or lost (p. 36) is revealed ; rain (pp. 16, 89), snow (p. 166), and wind (p. 166)

said, " This Olivella Flower takes out what meat he wants and throws away the rest. He thinks the deer costs nothing (i.e., is not precious). We have to do something about it. You younger boys here, who will be the one to kill Olivella Flower ? " " I am the one to kill him, " one of them said. "I am going to make a big deer. " He said to one *pinandi* who was Coyote (*posew'a*), " You have to call a little snow tonight when it is getting dark to cover the ground. I will go over to Olivella Flower's house to tell him a big deer is near at hand. " So they do it. That *pinandi* made a deer. There was a big *kaye* ¹ near there, that deer jumped near there. Then that *pinandi* went to Olivella Flower, and he woke him up. He said, " I came to tell you a big deer has just passed near here. " — " Yes. I will catch it. " He dressed, he got his arrows, he went down, he went where that deer had gone. He saw him jumping. He was a big deer. He went after it. Then as he went Spider old woman spoke to him, " Olivella Flower, what are you going after ? " — " I am going after a deer. " Then she said, " That is not a deer, that is a kind of *pinan* boy. These *pinan* are coming after you, they are angry with you, and working against you. Listen to me. They are working to kill you. As for that deer, catch it. " She gave him medicine. " Go down a little hill and so on down three hills, then on his tracks spit medicine, also spit medicine all over yourself and your hands. " On the fourth hill he saw that deer. That deer was falling down and rolling over, he could not walk. He was a big deer, his eyes were very red. He hit him with an arrow, looking at him. And that deer spoke, " *Hewemboharahi'* ² elder brother, Olivella Flower, you have more *pinan* than we have. I am having a hard time, I am almost dying, but I cannot die, kill me ! " And Olivella Flower shot him and killed him. Those *pinandi* had a fire in their kiva, waiting for Olivella Flower. They thought they were going to kill Olivella Flower. Olivella Flower was carrying the deer. Then Spider Old Woman told Olivella Flower to carry the deer to the kiva and throw it down. So he carried it. As he went up, they said, " He is bring-

are caused, corn and melons are made grow (p. 89), life is given to the inanimate (p. 94). Society members or persons in ceremonial retreat have or work *pinan* (? *pinandi*) (pp.40, 108), also the dead who are without a heart (p.116), also witches (pp. 37, 62), including the foreigner, whether Hopi, or Navaho (p. 25), or Snake People (p, 19). There may be competition in *pinan* (pp. 21, 38, 87-9, 92), and *pinan* is good or bad (pp. 36, 40).

Although so frequently used by the Northern Tewa, the term does not occur in the Arizona tales at all. But it is not unknown on First Mesa (See Robbins, Harrington, Freire-Marreco, 105) where a woman chief at Moenkapi was credited with *binan* because she smoked.

1. Shrine of stones.

2. *Hewembo*, because, *harahi*, why, " I wonder why. " This very common exclamation is translated, " My goodness ! " or " Oh my ! "

ing Olivella Flower. " He said, " I am bringing you a deer, " and
he threw it down. And they scolded their old man (i. e. Chief).
" Olivella Flower has beaten you, " they said. " There are lots of
good boys here. I will kill Olivella Flower, " he said. " Get ready.
I will make a mountain lion (*kǽ*), nobody can beat Mountain lion. "
He told Coyote to make a little snow. When Coyote called it,
snow came. Another boy went and knocked at the door of Olivella
Flower. He said, " Good morning, elder brother! A mountain lion
passed by here. " He said, " Yes. We will catch it, to make a bed
of the skin. " So he took his arrows and went down. Then he went
after it. And Spider old woman talked to him, " Olivella Flower,
what are you going after ? " " After a mountain lion, " he said.
" That is not one, that is *pinǫndi*. " So she gave him medicine for
that lion. " As you did to the deer, so do to the lion. Spit medicine
on its tracks, and all over yourself. Go down on two hills, and spit
on the tracks. " So he did it. On the third hill he saw him where
there were some sticks. Lion was turning around and falling over.
He said to him, " You have more *pinǫn* than we have. Kill me. " So
Olivella Flower shot him, when it grew dark, and killed him and
carried him back. Those *pinǫndi* were in their kiva. Then they said,
" Wonder why he did not come, that lion ? Maybe he is waiting for
it to get dark. That lion will kill him. " Then Olivella Flower carried
him to the kiva to throw him down. " I bring you a deer, " he said
and threw him down. They fell to scolding one another. "I am going
to make up as a jack-rabbit, " said one. He called Coyote to call the
snow. This jack-rabbit passed near Olivella Flower's house. One of
those *pinǫndi* went in and said, " Elder brother, a jack-rabbit has just
passed by here, it went close to your house and passed on. " ―
"I will catch it so we can eat rabbit meat. " So he dressed up and ran
after that jack-rabbit. As he was running, Spider old woman talked
to him again, " Olivella Flower, what are you going after ? "
" After a jack-rabbit, " he said. " That is not a jack-rabbit. That is
pinǫndi. I will help you. We *have* to help you because you never
forget us. [1] Come on, I will give you something. You will catch that
jack-rabbit. Go down one hill, and spit the medicine on his tracks. "
She gave some bees and some bumble bees to Olivella Flower.
" When you are having a hard time, let them out. If the big ones do
not help, let out these little ones. " So he put them in a cloth in his
belt. Then he went after that jack-rabbit and he spit the medicine on
his tracks. That jack rabbit got tired, and on the second hill he saw
him. There was a crack in the big hill and Jack-rabbit ran into it.
Olivella Flower could look in, not very far. He put his hand in the

---

1. A good illustration of how, to the Pueblo Indian, gifts may have a compulsive
character.

crack and Rabbit caught him and pulled him in. He was caught tight.
Then he remembered those bees. He took them out. " Help me ! "
he said. The bees went in and began to work on the crack. They
could not do much, they flew out tired, almost dead. He put them
back into his belt. He took out the little bees. He said, " Like a man
you have to help me. " They made a big noise way under. They
forced that jack-rabbit out. They bit him all over, in his mouth and
ears. Then he caught that jack-rabbit. He tied the bees up well and
put them into his belt. He carried the jack-rabbit in his hand to the
house of Spider old woman. " Good evening. They helped me,
I caught it. Here I bring it. I am glad that you helped me. " Spider
old woman said, " Because you believe in us, and always take those
feathers out, our clothes, ¹ we help you. Never forget us. Those *piṇạn*
wont do anything more to you. " Olivella Flower went to the kiva.
" Here I bring you a deer, " he said, and he threw down the jack-
rabbit. When they saw the rabbit they did not try to do anything
more to Olivella Flower. That is what happened to Olivella Flower.

5. HE FOLLOWS HIS DEAD WIFE. ²

They were living at Okeowinge kọochute'e, Olivella Flower and
Yellow corn girl. They were living nicely, they loved each other.
Then Yellow corn girl died. She left one little boy. One day they
buried her ; two days, three days, on the fourth day in the evening
the little boy was crying. They could not make him stop crying. So
they carried him way up past the corrals on the east side. Olivella
Flower saw a fire at K'ụwhanoge (it is down south). So he took the
little boy to the house of his *ko'o* (mother's younger sister). He left
him there. Then he said, " I wonder why there is fire there. I better
go there. " It was getting dark. So he went. When he came there·
where the fire was, there was a house, and he stood up by the window and he looked in the house and he saw Yellow corn girl in
there ; she was combing her hair. When she was living she would
comb her hair, and now in that same way she was combing her
hair. He talked from the window, " *Hewemboharạhi'* ! Yellow corn
girl, you are mean ! You are not far from home, why don't you go
home ? " Yellow corn girl said to him, " *Hewemboharạhi'* ! What are
you doing here ? I am getting ready to go home tonight. Are you
not getting ready to send me away ? I do not belong here. I am a
kind of wind. Are you going to send me away from here ? "
"No, I love you, " said Olivella Flower. " I will not send you away

---

1. A very interesting reference to the significance of prayer-feathers as clothes for
the Spirits.
2. Informant I of San Juan.

from here. " — " No, do not say that. Be a man and a woman. But
if you stay with me, in three or four days you will get angry with
me. " — " I think not, " he said, " because I love you. " — " You
will be a woman and a man ? " she asked. " Yes, I will be, " he
said. " If you are a woman and a man, " she said, " come in. " So
he went in. And that night they slept together and he put his arm
around her, and he smelt her (in the mouth) and he drew himself
away. " What are you doing that for ? " she said. " Why did you
say you would be a woman and a man, and now you turn away ? "
" No, " he said, " I get tired on one side, that is why I turned
on the other side, " he said. But he kept smelling of her. " That's
why I told you to meet me at home, and send me away. But you
said you were a woman and a man, and now you have to stay with
me. " But he could not stay, and he got up and went down and ran
away. " Why are you running away? " said Yellow corn girl. He
ran, and she ran after him. He came to a shrine, he could not hide.
He went to another shrine, he could not hide. He came to the house
of T'owa'e. He said to him, " Olivella Flower, Yellow corn girl is
running after you. Can't you find any place to hide ? " — " No.
Will you please help to hide me ? " — " Yes. " [1] He had a cane
arrow, he put him in it. He shot him up. He became Big Star
(Agoyotsoyo). She came after him. T'owa'e put her into another
cane arrow and shot her up. She followed on after him as Tsækįn-
kwiyio, Yellow going old woman. She had died, she did not give out
a strong light. Agoyotsoyo, he was alive, and so he gave much
light. Agoyotsoyo comes up first, Tsækįnkwiyo next. But sometimes
she passes him ; for Tsækįnkwiyo has no heart. That is the way it
passed with Olivella Flower and Yellow corn girl. That is why we
make four days, and then send the dead away from here, they do
not belong here. After four days and nights we cook good things, we
take a little bowl and put food in it and take it out. All their relatives (*matui*) are there and say, " Do not remember us, even if we
dream in the night. " They say when they take the bowl out, " You
do not belong here. Whether you become Kayapowaha (Warrior
cloud beings, i. e., the Outside chiefs or " war captains " of the
cloud beings of the directions) or Kayatsauwe (Blue spirits, i. e.,
Blue cloud beings), Kayatseyi (Yellow spirits) or Kayapi (Red spirits) or Kayatse (Speckled spirits or Dark spirits). From the big
mountains, from the foot hills, or from the east plain, [3] from there
you have to help your people. Do not remember us. Even when you
are moving about, we do not need to hear. You have no heart. You

1. Cp. for the pursuit by a dead woman, Zuñi, Parsons 7 : 156-158.
2. Cp. Harrington, 49.
3. There lies the cemetery of San Juan.

have to ask Josita' (like santu) to give us a good living. " [1] We make
one line [2] (with foot), and in the same line move the foot four
times, one, two, three, four, and say, " Go away from here ! " Thus
it was with Olivella Flower. *Huʻ* !

6. THE TAOS DEER HUNTERS AND THE GHOST. [3]

There was a girl having a baby. She died after the baby was out.
Yet they did not make any four days. Then Olivella Flower said they
would go after deer. They went north, twelve boys. They built a camp
where they thought there were lots of deer, and there they stayed.
They found lots of deer, and killed them. Then they said that who
ever came first into camp would have to make a fire and cook. They
went hunting deer. When they came back in the evening all was
cooked and ready. They asked who came first and cooked. Nobody
knew. " Wonder who came and cooked for us ? Maybe somebody
who is good. We come tired and all is cooked for us. " They ate
and lay down and slept. In the morning they cooked for themselves,
and went out hunting deer. In the evening, coming with deer, they
found all was cooked and ready. That is the way they spent every
evening. Then they got enough meat. They got ready to go back to
their home. They said, " Tomorrow we will go hunting again, and
take some meat on the way. " So they dried all the meat they had.
Then next day they were going. They got lots of wood and put it
near their camp. The boys were talking, " I wonder who has been
coming and cooking for us. What shall we do for them ? I wonder
who it is ? " they said. " We have to cut a piece of meat, each one
of us, and put it down for her, and call her, maybe she will come
and take it home. " [4] One man stood up and cut off a leg and put
it down for her. Each one put down a piece, there was a big pile of
meat. They said, " Who will call her ? " So they told one boy,
" You have to call. We will get lots of wood and burn it and see
from where she comes. " So that man stood up. " When she comes,
whatever she is, do not run away, stay like a man. " This man called, " Whoever it was who came and cooked for us when we came
back tired, come on ! This is for you. Come on ! Come on ! " He
called the fourth time, " Come on ! " Then somebody called, " I
am coming-g ! " He called again, " Come on ! Come on ! " — " I am

1. The Catholic doctrine of intercession. Stevenson noted it in Zuñi among the
spirits. I did not.
2. This line means mountains and hills that are not to be passed over. Cp. similar
funerary lines of exorcism made on First Mesa.
3. Informant I of San Juan.
4. In just this spirit offerings are put down for the supernaturals.

coming-g! " Again. That's the way she was coming. As she was near, he said, " Here we have got it ready for you to take home. " When she was coming near, he stopped, he got scared, nobody spoke. There was a big fire, they could see far away. She was coming from behind and the baby was on her back. They got scared, and they ran away. She said, " You are calling me, and you run away! " They ran home and she ran after them. Then they talked of what had passed. One old man said to them, " You have to make four days. When that girl died, we did not make four days, so she came. " So they cooked and called in their relatives. By making those four days, they took all the scare away from those boys. That is what happened to those Taos people.

7. THE HOPI GHOST KILLS AND GAMBLES. [1]

This story belongs to the Hopi. [2] Those Kosso (Hopi) have lots of *pinang*. There was fighting where they lived in their houses. They lived at Tsi' kwaiye. Then they beat those who came to fight them and they ran after them. A distance from here [3] to San Juan they went fighting, and one Hopi man was killed. They left him there. They did not tell him after four days to go away. [4] Because he had no heart, he was a kind of wind, he stood up then and he walked around all the world and he found no friends. So he came back to his house. They did not see him, because he was a kind of wind. He went into a hill, in a big hole there at the end of the hill he lived. So at night he went out from where he lived. He went into the town and into every house. And he had a broom. So while they were sleeping with their wives, he took his (broom) straw and put it into their nostrils and played with them. They did not see him, he was a kind of wind. Those he played with did not wake up alive. The people did not know why they were all dying. They said, " Wonder why this is going on? All the good girls and good boys are dying. " So the old ones called all the men and women into one kiva. All went, and that Summer chief said, " Now we have called all you children. I do not know why we are losing you all, boys and girls. They are not sick, and yet they die. That is what I am thinking about, " said the Summer chief. " We must find out why it is so. We must look around this place where we live. " So they said, " Yes, that is what is passing here. " They talked about it.

1. Informant I of San Juan.
2. But the narrator was unable to give any explicit Hopi source. The ghost references are in general reminiscent of Maasewi, Skeleton or Death ; but that term was unfamiliar to the narrator.
3. Alcalde, two miles and a half from San Juan.
4. That is, they did not exorcise him.

They got a big boy (*enu*). [1] " Our son, " said the old man, " you ought to think like a woman and a man. Now we have you. Look around this place where we live. If we think about good things, maybe we shall find out who is doing this. " So he said, " Of course I will be a woman and a man. Because in this place we do not have good times. " So they made him stay in that place. And he ate nothing but medicine (*wo'*), and the Summer chiefs and Winter chiefs and the old men and Outside chiefs were taking care of him. In four days he got thin from not eating anything. In five days in the night they went into the kiva. So they all stayed in the kiva. They began to sing. They took their eagle feathers and stood the youth up (with the ends of the feathers) and they sat him down on the road. [2] They said, " Think like a woman and a man and like our father. " So they smoked and gave him a smoke. [3] He fell down, stretching, to become strong like a man and a woman. Having got strong, he sat up, he began to walk two feet up from the ground. So they said all right. He began to fly along the walls, like wind. They said, " Think like a man ." So he said, " Ready. " They said, " Think like a woman. Look around all the place where we live. " So he went out and looked all around the town, like wind. So he saw that dead one. He could not meet him, he looked at him from all sides, he could not do anything to him. So he went back to the kiva. " How did you go, father and our son ? " He said, " Yes, I saw him, but I do not know who he was. I could not meet him. " They were thinking about how to see and catch him. The next night, too, it was just the same. They gave him a smoke and he stretched and got strong, and sat up, and flew around the walls and went out. They said, " Think like a man so you will catch it, whatever it is. " So he went around the town, and he saw that dead one. He ran away, he went on one side, he came on the other side, *all* night. He could not do anything. And he went into the kiva again. " How did you go ? " they asked him. He said, " I saw a big one. I could not meet him. I think he is the one doing this. He is killing us all here. I think he is the one. " The next night he went again. They gave him a smoke and he stretched and got strong, and sat up, and flew around the walls and went out. They said, " Think like a man so you will catch it, whatever it is. " So he went around the town, and he saw that dead one. He pretty nearly met him. All night he was chasing him. He went back to the kiva. He said, " All the people in here, you must think about it good. I pretty nearly caught him. "

1. Of fifteen or sixteen.
2. Presumably the road of meal to their altar.
3. In the long ritual pipe. Inferably there is a connection between smoking and *pinang*, as among the Tewa of Arizona. (See Robbins, Harrington, Freire-Marreco, 105).

The last night only the Outside chiefs and the old ones went in that kiva. They told the people to stay in their own houses. " There you can ask (pray to) our Father and Mother to catch him. " They gave him smoke, he got strong again, he stood up, he went up. He walked about only three times, not like other nights, and he went out and saw him. He turned, and met him. He said, " My friend, is it you ? " — " Yes, it is I. " — " My friend, where do you live ? " He said, " I live way down here. Where do you live ? " — " I live up there. " — " Do you remember, " he said, " once the fighting people came in here and we ran after them and some place way down there they killed me and they did not pick me up, they left me there and they did not make the four days for me or tell me to leave here. That is the one I am. I walked all around the world, I found no friends. So I came back here. " [1] — " Just because you walk around I am her to talk with you. I am your friend. " — " Let's go into this house, ' said the youth, " so you will know how I play with these people. " They were walking with *pinqn*, so the people in the house did not hear them. This man was sleeping with his wife. He said, " Look at me. " He put the straw into the girl's nostrils. She sneezed. He laughed. " That's the way I play, " he said. He was going to tickle the man. " Don't do it, " said the youth. " Let's go out. " They went out, they were talking. " Let's go to my house. " So his friend took him to his house. They went to the big hill, to the big stone ; he turned it over the door ; they went in, he covered it over again with the stone. He had everything in there — red beads, white beads, white dresses, black dresses, belts, buckskin, buffalo skin. " Look here, friend, I have got lots of things, " he said. " Tomorrow night you must come, and we will play (gamble). " So he said, " I guess I better go home. " He went out, and went back to the kiva. He came in. The old men were just staying at talk there saying (i. e. praying), so he would catch it. The youth went in, he did not step anywhere on the ground, but went like wind. They asked him how he had fared, their son and father. He said, " I went and I know him, I have seen him. " " That is good ! That is good ! That is good ! " they all said. [2] " Now you have to tell us about it, " and they put him down in the middle and they sat around him, and he told them about it. " Do you remember a long time ago they were coming into our town, fighting people, and some are living yet from that time. They ran after those warriors. They killed one man. Maybe you remember who he was. You did not pick him up. You left him. You did not make four days or anything for him. That is the one who

1. Cp. Dumarest, 170.
2. Just as Keresan ceremonialists would say to their messenger, " *Tauwa e* ". (That is good.)

walked around and then came back to his home. He is the one who
is doing this. He walks at night into every house; he sticks the straw
into their noses, they sneeze; and he laughs and the next morning they
are dead. I met him. He said to me, ' My friend is here, and I walk
around. ' I said yes. He said to me, 'Let's go into this house. ' A
man there was sleeping with his wife. He began to tickle her with
the straw. He laughed, he said, ' This is the way I play with these
people. Those are they who die the next day. ' That is what he did
there. He said, ' Let's go into my house. ' So he asked me to play
(gamble) with him. " So he said to them he must get ready some red
beads and turquoise (*konye*), and turquoise earrings (*konye oyekon*) and
white garments and black garments. They went into their houses and
got ready and made two large bundles. (That night his friend was to
be waiting for him.) He said to them, " When I say, 'get ready,' you
must be ready, too, and call all the people into the kiva. " So he said
he was ready. They got two Outside chiefs to go with him. He said
to them, " When I go where that dead one lives, you just sit alongside on the road. When the dead one is about to beat me, and I am
going to lose all my things, I will call up and you go in. " Their
" Mothers " gave the Outside chiefs medicine, too. They carried his
bundle. The dead one was waiting for him. He began to sound on
the stone. " My friend is coming, " said the dead one, and he turned
the stone. He threw in one bundle, and the other he carried. The
Outside chiefs stayed up on top. " I am coming with these bundles, "
he said. " I had a hard time; nobody helped me. " He took out his
things. The dead one said, " My friend, you are rich like me. " He
said, " Yes. " They had a big fire. The dead one said, " Let's play
popoyoe' (hidden ball). " — " No, let's not play *popoyoe'*, let's play with
our hands. " [1] He beat the dead one, the dead one had no chance.
He said, " Let's play with sticks. " [2] The youth threw the sticks into
the fire. So the dead one had to play with his hands. Then the dead
one began to beat. Again the youth was beating. After a little they
began to abuse each other. Then they laughed, then they got mad.
The boy won all the things the dead one had. He said, " Why did
you put the ball in the fire ? We ought to play with them now. You
have won all my things, " he said. " Let's play again. I bet you all
my things and the things I won from you, and do you bet me your
heart. " They sang, they called it, they laughed. He won the heart.
The dead one did not want to give his heart. They were pulling at
each other's heart. Then he caught the dead one's heart in his left

---

1. The hands held palms up behind the back, the object to be guessed held in one
hand.
2. Judging from parallel gaming bouts in other Pueblo folktales, the sticks were
magical.

hand. ¹ So he died, the second time. Twice he died. The youth took the heart and called the Outside chiefs and went into the kiva. He said, " Now we shall have good times. " They tried to open his left hand. They could not open it. At last they opened it and they took the heart. And they told the dead one to go away from there, he did not belong there. That is how those Hopi people had *pinang*. ² *Huʿ* !

8. THE ENVIOUS CORN GIRLS. ³

Owewehambaiyo at Okeowinge kǫochuteʾe, Olivella Flower boy was always hunting deer. Shrivelled corn old man (Kǫtsebu sendo ⁴) was his father, and Shrivelled corn old woman (Kǫtsebukwiyo) was his mother. He always killed lots of deer. Some time in the morning after they got their breakfast he would come with his deer. Blue corn girls (Kǫtsaweanyo), Yellow corn girls (Kǫtseyianyo), Red corn girls (Kǫpianyo), White corn girls (Kǫtseanyo), Dark corn girls (Kǫnokǫweanyo), Speckled corn girls (Kǫtsægeanyo), they would say, " Let us grind! Wonder who will be Olivella Flower boy's wife. " The Blue corn girls went first. They filled up their basket and carried it to Olivella Flower boy's house. They said, " *Sǽngi hamu*! " — " *Sǽngi hamu* to you, also, " they said. " Here we bring baskets of meal for you. " " When did you grind this meal? " said Olivella Flower boy. " Early this morning. " Olivella Flower boy said, " Thus early when somebody dies, you give them something to eat. " He did not want to marry them. (They had ground too early.) So they left. Next day they said to Yellow corn girls, " You go, maybe he will marry you. " They watched when Olivella Flower boy came with deer. They went. They said, " Good morning! " — " Good morning to you, also, " they said. " Here we bring baskets of meal for you. " " When did you grind this meal ? " said Olivella Flower boy. " Early this morning. " Olivella Flower boy said, " Thus early when somebody dies, you give them something to eat. " Red corn girls went. They said, " Good morning! " — " Good morning to you, also, " they said. " Here we bring baskets of meal for you. " — " When did you grind this meal? " said Olivella Flower boy. " Early this morning. " Olivella Flower boy said, " Thus early when somebody dies, you give them something to eat. " White corn girls went. They said, " Good morning! " — " Good morning to you, also, " they said. " Here we

---

1. Elsewhere, also, the left hand is associated with death.
2. If they had had no *pinang* they would not have caught the dead one.
3. Informant I of San Juan.
4. Cp. Harrington, 300. He also gives *si*, which I heard as *tsi*, as " wrinkle ", and *buʾu* as " large low roundish place. "

bring baskets of meal for you. " " When did you grind this meal ? " said Olivella Flower boy. " Early this morning. " Olivella Flower boy said, " Thus early when somebody dies, you give them something to eat. " Then Speckled corn [1] girls went. They said, " Good morning ! " — " Good morning to you, also, " they said. " Here we bring baskets of meal for you. " " When did you grind this meal ? " said Olivella Flower boy. " Early this morning. " Olivella Flower boy said, " Thus early when somebody dies, you give them something to eat. " So they left. All went. Fininianyo (Sweet corn girl) [2] was watching these girls, what they did. Sweet corn girl said, " I am going to beat these girls. " Sweet corn girl was by herself, the others were in one house. They did not call Sweet corn girl. She was watching for Olivella Flower boy to see when he came with his deer. So she went, when he came, and said, " Here I bring some meal to eat. " Olivella Flower boy said, " When did you make this meal ? " Sweet corn girl said, " When you were coming with the deer I began to grind. When you came here, I got through. " Olivella Flower boy said, " You are fit to be my wife. " All those girls were watching and saw Sweet corn girl go to Olivella Flower boy's house. They said, " We went first, he did not want us. Sweet corn girl, he liked her. We are good girls, but he does not want us. " They were watching, she did not come out. Sweet corn girl became his wife. When Olivella Flower boy went up the ladder to go after deer, Sweet corn girl would hold the ladder so he would not fall down. All these corn girls got angry with Sweet corn girl. They did not like her. She and her husband were living well. So those girls were looking for something to make her have a bad time. Once they went to her and said, " Let us grind. " They said, " Why don't you walk to our house. If you bring a big basket of corn we will help you to grind. " So she said, " All right. " So she went to White corn girl's house. Then they went after water. They came to the ditch. Blue corn girl had a hoop (*tembe'*). She said, " We have a nice hoop we are used to play with. Let's play a while, then

1. The color-direction associations of the Northern Tewas are given by Harring-ton (Harrington, 43) as north, blue; west, yellow; south, red ; east, white ; zenith, speckled or all-colors; nadir, black or dark. This is the order given for the Cloud boys in tale 10, but in this tale 8, Dark corn girl precedes Speckled corn girl, which is also Freire-Marreco's observation (Robbins, Harrington, Freire-Marreco, 82) and is, therefore, contrary to Miss Freire-Marreco's inference, to be associated with the zenith. The Tewa of First Mesa have the Hopi association for yellow and blue : yellow for the north and blue for the west. This is the association for all the Pueblos excepting in the Northeast and at Isleta where we find black for the north, yellow for the west, blue for the south. Unfortunately the color-direction association for the zenith-nadir in tale 14 of the Arizona Tewa is somewhat obscure.

2. See p. 35, n. 4.

we can go for water. " Sweet corn girl said, " I have been here so long. What will Olivella Flower boy say? " — " He wont say anything to you. " So they took out their hoop. It was a nice little hoop. Blue corn girl said, " Stand up on one side, we will stand on the other side. I will throw it. When it runs, just put your hand through and it will be yours. " So she threw the hoop. She put her hand through it and she stood up a fox (*popowindu*, yellow white-tailed fox). Then they got stones and threw them at her. They said, " You have to walk around like the deer. If you find something good to eat you will have a good time. Il you do not find anything, you will be hungry. We are going to live with Olivella Flower boy. " So they went home, those two girls. She went up, and Olivella Flower boy was coming with a deer. She was coming after Olivella Flower boy and crying. Olivella Flower boy looked at Fox and said, " I wonder why this fox is following me? Maybe she is hungry. She is crying. Maybe she wants some meat. " He put down the deer, cut it, and threw some to Fox. " Eat this meat, " he said. She could not eat it, it was not cooked; she just followed Olivella Flower boy. " I wonder why this fox is following me? " So he went on with the deer, and nobody came out to hold the ladder for him. " Why does not Sweet corn girl come out? " [1] he asked. " Perhaps she went after water. " He went in with the deer. " This morning those Blue corn girls came and asked her to go to their house to grind and she went and did not come back. " So they went to ask about her. They said, " She got through grinding and left. We do not know about her. " They were hunting all around for her. This fox came up to the house, and the dogs barked and she ran away. Olivella Flower boy grew sorry because Sweet corn girl did not come. He did not eat supper. He took his " lion " (*kæ*) (i. e. lion skin quiver), [2] and " buffalo " (i. e. buffalo skin cover) and upstairs he lay down. " I am going to lie here, I am very sad not to have my Sweet corn girl, " he said. " Maybe Sweet corn girl will see me lying up here, how I am grieving for her, and will come back, " said Olivella Flower boy. So those corn girls, Blue corn girls, Yellow corn girls, Red corn girls, White corn girls, Dark corn girls, Speckled corn girls, all said, " Wonder why Olivella Flower boy is grieving over that girl? Maybe he thinks he can get no other girl. We are good girls, better than Sweet corn girl. There he lies in heat and cold and wind. " Olivella Flower boy was there lying down grieving for Sweet corn girl. Those girls dressed up nicely and passed nearby where he was

---

1. At Zuñi it is conventional for a woman to go out to welcome her husband on his return from a day's expedition.

2. So " lion " was interpreted, but it was the lion stone fetish of the hunter, I surmise, that was referred to.

lying down. But Olivella Flower boy would not look at them, he was just crying for Sweet corn girl. That fox would run up to the house, and when the dogs barked would run away. She was getting thin. Sweet corn girl said, " I was walking near Olivella Flower boy. He has such a hard time in heat and cold, in the wind, under the sun. I am so sorry for him. I had better go away from here, to the east where the Kaiowa and Kumạchi live. " She went away, but as she hunted deer she was always thinking about her husband. " I better go back to see Olivella Flower boy. I wonder whether he is still up there. " She came back, he was still up there. She came near the house, the dogs were after her, she ran away. She said, " When I look at Olivella Flower boy I get so sorry. Better to kill myself. Better go to the north, where the Utes live. " As she killed deer, she was thinking about her husband. She came back. Olivella Flower boy was still lying down. All the hair was worn off his cover. She saw him lying there. She came close, the dogs were after her. She was sorry for him. " Better go to the south, " she said. She went to the big mountain in the south, Punyạepị. There Prayer–stick old man was killing foxes by trap. As this little fox was passing, she fell down into the pit. Prayer–stick old man would go in the morning and look at his trap. Sometimes there were four in it, sometimes three, sometimes two. That time there was only Sweet corn girl. In the morning he went, he saw the fox was looking up. " I have caught only one today, " he said. The fox was looking up, crying and crying. " I wonder why the little fox is crying, " said the old man. " Maybe this is not a fox. " He took a stick to hit her. [1] The fox went on crying. The old man said, " This little fox wants to talk, but can not talk. " Then he said, " This is not a fox. " Then he remembered that a long time before Olivella Flower boy lost his wife. " Maybe this is his wife. Maybe, " he said. " I am going to talk to her. " So he said, " You are Sweet corn girl ? " The little fox just nodded her head. " You are not lying ? " She shook her head. The old man went to his house. He said to his wife, " My wife, don't you remember long ago Olivella Flower boy lost his wife. I asked the little fox was she his wife ? She just nodded her head. " — " Go bring her. Be careful of her. Do not hit her, carry her carefully. " So he took a little step-ladder, and went down. " Come on, Sweet corn girl, if you are Sweet corn girl, I am going to take you. " So she came up to him. He put his arm under her and took her to his wife. They were just talking with their heads. He was looking for something on top of her head, patting her head. They were hunting for *pinang*. They found it, something round and hard like a pin, on top of her head. They took it off, and pulled off her skin. Sweet corn girl was all

---

1. The trapped animal was killed by a blow on the neck with a sharp stick.

ragged, she had no clothes. So they bathed her. The old woman said to her, " Olivella Flower boy is up there yet, he does not eat, he does not drink, he is living in cold, in heat, in wind, and all the hair is gone from his cover. " So Sweet corn girl told the old man and old woman how she became a fox. They said, " Yes. " He said, " You were always thinking good things about your husband, so you came here and I caught you. If you had thought bad things you would have been killed. Listen to what I say. You do to them just what they did to you. I will make you a hoop. " So Prayer-stick old man made one for her. " When I take you home to your house, they will treat you nicely. When you go after water they will go after you. When they see your hoop, they will ask you for it. You say, 'This I give to nobody.' They will ask you again. Say, 'This I give to nobody. You stand up on either side. Through the middle I will roll it, whoever catches it first hers it will be.' " Then they dressed her up well and took her home. And Olivella Flower boy was lying down. They took her down inside the house. Her mother said, " Sweet corn girl, have you come? Come in. " Sweet corn girl said, " I have come. " Olivella Flower boy had no strength to talk. So Sweet corn girl went up to see him and talk to him. " Olivella Flower boy, why don't you come and talk to me ? I am Sweet corn girl come to see you. " Olivella Flower boy could not get up. So Sweet corn girl held him up. The hairs blew off his cover. He took a step, he staggered. [1] After that he got well. Then those Blue corn girls saw Sweet corn girl again. They came where she was. They said, " *Hewęboharahi*ʻ! elder sister, Sweet corn girl, where have you been? We did not see you at all. " " I was just taking a walk, " she said. She had the hoop tied to her belt, a nice little one. " *Harahi*ʻ! Sweet corn girl, why don't you give us that hoop? " — "I give it to nobody, " she said. "Let us see what it is. " She let them look at it, but she would not let them touch it. They were saying, " Give it to me! Give it to me! " She said, " I am going to roll it. You lie on one side, you, on the other side. Whoever catches it first, hers it will be. " They lay down, she rolled it, each tried to catch it. So they came up blue snakes. They did not know how to move like a snake. She said, " Somebody may love you, but if nobody loves you, you will go around on the ground when it is hot and when it is cold. " They could not move like a snake. So Sweet corn girl took a little stick and threw it at the snakes. Then she went home. Those snakes, those blue ones, are the Blue corn girls. That is what happened to Sweet corn girl. *Hu*ʻ!

1. Informant acted this out.

3

(*Variant*) [1]

Owewehæmbayo White corn girls (Kųtseanyo) lived. Once they made meal of white corn and at night they went over to the house of Olivella Flower boy with their baskets of meal. So they said to them, " Here we bring some meal to you, Olivella Flower boy. Wonder if you want us to sleep with you? " Then his mother took in the basket of meal, and they went in. Then Olivella Flower boy went in and saw the basket of meal and he told his mother to empty the basket and fill it with meat. [2] So they picked up their basket and went home. Then those Blue corn girls (Kųtsaweanyo) heard of it and they said, " Let's go, too. Wonder if Olivella Flower boy does not need us. " Then they made blue corn meal and took their basket to the house of Olivella Flower boy. So they said to them, " Here we bring some meal to you, Olivella Flower boy. Wonder if you want us to sleep with you? " Then his mother took in the basket of meal, and they went in. Then Olivella Flower boy went in and saw the basket of meal and he told his mother to empty the basket and fill it with meat. So they picked up their basket and went home. Then the Black corn girls (Kųpęnianyo) [3] went. So they said to them, " Here we bring some meal to you, Olivella Flower boy. Wonder if you want us to sleep with you? " Then his mother took in the basket of meal, and they went in. Then Olivella Flower boy went in and saw the meal and he told his mother to empty the basket and fill it with meat. So they picked up their basket and went home. Then the Yellow corn girls went. Then the Pink corn girls (Kųpiawianyo), then the Speckled corn girls (Kųtsægeanyo), then the little Pininianyo. [4] " Sængihu, " [5] they said, " Here we bring Olivella Flower boy a basket of meal, I wonder if he will need us ? " His mother took in the basket. Then Olivella Flower boy said, "These are the ones I need. These are my wives. " So they stayed the night there. And the next day, they went after water to the ditch and when they were coming the White corn girls saw them. Then they said, " Hewemboharạhi' ! those Pinini girls Olivella Flower boy wants to stay with them. And we are nice girls, white and clean, and he does not need us. And those Pinini girls they are not so nice, and they are spotted all over, and yet Olivella Flower boy likes them.

1. Informant 2 of San Juan.
2. A like interchange of meal and meat occurs in the rabbit hunt.
3. The narrator is far from being the careful and stylistic story-teller her uncle is, as appears now in her departure from the accepted color circuit.
4. " A little white ear, not very good. " See Robbins, Harrington, Freire-Marreco, 82.
5. *Sængi*, happy ; *hu*, dark. Translated, " Good night ".

Let's tell them to come and grind with us. " Ana so when they were coming with their water, they called them to com and grind with them in their house. " All right, " said the Pinini girls. " I will tell Olivella Flower boy so he will let us come. " Now Olivella Flower boy had gone out deer hunting (he killed lots of deer), and only his mother and father were at home. So they said to them, " Yes, you may go. " So they went to White corn girls' house to grind. They stopped grinding and said, " We are tired grinding. Let's go outside. " Those two White corn girls had a hoop. When they went through one side they came out coyote, through the other side, they came out girl. So they said to them, " Come and do this just the same. " — " Why ? " — " So you will be some time coyote and some time girl. " — " All right. " Then they went through the hoop, and they came out coyote. Then the White corn girls took away the hoop and she[1] stayed coyote. They took her way out beyond the corrals. She did not know how to eat. She began to cry. Then her husband was coming and she tried to run after him. He said, " Coyote, you do not belong here by the corrals. But if you need meat, here is a piece, " and he threw it to her. But she did not know how to eat raw meat, and she just went on crying. Then when he came to his house and asked his father and mother where his wife had been, they said, " Down at White corn girls' house, and she is not back yet. " Then the mother went out to call her. Then the White corn girls told the old woman, " She went home long ago. She did not come to our house. She got through first and left here. " Then Olivella Flower boy began to cry, and he went up to the top of the house. He did not drink or eat, he just cried for Pinini girl. Pinini girl was just the same, without food, too. Once she went way down where lived Spider old woman (*awæ̨kwiyo*) and Spider old man (*awæ̨ sendo*). Spider old man was killing coyotes and skinning them and selling them. He had a trap. Pinini girl went in and was caught. When Spider old man went to kill this coyote, it began to cry. Spider old man said, " Maybe this is Pinini girl. " (Everywhere they knew that Pinini girl was lost.) Spider old man said, " Are you Pinini girl ? " Coyote nodded her head. So he took her to Spider old woman grandmother.[2] She boiled water and put Coyote in a big pot and poured water over her head and down. The skin cracked on top of her head and they pulled it off, and she stood up a girl. She was very thin. She stayed four days there to get strong. And Spider old woman grandmother was grinding. And after four days and nights Spider old woman grandmother said to her, " Get ready to go home. Your hus-

---

1. The girls are referred to sometimes in the plural, sometimes in the singular, but from here on only in the singular.
2. *Awæ̨kwiyo saya*, as Spider woman is regularly called in story.

band is crying lying up on the house, not eating or drinking. The sun and the winds are eating him away, but he is still alive. " So on the fourth day and night she went back and said, " Good night, father and mother, *Sængih tarainggiya.* " Then his mother called to Olivella Flower boy that she had come. He went down and cried and held her tight. He was very thin, he had been so sad about his wife. Then Spider old woman grandmother went home again. Before she went she gave Pinini girl a little hoop and said, " Take it home, and tomorrow morning go after water and play with the little hoop and when the White corn girls see you they will come after you. " So the next day she went after water and she was playing with the hoop, throwing it and running after it. And the White corn girls saw her and went to her and said, " Pinini girl, did you come ? " and she said, " Yes. " — " Let us have the hoop. " — " No, I can't. Come on, if you go through it, I will give it to you. " So they came near her and they both went through it, and became snakes, big live snakes. So she took the hoop again. Then Pinini girl said to them, " You stay snakes, because you were so mean to me. You can go through what I went through. You can go zigzagging your way, whether it be cold or hot. " So they stayed snakes and Pinini girl went home with her water.

9. FALSE FRIEND .[1]

From Yungeowinge [2] some people came up to San Juan. They stayed *pinan,* they were good ones and so was also their *pinan.* Wherever men walked and got lost, dead ones, too, they would find them and bring them back. And there were three boys who went to the Utes. One boy was married and one was his friend, he was not married. The two were always together, these two friends. They went to the Utes to sell meal. The whole day they walked and then they stopped in the middle of the mountain where an eagle had his little eagles. They saw them. So they said, " When we are on our way home let us take the little eagles home. " They reached the Utes and had a good time there. They got lots of things there to bring back, buckskin, cow-hide, horse-hide, things their friends there gave them. They were coming back. At one place they slept and they came to another place. Then they came and stopped where they had stopped before. His friend said to him, " Let's get those two little eagles, one for you, one for me. " So his friend said to him, " How can we go up ? It is too dark to go up. " " I know from where to

1. Informant 1 of San Juan.
2. Chamito. See Harrington 214, 227-8. The pueblo was relinquished to the Span-iards in 1598, the people going to San Juan.

go, we wont find it hard to go up, " he said. To the other boy they
said, " Stay here. " They did not tell him where they were going,
because there were just the two eagles, one for each. They came to
the mountain. It was very high, very steep. " How can we go up ? "
his friend said to him. " I know how we can go up. Get on top of me,
and shut your eyes and keep them shut til I say to open your eyes. "
So he got on top of his friend and shut his eyes. The other boy was
a kind of *pinan*, so he took him up to the little eagles, and he said,
" Open your eyes. " The two little eagles were there, looking so nice.
Then his friend said to him, " You have to stay here. If you can go
down by yourself, you can ; otherwise you must die up here. And I
am going to live with your wife. " And the poor man stayed up there.
He (the false friend) was a kind of witch (*chuge*). Then he came to
the camp where the third one was staying. The boy in camp opened
his eyes and saw the other boy sleeping there. It was early in the
morning. So the boy got up and made a fire. He asked for the other
boy, " Where is your friend ? You are sleeping by yourself. " (The
two friends used to sleep together.) He said, " Last night when we
went to see if the horses were near, he went on one side and I on
the other and he did not come back. " Then he cooked. Near sunrise
(sun out) they got their breakfast. The other boy said, " Let's go
hunting for him. " He went to look for him. When he returned to
camp he saw the friend there. The friend said, " Did you find my
friend ? " He said, " No. Let's take his horse and tie him back of our
horses and go, maybe he may meet us. We will take his things with
us. " The other said, " Let's hunt for him again, we don't want to
leave him behind. " So they went hunting again. They were hunting,
they could not find him. Then they got their dinner. The (innocent)
boy said, " I wonder where he is. " They got ready and brought in
the horses. They took his horse and his things. He said, "We can put
his things on his horse and take them home. " They stopped at
their next camp and the next day they came (home) and that other
one did not come. When they came, his wife went to ask for her
husband, where was he ?

So the friend said, " When we stopped, after a while he went after
the horses and did not come back and the next day we hunted for
him until dinner time and he did not come. " And she went to the
house of the third boy and he said the same words. So the friend
went into the wife's house. Then he said to the wife, " I don't know
whether your husband will come home or not. I guess he died. Don't
you want to live with me. " And the girl did not want to. " Maybe you killed my husband. You wanted me and so you killed him.
I do not need you. "

The man was way up high. The mother eagle brought rabbits, and
the man ate with the eagles. Now the man had a shirt of buckskin and

gathered up a piece and caught the rain to drink. When it did not rain, he had a hard time. He ate raw what this mother eagle brought the little eagles to eat. When the eagles got big they began to fly out. Then the man had a hard time. He had nothing to eat, he was getting thin, with no water, nothing to eat. But he was still alive. His wife was thinking about it, she called all her relatives. She said to them all, " Father, uncle (*Tara, meme*) I am thinking this way. Let us go to the house of those *pinandi* to find my husband, I wonder if they can bring my husband, living or dead. That is what I am thinking. " All the relatives said, " That is good, what you are thinking. " So they went. They carried with them to their house *pochashu* [1] (black dirt), pollen, and meal. [2] So those old men said, " Yes, we will help you. In four days and nights you must come with all your relatives to our house. " So in four days and nights they went, all of them (because that night they were going to have *pinan*). Then *pinan sendo* said to the relatives, " Don't think about any thing wrong, so we can perform well. " So they stood up two *pinan* boys. " Think like a woman and a man, so wherever he is, bring him. " So they went out to search. They stopped at the same places where the three boys had stopped. Then they came back. The next night another two went out. They went to the Utes, they found out all about the boys. But they could not find him. Two more went; on their way back, they stopped at that camp by the mountain. They did not find him. The last night another two went out, these had more *pinan*. " Maybe our Mother will help us and maybe tonight we will find him. " They came to the Utes. They looked around, they did not find him. They found where he had stopped hunting. They came near to where the eagles were. So they went up into the mountain. Then they found where he was. They brought him down. He was nearly dead, only bones, very thin. Early in the morning they brought him, and took him in. They layed him down in one corner of their room. They said, " You people may be excused, to go to your beds. Tomorrow you will learn where we got this boy. " So all went out. They had a road of black dirt, pollen, and meal, and they set him in the middle. He was so weak he could not sit up. They gave him a medicine to get strong. Then those *pinandi* told him, " You must tell us the story of what happened when you left home with your friend. " So he told all the story of what happened with his friend. So they said, " Your friend has *pinan*, but we beat his *pinan*. The other day maybe he got ashamed, and he died. " They sent word to his wife that he was there. Four days he was to stay there and then his relatives came for him and he went home with them. That was good *pinan*. That is what happened to that man. *Hu*' !

1. See p. 10, n. 3
2. The characteristic way of asking a society or doctor for aid.

(*Variant*) [1]

Olivella Flower boy had a friend. He asked him to go hunting. They went hunting together and the friend became an eagle and carried Olivella Flower boy up on the side of a cliff and left him there. Then the friend went to the house of White corn girl, the wife of Olivella Flower boy. Olivella Flower boy stayed on the edge of the cliff. *K'uyemo'e*(? Squirrel) found him there and fed him from a little cup. Then Squirrel planted a seed which grew into a tree, and on that tree Olivella Flower boy came down from the cliff. Squirrel gave him an ear of corn to eat and to spit on his wife, she was going to marry his friend.

10. THE FAITHLESS WIFE. [2]

At Tekeowinge they used to live. They were getting ready to have a dance, *puwǫre* dance. [3] Olivella Flower boy had the dance in mind. (He was the Summer chief. See below). So he called all the men into one house and told them why he had called them. " Now we know why you need us, " they said. " That is a good dance you have in mind, " they said. " We shall have lots of fruit, lots of corn, lots of everything we have planted. " So those men said, " We need parrot downy feathers (*tanyi po*, parrot hair) and parrot tail feathers (*tanyi w'ǫ*), and we have none. " Then Olivella Flower said, " That will not keep us from having the dance. I will go down to the South where it is warm and the parrots live and get those feathers. " And he said, " Now we have to work, everyone has to bring feathers of the summer birds. Our Mother will help me, and I will bring back those parrot feathers, so we shall have what we need. " So they brought in their feathers and tied [4] the feathers themselves, for Blue Oxuwah, for Yellow Oxuwah, for Red Oxuwah, for White Oxuwah, for Speckled Oxuwah, for Dark Oxuwah. Then they took the feathers out to the hills, so the Oxuwah would help them. Those Oxuwah remembered Olivella Flower and loved him. Olivella Flower had a

1. Informant 2 of San Juan. She heard this story from one Antonio who was in a lumber camp in Utah. Antonio had read the story in a book of Hopi stories. This is the first time I have heard a Pueblo Indian story from a literary source.

2. Informant 1 of San Juan.

3. Danced at Santa Clara, sporadically, when there are girls to be initiated into the woman's society in charge. Formerly there were men in the society, which appears to have been a warrior society. (See p. 61). Burlesque is the outstanding feature today, the sexes changing roles. *Puwǫre* is no longer danced at San Juan.

4. Presumably to prayer-sticks. Tying feathers is the form of reference for this elsewhere, e. g., at Jemez and Zuñi.

father. Olivella Flower was Summer chief. Some of those boys were to stay working *pinạn* in the house of Olivella Flower until he came back, in order to help him on his journey. He told White corn girl (his wife) to take care of those inside, to bring them water and food, to sweep the room, then to take care of them until he came back. He said, " These boys are *pinạn* in here because I want to come back quickly and they are helping me. " Then he went out to the west. He went up Tsikomo on top (*tsikomokwaiye*). When he was up there came Oxuwah tseyi powaha [1] (Oxuwah yellow servant or errand man.) Yellow Oxuwah's errand man told Olivella Flower to go in. So he went in. Yellow Oxuwah's errand man said, " White corn girl, she has failed you. You told us to help you. We were going to help you, to give you parrot feathers. But what you told White corn girl to do she did not do. She has failed you. When she went after water she went into the ditch, and a boy came after her, and she went with him and she has not been carrying water and food to those boys doing *pinạn*. She is just going with that boy. " Olivella Flower said, " Even if my wife has failed me, I have to do what I said I would do. " Yellow Oxuwah's errand man said to him, " I do not know when you will arriye where you are going. You will become an old man on the way. " — " I have to do what I said. I do not care if I die on the way. " So he went on. He came to a big wide river. He could not see across, no dry place. " *Hewembohaṛahi*[ʹ] ! What am I going to do here ? " Then he met a water snake (*popanyu*). The water snake called him by name. Olivella Flow r did not know who was talking to him. " I am the one who is talking to you, Olivella Flower. Your wife has failed you, so you are going through a hard time here. " — " Yes, my wife does not love me, she does not like me, she does not need me. So I am having a hard time here. But I have come. " He said to the water snake, " Will you not pass me over this river ? " — " Yes, I will pass you over. But you have to go very far. Maybe our Mother will help you and you will arrive where you are going. " So that snake passed Olivella Flower across the river. Before he knew he was on the other side ot the river. Then the snake talked to him. " Just look at it (consider). The first house you will reach will be Snakes' house. Don't be frightened because you see snakes, yellow snakes. Then you will go to Ants' house. There you will be near *w'aiyege*. " [2] So he went on.

---

1. Each of the six Cloud beings or kachinas has his errand man or guard. These may be equated with the *salimobia* of Zuñi. As Tsikomo is in the west, it is associated with the yellow kachina. See p. 30, n. 1. Tsikomo is in fact called the cardinal mountain of the west. Harrington, 44.

2. " There is no winter there, summer all the time. "
Probably a reminiscence of *wenima* (*wainema*), paradise of the Keres (Dumarest, 173). Cp. Harrington, 571.

He came to Snakes' house, and he could find no place to set down his feet, the snakes were so many. Then he gave them corn meal. He said to them, " Do not bite me, Snakes! I am only walking by here. " They said, " *Hewemboharạhi*! Your wife failed you, so you are going through a hard time here. " So they took him to the Snake chief's house. Snake chief said, " Olivella Flower, your wife failed you, but our Mother will help you. That is why you have been able to come so far. " Olivella Flower said, " What I said I would do I have to do, even if I have a hard time. I told my wife to do certain things until I returned; but she did not love me and did not do them. " Snake chief said, " We will help you. You will arrive at Ants' house. " So he went on, and he came to Ants' house. There were lots of ants. He gave them corn meal. " I am very poor, " he said. " But what I had in mind to do, that I am doing, that is why I am walking here. My wife failed me. She did not do what I told her to do. That is why I am going through a hard time. " — " Your wife failed you; but our Mother loves you. That is why you have been able to come here. " Then he went on and approached *w'aiyege*. It was like a mesa; he looked way down, way down. It looked very green; the trees were very green. By that time he had been walking ten years. " Maybe this is the place I was to come to, " he said, " but how can I get down there ? " There he sat and looked down into the green. There came to him a *potse* (water-dog i. e., otter) [1]..... That otter said, " You are still walking because you wanted to do what you said you would do. That is why you have come here. That is the way men should do. Whatever they say they will do, they should do. Your father is sitting doing *pinạn*. That is why I come to help you. Think like a man, I will take you down. " So that otter took him down, and he came to the house of Parrot chief (*tanyitonọ*). He was carrying pollen (*k$̣e$*) and he gave it to Parrot chief. Parrot chief said, " *Hewemboharạhi'*! Olivella Flower, Summer chief of Tekeowinge (tekeowinge po'ingtuyo), having it in mind you came here. You came this long way because your wife failed you. You have had a hard time, yet you have come. In two days you will be back in your house, because Blue Oxuwah, Yellow Oxuwah, Red Oxuwah, White Oxuwah, Speckled Oxuwah, Dark Oxuwah will help you. You have been so long coming because your wife failed you. Your father is seated asking our Mother to help you. You are to take back what you need. " Then the parrots came in, and very prettily they spread their tails. " Take out what feathers you like, " said Parrot chief. So Olivella Flower plucked their feathers, new feathers. Then he thanked them. Otter had told him to come back to where he was. So he found Otter waiting there for him. Otter said to him, " Now you are taking

1. Henderson and Harrington, 23.

home what you want, because our Mother is helping you and your father is helping you. " Otter put him on the back of his neck, he carried him past the Ants' house and the Snakes' house and to the river. Snake was waiting for him, so Snake came and said, " Have you come ? " " Yes, " said Olivella Flower. " Your father is still working for you. Our Mother is helping you. You are having good fortune. " Snake passed him over the river, to this side. Then he went on. He walked until he was tired. Then he lay down and went to sleep. He slept as if he were dead. As he lay sound asleep Oxuwah *pinandi* (the supernatural cloud beings) took him up from there and carried him to a little hill near his home, and laid him down. When he awoke he looked around, saying, " Where am I lying, where am I? " He did not know where his home was, so long had he been gone. So he sat there and thought about it. " Maybe this is the place where my home is. It looks like my home. But how did I get here while I was asleep ? " Then he went up the hill and looked closely. " This *is* my house, " he said. " I wonder who brought me here and helped me, " he said. As he approached his home. they saw him. Everybody said, " Olivella Flower is coming! Olivella Flower is coming! " They were glad to see him. Then he went into where his father was *pinąn.* (They told him, " When you reach home White corn girl will come and try to embrace you; but do not let her embrace you, go first to where your father is. ") So he went and found his father, now an old man. Then he told of what happened to him on the road. Then they looked at his parrot feathers. Next day they called all the men. Then he stayed in four days. *That time* White corn girl carried in water, and brought them something to eat and went in and swept the room. " Do not give me your hand (? touch me) for four days, " Olivella Flower said to her. After four days they began the dance. White corn girl and Olivella Flower were sitting on the roof and looking at the dancers. " Do you love me ? " Olivella Flower asked White corn girl. " Of course I love you. " — " Will you do what I tell you? " She said yes. He said, " All right. Take off your turquoise earrings and take a big round stone and break them. " She did this. " Now smash your red beads. " She did this. The dancers and the people saw what Olivella Flower and White corn girl were doing. " *Hewemboharąhi*'! " they said, " White corn girl is going to have something bad with her husband. " Olivella Flower said to her, " Go down into our rooms and bring up a buckskin. " She brought it up. He slit the skin for the neck, and made a dress such as the Utes used to wear. He said, " Take off your dress and belt [1] and put on this deerskin. " So she did it. Then he gave her a

[1]. " They used to wear large, wide belts. "

sack of red paint [1] and put a little lard in her hand so she could paint her face all over. In this way her husband made her a Ute. Then he said, " Up there live those Utes. You belong to them. To them you have to go. Tewa never have two husbands, only Utes. Utes have two husbands and two wives. You belong to them. " Then he sent her away. " Take a sack, " he said, " and go into every house and get food, and go. Go to those who marry two by two. " So she went to the Utes, and she became their Mother. That is how the Utes got White corn girl for their Mother. *Hu'* !

II. THE TAOS BOY CAPTURED BY CHEYENNES : [2] THE BEAR DOCTOR [3]

Long time ago they went hunting, those Taos people (Tawin [4]), they went buffalo hunting. Against them came fighting the Shaiyeno (Cheyennes). They killed the Taos people, all of them, except one boy. That boy the Shaiyeno took to their home. Their chief took him and cared for him, like his own son. He grew up big and stout. He had a friend with whom he went buffalo hunting and killed buffalo.... When these Shaiyeno took a captive they would tie the captive, whether boy or girl, to a stake in the ground. [5] They would make a big fire, and around the fire and the captive, who was bound maked to the stake, they made a big dance. After they began to dance they would call out the dancers by name, and as the name of each was called he would go and cut out a piece of flesh from the captive at the stake, cook it at the fire and eat it. This is what they did at their war dance (*hemi share*). At this time they would hide away their other captives in the mountains so they would know nothing about it. This Taos boy had been taken away in the mountains, too, so he would not know what they did. Whenever they wanted to take him to tie to the stake, their chief would say, " Take him next time ! Next time ! " He put them off because he liked the boy. Now the other men began to grow angry about this. They were having hard times, and they thought it was because they had not taken that boy. " We are going to take him, " they were saying. The boy's friend saw the stake that was being made ready. They had been buffalo hunting and had come home. His friend saw the stake and said,

---

1. *Pi'mu*, red sack. Rabbit hunters, men and women, use this red paint " so the sun wont burn them. "
2. Informant 1 of San Juan.
3. Cp. in particular Dumarest, 234-6.
4. Meaning " rats, " which is the nickname the Tewa give the people of Taos. " If they call us ' rats ' " they say at Taos, " we will chew them up like rats. " And the Taos people in turn nickname the Tewa " Wolf droppings. "
5. Cp. Dorsey, 49.

" Let us go hunting again. " They went, and when they made camp
his friend said to him, " My friend, I like you. Now I am going to
tell you something I know. Did you see a stake in the ground? Do
you know why they put the stake in? " — " I do not know why
they put in the stake. " — " Now since you are my best friend, I am
going to tell you. When they go to fight and bring back a boy or a
girl or woman they make a big fire and eat this one. They cut off all the
flesh, only the bones stand up. Your father likes you very much and
he has always said, ' Next time, take him next time. ' But now it is
your time, they are going to do it to you, in just two days. You had
better run away from here. My poor friend, I will hide you. Leave
tonight. Look at those three stars in line. [1] Go by them and you will
reach your home. Let us get supper, and then you go. " So they said
goodbye to each other. He took two pairs of moccasins and lunch and
a good horse. He went all night, till sunrise, and all next day. Then
he slept, he was tired. After two nights and one day his horse was
tired, he turned him loose, he went on, on foot. . . . His friend went
home, alone. He said, " My friend stayed back in the mountain. He is
still hunting. He has not yet killed a buffalo. I killed one and came
back. " They went after him; but they did not find him. They said,
" Maybe somebody told him and he ran away. " So they followed
him. on good horses. They found the horse he had left. . . . He
saw them coming. Then he saw a fire. He came up to the fire. He
was not very far from his home, he had maybe six days still to go.
Well, he drew near to the fire. He saw an opening in the cliff wall
and a light. He looked underneath towards the light and he saw a
girl. Her hair was hanging down and she was brushing it. She was
a nice looking girl. She was brushing her hair with a brush broom
(such as they used long ago). [2] " Here are people, " he said, " but I
don't know what kind of people they are. I am going to knock. " So
he knocked. They did not say anything, so he knocked again. She
said, " Who are you? " She opened the door to see. He said, " It is I.
Let me in. I am running home from the Shaiyeno. I saw a light here.
Wont you let me come in? " She said, " Come in then. " So he
went in and sat down. She gave him to eat. Then she said, " Nobody
comes to our house; but you have come. I don't know what my
father will say to me, I don't know what my mother will say to me,
because you have come in here. My father is very mean. We are
bears, but you saw me as a girl; that is why I let you in. " Then she
said, " My father and mother went to help those *pufona* (doctor

1. *Wirini.* These are Winter stars. They are watched by the two Town chiefs.
If these stars come out in leaf open moon (*kapawepo*), May 4 or 6, it will not freeze,
the summer will be good. If they are later, the summer will be bad. These stars are
supernaturals, as at Jemez.
2. And in many towns still use.

society). ¹ My father and mother will come back early in the morning. I don't know what to do with my father and mother. Just because you saw me, I let you come in. Do not be afraid of my father and mother. I will manage them for you. " The boy was sitting there afraid. She said, " Are those Shaiyeno coming after you ? " " Yes, that is why I ran away, " he said. " The Shaiyeno will not find you because you are in here. " . . . . Now her father and mother were coming early in the morning. From down at the foot of the hill they smelled somebody in their house. They came up to the door. " Whom have you in here ? " they said. Then the girl said, " Do not be angry, Father. A boy came, the Shaiyeno were after him, poor boy ; that is why I let him in. " Then they went in. With them they were bringing lots of paper-bread and lots of sweet corn. Those who were making *pinang* had given all that to the bears. ² So they gave the boy something to eat again. Because of their girl they did nothing to him. They took off their skins and hung them up, and sat up, people. They said, " You were fortunate to come here. The Shaiyeno are coming after you in anger. " They said, " You are to stay here six days. " ³ They went to sleep inside their house. Then those Shaiyeno passed by ; but they did not find him, and passed on. So they said, " The Shaiyeno wont come after you any more. Now you have to think about what you will do. " So he said, " Thank you very much. I will never forget it. " So now he went on, but no longer running. He reached Taos. At first the Taos people did not know him, they were scared. But he was the little boy taken captive. His mother was still living ; his father had been killed. Then everybody wanted to see him, and came to see him. He told them the story about those bears, how they were people.

12. THE WITCH DOLL. ⁴

There was a boy married to the daughter of *Pu'fona sendo* ⁵. This *pu'fona sendo* had *pinǫn* to catch witches. The boy did not believe that *pu'fona sendo* had *pinǫn*. The boy was a fast runner, nobody could beat him. *Pu'fona sendo* stayed in four nights, and after four days everybody would go into the big kiva, men and women, and

1. Among the Keres and at Jemez and Isleta the bear is a tutelary spirit of the medicine societies.
2. An illustration of the idea that the payment to the medicine men is to be passed on by them, in part at least, to their Spirits.
3. *Wi* (one), *jare* (six days), translated, one week. The count is from Monday to Saturday, Sunday excluded.
4. Informant of San Juan. For a close Keresan parallel in witch-catching, also for a picture of a witch " doll ", see Dumarest, 163-165, fig. 1.
5. Old man or chief. The chiefs are frequently thus referred to.

pu'fona would give them medicine. The Outside chief would go around to every house to call them. About this time (4 P.M.) this girl was washing her husband's head, and he was thinking, " I am going to see if they have *pinąn,* if it is a lie or the truth. I am going to make a doll (*suwi*), and I wonder if they can catch me. " She combed his hair well. He got a rag and shook it well and put it under his blanket. He got another and put it under his blanket and he got another and put it under his blanket. " This is enough, I can make a big doll. " He went to the river, and sat down and began to make the doll. He made ears and eyes and mouth and he held it out and looked at it. " I think it is good, " he said. He made arms, too. " I am going to lay it here, and after supper I will come after it. " He lay it down and covered it with earth. He left and as he went he looked back and there was the doll running after him. " *Hewem-boharąhi'*! it lives, " he said. He caught it and laid it down and covered it. This time it did not run after him again. He came home. That night his wife and father and mother were bathing and washing their head to get ready. " Where were you so long ? " said his wife. " Just taking a walk, " he said. They got ready. It was growing dark. They said, " We will go first, so the women can get good seats, the men last, when you come, lock the house. " — " I am going to get ready now to go *chuge* (witch). " He took off his shirt and trousers and tied up his hair way up on his head and got *tǫ* (white clay) and put it all over his head. He had a looking-glass. " I need something yet. " He got a ragged old dress. He tied it around his arms and legs, under his knees. He put black paint (hand prints) over each shoulder. " If they catch me, they have *pinąn.* If they do not catch me, they have no *pinąn.* " As he was getting ready, in came the doll. "*Hewembo-harąhi'*! this is living. " He caught it and went out. Those *pu'fona* were at work now. Those Outside chiefs were up on a roof and looking around. This boy, nobody saw him, he got a little stone and threw it at the Outside chief. Nobody saw him, the witch helped him. Then they looked in their medicine bowl, and saw that boy, what he was doing. The *pu'fona* got mad and threw out their arms, and that hit him outside. So he went to his house, running into his father's house, the doll under his arm. He hid way up high behind the corn store. They went in, those *pu'fona,* and took him down. He was struggling. There were lots of people in the kiva and they took him in with his doll. They did not know who it was. They sat him down where those *pu'fona* were sitting. That *pu'fona sendo*! it was his *soningi.* ' His mother and his wife they did not know about it as yet. Then he said, " Here they are all together. You must believe what

----

1. Male connection by marriage; i.e., son-in-law. Laughter here, the situation seemed very comic to both narrator and interpreter.

our Mother is working here for us. But my own son does not believe it. Now he will see it. " And he gave him medicine. And the boy looked in the water, and he saw himself in there. " My wife is combing my hair. " He thinks how he was shaking out the rags. He sees himself shaking one rag, then another. He thinks of how he went up to the river, and made a doll. " There I am hiding the doll. Then I went along with the doll running after me. I caught it again and hid it again. And I came in my house and my wife gave me to eat and my wife went to the kiva with my mother and sister. And I was painting with white, and putting on black hand prints, and tying an old dress on my arms and legs. Then came the doll and I took him. " He was talking of all he had done. " I came out and threw a stone at the Outside chief and ran away, and when the *pu'fona* shook their arms at me I nearly fell down, and ran away and hid way up in the stack. They followed me, caught me, brought me into the kiva. " So now he believed, and he became *pu'fona*. All this he saw in the bowl. [1]

13. LITTLE DOG TURNS GIRL. [2]

At Yungeowinge they lived, Yellow corn girls Agoyone', [3] Rising Star, lived where the school-house is now. [4] He had turquoise earrings. [5] He was not married. He had two sisters, big girls. Rising Star made a dance, [6] and he sent word to everybody to come. He made the dance that he might find a girl to marry him. So they came, all the Tewa (*tǫki w'ǫne*). Those Yellow corn girls they, too, came to the dance. The Yellow corn girls had nice clothes, they had black dresses marked red along the edges, but these dresses they did not wear. They had a little dog. That little dog they left at home, to keep the house. As they were dancing there came there a maiden. They did not know who she was. " She has on a nice dress, " said the Yellow corn girls, " just the same kind of a dress as we have at home, " they said. " Just look at it! " They did not know the girl. Then they went home. The little dog had turned into a girl and had dressed like a girl and had gone to the dance. There Rising Star had liked her and had taken her. Well, the Yellow corn girls went home. After a while the little dog came. She came carrying earrings in her

1. This story was told in response to a question I put about second sight through a medicine bowl.
2. Informant 7 of San Juan.
3: " Star now ", i.e., rising (?)
4. Southwest edge of town.
5. Not worn today ; but they were worn within the memory of our middleaged woman interpreter.
6. As individuals or rather families may do on First Mesa.

mouth. They said, " Just look at our little dog bringing Rising Star's turquoise earrings! " They said, " The girl we saw, we guess, was this little dog. Maybe this dog is that girl because she is bringing Rising Star's earrings. " They took the earrings. In about three moons the dog fell sick [1] and two puppies were born. The Yellow corn girls said, " Now we are going to the house of Rising Star. There were lots of nice girls, and he did not want them and he took a dog. Let's go to his house! Maybe he will be ashamed. " They made paper-bread. They said, " We have to take the dog to her husband's home. " So they put some corn meal in two baskets and each girl carried a basket and under her arm one of the puppies. The mother dog followed them. They came into the middle of the town. People saw them and said, " Those Yellow corn girl are coming to the house of Rising Star with baskets of meal. " So they came and went up. The *s'ai* (woman married into family i.e., the dog), stayed below. They went up and in. The said, " *Sæ̜ngi tsamu* ! " Rising Star said, " Sit, Yellow corn girls. " The little dog was below, looking up and crying, " *Agoyoné-é* ! " They talked, they said, " Here we are bringing these children. They are Rising Star's children· " Rising Star's father asked, " Which of you is our *sa'i* ? " They said, " We left your *sa'i* down below. " Rising Star was lying down, his arms crossed behind his head. His two big sisters were asking, " Which is our *sa'i* ? " They said, " Not we. Your *sa'i* is down below. Here are the children. " They left the puppies there. Rising Star got very much ashamed, and did not want to be seen by anybody. He was waiting for it to grow dark, in order to go away from that place. There were lots of good girls, and yet he had liked a dog. Thus it happened. *Hu'* !

(*Variant* [2])

There was a feast, and they had a big dance, and Agoyone' called all the people to come, ane they all got ready. Rising Star was a nice boy, no boy was equal to him. He looked at the girls ; but he saw none among them he wanted to marry. That is why he told all the people to come to the feast. The little dog (*chulae*) of the White corn girls heard there was a feast (*shɑkeri*). [3] Then the White corn girls went to the feast. And then the little dog said, " I guess I better dress up, too. I wonder if Rising Star would like me. " It was a little white dog. So she dressed up and went and stood up at the south-west corner of the court, looking at the dance. And all the people

1. " Got sick to have baby. "
2. Informant 2 of San Juan. Heard from Informant 1.
3. *Oke shɑkerina'* " Feast at San Juan ", Santa Clara people would say of San Juan day.

saw her and wondered where that nice girl came from. And Rising Star was out there too, and he saw that girl too, so he went around the house and to the girl and called her, and said, " Let's go to my house. " So they went to Rising Star's house. And that little dog stayed all day in Rising Star's house, all day, and Rising Star stayed, too. So in the evening when they got through the dance all the people went home, and the little dog went home, too. And after the little dog took off all her clothes and stood up as a dog again, came Yellow corn girls and they began to talk together. The little dog heard them. " *Harąhi*! One girl came, I wonder who she was, a nice girl. Maybe Rising Star took her to his house. We were thinking Rising Star would want us and we dressed up nicely. But he did not want us, because he saw that girl. " In about nine months or eight months that little dog had a little baby. Yellow corn girls said, " I wonder whereever little dog got that baby ? " It was a little boy. So they washed it and dressed it and laid it by the fire. And the baby cried Agoyone'! Agoyone'! They got scared. " *Harąhi* ! " they said. " Maybe this was the girl. We have to grind meal and take it to Rising Star with the baby and the dog. " They ground all day. In four days they washed the dog and they washed the baby. " We must go, " they said. They filled one basket of meal and one Yellow corn girl carried the baby, and one the basket of meal, and the little dog just ran after them. So they went to Rising Star's house. So they went up, with the baby, and the little dog stayed below. So they said to him, " *Sægi tsamu* ! We came with our basket of meal and our little dog and the baby she had. The baby cried Agoyone'! Agoyone'! So you are its father. " So Rising Star went up and went down and got the little dog and took her up. And the Yellow corn girls left them. And they do not know what Rising Star did with that dog and little baby. Rising Star was ashamed. He was a good boy and he believed the dog was a girl. *Hu'* !

14. DISOBEDIENT GIRLS. [1]

There were two Yellow corn girls way down at Achuga, [2] and the Governor (*toyo*) said, " Everybody has to go and get onions (*sih*). " [3] So everybody went, except those two Yellow corn girls, they stayed home. They said, " We will go afterwards and bring the onions. " In the evening they went, when the others were coming back. " Let's run, " they said. They ran and ran and ran far away. The others were coming with their onions, and they were just going.

1. Informant 2 of San Juan.
2. Probably Ashu'ge See p. 80.
3. See Robbins, Harrington, Freire-Marreco, 53.

And they went where the onions were. They began to take them
up. The sun was going. So they took up just a few of them. So they
said, " Let's go, the sun is going. " The younger said, " Somebody is
singing. " The elder said, " Nobody is coming, they all went home. "
— " Somebody is singing. " — " No, " said the elder, " I am singing
from my nose (*nashito'otǫ*). " The younger said, " Let's wait. " It
was getting dark, and they were still there. Then one of those Tsa-
biyu sendo [1] came with long jucca (*pa*) blades. He came and he said,
" *Sǫngi tsamu*! You do not mind the chiefs (*tuyowa*, pl.). " They
said, " We will go with you. " — " No, I did not come to bring
you home. " Then he drew out his whip, and whipped one and then
the other. They ran and cried. And he ran after them and whipped
them, and they ran and he after them. And the laces of their moccasins broke and their leggings fell off, and they left them there and
ran, and their belts came off and they left them there and kept on
running. He was after them and whipped them. And they threw off
their shawls and dropped their onions. And he ran and he whipped.
Their under belt came off and dropped. He used up all his blades.
Then he said, " Yellow corn girls, next time you wont do this again.
When people go out, they should all go together. This is what
happens to girls who do not obey their chiefs. Now go home! "
They went home, without onions, without moccasins or belts or
shawls.

15. AWL BOY. [2]

At Puye [3] they lived, Prayer-stick old man and Shrivelled corn
old woman. They had one son, Olivella Flower boy. He had a wife,
Yellow corn girl. Olivella Flower boy went hunting every day and
killed a deer. All the people there ate meat. For some time they wanted to go to the Kosso (Muki, i. e. Hopi). Yellow corn girl was going
to have a baby. They told everybody they were going to the Hopi
to get ready. In the morning they got ready, that night Yellow corn
girl had her baby. So she went, too, and left the baby. An old woman
was left, too, because she could not walk. The old woman went out
looking for something to eat, from house to house. She went all
over the houses. She went in to the house where Prayer-stick old
man and Shrivelled corn old woman and Yellow corn girl lived. She

---

1. Two kachina-like spirits who live in the eastern mountains. They are bogeys
to be equated with the Atoshle of Zuñi, and Suyuku and Tcabaiyo (Fewkes 3;
pl. XIII) of the Hopi. At Zuñi I have seen young girls run away from Atoshle very
much as these corn girls are described as doing.

2. Informant 3 of Santa Clara.

3. Believed by Santa Clara people to be an ancestral home. (Cp. Harrington,
236-8).

found a baby in there crying. She said, " I have found a baby. " She took it out. She took it home. She lay in, with the baby. In four days she got up. After a while the baby grew up. Then the little boy went out in the houses, looking for something to eat, killing mice and rats to take to his grandmother. He came in where his father had lived. Somebody called him from the roof beams. It was Awl [1] calling to him to take him down and to Grandmother's house. So he took down the awl. He could not reach, so he took a stick and got it out. He took it home. Awl told the little boy, " If you have some cowhide, wrap me in it. " So the little boy picked it up and wrapped it and took it to Grandmother. Awl told the little boy, " If you go hunting, take me along, and I will help you. " [2] After that when he went hunting he took Awl along. He killed lots of rabbits and jack rabbits. After some time he told Grandmother he would go hunting deer. He went to Kwæ sabokwaiye. [3] Awl said, " If you find a deer, throw me so I can kill the deer. " The boy's name was Kækopiri e'nu (Awl boy). So he threw the awl, and they got the deer. He wanted to bring it home, but it was heavy. So Awl told the little boy, " I will help you carry it home. " So they brought the deer home to Grandmother. When he brought the deer, she was very happy. After that he went deer hunting every day. After that they had a good time. After that they had lots of deer meat. They dried the meat. The little boy said to Grandmother, " I am going to the Hopi. " The little boy got ready. In the morning he went. He was going along for about five days. In five days he came to the Hopi. So Awl told the little boy where his mother and father lived. " You will come into the middle of the town and upstairs live your grandmother and grandfather and mother and father. They will not know you when you come. They have forgotten you. If they do not know you, tell them, 'I am the baby you left, I am Awl boy. My grandmother put that name to me.' " Then Yellow corn girl remembered the time she left the baby and she cried. They treated him very well, and he had a good time. In the morning when Awl boy went out he saw his people were poor and the other people, the witches, had everything nice, parrot feathers were tied to their ladders. He asked his grandfather, " Why are you all poor and those witches have everything nice? Now we will do the same. Now you call all the men, all those who are poor. " They had a meeting that night. Awl boy told all to get ready. " Bring me a lunch. I am going to wear parrot feathers (*tanyi po'*). " Awl boy got ready, they made moccasins for him. He asked an

---

1. An awl is made from a lion's foot-bone, and so named; *kæ*, lion; *ko*, arm, foot; *piri'* ?
2. In this tale and the two following, awl is obviously a hunt fetish, presumably because it is made from mountain lion, the great hunter.
3. Height in the Jemez mountains, near Mount Tsikomo.

Outside chief (*akonotujo*) to go with him. When they went out, they found a deer. They killed it. They went far, they came to a mesa. Awl boy told Outside chief, " Now you shut your eyes. Do not open your eyes until I say. " From there the little boy put Outside chief and the deer on his back. They went down off the mesa, he told the Outside chief to open his eyes. They were down. The boy said, " There are some feathers, *tanyi wæ* (parrot tail), *tanyi po‘* (parrot feathers), but do not pick then up, we are going for better ones. " So they came to where those parrots lived. They met a man who was a Parrot man. They asked where the chief (*tunjo*) lived. He took them to where the chief lived. He brought them in. So they went and told the chief, " We bring you a deer and we want some feathers. " The chief said, " Yes, thank you. So you brought me a deer. " Then the chief told the first Parrot they had met to call all the people to his house. They all came in. The chief said that they had brought some deer meat, and they gave everybody a piece. The chief said, " Now you have to give some feathers to Awl boy. Everybody give him some. " So all those Parrots put down a white blanket and picked out feathers and put them down on the blanket. Each gave one or two feathers. They said, " Thanks, for giving us feathers. " Then they went. They came back to the same mesa. The little boy told the Outside chief to shut his eyes. So he did the same, he got on Awl boy's back again. He took him on top of the mesa. He opened his eyes, and they went on home. They came home, where the Hopi lived. They brought feathers. That night they had a meeting and called everybody. The little boy (*enuke*) told them to get ready for the feathers, to bring some strings (*pá*, jucca) to tie the feathers. They worked all that night and next day tying the feathers. Some time in the evening they got through. He said, " Now tonight you tie the feathers to your doors and windows and ladders. " [1] So they gave the feathers to everybody. Now their places were prettier than those of the witches. From then on Awl boy was their chief. And that is all. That Awl boy made everything nice in the pueblo for the poor people.

(*Variant*)

Owewehambaiyo, at Posųwa (Pow‘aki, i.e., Pojoaque), they were married, Yellow corn girl and Olivella Flower. One year nobody found anything to eat. So they were very hungry, and they went up to the big hills. They went looking for green plants in the hills. All

---

1. Feathers are actually thus tied by the Hopi, but not, so far as I know, by the Tewa.
2. Informant I of San Juan.

the people went out hunting for something to eat, and only Yellow
corn girl and Olivella Flower stayed home, and Yellow corn girl was
sick to have a baby. They did not go out because she was waiting
for her baby. She had not yet had her baby. Olivella Flower wanted
to go with the other people. So one morning he went down. Then
he went where those people were. Yellow corn girl said, "Maybe
Olivella Flower is going to leave me. " Olivella Flower did not come
back that day. She said, "Maybe he has gone. " So she got sick to
have her baby, and she gave birth. It was a boy. So she dressed up
well, and she fastened up her clothes between her legs, and she
went after the people in the hills. She made a fire in her room, and
left the baby before the fire, so the baby would not get cold. The
little baby would not eat, he only cried and cried. Now he was
getting big. He got up and sat down, he began to move around, in
all the rooms. He began to stand up. Nobody knew why he was so
strong, because he did not eat. He began to walk. He walked around,
as big as this (indicating four feet). He did not know what they
ate. He was getting bigger. So when he was grown into a boy he
went into the back room. There he saw the Mother (*yakwiyo*) hanging up. His father Olivella Flower belonged to the Summer chiefs.
The Mother (*yakwiyo*) said, " Little boy, hurry up, take me down,
I am very hungry. " — "I can't reach up, I can't take you down, "
said the little boy. "Take a stick in there. You can pull me down, "
said the Mother to the little boy. So the little boy got a stick and pulled
the string which was fastened to his Mother and took down the Mother.
Then the Mother said to him, " Go in and give me something to eat
which is in the back room in a little basket. (That was corn meal,
kǫboa). When you take me down, put me in the middle of the
basket. " So he took off all the cover from the Mother and put her
in the middle of the basket. So the Mother said to him, " Go into
the other room, and bring the awl. " And so she said, " Bring a
basket and put the awl into it. Then you go up from here and go
down, " the Mother said to the little boy, "and get some arrow
points (*tsie* or *tsipenu*). " And he went down and he found them, and
he put them in the basket with Awl. Then the Mother told him that
Awl would make him clothes, and he must put them on and get
ready to go out, the next day. The Mother told him to take a piece
of deerskin and cover the basket Awl was in. So he covered the basket
with the deerskin, and went into the next room and got out his bed
and went to sleep. (It was evening.) When the day was coming he
got up. The fire was still burning and keeping the room warm. In
the morning when he got up he found a shirt of deerskin and trousers of deerskin and deerskin moccasins, and they were all over
covered with [?] badger skin trimming. Then the Mother said,
" There are your clothes. Dress up. " That morning when he got

up, he got up a big boy. "Now you are ready, " the Mother said to him. " Put me in my bed, and cover me up well again, and bring Awl from the back room. " With the boy's clothes was a buffalo hide. He put it around the middle of his body. So he looked nice, all fixed up. He got all ready. Then the Mother said, " I will lead you when you go out. ¹ Go straight East. I will take you where there are good people, lots of people. " And they went straight to where the Sun comes up. (Awl was also along.) They went a long way, in one direction. And the Mother took him to where lived ǽ'yotsañyotse ² and Ke'tseyase' (Yellow Bear Man) and Kųyo (Wolf) and Kǽ (Moutain-Lion). They came there. In that place these four were their old ones (their old men, *sendo*). These four were ruled by Tsiguwenuke' (Lightning). When they made mistakes [i.e. did wrong] Lightning man was told and he would throw light-ning-sticks against them. Then when they came there, they stayed there and they had a good time there. And that was the place where the boy began to eat. They gave him to eat, blue paper-bread, and yellow, and red, and white, and deer soup. So the Mother would talk to him about what he was to do. And similarly Awl would talk to him. So Awl said to the boy, " In the morning you must get up early, and go to the river and bathe. " So Awl said to the boy, "Why should these people give us all they have and we give them nothing ? We must go out hunting, and give them something, too. We must give them some deer meat. " So the boy went out hunting and brought in deer every day. Then Yellow Bear man, got angry with the boy because he brought deer every day. So Yellow Bear man said, " You need not stay here. Go back from where you came, " said Yellow Bear man. " You better go home. " And he called the others, the two of them, Wolf and Mountain-Lion. They were going to talk to the boy about going home. But Yellow Bear man did not call Wildcat man. However, he knew about it (he was *pinang*). When Wildcat man went to call the boy, Wolf said to Yellow Bear man, "What kind of entertainment have we made for this boy ? " The boy came with Wildcat man. Wildcat man said, " Here we are; what do you want this boy for ? Tell him. " Then Yellow Bear man said, " He will not do what we tell him. That's why he better not stay here. " — " He is a good boy with all of us, " said Wildcat man. So they said, " If he does not want to go home, we must call Lightning man and he will know what to do to him. " Wildcat man said, " Don't you know ? A long time ago don't you remember we said some words and the other said other words, and we can never do good of ourselves ? ³ We have to let Lightning

---

1. See Harrington, 501.
2. See p. 11 n. 1. White mountain lion, i.e., wildcat.
3. This is obscure, but even on returning to the passage at the conclusion of the narrative, I failed to get anything clearer.

man know. " ¹ Then Yellow Bear man said, " All right. " Then
Wildcat man and Wolf said, " Go ahead and do it. If it come after
you (if there is any consequence), you will suffer for it. " Then they
went out from there. So that boy went home to the house of Wildcat man, and stayed there. Then Awl said to the boy, " Tomorrow
you must get up early and bathe and go turkey hunting. We must
work and bring all the feathers ² to Wildcat man, and he will hold
them in his hands ³ and the feathers will talk. ⁴ Wildcat man took
the feathers in his hands, and talked over the feathers to Lightning
man and from a distance Lightning man answered, " What do you
want with me ? " — " This Yellow Bear man is not doing right,
to send away this boy. What will you do about Yellow Bear man,
That's the way he is doing. " Lightning man said, " The boy must
come here where I stay. If he comes here, I will talk with him, and
do for him whatever he needs. " So this boy made himself nice and
clean and Wildcat man sent him to where lived Lightning man.
He told him to go straight there. Wildcat man told the boy, " When
Lightning man moves, the ground moves, and when he speaks, fire
comes out of his mouth. But don't get scared. " Wildcat man told
him to get downy eagle feathers and black dirt (*poshu*), and meal
(*kæboa*), and pollen (*kætu*), and to take all these to Lightning man.
So the boy got all these and carried them with him. As he was going
along, Coyote came up to him. " Where are you going, friend
(*k'ema*) ? " asked Coyote. " I am going where Lightning man lives. "
— " I will go with you. " He said, " All right. " So Coyote went
along with him. Then came another Coyote. " Where are you
going ? " — " We are going to the house of Lightning man. " —
" I will go with you. " Coyote said, " We are three now, Lightning
man wont do anything to us. " As they walked along, came up
another Coyote. " Where are you going ? " — " To the house of
Lightning man. " — " I will go with you. " Now there were four
of them. When they were drawing near to where Lightning man
lived, Lightning man smelled them. He began to call, and the
ground shook. Coyote said, " Excuse me awhile. " He stayed back,
he was scared. Lightning man called again. Then another Coyote
said, " Wont you excuse me ? " He went, he stayed back, he got
scared. Then the other Coyote said, " Excuse me, " and he left.
All these friends left him. He went on alone. He was very near
Lightning man. Lightning man came out. When he began to speak,

1. Everywhere arrow points are usually fastened to the fetish animals. Between
this ritual fact and the theory of relationship in this tale there is probably some connection.
2. *Pe*, stick ; but there is no stick to which the feathers are fastened.
3. In both hands together, palms up, the gesture of giving.
4. " Like telephone ", i.e., carry the message to a distance.

the ground moved, and fire came from his mouth. Then the boy,
said, " Lightning man, don't be mad. " — " I am not mad. " The boy
threw all the things to him, all the downy feathers. The feathers
flew all around him. He said, " Yes, yes, yes, I love you. I heard
about you. I heard what Yellow Bear man did to you. Wildcat man
told me all about it. " Lightning man said, " You have a good heart ;
now you will know what is going to happen. Now we are going
from here, " said Lightning man. " Run as fast as you can, and I
am going after you. And you run, and I will throw lightnings alongside of you. We will come into the house where they live, and go
into the house of Yellow Bear man. When I go in the house, I know
what I am going to do. " So in that way they were coming. So
when Yellow Bear man heard Lightning man coming, he went in
to hide, and Wolf went in to hide. Lightning man stopped in
the house and Yellow Bear man went out to see him. So Lightning
man sent lightning against the house of Yellow Bear man and took
him out, and against each of the other two houses he sent lightning.
When lightning came, all their clothes fell off and they dropped
dead. Then he got all their bones together and put them in one
place. Lightning man is *pinandi*. When he put the bones together,
they began to stand up alive, as men again. Lightning man said,
" They must not do it again. " That Wildcat man said, " What you
wanted to do to the boy, this you had to undergo yourself. So you
must be careful next time. " So that is what happened to that boy
in that place, he had a hard time. Then the boy married the daughter of Wildcat man. After they were married, Wildcat man said,
" You must go back to your own home. Your father and mother
are still hunting for greens, having hard times. You better go back
and help them. " So they went. Then the people who were hunting
were coming. So they came where they stayed. Where were his
father and mother, there was nobody there, except one old man and
one old woman. So they said, " Good evening, Grandfather and
Grandmother. " — " Who are you ? I do not know who you are. "
The boy said, " My mother is Yellow corn girl. When I was born
she left me in the house. Olivella Flower is my father. And I have
had a hard time in growing up. Now I am a man, and I came to
look for my father and mother. " In the evening they came with
their green things, Yellow corn girl and Olivella Flower. Then they
were ashamed before their son and their *sa'i*. They did not look
good, they were thin and miserable, and they did not know them.
He said to Yellow corn girl, " Don't you know me, Mother ? I am
your son, " said the boy. " You bore me and left me in the house.
After I was born, my father went away so I had a hard time to grow
up. " Then he said, " This is your *sa'i*. " Then they cried, and they
knew then who they were. And they held them around (embraced

them) and cried. Then he said to his father, " You must call all the men to the camps. " So they went out to call all the men, and the boy came. He told them all to clean all the town, and sweep all the houses. So they came down to sweep. " When you get through sweeping, you must let me know, " said the boy. So the boy said, " We are going down first, after us all you must go. " So they came there, to Tekeoŋgi, ¹ to his father's house. Wildcat man had given him grains of corn. So he said to his wife, " Bring the corn. " He took the corn in his hand. In every house that was open, he threw seeds of corn into the door. Then they were coming home. When they came in they saw their house full of corn and wheat. ² They got so glad. When they came home they said, " We did not know how we were to live in this world. Now you are our father and you are our mother. " So everybody got their corn and they made him *yakwiyo* (the Corn Mother), he became their Summer chief (*po-ętoyo*.)

Variant 2 (from Tesuque).

They were living at Perage owinge, some good people (*hiwanin t'owa*) and some bad people (*hawinwemba t'owa*). The bad people were envious of the good people who had lots of corn and wheat, and killed lots of deer. Uroto seno said, " If they are envious of us, we will go to another place to live. " They were going to Tsirege, and all the poor people were going to go with them. " In four days we will go, early in the morning, " said Uroto seno. In four days they all went except White corn girl and one old woman who could not go. White corn girl had a baby the morning they left, and she went on and left the baby behind. There were houses on the west side and houses on the east side. The old woman who was left behind went from house to house to look for something to eat. She found the baby crying, a baby boy. She bathed the baby. She named him Nuenu (Ash boy). Every day the little boy grew bigger. The old woman could not walk, she could only creep about like the baby. When the boy grew up he said to his grandmother that he was going up to the mountain to get a deer for them to eat. He asked his grandmother, " Who is my mother ? " —" Your mother is White corn girl. She went with them to Tsirege. " After four days the boy went to look for his mother. His mother lived in the middle room of the house. When Ash boy came he said, " How are you, Mother ? " But White corn girl did not know her boy. Then she said, " Yes, when we were going to come here I had a baby. Maybe this is the one. " — " Yes, an old woman found me and fed

1. Probably *teke'oŋgwi*, cottonwood pueblo. See Harrington, 336.
2. Cp. Zuñi, " The Deserted Children. " (Parsons ms.)

me and I grew up and I asked her who my mother was and she told me and I have come to see you. " His mother asked him, "What is your name ? " He said, "Ash boy. " He said, " Tell all the men to come to this house, so I can talk to them. " (He wanted to dance with them.) He said to the men that in four days they would dance with the bad people. They danced the Deer dance, his people ; the others danced the Basket dance. The Basket dancers came out first. Then after they went in, the Deer dancers came out. They danced three times. The fourth time Ash boy and his people beat. They said to the bad people, " You need to be beaten again. Let us race. " The good people ran from west to east ; the bad people from east to west. Again the good people won. The bad people said, "We thought you did not know anything; but you know more than we. You have beaten us. "

16. BLIND MAN AND LAME MAN AND AWL.

All the people were coming up from the big lake. They built camps. They said, " Let us stay in one place twelve days. " [2] (That meant twelve years.) They stopped first at Tsæpæwiri. [3] From there they moved on to Ritos. At Ritos they lived. [4] At twelve towns they lived, and they had with them two men, one was blind, the other was lame, his legs cramped and his arms cramped. And Olivella Flower carried them. And when twelve years passed they started to walk again. They went far to the west. That blind one and that lame one they left them behind in a house with lots of water and wood and food. Olivella Flower had an awl which he had left stuck up in the rafters near the door. And he had left behind his arrows. So they finished up their food and wood, it was all gone. So the blind man carried the lame man to fetch water and to fetch wood. Then at supper time they ate the last food that they had. So they said, " What shall we do ? All that they left us is gone. Let us think about what we shall do. " Then the awl spoke to them, " Do not worry, bring me down ! " So the blind man got a little stick, with a nail on it and they moved it this way and that and the awl fell down. When it fell down they picked it up. And Awl said, " Wrap me up well and I will tell you what to do. " So the blind man picked up the lame man and carried him down. The blind man could not

---

1. Informant I of San Juan.
2. Here the count was in some way by the twelve feathers in the eagle's tail (*tsewæ*) ; but our interpreter failed in translation and the narrator grew impatient and went on. Compare the count by the twelve feathers in the tail of the chaparral cock for the Zuñi taboo after killing. Parsons 7 : 158.
3. See Harrington, 144.
4. There is another Tewa ruin near El Rito, but it is north of Tsæpæwiri.

see well, the lame man told him where to step. They were passing a hill and saw a deer, standing asleep. So he told him to take the arrows. " I wonder could we kill it ? " He took the arrows out and he moved the bow this way and that. And the lame man directed the arrow. And he shot straight. He shot the deer under the right arm [leg]. It dropped down. They killed it. They came up to it and the lame man showed the blind man where to open it. And they spread it wide open, and took out the stomach and everything. So the blind man carried the lame man to hunt wood. They carried in lots of wood and made a fire. When they got a big fire, they put into it all the stomach and insides of the deer, and covered it all up, the fire. The fire was out and all covered up. Then the fire sparked out, and they were scared, and the blind man opened his eyes and the lame man began to walk. The lame man said, " Dry the meat, the deer has lots of meat. " Awl said, " Olivella Flower led all your people away, but they are very hungry, they have nothing to eat. They eat any green thing they find. Go after them. You will over-take them soon. " So when they dried their meat, they packed it in packages and carried it and went up after them. As they went the blind man was looking all around and the lame man was walking. They walked and they came near the people and they saw the people and the people saw them. And they said, " There are two of them, what kind of people are they ? " They came very near to them ; so they knew them. They said, " The blind man and the lame man are coming. " Then they were close to them. Then they came up to where the people were going. When they came, they took off the bundles and opened them and laid the contents on the road. Then Olivella Flower said to the blind man and the lame man, " We are going about very hungry because I left my awl behind. When I have my awl, I kill lots of deer. Now we are going about very hungry. " Blind man and Lame man said, " We have it, that awl, and now we can kill lots of deer. Why did you leave it ? You made a mistake to leave it. Now we have it. It is ours. " So Blind man and Lame man went out hunting with some other boys, and they killed deer, killed and killed. And they brought meat to the people. That is what happened to the blind man and the lame man. *Hu'*!

17. BLUE CORN GIRLS ARE SENT TO WAR. [1]

Owewehadita, far away they lived, at Pow'ạki (Pojoaque), Prayer-stick old man, Shrivelled corn old woman, Blue corn girls. They did not want to marry anybody. One time they were at war.

---

1. Informant 4 of Santa Clara. Heard from a man who said that his grandfather's brother was alive and present on the occasion.

The Outside chief said to the girls, " You do not want to marry the boys. I think you are men, and you have to go to the war. " They cried, they did not know what to do. So after four days he told them to get ready bows and arrows. So they went in four days. As they were going along they found a hole and went into it to Saya awǫ kwiyo, Grandmother Spider old woman, and they asked her what they were to do in the war. They said, " We do not know anything about war, we are women. Can you not tell us what we are to do ? " So Grandmother said, " I will tell you, my children, what to do. I do not know much about war, but I will tell you something. You go tomorrow, do not go today. I will give you some songs. " The song said :

> hæda kutsanyoanyo omu
> nea agoyonohųtse gamu.
> Formerly we were Blue corn girls,
> Now we are Dark Star Man. [1]

They went out, Spider woman gave medicine (*wo*) to them, plant medicine, and they went to the war, and killed a lot of men, and took off their hair (i.e. took their scalps.) Then they came back to Pow'ǫki. And when they came close to the pueblo they sang :

> hæda kųtsanyoany(o) gamų
> neanandi agoyonohųtsęgamų. [2]

So they brought that hair into the town and sang that song. Then the Governor came out and built a fire in the kiva. And they called all the men, and they told all the story of how they went to war. They said, " We went from here to where lives Grandmother Spider old woman and we stayed there and the next morning we went from there. We asked her how men fought and she told us and gave us some medicine and she told us to chew that medicine and spit it all around and on our bow and arrows and on our body, all over. And we went to the war. Came out men, and we fought with them and we killed them and we got their hair, and came back, and stopped again where our Grandmother is, and she told us when we came near the pueblo to sing that song. And we sang the song as we came through the pueblo. And then the Governor came out and built the fire in the kiva, and we went in there to tell the story of how we went. And they called all the men and we told all how we fought and how we came and how we killed the men. We asked them, Summer chief and Winter chief, if we did right, if we did what they

1. Described as Morning Star, who " used to be asked to help in war. " On First Mesa scalps are called " Morning Star. " (Robbins, Harrington, Freire-Marreco, 50).

2. " This time sung a little differently, " but the difference I could not get in translation.

told us to do. So they said, ' Yes, my children (*nabi e*). ' They asked us if that was all. And they said if that was all they would bring some food for us. We have told all our story. " Both those men (Summer chief and Winter chief) said, "Now in four days we will have a dance, and they have to stay in there those four days. " (That time they were men.) In four days they made a feast and had a dance. They had *pu 'ware* (the scalp dance). Then those two girls sent word to their father and mother to prepare lots of food. (They throw everything in this dance — corn, dishes, everything. [1] And they had the dance. The first time came out the elder (*pare*) with the hair (scalp), she carried the scalp on a pole, and she sang :

> hǽnananda kųtsañyoanyogamų
> nenananda agoyonohųtsęgamų.

She went in, and the younger (*ti'u*) came out and she sang the same song :

> hǽ nananda kųtsanyoanyogamų
> nenananda agoyonohųtsęgamų.

And that's all I remember.

18. WITCH WIFE. [2]

At Okeowing kǫochute'e they were living. Olivella Flower and Yellow corn girl were married. Olivella Flower would go out hunting deer, and Yellow corn girl would make wafer-bread. She never gave any to Olivella Flower, she gave him only *s'akewe*, [3] every day only *s'akewe*. Once Olivella Flower said to Yellow corn girl, " For whom are you making wafer-bread ? Whenever I come with deer you give me only *s'akewe*, " said Olivella Flower. Yellow corn girl said, " I make wafer-bread every day, but I can not make much, because it is so thin. After I get a lot, then you can eat it with stew. " So Olivella Flower was thinking, " Maybe this Yellow corn girl knows something, that is why she acts this way. So today, " he said, " I am going deer hunting, but I will just lie down and not get tired. So tonight I will not sleep but watch her. " So he went into the sunshine, and lay down and slept all day. In the evening he came, he brought no deer. So he said, " Yellow corn girl, *hewemboharǫhi'* ! I got so tired. I hunted a deer. I could not catch it. Give me something to eat and put out my bed. I am so sleepy. " So she gave him *s'akewe* again.

1. Today in the Santa Clara dance, women carry baskets of food on their heads, and throw it, saying, " My *pare* is dancing, and I throw this bread. "
2. Informant I of San Juan.
3. See Robbins, Harrington, Freire-Marreco, 91, 93. Cornmeal cooked in boiling water, " the conventional breakfast food. "

That time they were going to *pinan*. Then he lay down to sleep. But he was just watching what Yellow corn girl was doing. In the middle of the night somebody came to the window and knocked and said, " Yellow corn girl, it is time to go. " — " Come in, " said Yellow corn girl. " Olivella Flower was out catching deer, tonight he is tired and sleeping soundly. " — " Hurry up. Come out. " Olivella Flower heard what they were saying. Yellow corn girl dressed up and took a basket of wafer-bread and covered it with a shawl. She dressed up in a new dress. She came to where Olivella Flower was sleeping. Yellow corn girl thought he was asleep. She pulled a hair from his toe, ¹ but he did not move. So she said, " He is asleep. " She had a niche in the wall. She took out her eyes and put them in the wall niche. She put in owl eyes. ² Olivella Flower was just looking on. Her friend knocked at the window. " Ready ? " — " Wait a little while. " Yellow corn girl went into the back room. She got a big bowl, in it she kept a skeleton (*penita*). She took out the skeleton and laid it alongside of Olivella Flower. She said, " You have to take care of him well and say to him whatever I would say to him. I am going where they need me. " She went out. As soon as she went out Olivella Flower picked up the skeleton and threw it away. Skeleton said, " Olivella Flower, I will help you. " It said, " Yellow corn girl always goes to some place they send her, and always leaves me with you. I have been here a long time. I want you to bury me. Watch where she goes. I will help you. " So Skeleton gave him medicine. " Go from here to where they went in. Paint yourself all over with this medicine and they will not see you. They are calling all who belong to them. A girl died and only today they are making her four days. They are going to take her out and make her live. That is why they are calling everywhere. " He took those eyes which Yellow corn girl kept in water and put them into his belt. He went to Tsemata. ³ There they had a kiva. When they opened the hatch one could see a light. Olivella Flower went after them. They came there with this wafer-bread. The light shone out, so they went in. Then Olivella Flower came, he was covered with the medicine. They had a basket-like door [i. e. straw over the hatch], and in it he hid. He watched them, men and women, in the big kiva. They came there, those witches, from everywhere, from very far, Nambé, Cochiti, Santo Domingo, Santa Clara, San Ildefonso, Taos, Picuris. Some came as foxes, some as eagles, some as vultures (*okáma*), some as *humatige*, some as *popowęnde* (a kind of crow), ⁴ some as mountain

1. Cp. pp. 65, 67.
2. Cp. Dumarest, 165.
3. Near Ranchitos, a hill there between San Juan and Alcaede.
4. But see p. 123.

lions, whatever they liked to be. When they went in they took off
their skin and hung it up. Men came with meat, and women with
bread. So they put the baskets of bread in a row, and the meat on top
of the bread. And the old man was Hopi. They said, " Wonder
why he has not come. He ought to be here the first. ¹ Yellow girl is
here. " That man was Hopi Summer chief, and he was Yellow corn
girl's friend. An eagle (that was Yellow corn girl's friend) came. He
said, " Who is in here? " he asked. " Nobody is in here, " they said.
" Only those we know. " — " No. Somebody else is in here. " —
" Come in, and sit down, and stop talking. " He went and got a seat.
He brought lots of meat. He took off his skin and Yellow corn girl
took it and hung it up, and he sat down next to Yellow corn girl.
He said, " I guess we better eat, and after we have eaten we can go
and bring the girl who died. When she comes to life she can eat with
us, too. " That girl had died of *pinąn* (not because she was just sick).
So they stood up two boys and said to them, " You have to stand up
a man and a woman and go after that girl. They made a kind of bur-
row underground, and brought her through and brought her there
and laid her down. Olivella Flower saw her lying there. Hopi Summer chief said, " Wake her up, this sleeping girl. Wake up! " So she
sat up and began to scratch her head, and one held her by the hands
and stood her up. Olivella Flower jumped down to where the girl
was standing, he took her hands, then all the people in there all
vanished [" got loose "] and they were standing there by themselves.
And Olivella Flower took the girl home, to her brother's house. Her
brother was sitting by the fire, still crying because his sister had died.
He called, " Here I bring your sister. These *pinąn* people took her
from where she was buried and made her live, and I jumped down.
I did not know what that Hopi Summer chief was going to do to
her. I took her by the hands. The people disappeared and the kiva
disappeared and we stood up alone. " — " Thank you, Olivella
Flower, for bringing my sister. " For this girl, night was her day, day
was her night and in the night she worked. Then after a long time
she died again. Olivella Flower went to his house, and came in and
Skeleton was where he threw her. So Skeleton said, " You have to
take me home, too. For a long time I have been here. Yellow corn
girl brought me here. " — " Where shall I take you ? " — " Take
me some place, where the hill is falling down [i. e. on a crumbling
slope], put me in and cover me and then leave me. " So he took her
down, and covered her. Olivella Flower came back to his house, and
Yellow corn girl had not come yet. Her eyes were fastened tight
into his belt. Olivella Flower lay down, waiting for his wife. Then

1. Actually in ceremony, the chief of the society precedes the others even to the
extent, in a Hopi eight-day ceremony, of four days.

Yellow corn girl was ashamed to go in. The day was coming. She was ashamed to have the people see her, so she went up and went down and lay down in the middle of the floor (on her stomach with her arms over her eyes). Olivella Flower said, " Yellow corn girl, why are you sleeping there? Come to your bed. " She did not move. Then Olivella Flower said, " What shall I do? " He went to call Yellow corn girl's relatives. All were thinking that there was something good, that Olivella Flower had killed a deer. " We will go, " they said. They knew nothing about it. He told them to sit down. Yellow corn girl was still lying down. Her relatives were asking what was the matter with her. Her father and her uncle (*meme*) said, " Why are you lying down? " they said. Olivella Flower said, " Now you will know what kind of a wife I have. " So her father got mad. He scolded her, he made her get up. He held her by her hair and pulled her head back. Olivella Flower said, " Now you will see with your own eyes and not think that I want to talk about her. " [1] They straightened her up, they saw that she had yellow eyes. " Here I have her eyes. Just see! " He held out his hand with her eyes and showed them to everybody. Just as they straightened her up, she died, of shame. " We thought she was a good girl, we are not sorry for her. You need not bury her. Throw her in the yard so the dogs and foxes can eat her, and the flies. " Now you have heard how Yellow corn girl was a witch.

Variant. [2]

Olivella Flower and Yellow corn girl were living, and Olivella Flower always went out hunting and every day he would kill deer and come with them in the evening. He had an eagle. Every day he cut a piece of meat and gave it to the eagle. Once when he went hunting, he killed a deer and brought it home and he was very tired and he told Yellow corn girl to cut a piece of meat from the deer and give it to the eagle. She cut a piece from the neck, and that meat was tough, and the eagle did not eat it. Next day he went and said, " Greetings, my eagle. " (*Sǽgihamu, nabi tse.*) And he saw the meat lying there and he said, " Why did you not eat, my eagle? " He picked up the meat and saw that it was from the neck. He threw it away and went in and cut another piece. But the eagle got mad and did not eat the meat. So he said to him, " You are going hunting today, but do not hunt, just sleep, in order that tonight you may see something. " Then he went out hunting, and he saw that Spider old woman and she said, " Olivella Flower, where are you going? " — " I am going

1. I am reminded of a certain young woman at Jemez who *is* talked about as a witch, by her family-in-law, and accused of killing her husband.
2. Informant 2 of San Juan. Heard from Informant 1.

hunting. " — " Do not hunt today, go and lie down and when you come back, come to my house. I will give you something. " So when he was coming back he stopped there and Spider old woman came out and gave him a little stick of medicine (*wopepue*) and said, " Your wife goes away in the night, you will see tonight. Go after her when she gets up and you will see where she goes. She will turn the stone and go in under, and you can sit on one side of the stone and when you eat this medicine stick you will be hidden. " So he took the medicine stick and went home. When he came, his wife gave him something to eat, and he lay down as if he was sleeping, but he was watching what his wife was doing. And that woman was making blue wafer-bread every day, but she gave her husband only *tsakewe*. Then a girl came to the window and said, " Yellow corn girl, it's time to go. " And Yellow corn girl said, " I don't know if my husband (*nabi t'owa*) sleeps or not. Wait a while! I will see if he is asleep or not. " She went to her husband and pulled the little hair on his toes. It hurt him, but he did not move. " I guess he is asleep, " she said. Then she got a basket of blue wafer-bread, folded the bread, and put it in a basket and on her shoulder. She got a clean plate, and took out her eyes, and put in their place owl (Tewa, *mahu*; Mex., *tekolote*) eyes and put the plate in a niche in the wall. She took two ears of black corn and laid them by the side of Olivella Flower and said, " Now you are going to lie by Olivella Flower and you must do whatever he pleases. " She went out and left the corn. Olivella Flower said, " *Humbaharahia*! Mother, you are mean with me. That's the way you treat me. I am going to burn you. " — " No! I will tell you where your wife has gone, " said the black corn to him. " She has gone to a place where lots of witches [1] (*bayeke*, lots of, *chugee*) are going tonight. That's why she took lots of wafer-bread with her. When you go, you will see what they are going to do. I will tell you. Her eyes are up here. If you want, I will bring them to you. " So Corn got up and brought the eyes, and he put them in a cloth and tied it tight and put them in his belt. And Corn gave him one stick of medicine. " Chew it here, and put it all over your head and body so nobody will see you. " Then Olivella Flower went after Yellow corn girl and he followed her, and found her moving the stone and going in, and Olivella Flower lay above on one side and could look down and see well where they were, and he ate the medicine that Spider old woman gave him. And he saw his wife and lots of men and women he knew, they were in there. They said, " Wonder why that man is so slow to come, " they said. Then that man came. That was Eagle, and he came down and took off his skin. He had lots of dried meat and he put it down. And Yellow corn girl

1. Given first as " devils ".

came and washed Eagle's face. She was married to Eagle man. And they asked him, " Why are you so late ? We thought you were not coming ? " He did not answer them. And that day a girl had died. Two boys were to go after that girl to bring her where they were. And so those two boys went and they put on the skins of badger (*ke*) and they made a hole to where that girl was, and they pulled her out and brought her underground till they came ;where the others were. When they came, they shook off the earth. They got hot water, and put that girl into the boiling water and she moved — and that Olivella Flower was looking on — and she stood up. Olivella Flower said, " *Humbaharahia*! I guess they have taken her heart. " And he was eating his medicine. They said she did not want to marry one of those boys. They asked her why she did not want to marry, and she did not find anything to say. Olivella Flower was eating the medicine and he spit it around and he reached his hand down and snatched up that girl and carried her home. He took the girl to her mother's house and told her mother about what had happened. He went home. Then Yellow corn girl came back, and took up the black corn and put it back in the corn room. And she looked for her eyes and she did not find them. So she lay down on one side of Olivella Flower. Day was coming. He woke up and said, " Yellow corn girl, why don't you get up ? " She covered up her head. " Get up, Yellow corn girl ! " — " I have a headache, " said Yellow corn girl. So Olivella Flower got up and took off all the cover and Olivella Flower held her head up and said, " Yellow eyes ! " and said, " Look at me ! " But Yellow corn girl could not see in the day time. Then Olivella Flower went to call her father and mother and her relatives to come to his house and he told them what he saw that night, and that she had not her eyes. " That is why she will not take her hands from her eyes. I have her eyes, " said Olivella Flower and he showed the eyes to them. Then the father and mother and all the relatives began to cry. They said, " *Humbaharahia*! Yellow corn girl, what are you thinking of, to do such a thing to your husband ! What shall we say ? We have nothing to say. We can not help you. All we can say is to burn you with wet wood. " So they went out for wet wood and brought in lots of wood and put her in the middle and burned her. That is the way. (She was a kind of witch). I throw it to you, *hu*ʽ !

Variant 2. [1]

At Koochuteowinge lived Prayer-stick old man, Shrivelled corn old woman, Yellow corn girl, Olivella Flower boy. Olivella Flower boy was their son and Yellow corn girl, their *sa'i*. Olivella Flower boy

1. Informant 3 of Santa Clara.

went hunting every day. Every day he brought a deer, and Yellow corn girl made blue wafer-bread every day. So every day when Olivella Flower boy came, she gave him *sa'kewe*. That is the way she did. After a time Olivella Flower boy began to think about it, about what Yellow corn girl did with the meat he brought and with the bread she made. One night Olivella Flower boy could not sleep. He was lying down as if asleep. That time a girl came in and told Yellow corn girl to go to a council (*wænge*), Yellow corn girl was to be a witch. So Yellow corn girl pulled a hair from the face of Olivella Flower boy. He did not do anything. She pulled a hair from between his toes. He did not do anything. She said, " He is asleep, time to go. " Yellow corn girl had owl eyes. She had a dead person (*penita*) in the other room. She brought out that Skeleton alongside Olivella Flower boy. She said to that Skeleton, " You act as I act to Olivella Flower boy, whenever he wakes. " Olivella Flower boy was just listening to her. They went out. She took out wafer-bread and meat stew. After they went out, Olivella Flower boy got up, he picked up that Skeleton and threw it up against the wall. She said, " No, elder brother, do not do anything to me. I will help you. " Skeleton said, "Elder brother, now you go. Here is some black corn, put it in your mouth. " She gave him a root, too. " When those witches are in that kiva, [1] spit that root around them, so they do not see you or know you are coming. " So he went and nearby he spat the root, and the black corn he put under his tongue. He lay down in the hatchway of the kiva, under the willow of the roofing. So everybody came into the kiva. The last one was *sǫwǫdi*. [2] They asked her, " Has somebody been in here ? " Then those people said, "Nobody here, only we who belong here. " So she sat down. Then they told the witches, (those *p'atowa*), " You get ready to go far away. " So they took down the skins that belonged to them. They went forth as Crow, Eagle, Owl. Then the chief got ready to go first. He took down an eagle skin and put it on. In the middle of the kiva they had a big bowl. They had water in the bowl and a heart, a human heart in the bowl. (When they are going to become witch [i. e. to be initiated] they take out the heart from one they like best, father, mother, sister, etc. [3] *That* heart they put in the bowl.) They had to jump over the bowl, then they became Eagle, Owl, etc. So Olivella Flower boy watched them, what they were doing there. Then they jumped across the bowl, those witches, but they could not turn into the creatures they wanted to be. The chief told them to go out and look for somebody who was watching. They went out and looked, they could not find anybody.

---

1. Cp. Dumarest, 208.
2. Little grey bird spotted with white, in rocks.
3. Said of witch practices also by the Keres and at Zuñi.

They came in, they tried it over the bowl, but they could not fly. They tried again and again. So their chief said, " You are not a woman and a man, you can not go. " So they could not do anything that night. When the witches were ready to go, Olivella Flower boy went home. When he came home, he put back that Skeleton by him as if sleeping. Then his wife came, Yellow corn girl. She went to bed. Then in the morning, Olivella Flower boy went hunting deer again. He found a deer and killed it. When he was coming home he came where Grandmother Spider old woman lived. She called him, " My child, you are going to be killed by the witches. They are going to kill you with a lion ; but if you come back tomorrow morning, come by here. I'll give you a root, so they can not do anything to you. " That night Yellow corn girl went back. Olivella Flower boy went back also to that witch kiva and listened to what they were saying. Their kiva chief said, " Any one of you, man or woman, go tonight and get Olivella Flower boy. " So a man said, " I am going Mountain Lion. I will kill Olivella Flower boy. " Another man said, " I am going Eagle. " Another man said, " I am going Eagle, too. " So Eagle said to Mountain Lion, " If you fight with Olivella Flower boy, I will fly down from above, and kill him. " So he heard how he was to be killed. So next morning Olivella Flower boy went hunting again. He came by Grandmother. Grandmother said, " You have come back ? " Olivella Flower boy said yes. So she gave him breakfast. After breakfast she gave a root to Olivella Flower boy. " When you go up the mountain and see the track of Mountain Lion, spit on the track with this root, Mountain Lion will not be able to see you. You will kill Mountain Lion. Eagle will come down. When you see him, spit with this root. Eagle will not be able to see you. Then you shoot him with an arrow. You catch the eagle. " Then he killed the mountain lion and the eagle. Then he carried the mountain lion and eagle on his back. He came by Grandmother again. He said to Grandmother, " There they go! " So he brought the eagle into Grandmother's house. " So Grandmother gave him dinner. She said to him, " Now don't you go yet. Go when it grows darker. Bring the mountain lion and the eagle to the witch kiva, throw them inside, to the witches waiting for you. " So he went very late in the evening. When he came near the witch kiva they heard. They said, " Olivella Flower boy is coming, he is being brought down dead. " They thought that he was killed. Yellow corn girl went early that day to the kiva to wait for Olivella Flower boy, thinking he was killed. Olivella Flower boy came by the door of the kiva. Olivella Flower boy said, " Here they go in ! " Then he threw in the mountain lion, then he threw in the two eagles. Then Olivella Flower boy went in. He told the witches, " I have brought a deer. Now I am going to kill you all. " So he picked up his arrow and bow and he shot the chief

first. Then he began to shoot all. So all the witches in the kiva were
killed. One woman belonging to them was having a baby and she had
not come in. From them more of these witches were raised. [1] Then
Olivella Flower boy's father and mother, Shrivelled corn old woman
and Prayer-stick old man, asked Olivella Flower boy where Yellow
corn girl was. Olivella Flower boy said, " Yellow corn girl is dead. I
killed her. " They cried. Olivella Flower boy said, " Do not cry for
her! She was a witch. " So they stopped crying. Olivella Flower boy
said, " Yellow corn girl wanted me to be killed. I was not killed and
I killed all the witches. " And that is all.

Variant 3. [2]

At Perage onge they lived, Shrivelled corn old woman, Prayer-stick
old man. They had two girls, Yellow corn girls. There were lots of
people in the pueblo and lots of witches. They had a meeting every
night, they went into the kiva.

There lived another Shrivelled corn old woman and Prayer-stick old
man. They had a son, Olivella Flower boy.

If a bear or lion came down, they would say, " We will make
rain or snow, to see the tracks. We will go tell him, Olivella Flower
boy. " Yellow corn girl was making bread every day. Olivella Flower
boy went hunting every day. Olivella Flower wanted to marry the
girl. One day he went and asked her father and mother if they would
let him in. So they did. In time he married one of the Yellow
corn girls. In the daytime she was married to Olivella Flower boy,
at night she went to eat with the witches. They would tell
Olivella Flower boy that lions or bears or deer would come down.
Yellow corn girl would make bread, and not tell how it was
used. She would serve only mush. One night he did not sleep, he
watched his wife. The witches were going to hold a council, from
everywhere — Taos, Cochiti, Navaho, everywhere. Yellow corn
girl brought meat and corn bread to them. They were trying to kill
people in Santa Clara and San Ildefonso. They boiled gum in an *olla*,
to kill with. Olivella Flower boy met Spider old woman. " I feel
sorry for you, because of the witches, " she said. She gave him some
roots. " Every night your wife puts a corpse next to you. Tonight is
the last night, for the boiling of that *piñon* gum to kill with. They had
five or six big *ollas* in their kiva. " Spider old woman told Olivella
Flower boy, " You take this root and go tonight and watch the witches.
They have a large flat stone to cover up the kiva. Go up the stone
steps, turn over the flat stone, lie under there. Spit this root inside

1. Cp. p. 180.
2. Informant 4 of Santa Clara.

the kiva. When it is time to take off the boiling gum, go in, into the kiva, hold ashes in your right hand. You will see your wife, with a rich Navaho *capitan*. Put the ashes in the *ollas*. I feel sorry for my children. "... They were coming, the witches. Olivella Flower boy was there listening. He did what Spider old woman told him. There was a big bowl in the middle of the kiva. First thing he saw his wife sitting with a big man, she was married to him. Olivella Flower boy went inside, he got ashes, and put them in the four *ollas* and at last into the bowl, in which was the heart. So they could not do anything, that is why they did not get killed, the people. The chief in the kiva said, " What is the matter? You people are sleepy. I told you this was the last night to boil. To morrow everybody will get sick. " Soon those *ollas* cracked, and spilled out all the bad medicine.

Variant 4 (from Tesuque).

They were living at Tegike owinge, Kofedi anyo (Black corn girl) and Olivella Flower. Black corn girl would always make wafer bread when Olivella Flower went hunting. But when he came back she did not give it to him, he had only *koboa* to eat. Black corn girl was a witch, and she carried the wafer bread at night to the kiva. One time as he was about to go up on the moutain, Black corn girl said to him, " Do not go. I want to wash your head. I never wash it. " The witches were planning to kill this boy. So Black corn girl washed his head. The bad people saw him sitting outside. " This is our deer. Tonight we will eat him up, " they were saying. The next day as he was hunting, Spider old woman called to him, " Oh my boy, where are you going? They are going to kill you today when you go up the mountain. They will send a big deer, but it will not be a real deer, but a witch. I will help you. " So she gave him a bow and arrows. With them he killed the witch deer. At night when he went to his house Black corn girl was not there. He went to the kiva where all the bad people were waiting for that big deer to bring Olivella Flower. But Olivella Flower brought the.big deer and threw it down into the kiva. " There is your deer ! Catch him ! " The men stood up to catch him. Olivella Flower went into the kiva and killed all of them.

19. BLUE CORN WOMAN MARRIES

BLUE KACHINA WHO BRINGS A MEDICINE SONG [1]

Kotsanyokwi, Blue corn woman, went to the river bank [2] (*pokege*), for water. She got water, and they talked to her. She did not know

1. Informant 5 of San Ildefonso.
2. See Harrington, 85.

who talked to her. And she went home, and told Poseyemu seno, [1]
" They talked to me when I went for water down to the river. " And
Poseyemu asked her, " Who was it ? " and she said, " I do not
know. He said to me that he wanted me to marry him, but I did
not answer him because I did not see who he was. " There was a
boy (*enu*), Blue boy (*enu tsǫwe*), he was standing beside the cottonwood tree. He was ashamed to go when Blue corn girl was getting
water. She did not know who was talking to her. Then said
Posew'a sendo (Coyote old man [2]), " You ought to go to the river
again and get some more water. If they talk to you again, you answer,
so you can see him and call him to talk with you. " So she went
down to the river again. By that time the boy was waiting for her.
" Blue corn girl, what did you say about what I said to you yesterday ? Answer me, please. " — " Yes, I could answer you, but I do not
see where you are standing. " — " Why, Blue corn girl, don't you see
me ? I am standing here, just beside you. " — " Well, come over
here while I am getting this water. I am not going to fill up my
pompé (water jar), you come over here. Then after we talk, I will fill
my jar. " — " Please, Blue corn girl, just turn towards the north
side. " [3] — " Oh what a nice pretty boy you are ! " — " Surely I
could marry you. " — " Yes. If you want to go to my home, I will
marry you. " — " I do not know, Blue corn girl, if I will go with
you. Because I am not to go there, because nobody may see me. But
I would like you to marry me, and stay with me. I can not go out.
This river bank is my home. " — " Well, I have to think before I
marry you. I am sure I can not promise you before I talk with Coyote
old man. I am going home. " — " I will wait for you tomorrow
afternoon again. " — " All right. " Well, she went home and said to
Coyote old man, " I talked with the boy again. I saw him. He is a
very nice boy, and he wants me to marry him. But I told him that
until I talked with you I would not marry him, because you might
get angry with me. " — " No, Blue corn girl, why should I get angry
with you ? If you want to, you can marry him. It will be very
good for you, so you wont be by yourself. " — " I told him I
would marry him, but he does not want to come here and stay with
me. He says, ' I live here at the river bank and I can not leave my
home. I would like you to come here. ' That is what he said to me. "
Then Coyote old man said, " That is all right. You can go when you
want, if you want to marry him. " — " All right. Then I have to go
for water to morrow, so I can talk with him again. " Next day she
went down there and talked with him. And she said, " I will go with

1. See p. 110.
2. Through forgetfulness informant changes Poseyemu into Posew'a (coyote).
3. See p. 30 n. 1.

you now. " — " All right. I will take you to my house, so you can
see where I live. " He went a little way. Then she saw the pretty
nice house he had. She married him. He brought a deer and wafer
bread (*bowaiyawe*). They cooked the deer, for all the people to have a
good time at Blue corn woman's. They got married. They had a nice
time. Everybody was happy that Blue corn woman was married.
They went out to the mountains. They had a nice time on horseback.
Blue boy showed Blue corn woman the big *okwinge* (spring) and how
Okuwah tsanyose (blue man) sang. Then Blue corn woman said,
" That is a nice song. I wish we could stay here for four days. " Then
he said, " Yes, Blue corn woman, we might stay four days; but
no, I do not want you to hear that song, because that song
is never sung that way at home, it is sung here only. That song
belongs to the medicine people, *pufona towa.* " [1] Then Blue corn
woman cried. She wanted to learn that song, but her husband did not
want her to. Then she came out. She said to Coyote old man, " He
took me over to the mountain by *okwinge*, and I heard a song that was
a nice song, and I said to him, 'I wish we might stay four days so I
could learn that song', and he said, 'No, I do not wish you to learn
that song, that song is for the medicine men.' " — " That's right,
you do not need to learn that kind of song. He was right, your husband. You can learn another kind of song when you grind. You have
enough songs of another kind. But you tell Okuwah man to come
over here, so I could learn it. " Then Okuwah man went over to
Coyote old man's house, and Coyote old man said, " Blue corn
woman told me she heard in the mountains a very nice song, but she
did not learn it, you told her it was a medicine song. " So he sang
it.

Heni e ya he
a ya a he.

" Now in four days we will have all the head men (*tarae*, fathers)
meet in the kiva, and you sing that song, to see what they will say
about that song. " They called all the fathers into the kiva and said to
them, " Okuwah man has brought a song from the mountain spring
that we have never heard here. I think you fathers have to think
about the song to sing it for us. " — " All right, we are all together
now. You had better go after Okuwah man, so he can sing for us. "
So they sent out Outside chief, and he went in to the kiva of Okuwah
man and sat down. " Well, Coyote old man he had a meeting with
the fathers and he told them that you have brought a song from the
mountain spring, and we want to hear the song you have brought. "

---

1. Here may be a reference to the Lake of Emergence and to Wildcat man and
the curing animals. Cp. p. 10.

— " All right, I will sing to you. " He said to Outside chief, " You have to go outside the kiva and sit there. And you, father, you can hear what I am going to sing. " So he sang :

> Heni e ya he
> a ya a he.

" That's a nice song you sing, Okuwah man, we are very glad that you have brought that song. We had almost forgotten it. We asked each other about that song and nobody remembered it. But we have got it now. We wont forget that song now. Thank you very much, Okuwah man. "
That's all I know.

Variant (from Tesuque.)

Eó there were living an old man and an old woman and Tinini-powienu (Olivella Flower boy) at T'aba owinge. On Tsikomo there is a spring, and into it one day went Olivella Flower boy. He did not come out. His mother and father went to look for him. After four days Olivella Flower boy came out, and those two Yellow corn girls heard him singing. The elder said to the younger, " Our brother is coming. " He went to the moutain, *kyæpị*, and thence he went to T'aba owinge. His mother and father saw him when he came and they took him to their house and they were crying. He stayed only four days at home, and then he told his mother he had to return to Tsikomo. His mother cried again. He went back to Tsikomo into the spring. Early in the morning he would sing. Uroto kwiyo lived near the spring and she heard him sing. She would go and fetch water and hear him sing. He spoke to her but she could not see him. She went back to her house, ground some blue corn meal and made bread and carried it to the spring and left it there for this boy. He took the bread, but the old woman did not see him. She stayed there four days to see him. He spoke to her again. She said, " Come out, boy ! " He came out, and she said, " Come and be my son. " She was crying. He said, " I wish I could live with you, but I have to stay here. " She went back to her house. The boy would come out to plant corn and wheat...

20. SUMMER CHIEF TESTS COYOTE WHO GETS A KACHINA SONG. [1]

At Potsuwi they came out with Okuwah. Coyote old man went to get water for his children. The birds were singing about *potsuwa e.* They were singing about rain. He went back again to get that song, to sing the song of the little birds. He sang for them. The birds sang

---

1. Informant 5 of San Ildefonso.

again. He went to the same spring. Coyote old woman got water the same way for the girls. Then they said that they wanted to hear the same song, that was a very pretty song. " We are going to grind corn. We will sing that song so we can finish grinding green corn. " Coyote old woman said, " We will be happy to hear that song. Let us start it. " A woman was to have a meeting that night so they could grind green corn for Coyote old man, so he could go hunting deer for them. That Coyote old woman they gave her the song. " Where did you get it ? " — " From the same spring. And I think we have learned the same song as the boys. " — " Yes, it is just the same. " [The song followed, but it was not recorded.] Coyote old man raised his hand and cried, " I am very glad to have you girls learn so quickly. " Coyote old man said, " Now you boys have to go and sing for the women as they grind. " [1] .... Coyote old man brought the deer. They had a meeting of the head people, so they could cook the deer that Coyote old man brought for all the people. Coyote old woman brought red corn and ground it for all the people to make wafer-bread, and give it to them, all the head men first. First Summer chief went in and got his supper first. He got a piece of meat and some purple bread. To the east he threw it, and he stood about half an hour in prayer for Coyote old man to have the Okuwah to help him. And then he went inside and he sat down and had a little talk with Coyote old man. He asked him how he got the deer. And then Coyote old man went inside and got his arrow and bow. " This is the one. I shot with this arrow and killed it. " And Summer chief did not believe he could kill deer with arrow and bow. Then Summer chief told Coyote old man to call them, all the head women, to Summer chief's house to have supper. Coyote old man and Summer chief went out, and Summer chief put a horn up about a hundred yards off and then he said to Coyote old man, " Well, I have put up that horn for you to shoot with your arrow. If you knock it down, then I will believe it. " — " All right, Summer chief, I will do it. You go over there where the horn is standing and I will shoot from here. " Then Summer chief stood near the horn. He said to him, " Summer chief, I am ready. You just watch. " And he shot it and hit it right in the middle, just as he would shoot a deer. " That's the way I shoot a deer. " — " I believe it. But tomorrow we will have another meeting, you and myself. Okuwah will come, and see you and me. You have to get up very early in the morning and go to the river and wash, and throw the corn, yellow ones, to the east and go to the *te'e* (kiva) and stay with us. " .... Okuwah tsąwaye (Blue kachina) came and said, " Coyote old man, do you remember me ? I am the bird that sang for you when your boys were very thirsty and you went for the water

1. As was the practice at Laguna, at Zuñi, and probably elsewhere.

down at the lake (*pokwinge* [1]). Then I sang for you that song that you sang for your boys. And when you were going along you were just thinking about the song and then you were going to sing and you dropped the water and forgot the song. And then you went again, then I sang for you again and you did the same thing. " [2] — "Okuwah, are you the one that sang? Are you sure that you sang for me ? " — " Yes. I am the one that sang for you. " — " Well, I want to hear again the same song. " — " All right. I will sing for you. " Then he sang the same song. " Yes. Now I believe it is true. Thank you, Okuwah, that you sing for me. Summer chief told me that I would not see you, but I am very glad to see you. " — " Well, Coyote old man, why did you not believe what Summer chief told you ? From the sky, I saw you, how you shot the deer, for your boys to bring the deer so they could eat. Now I am going again to the same spring. Do not forget me, now you know who I am. If you want me to help you, just talk with Summer chief. I have to do what Summer chief tells me. *Poingtuyokwiyo* in *okuahkwi*, she is the old head woman. Just the same she has to do what Summer chief says, in *okuahkwi*, Kǫtseyi (Yellow Corn). And Kǫtseyi, she says the same word. They are all together sometimes. You go, Coyote old woman and old man, together to the same spring where are Okuwah old man and Okuwah old woman. You will hear this song, but do not drop the water when you go to this spring, because you know who we are now. And now you see us. We have some people just like you, people inside the spring. We are helping you, all you people. If you ask for rain, we give it to you. When you people are good, when you believe in your ceremony, we are the ones that help you people all we can through Coyote old man, that he bring the song for you people. And you have to believe what Coyote old man says. And that is the way we help you out, you people. If you have the ceremony (*kaye*) for me. " — " And that way, what we believe, our people, is very true, " that is what Coyote old man said to his people when he came out from the kiva. He had all the people and the head men meeting with Coyote old man for him to tell them what Okuwah said to him. And the head people were very glad that Coyote old man saw what kind of people they were. " Now it is very true. You boys and girls ought to believe it. So they could help us all they can, and we do the best we can for it. So we can raise corn, and wheat, everything that we plant. " And just the same the head woman of Summer chief, our head woman, sent word, and Summer chief got it the same night at his meeting and he told all the boys to practice a dance for the Okuwah so he would help us. They had a dance in four days, and they

---

1. Harrington, 85.
2. A reminiscence, here, of the tale of the water carrier. See pp. 160-161.

had rain, too. Then Coyote old man was thinking to himself inside the kiva, that he was very glad that they believed what Summer chief said. Then he went out from the kiva and he went to the north, down to the lake he went, about two o'clock in the afternoon (*tsąwawiri*), and he heard the same song again. Then he went home and inside there were all the head men. And he went in and told how he had heard the same song.... " Now we Summer people, we are right. That will be for us rainbow on top, *pùkano kwage*. We are going to the south, to Shumak'ere, [1] Black mesa, we are going. There we will see *kaye*, Bear, Mountain Lion, and Okutsąwe (Blue kachina). " That's the end.

21. TALE FRAGMENTS FROM SAN ILDEFONSO AND TESUQUE.
San Ildefonso. [2]

At Taba [3] Yellow corn girls (Kǫtseanyo) lived. They broke a jar. Olivella Flower was trying to get Yellow corn girl to marry him. Olivella Flower brought them a deer. Olivella Flower's people (Pink Quartz people, [4] G'uhpintowa) lived way up on the hill... Pewa old woman [5] was trying to get all the children. Pewa old woman was beaten, and Salt old woman (Akwiyo) was not beaten... Pink Quartz girl was trying to get rabbits. Olivella Flower was trying to get the jar... Pewa old man was trying to get the crow (*odo*). Pewa old man got the rabbit, and he ran away with the rabbit... *Owewehen* on the other side of the river there lived some people. Grandmother and Yellow corn girl lived right there. Eagle Woman (Tse akwi) and Olivella Flower went to hunt for rabbits. In four days Yellow corn girl was going to get married and Olivella Flower went to hunt for a deer. Olivella Flower told Yellow corn girl to go to the river and get some water. Yellow corn girl (took her jar) and Olivella Flower girl (Tininipowianyo) said it was a nice jar. " It is a nice jar, " said Olivella Flower girl. " If I knock it over, you will get it (suffer for it). " Yellow corn girl said to Olivella Flower girl, " If you lay your hands on that jar, you will suffer. " Yellow corn girl knocked the jar over, and Olivella Flower girl put her hand in the jar and turned into a coyote (*de*).

Then Eagle woman asked, " Where is my daughter ? Why has she not come ? It is a long time since she went. " Olivella Flower came and

1. Harrington, 323. " On top of Shuma ".
2. Informant 6 of San Ildefonso.
3. A ruin associated with San Ildefonso. See Harrington, 310.
4. Note the first and only reference to clanship in these tales of the Northern Tewa.
5. Pewa old woman and Pewa old man are the same as Tsabiyo or Awelito (Mex. *abuelito*, little grandfather), the bugaboo that steals children See p. 50.

asked, " Where is my wife ? " Eagle woman said, " There she is coming, near the house. " Olivella Flower girl went into the house, to see if Yellow corn girl was coming. Olivella Flower was talking with Olivella Flower girl and Olivella Flower girl went down and told Eagle woman that Olivella Flower was coming. Olivella Flower girl was beaten. So Olivella Flower girl got married. After they married they had children. Then Pink Quartz clanswomen (G'uhpintowa *kwiyo*) came to their house to see them. And *bianyo* (? her girl) went away, ran away. That's all.

Tesuque.

1. They were living at Perageowinge, the two boys Pateenu (Ash boys) and Pa'powienu (Fire Flower boy. Ash boys said to Fire Flower boy, " Let us go up to the mountain. Whoever gets the most deer will beat the other. " Fire Flower boy never went out hunting. " He wont beat us, because he never goes hunting, " the Ash boys were saying. They stayed in the mountain four days. Fire Flower boy caught ten deer, and the Ash boys caught only four deer. They caught turkeys, too. " You have beaten us, " said the Ash boys to Fire Flower boy. Then the boys went home and told the other boys to bring in the deer.

White corn girl told the other girls to come to her house, all but Fininianyo (Sweet corn girl), she lived with her grandmother. They were poor and the people did not like them. The Corn girls ground corn, twelve baskets of meal; and they took the meal to the house of Fire Flower boy. Sweet corn girl saw them baking the bread, and she ran and told her grandmother she was going to grind too, and take the meal to the house of Fire Flower boy. " No, " said her grandmother, " they wont take it because we are poor. " But Sweet corn girl started to grind and she ground quickly and took the meal to Fire Flower boy. Her meal was finer than that of the other girls. Fire Flower boy tasted it and it was sweet. He said, "Now you have to stay here and be my wife. " So she stayed and lived with him. Next day she went to her house to fetch her grandmother. They lived there. Every morning Fire Flower boy went hunting and each day he would bring back four or five deer. The other Corn girls got angry with Sweet corn girl.

2. At Tsire owinge the White corn girls were living, and every day they would grind corn. They went out only at night. They lived in the upper room. The boys would play with their bow and arrows around the house so they might see the girls ; but the girls never came out. Then the Towae heard that these girls never came out and that the boys wanted to see them. So in four days the Towae came and played there and stayed until sunset. Then the girls came down, and

the Towae were sitting there by the fire. The girls said, " We have found two little boys, " and they took them to the upper room and put them to bed. They told their father, Uroto seno. He said, "Well, put them to bed, so they will be warm and go to sleep. " At night the girls would not grind, but they would get up early in the morning to grind. This morning they did not get up. Their father said, " What is the matter with you ? Get up ! " They got up and put the little boys in a big jar. In the day time they kept them in the jar, and at night they would take them out to go to bed with them. After four days their father found the boys at night, and he threw them out of the window and told the other boys to get their bows and arrows and shoot them. The Towae ran off, calling to the other boys, " We beat you ! " The other boys got mad. The Towae ran to Tsikomoping, and there they lived. After four days the two girls had babies. These baby boys were growing up, bigger and bigger. Then they asked their mothers, " Who are our fathers? "... Their grandfather made them bows and arrows. They grew bigger and bigger. Then they went to Tsikomoping to find their fathers. There they found their fathers. They told them, " We are your sons. " The Towae made them bows and arrows and moccasins. They said to the boys, " Now stay here four days to hunt rabbits and deer. " So they stayed. Then their fathers said, " Now go back to your mothers. " And they went back, hunting rabbits and deer. Their fathers told them to dance *tumshare* after they got home. " Dance four days and after four days we will come down to see it. " So they were dancing, and after four days the Towae went down and during the dance took away the boys' mothers to Tsiko-moping. They finished dancing. Then the boys went to look for their mothers; but their mothers told them to return to their grandfather and grandmother.

The White corn girls stayed there on the mountain with the Towae. One day they went for water, and the elder girl told the younger to put her hand into the water. When she put her hand in, somebody seized her hand and drew her down into the water. The older one went home and began to grind. The Towae came back and the younger one did not find his wife. " Where is your sister ? " he asked. " When we went to get water some one seized her hand and drew her down into the water. " They went to look for her, but they could not find her. It was Coyote who had taken her. Towae the older would sit still and not go out to hunt. After four days the girl came back, not as a girl, but as a deer. She spoke to Towae the younger while he was out hunting. He went back to tell his brother that he had found a deer that was a girl. They went to look for her, but they could not find her. She had gone back into the water. Then they lived sadly, Towae and his brother and sister.

3. Once at Tanowe' unge lived a boy who was lazy, Olivella Flower

boy. He got married, to Kǫfeti, Black corn girl. This girl was rich, but Olivella Flower boy was poor. The morning after they married the boy told his wife that he was going out to work, and to make him some bread. Black corn girl did not know how to make bread. She went to her mother who said to her, " You have got to learn to make bread now you are married. "... Olivella Flower boy went to work at a farm where other boys were at work. They said to him, " You are not married to a rich girl. " He said, " In a little while you will see her. " He had told his wife to bring his dinner to where he was at work. So she came... Olivella Flower boy had never worked, but when he married he had to learn to farm and to weave blankets. He got rich, too. He got cattle and horses. He was the richest man in the pueblo. He became *pocętuyo* (Summer Chief).

4. Once at Tsæwa'unge (Chimayo) were living two White corn girls. At Posǫa they were going to have a feast. The girls told their mother and father they were going to the feast. They said, " All right, you may go. " They came to Posǫaunge. There was living there a boy, Kųkąbienu (Corn hard boy). They were dancing at night in the kiva, *kupishare* (red corn dance). This boy was sitting by the ladder. After they finished dancing the *pocętuyo* told them they could all go. Two girls went up, and Hard corn boy followed them. He invited them to his house, thinking they were the White corn girls, but they were witches. He slept with them, but in the morning when he found out they were witches he cut off their heads and threw them in the fire. Meanwhile the White corn girls had returned to their house. Their mother and father asked them why they had not stayed. They said, " Hard corn boy asked us to stay, but we did not stay, because he went away with two other girls. " After a while the White corn girls went again to Posǫa, and they saw Hard corn boy again. He took them to his house and they lived there. After four days they wanted to wash his head. They went with him to the mountain to a water hole to wash his head with jucca. Then into the water hole they pushed him, because that first night he had not taken them to his house. Then the two girls returned to Tsæwale.

5. Once at Posoæ owinge lived some people who were envious of the others, and the *pocętuyo* said they were to play top (*petinin*), the east side against the west. They played and the men of the west side won. Poætuyo had said that who won was to dance *t'anshare* (Sun dance), in four days. (In this dance, they throw things they want, blankets, shoes, beads.) After they finished dancing, they went to the kiva to talk. " We will not play top again, " said the boys who were beaten. " We have had enough of the top playing. " Since then they have not played Indian top.

6. They were living in Perae. There were some bad, envious people. The bad people, witch people, had feathers fastened to the ladder of

their kiva. The good people had no feathers. Olivella Flower was living at Tsiguma, but he came to Perae where his mother lived. When he came he wanted to dance, to beat the witch people. He went with another boy, with Towae, to get feathers, parrot tail feathers, to Okuping (Turtle mountain). He went to the birds to ask them for their feathers. One of the birds was their father and he told the birds to shake their tails on the blanket Olivella Flower put down for them. Towae stood waiting for Olivella Flower. In the middle of the night they returned to the kiva. Those good men were fixing strings of jucca to tie the feathers on to the step-ladders and to put in their hair. In the morning when the bad people got up they saw the feathers tied to the ladders and they were envious of the nice new feathers...

7. They were living at Tepo owinge, White corn girl and Olivella Flower. He went up into the mountains to hunt deer, and the clouds were all around. It was lightning and thundering, and Olivella Flower was killed by Lightning. White corn girl was waiting for him, making bread. "I wonder why Olivella Flower does not come, " White corn girl was saying. "I have finished my work. " She went on top of a hill near by. There Spider old woman said to her, " What do you want, my girl ? "— " Olivella flower has not come yet. I do not know what is the matter with him. " Spider old woman said, " Lightning has killed him. Do not cry. In four days he will come back. In four days you must come here and stay with me. " After four days White corn girl went to Spider old woman. That night Olivella Flower was coming singing, coming out from the lake. Spider old woman was the first to hear him. Not until he had sung four times could White corn girl hear him. Spider old woman went out and said to him, "Olivella Flower, where are you going ? White corn girl is here. You must go back to your house with White corn girl. And hurry lest Lightning get you. "...

22. SALT WOMAN GOES AWAY. [1]

At Ashu'ge [2] they used to live. At Yungeowinge they had a big feast and a dance. All the people from all over went to the feast. So Salt Woman (*anye kwiyo*) she, too, stood up a woman. Then they gave food to the people. One woman said, " This stew has no salt. " Salt Woman said, " If the stew has no salt, I will put some salt into it. " She blew out of her nose into the stew. [Shown by gesture]. " Eat! " she said. They just looked at her. " You are a dirty woman ! We do not eat that way! " They got angry. Salt Woman wanted to go away from them. That is why she did that. She said to them, " Now

1. Informant I of San Juan. Cp. Harrington, 536-7.
2. " Down at the alkali point " (Harrington, 229). A place across the river which still looks salty, near Chamita.

if you need me, you will have to go far away [1] and get tired and hungry, if you want me. " They did not know that was Salt Woman. So she went away from them. She spoke the truth. They get tired now when they go for salt. [2] That is all. *Hu'* !

23. SKELETON BOY : STAR HUSBAND :
HIDING TESTS AND DISTRIBUTING THE ANIMALS :
THE BOY SACRIFICE AND TRIAL OF MAGIC. [3]

Owewehambaiyo they were living at Yungeowenke. There were two Yellow corn girls. Their father was Prayer-stick old man, and their mother was Shrivelled corn old woman. They were going to have a big dance. They had a big building to dance inside, and everybody would go into that kiva. They were coming into that kiva. Up in the hills to the west was living Skeleton (*penit'a*). He heard of the dance and he got ready. He fixed himself up nicely ; he put on abalone (*eyi*) earrings ; he wore a skin of white buffalo. Then he came and went down into the kiva. He stood up by the side of the ladder. When the Yellow corn girls saw that boy they were asking, " Whence comes that boy ? He is a nice boy, " they said. " Let's go out and urinate, " they said. " When we pass him, we can ask him to go with us. " As they passed him they pulled at his mantle. So he went out after them. So they came down and went out to the corrals. They were asking, " From whence are you ? Where do you live ? " He said, " I don't live far ; I live near by. " So they liked that boy. Then the girls said, "Let's go to your house, if it is not far. " They went, one on one side, the other on the other. They came to his house. He had a white house. So they went up. And Skeleton went in first. So Skeleton said to his mother, " I have brought you two *sa'i*, tell them to come in. " — " From where are you bringing *sa'i*, Skeleton ? " — " Do not say that word, they are standing up there, they might hear it. " So his mother said, " You are two *sa'i* up there, come down. " So they came down, putting down their legs, in nice boots. They told them to sit down. He had lots of things, buffalo hide, buckskin, black dresses, belts. They took out wafer-bread and dried meat. They got through their supper and they got out their beds. So the boy put his bed in the middle and on each side a girl. When the day was coming, the younger one woke up. When she woke up, the boy lay there as a skeleton, his eyes way

1. When the U.S. Government moved the Apache from the northwest southward to the Mescallero country, Informant I and other Pueblo men went on burros to the Mescallero country to sell grain. On this trading journey they found salt.... The Apache returned to the northwest because their children were dying in the Mescallero country.
2. *Anyage*, salt place, but no definite place is referred to.
3. Informant I of San Juan.

down in his head. She got scared. " *Hewembohạrahi!* what kind of a boy are we sleeping with!" She aroused her sister and said, " Just see what kind of a boy we are sleeping with ! " They got up very softly and put on their clothes in a hurry, and put on their boots. So they noticed he was wearing not abalone earrings, but earrings of gourd, big ones. So they went down and ran fast. They were coming way down here at Tatunggere. [1] Then Skeleton woke up and called, " Yellow corn girls, my friends, why did you leave me in my bed ? " Then he went after them. The younger said, " *Hewembohạra hi*' ! elder sister, that skeleton has awaked, he is calling and running after us. Run just as fast as you can, and I will run, too. " So they ran. He called again. " Elder sister, he is gaining upon us ! " When the sun came out, he was getting near them. When he was very near, from out the sky Agoyonohụ (star dark [2]) threw down a string with an arrow. Dark Star said, " Yellow corn girls, do not believe in everything. You believed in that boy, do not do it again. Catch the arrow. " They took the arrow, and Dark Star pulled them up, [3] and it sounded like wind. And Skeleton cried and cried and went back into the ground. He did not catch them.

So they went up into the sky. There they got sick to have their babies. They had their babies. Both of them were boys. When they were big boys, they made them arrows. So they went out and played with the arrows and killed rats and took them in to their grandfather (*t'et'e*). Their grandfather made them arrows. They went hunting farther and they began to kill rabbits and jackrabbits. They were now big boys, and began to kill deer and buffalo and white-tailed deer [4] (*ohụ*). Then their grandfather told them not to go to the north, to go only west, south, and east, there they could go. " I wonder why our grandfather tells us not to go north. I do not care if he tells us not to go, some day we will go, hiding behind the trees, " they said. One morning they went out hunting deer, and their grandfather said not to go north. So they went south, and went a little way and hid and then went on north. They went shooting their arrows and going after them, and shooting again and going after their arrows, that is the way they went. When they had gone a little distance, there were lots of deer and buffalo and mountain sheep. " Maybe in this place there are lots of deer and that is why our grandfather does not let us come this way, " they said. There was a man, Pineto sendo (mean old man), taking care of those animals. Crow (*Ọndo*) was on guard. When anybody came he would let Mean old man know. At the time the little

---

1. " Way up, this side of Chamita." See Harrington, 228.
2. Morning Star.
3. Cp. De Huff, 55.
4. Henderson and Harrington, 17.

boys were coming, Crow was asleep and did not see them. They were
playing and shooting. In the sunshine Mean old man was sleeping,
and when they came he woke up. Then he said, " Why did you
come here, you *penibie* (Skeleton, his child)? " They said, " We are
not Skeleton's children, we are *agoyŏnohusendbie* (star dark old man his
child)" — " You are not Dark Star's children, you are Skeleton's
children, " he said to them. Mean old man ran after Crow, and said,
" You were on watch here, why do you sleep ? " He took a big stick
and hit the bird in the neck and knocked him down. So he said,
" Now I will see if you are Dark Star's children. " He said, " Now
we are going to play at hiding. " The boys said, " We don't know how
to hide. " — " But we are going to play, " said the man. " I bet you
all what I have here, deer, buffalo, sheep and turkeys. " The boys
said, " You have to hide first. " He put over their heads a buffalo skin
and he hid. So he stood up buffalo, in the midst of buffalo. He called,
" Ready, hunt me. " Then they took off that hide. They had *pinang*,
too, so they looked and saw the buffalo. The elder said, " You are
over there, walking as a deer. " The younger said, " *Hewemboharạ hi‘ !*
elder (brother), I guess you want Mean old man to beat us. You should
say, ' There you are walking buffalo. Come on ! we have found you ! ' "
So he said it that way and Mean old man said, " *Harạhi‘!* Skeleton's
children ! " — " We are not Skeleton's children, " they said. " Now
you hide and I will find you. " So they hid, they covered him with
the buffalo hide, and they stood up antelope [1] (*t'on*). They said,
" Ready, hunt us ! " He was looking around. Then he said, " There
you are, walking buffalo, Skeleton's child. " Nothing came. " There
are the Skeleton's children, walking deer. I have found you ! " Nothing
came. He said, " I have not found you. Come on ! You hid well. "
They were walking antelope and they came. So he said, " If you hide
well four times, you will beat me. You have beaten me once. " He
covered them with the buffalo hide and he hid, and walked up wolf.
" Ready, hunt me ! " he called. Then they saw him. The elder said,
" I have found you, Mean old man, walking white tailed deer (*ohụ*). "
The younger said, " *Hewemboharạhi‘!* elder brother, you always do it
wrong. You ought to say, ' There you are, Mean old man, walking
wolf. ' You ought to say it that way. " So he said it that way.
" *Hewemboharạhi‘ !* you have found me ! " So they covered him
with the buffalo hide, and they hid, those boys. And there
was a big lake there and they became ducks (*owị*), swimming in
the water. They called, " Ready ! " And he took off the cover and he
was looking around. " I have found you, Skeleton's child. There you
are, walking goose (*kạgi*). " Nothing came. Then he said, " I have
found you, Skeleton's child, walking turkey (*pindi*). " Nothing came.

1. Henderson and Harrington, 15.

" Come on! boys, you hid well. I did not find you. *Harahi*! these Skeleton's children are going to beat me! Come on, Skeleton's children! " — " We are not Skeleton's children. " Then they covered up, and he hid. They took off their cover. And he was just the same as they had been, swimming in the water. " We have found you, " said the elder. " There you are, walking heron, come on. " The younger said, " *Hewemboharahi*! elder (brother), you always do that! Why don't you say, ' You are swimming in the water. Come on' ? " So they found him. So then the boys hid. They made themselves into rabbits, one into jack-rabbit, one into little cotton-tail rabbit. So they said, " Ready! " And he took off the cover. He said, " There you are walking crane (*puga*). I have found you. " But they did not come. He did not find them. He said, " There you are, Skeleton's child, walking elk, (*t'a*). " Nothing came. So he said, " Come on! I have not found you. Just once more I have to hide. " So Mean old man hid once more. He made himself into a cotton-tail rabbit. He said, " Ready! " They took off the cover, they saw him. The elder said, " There I have found you, Mean old man, walking jack-rabbit. " The younger said, " You always do that. Why don't you say, ' There you are, cotton-tail rabbit'? You ought to say that. " So they found him. [1] Mean old man was beaten. " Now you have beaten me. All these walking here are yours. " They said that they still needed something. Mean old man said, " You ought to go on a little farther north. There lives Mean old woman (Pineto' kwiyo.) [2] " So they went on walking north and shooting their arrows in play. Owl (*mahu*) was taking care of that Mean old woman. If anybody came he would always let her know. And Owl was sleeping too. And that Mean old woman was asleep in the sunshine. And they shot arrows near where she was. When they came, she said, " Why have you come, Skeleton's children? You ought not to come here. " And she got mad and took a stick and went after Owl. " You don't take care of me, to let those boys come into my house. " And she hit him with a stick in the neck and he fell down. " Well, Skeleton's children! " she said. " We are not Skeleton's children, " they said, " we belong to Dark Star. " — " I will see now if you are Dark Star's children, " she said. " Let us play at hiding. " — " We don't know how to hide, " they said. Then they said, " All right, you have to hide first. " She got a blanket dress (*tsega*, the Hopi white dress) and covered them with that. And she hid. She made a great big lake. When she said ready, they took off that blanket and they saw what it was. Said the elder, " There you are, walking fish (*pa*). We have found you, come on! " The younger said, " *Hewemboharahi*', elder brother! You always get it wrong. Why don't you say, ' There

---

1. Here our interpreter queried, " Is that four times? "
2. Cp. Henderson and Harrington, 46.

you are, turned into a lake ' ? " So he said, " There you are, a lake. " Then she covered up. So they hid. They stood up a tree. They said, " Ready! " She took off the blanket. She said, " There, you are swimming in the water. Come on. I have found you. " As there were two of them, she had to say again, " There you are, *o'k'ama.* " [1] Nothing came. She said, " Come on! I did not find you. You have beaten me once. " Then they covered up. She came out goose. "Ready!" When they uncovered they saw what she was. The elder said, " There you are walking heron. Come on! We have found you. " — " *Hewemboharqhi'*! elder (brother). You always do that. You want us to be beaten. You ought to say, 'There you are walking goose ! ' " So he said it. " Come on. We have found you! " Then she covered them. They stood cedar (*hʉ*). " Ready ! Hunt us. " She said, " There you are, walking jack-rabbit. " Nothing came. She said, " There you are, walking cotton-tail rabbit. " Nothing came. " Come on. You have beaten me. " So she covered them up. She stood pine (*wę́*). They uncovered themselves. They saw her standing there. " There you are standing piñon (*t'o*) ", said the elder. — " You ought to say ' There you are standing pine. ' " He said it. " You have beaten me, " she said. So they hid. They made themselves *pętotsirį.* [2] So she said, " There you are, walking turkey. Come on. " Nothing came. The second time she said, " There you are, walking heron. " Nothing came. She said, " You have beaten me. Now I believe you belong to Dark Star. I know you are his children. " She said, " You have beaten us. All the goats we have here are yours. You have to take them way down to the earth. "

Their grandfather was saying, " How long they are gone! They have not minded me. " They came home at night. Their grandfather scolded them. Their grandfather called their father, Dark Star, and said, " You ought to take them home. If you do not take them to their own home, they will do even worse than this. " So Dark Star told Yellow corn girls to get ready to take them back. They brought them and hung them up by the same string they took them up by, also the goats and deer and buffalo and elk and turkeys and birds of different kinds. Because Yellow corn girls' children won, we have different kinds of animals and birds. That is why we have them every-where. [3]

Yellow corn girls' father and mother were still living. They came with their sons, they said, " *Tsę́ngtsamu*, father and mother! " They cried because they had come back. " We did not expect to see you again, " they cried. " We are very glad to see you. " So they said to

1. Swimmer bird, with white beak.
2. A little brown bird that flutters on trees.
3. On First Mesa Morning Star is himself associated with all the animals and asked to give them to men, both hunt animals and domestic.

the boys, " These are your grandmother and grandfather. Know
them. " The boys went out and played with the boys there. The
other boys did not like them, but they always tried to go with the
other boys. They were *pinang*. The other boys treated them badly.
They found one little boy, with whom they would play and walk.
They heard that Lightning was their Mother. He was living near by,
on the big hills. To Lightning every year they gave one little boy ot
that town. Those two little boys heard of this and asked their grandfather, " Why do they do this? This place will not grow, because you
give boys. Winter chief and Summer chief do not take care of their
children well, because they give a boy to Lightning to eat every year. "
Their grandfather said, " We have done this for a long time. What
shall we do now, if you do not think well of this? " asked their grandfather. They were going with their friend, that little boy. He liked
them, and they liked him, too. The little boy said, " Friends, I want
to take a walk with you and a good walk, for to-night they are going
to bathe me [1] and to-morrow take me to Lightning to eat me. " So they
thought, " Lightning is not going to eat our friend. " Their friend
went to eat in his house. So they talked to their grandfather, " Tomorrow Lightning is going to eat our friend, our poor friend, " they
said. They did not say to their grandfather what they were going to
do; but they were thinking about it. They took their arrows. Their
grandfather said, " Why do you take your arrows? Are you going
far from here? " — " No, maybe we shall find a big deer and that
is why we take our arrows. " They went south and they turned and
went to find Lightning, and they were searching in the big hills. They
came from the west and found Lightning in a big house and he was
lying down, his arms crossed behind his head. The elder said, " Younger brother, do not run away, think like a man! " He was lying
down. The boys had a flute (*pipi*) (made of turkey leg bone). The
elder said, " I am going to blow it. When I blow it, he will move
and stand up, and then you shoot him. " So he got ready to blow.
He heard it, he got up and the younger shot him and killed him.
And they came up to him, and they took their lightning stones [2] and
opened him down the middle and took out his stomach. In his stomach was nothing good, only stones and sticks and pointed things.
They said, " *Hewemboharqhi* [*] ! these people here have a Mother like this,
without a heart ot any good " [3]. So they put in a good stomach and a
good heart and made him live again. " You do not need to do that, "
they said to him, " to eat boys and children who do not belong to you.
You must go away from here. You do not belong here. You must go

---

1. The ritual bath is common in Tewa ceremonialism.
2. *Tsiguwenuku*. Arrow or spear heads which are supposed to have fallen from
the sky.
3. Cp. p. 13.

into the high mountains and eat deer and whatever you find, away
from here. " So those two little boys took him away. Now they said,
" We will take our friend out. Lightning will not eat him. " Their
friend was in the Big kiva, well washed and ready to be eaten. They
came into the kiva and there their friend was. They were saying in
the kiva, " Wonder why our father Lightning does not come. The boy
is ready for him. " All morning they were waiting. It was near dinner
time. So they took the boy back to his house. " I wonder why our
father did not come, " they said. They went to find Lightning. They
did not see him. They saw the tracks of those two little boys. " They
must have killed him and taken him away. They are our father and
mother, " they said. So they came back and called all the men into
this house. One of the Outside chiefs went after the two boys. They
were not afraid, they knew what words they were to use. Their grandfather said, " *Hewemboharąhi*! I wonder why they want you. May be
you have done something wrong in the court. " They said, " Do not
worry about us. We know what to say. Why do we stay here? These
people do not like him. " So they went in. There were lots of men.
They told them to pass. They said, " No, we do not need to pass in
front of you men, from here we can say whatever you want to hear."
So they sat down there. They said, " We need you here because
Lightning is lost. That was our mother and father. You are the ones
who killed Lightning and you have to say like a man if you killed
him. " They said, " We killed him. " — " That is what we wanted to
ask you. That is why we called you here, you boys. " — " Is that
what you wanted to ask us ? We have said like men what we have
done. " So those little boys said to their Summer Mother (*poyokwi*),
" Is that the way you care for your children ? You give them to
Lightning. Is that the way to do ? If our Mother is good, he will take
care of his children, he does not give them to anybody to eat. There
is no need of our Mother to give them to be eaten. Mother and father
have to look after their children, not give them to be eaten. Now you
hear, everybody here asked if we killed him. We took him far from
home, not to eat children who do not belong to him. And we are the
ones who killed him. " So they said, " Let us bet. If you have *pinang*
too, let us bet. If you have good *pinang*, you kill us all, if we have
good *pinang*, we kill you. In four days it will be. " So they said,
" Maybe they will kill us. " So they came to their grandfather's house.
Their grandfather asked them, " How did you fare? " They said,
" They told us in four days we must get ready. If we have *pinang*, we
kill them. If they have *pinang*, they kill us. " Their grandfather said,
" *Hewèmboharąhi*! poor boys, we are going to have a hard time. " He
said, " Let's go out, it is winter time, but maybe near the river we
can find some green things. " They saw a little butterfly flying by the
river. They said, " Wish we could get this little butterfly. Maybe

with this we can beat, " they said. It was *oyipo* ice month (Sp., *Yenero*, January). So they ran after Butterfly and nearly caught him. Butterfly led them up to the west. When they thought where they were, they were way up in the mountains. Butterfly flew around some big stones and then he stood up a man, water running off his face. " *Hardhi*'! you boys are mean, see how tired I am with you running after me. " — " We did not run after you, but after a butterfly, " they said. " That's me, " he said. " Dark Star heard you were having hard times here, maybe he will help you. " Then he turned over the stone and took them in. Under the stone were Oxuwah tsauwe (blue) and Oxuwah tseyi (yellow). They asked them what had passed. They talked about what had passed here. Then they asked what the boys had told the caciques. " They asked us to display *pinang* against each other in four days. If we have *pinang*, we kill them; if they have *pinang*, they kill us. Maybe we are going to be killed. " Then they said, " Do not be scared, we will help you. And now you have to ask what kind of *pinang* you are going to use. " They said yes. They opened the door to the north, they took them in. It was raining lightly in there and lightning. " Do you like this? " They said no. They opened the door to the west. It was raining, too, but heavier rain, with lightning and sounds of thunder. " Do you like it? " — " No. " They opened to the south. It was raining, heavy rain, it was lightning and hailing. " Do you like this? " — " No. " They opened to the east. Hail was falling, sounding hard, very bad. " We like this, " they said. " That night when you have *pinang*, this will go. " They said, " All right, do not be scared of them. " So they gave them skins (rind) of watermelon and of muskmelon, deer meat, buffalo meat. They gave them a little piece of black cloth for their grandmother and grandfather and their two mothers. " And that night when you have *pinang*, you must wear these clothes (little miniature garments). If anybody comes over to your side, say, ' Come on.' " Then they went home. When they came home they took out their bundles and opened them. There were lots of meat, lots of melons, lots of corn. There was corn on the stalk also, to put in front where they sat. And there were clothes, lots. They put those clothes to one side, so if anybody joined them, they could give clothes to them. Those other people were trying with sticks to make melons and corn, with that they wanted to beat the boys. They thought they could beat the boys. Then the day came. The people of the boy who was to have been eaten came to the side of the little boys. So they gave them clothes. That night was the night it was to be. The kiva was full of people. They had an altar (*sen'te*) there where they sat. They had a niche in the wall, on both sides. In one niche they had a little boy. He had a little bowl of water in his hands to sprinkle from his mouth on a little grass. There were melons there made of sticks. So they went to call them, Outside chief. They were eating melons and meat, those people with the little boys. Outside chief said, " I have come for you people. It is time to go. " — " Sit down and eat melon, and then we will go. " He sat down and ate. He said, " I am going with you. If they have much *pinang* they will kill us. " — " Go and bring your children then. " So he brought them all. They gave them melons and everything. In Big kiva they were angry, they stayed so long. They sent another Outside chief. To him they said, " Come and eat. " So they sat down. He said, " I am going with you. " They gave him clothes, too. " Why do they stay so long ? Go and bring them, " they said. They sent another Outside chief. " Sit down and eat, " they said. " We will go after a while, " they said. So he sat down. Another Outside chief came, the fourth one. He got mad. " Don't be mad, " they said, " eat. " — " I have not come to eat, " he said. So there were three Outside chiefs on each side. They went into the kiva. They sat down. They carried in their melons and corn. They were eating there, in the kiva. The other people said, " Those things are made of stick. They are not really eating. They want us to believe they are melons. " They saw the little boy standing in the niche with water, and green fake melons. They said to the little boys, " You believe now that we have *pinang*. Now we want to see your *pinang*. " — " All right. Now we are going to have *pinang*. " They did not show them melons or green corn, they had another kind of *pinang*. The people in the kiva were looking on. The two little boys took some ashes, put them in one place, with ashes they painted themselves black and white like *kossa*. They faced the east. They took ashes in their hands like this (narrator makes a kind of slicing movement by passing his palms rapidly against each other in contrary direction). They said, " Those Oxuwah are coming. They are coming with rain and hail. " The other people said, " They will not bring anything. " They brought their sticks to kill the little boys. " They will not bring anything." The Outside chiefs said, " Just wait a while. " They were coming. They heard the sound of the rain, when it sounded harder it was hailing. Still they did not believe it. When they were very near to the kiva, lightning came near the building, they could see it. " They will not bring anything. Kill them ! " The Outside chiefs would not agree to it, yet. When they were close to them, it was raining hard, and hailing. Those upstairs went in. The boy in the niche they struck with lightning and threw him down, with his bowl. They said, " Come in ! Come in ! our Fathers and Mothers. " They were carrying green jucca (*pa*) in their hands and they whipped the caciques and all the people. [1] So the caciques were crying, and they gave cigarettes to the two little boys and said, " We have done bad things. You belong to our Mothers and Fathers. We will not do this again. " They

1. Just as elsewhere the kachina may whip for ritual violation.

said to the Oxuwah, " You must not be mad. " So they went out. Then came in one Avanyo, [1] and water came out from his mouth and the water rose. It rose six feet up, on those not believing, who held their children up in the air. The water stayed away from the other side. " Do not get mad, " they cried. Then the water dried up. They said to them, " You had hard times because you wanted these little boys to have hard times, " said the three Outside chiefs. Then they gave the Mothers to the little boys, one to be Winter chief, one to be Summer chief. *Huʻ*!

Variant : Skeleton Boy. [2]

Owewe'hę̨mba Yellow corn girls were living. They were grinding, and their grandmother said to them, " Hurry up! Get through with grinding so to-morrow morning you may get up early and go for *pe'pe'* (berries) [3]. " — " All right, " they said. And so they went for berries. And when they were getting berries they heard singing, and the younger said to the elder, "Elder sister, I hear singing, " and the elder said, " I am singing through my nose. " — " Just listen! " And they heard, and they said, "Wonder who it is? Let's wait to go with him. " So he was coming near. And they said, " How nicely he sings, that boy. I wonder who he is? " Then he came to where they were and he said, " *Sę̨ngit tsamu.* " And they said, " *Hǫ* (yes). You are the one coming singing? " And he said yes. " How nicely you sing, " they said to him. " Sing for us, so we can hear you sing. We like that song. " So he sang it. " Let's go. " So they went, the three of them. So the girls said to him, " Let's go to our house. So you can stay and live with us. " And the man said, " Surely I will go with you. " So when they came, their grandmother did not see the man, they hid him. So their grandmother scolded them, they were gone so long. They went in the morning, in the evening they came back. So their grandmother said, " Hurry up and cook the berries, so we may eat, and go to sleep early so you girls can get up early to grind. Get up when I call first. " And the man was in there, hiding. So they said to their grandmother, " All right, we will put our bed in here in the back room and you stay in the front room. " So in the night they slept with that boy, they put him in the middle, one on each side. So in the morning when their grandmother called them the younger woke up and called the elder. The boy was sleeping very soundly. She said, " Elder sister, wake up! look at what we are sleeping with! " They looked at that boy. He was a skeleton boy (*penit'aenu*) with earrings of gourd. He was

1. The horned watersnake. Among the Tewa he sends flood, and has a punitive function. See p. 148.
2. Informant 2 of San Juan. Heard from Informant 1.
3. Robbins, Harrington, Freire-Marreco, 114.

called from that, Poka'be enu (gourd break boy). They were scared, and they cried and ran away, and left Broken gourd boy sleeping. Then he woke up, and he said, " I wonder where they are gone. I better go home. " So he got up and went home. Then they came back, these two girls. When they came back their grandmother scolded them. She said that even a stone or stick could look like a boy and talk to a girl and they must not talk to anybody or bring anybody to their house, this their grandmother said to them.

Variant : Trial of Magic. [1]

Pategee, Ash boys, they lived with their grandfather and grandmother in Kụochute'e. And the people always treated them badly. They threw them dirt and ashes. So those little boys were very poor, they did not have enough clothes, they did not brush their hair, or wash their faces and clean their noses. Once Winter chief and Summer chiet called all the people to go at night into one big kiva. So they called these Ash boys too. So they said to their grandfather, " I wonder why Outside chief calls us to go to Big kiva ? " Then their grandfather said, " You must go. Do not pass clear where they are, sit down on the step. Whatever they ask, say, ' We do not know anything. We do not know even how to clean our noses. We do not know anything.' " They went to the kiva. Winter chief and Summer chief said, " In four days and nights you must come again because you never believe what Summer chief and Winter chief say. And Avaiyo sendo and Oxuwah are coming. And I wonder it you can do the same as we do ? " The boys said, " How can we do anything ? We are too little. We never think of those hard words. But maybe our Oxuwah will help us. " — " All right, " they said. " You be ready to come in four days and nights. " So they went out from there and they went home, and their grandfather said, " Why do they want you ? " — " Grandfather, I guess we wont tell you. " — " You tell me. " — " Our Winter chief and Summer chief want us to bring Oxuwah and Avaiyu. How can we do that ? " Their grandfather said, " Don't you think about it. We will work for it for four days. " For four days they were getting ready in Big kiva. In four days the little boys said to their grandfather, " Don't you go when first those Outside chiefs come, we will be the last ones to go. " Those Winter chiefs and the other chiefs (*pu'fona sendo*) made two little boys like Avaiyu in Big kiva, one on one side, one on the other side. In four days and nights one Outside chief came and called them to get ready to go to the kiva. He saw them eating watermelons, melons, everything. He ate with them. He said he would go with the little boys. " All right. You must bring your wife (*umbi kwiyo*). "

1. Informant 2 of San Juan. Heard from Informant I.

Then the next Outside chief called them. Then he 'saw their watermelons and he stayed with them, and he got his wife. So those two Outside chiefs and their wives stayed on the boys' side. Then came the third Outside chief. He saw watermelons and he sat down to eat and he stayed and went on the boys ' side. So they went to the kiva. It was full of people, and they saw those two little boys making Avaiyu · They brought those Oxuwah with jucca switches and tried to whip those two little boys. The boys said, " Don't be mad ! Don't be mad! " They [Oxuwah] went home. Then those Ash boys they brought their Oxuwah. Real Oxuwah came, very angry, and real Avaiyu. And all those people they killed with their water, and those two little Avaiyu made by the Winter chief and Summer chief they killed them. So we must not treat poor boys badly because those poor ones they have more *pinang*. God and everybody helps them.

24. THEFT OF MASKS. [1]

At Tekeowinge were living two boys. At K'ut'ihgeowinge (stones, lots of, pueblo) [2] they were going to have Oxuwah move (*dingoxuwahhina*). [3] When their mother went to K'ut'ihgeowinge she left them behind with a pail into which they might urinate. She told them not to go out. She covered up the hatchway so they could not 'go up. Then their father and mother went to *oxuwahhe*. [4] The two little boys opened the hatch and went also to *oxuwahhe*. Then they arrived. That day those Oxuwah came. The two little boys went into the same house the Oxuwah came to. They were naughty boys. The people did not see these two little boys. The Oxuwah [masks] were hanging up. The people were asleep. The boys took down the masks and took them home. Then they arrived. They took the masks in and put them down in their house. Their mother and father did not know what the boys had done. The people (of K'ut'ihgeowinge) said, " What has happened, we wonder. We have lost all that we have used. Who came in here and took them down and away from here ? " They said, " Maybe Towaé will know where they took them. We must go to Towaé and take him something he uses. " So they went to Towaé. They said, " *Na embi sendo*, from K'ut'ihgeowinge the Oxuwah are lost. We have to find them. " They gave Towaé some meal and downy feathers and tobacco. Then Towaé said, "I do not use these. They do not belong to me. I can do nothing. " So they went back. Then one man said, " Towaé uses arrows and shinny

1. Informant I of San Juan.
2. The town from whence the present San Juan was removed. Harrington, p. 210, 212.
3. In other words, a kachina dance.
4. "Same as *oxuwahhina*. "

sticks. He plays ball and goes hunting. " So they got ready arrows and shinny sticks. They took them to Towaé. So he said, " All right. Now I will help you hunt for them. " So he went searching. He came back, he said, "I saw nothing. " He said, " Maybe Skunk (*poæsœ*) will know where they are. " So they went to Skunk's house. That one had seen those two little boys. He said, " Those boys took those Oxuwah to Tekeowinge. There they are having summer all the time and rains. " Those people of K'ut'ihgeowinge were having a dry summer because they had lost their Oxuwah. So they said, " We must go and look for them. " Then they came to Tekeowinge. They prepared only good words to speak when they should come. They said, " You people, when you slept, you did not take care of those Oxuwah. Now if you want them, you must pay for them with good words. " They opened a door and took out the Oxuwah. They said, " You must take care of those Oxuwah, watch them well. You have had a hard summer because you did not take care of them. " If that Skunk had not seen those two little boys, they would have lost their Oxuwah. Thus it happened. *Hu'* !

25. THE OXUWAH ARE LET OUT. [1]

This little boy was hunting rabbits and he came to the house of Puga [2] sendo. He said to him, " Good-evening, grandfather. " He said, " Yes, get a seat. " Little boy was looking round everywhere. He said, " Grandfather, I want to live with you. " — " Yes, if you will live with me you will not have a hard time. " So that little boy stayed there. It was October and everybody was carrying in his corn. Then Puga old man said, " I am going to San Juan. The people there are getting in their corn, maybe I will get some. All I ask of you is not to go into that room. " After Puga old man left, Little boy said, " I wonder why my grandfather told me not to go in there. " He opened the door. All around there were big bowls all covered up. He went up to one bowl and uncovered it and up jumped Kossa (members of clown society), lots of them, and Little boy ran after them to catch them and put them back, but he could not catch them. [3] Little boy uncovered another bowl. From it out came Oxuwah. They began to dance. Then it began to rain. Puga old man was caught out in the rain. It wet him and he could not fly. [4] He said, " Maybe that little

1. Informant I of San Juan.
2. Unidentified bird — brown, tall with long tail and long neck, as large as a turkey. It comes in October and picks up corn. Cp. Henderson and Harrington, p. 46. Crane ?
3. Perhaps reminiscent of the chasing of the clowns by the children, which occurs on First Mesa, at Jemez, and probably elsewhere.
4. Cp. Parsons, 9.

boy did what I told him not to do. " Then he went home. Little boy was running after those Kossa, and the Oxuwah were dancing. Puga old man scolded little boy. He caught the Kossa and the Oxuwah and shut them up again. He said to Little boy, " Next time I leave you home, you must not do that. " Next time Puga old man went away he did not leave Little boy alone. (Puga ¦old man had wet his wings and could not fly). That is all. *Hu'* !

26. ASH BOY HUNTS A MAGICAL RABBIT. [1]

At San Juan lived Patee'e', Ash boy. Way down on the other side lived Shrivelled corn old woman. Now Ash boy was always going rabbit-hunting to the big hills (*yopepiŋ*). In the evening he carried back the rabbits. Some he carried strung around his body and shoulder, and some in his hands, his rabbit stick ·behind in his belt. In the evening Shrivelled corn old woman would come and see him. " *Haṛahi'* ! " said Shrivelled corn old woman. " Every evening that little Ash boy comes with rabbits, but he gives me none, not one. I am going to make a rabbit. " She made one and filled it with grass, and she got green things and set it up in them. She went upstairs and she began to sing,

tama [2]	uwa	suwa	tende
		warm	hopping
tama	uwa	suwa	tende
		warm	hopping
takete	pepe	suwa	tende
grass end of	pick up	warm	hopping
oye	mahų		owirioge
ears	twitching		scratching

She sang this kind of *pinang* song. She sang again. She sang three times, so he began to move one ear, his right ear, she sang the fourth time, he moved the left ear, and began to jump. He jumped around and jumped on the green things. In the evening came Ash boy with rabbits again. He was passing close. He saw the rabbit jumping around on the greens. He took his stick and threw it and the little rabbit fell down. He picked it up and took it along. The old woman got mad, she said, " Who is that boy who kills my rabbit ? " He took the rabbit and went home and left her mad. That is what happened to the old woman.

1. Informant I of San Juan.
2. No meaning.

27. ASH BOYS HUNT RABBITS TO THE NORTH. [1]

Prayer-stick old man, Shrivelled corn old woman, Yellow corn girls, at Nambé they lived, and Olivella Flower boy. Then Yellow corn girl had twin babies. Then they put a name to them, Pategee 'nye, Poker (? Ash) children. In time they grew up, and went out hunting rabbits. Then their grandmother and grandfather told them not to go to the north. " You go west, south, east, but not north. " Once they said, " Why did grandmother say not to go to the north. " To-morrow we will go, first to the east, then to the north. Why did grandmother tell us not to go ? Maybe there are more rabbits up there. " So they went to the north. They found lots of rabbits and they killed lots. It got late and dark. So they built a fire and cooked a rabbit and ate supper. As they were eating supper they heard something coming. Somebody said, " Which way ? " The little boys said, " This way ! " Something was coming nearer. " Which way? " Poker boys said, " This way ! " So that thing came nearer to Poker boys, and said again, " Which way? " Poker boys said, " This way ! " Coming nearer to Poker boys, it said, " Which way ? " — " This way ! " So it came. They were through their supper, they were scared. That was Singwæ kwiyo, Teeth old woman. [2] So she told the little boys, that witch old woman, to give her the rabbits. Poker boy said, " Eat it up ! " he gave her one. She ate that one. She told Poker boys to give her another. They gave her another, she ate it up. She ate up all the rabbits the Poker boys had. She said, " Now I am going to eat you up, little boys. " The little boys said, " Wait ! I have to go out first. If you are afraid, tie me up with something. " So she got rope and tied up the little boys. So they went out, at the back. Then they relieved themselves. " Every time she calls, you say yes. " She called, " Are you through ? " Then the faeces said no. She asked again, it said no. She asked again. It said no. The fourth time it answered very slowly. The fifth time, it did not answer. She pulled the rope. She just pulled in the faeces. She said, " I am going after those little boys. I don't care where they went, I am going to catch them. " The Poker boys ran fast, they came to where some Turkey girls (*pindianyu*) were grinding corn. The Poker boys said to them, " Hide us ! " The Turkey girls hid the boys. That witch woman came to where the Turkey girls lived. They said nothing to her. They ground faster when she questioned them. They only ground faster, they did not answer her. She got tired and went back. The boys ran away from there. The witch woman came back after those two again. The two came to

---

1. Informant 3 of Santa Clara.
2. "Like *pendi sendo* or *chuge kwiyo*, witch old woman. "

where the Gophers (*chunge*) lived. They told the Gophers to hide
them. So they hid them. The witch woman came to where Gopher
lived. She said to Gopher, " Did my children come here? " Gopher
said, " I told the children to take out the dirt. They never did. " She
asked again, " Did my children come here? " He only said, " I told
the children to take out the dirt. " [1] She got tired and went back. So
the Poker boys came out and ran away. They came to where grandmother Spider old woman lived. The witch woman came to where
grandmother Spider old woman lived. "Did my children come here? "
She said, " They came here. " She had a niche in the wall. " You see
them up there in that niche ? " — " You bring them down. " — " No.
If somebody wants something he has to do it himself. " Witch woman
went to reach up to the boys and when she reached up she turned
into a deer. She went away a deer. She never got those two little
boys. They went back to their grandmother. She scolded them. " You
two little boys, I told you not to go, and you went! " That's all.

28. TOWA'E HUNT RABBITS TO THE NORTH AND PLAN TO GO TO THE SKY. [2]

Grandmother (*saiya*) told Towa'e not to go out hunting over to the
north. " You can go hunting to the west and to the south and to the
east, but not to the north. " Towa'e brought some rabbits for grandmother and said, " I wonder why grandmother does not want to let
us go to the north, elder brother? " — " I don't know why ; but
to-morrow we will go to the north, younger brother. Don't you tell
grandmother that we are going to the north. " Every evening
grandmother was very happy because they brought rabbits. The
next day they went out to the north. They climbed up the hill
and they found Puwąhą kwiyo (Wind old woman). She said
to them, " Did not your grandmother tell you not to come
over this way? You boys are going to be killed to-night. Puwąhą
(Wind) is very mean, he likes to eat people. He does not like to
have people come around this way. For that reason your grandmother
told you boys not to come hunting this way. " — " Well, Wind old
woman, we are not afraid of your husband. There are lots of rabbits
around here, we are going to take all we can. " — " Well, you boys
better go home before my husband comes. " In the afternoon her
husband came, he was very mad, he blew fire from his mouth. He
said, " Who has been here, after my rabbits? I am going to eat them
up. " Towa'e hid behind a big stone, with the rabbits on their back.
Wind found them. He said, " Come on, boys, what are you doing

1. Spanish. Cp. pp. 130, 156.
2. Informant 5 of San Ildefonso.

there? I am going to have a nice supper off you boys to-night. " Towa'e, they just laughed. When the Towa'e did not come home, their grandmother was thinking about them. " The boys went, I think, where I told them not to go. Surely they are going to be eaten up. " ..... " Now, boys, let's go over to my kiva. That is the place where I am going to eat you up. " — " All right. Let's go. " They went. Wind sat in his *po'tsuno'* [1] seat. Then he took out his pipe, and he said to those Towa'e, " Now you smoke, and talk like a man. " They took out their pipe. It was a very small one. They gave it to him. " You smoke first. " He smoked first. Wind old woman said, " Oh my husband is going to die, I think. He thinks he is going to eat them up. But I do not think so. I see the smoke coming out from the kiva. They gave it to him first. " Then the Towa'e came out laughing from the kiva. Wind lay down for about two hours and a half. The elder said, " You see, younger brother, what we have done. Our grandmother thinks we are killed ; but we are going to bring her rabbits. " ..... " Good evening, grandmother, why are you crying ? " — " I am crying because I told you Towa'e not to go to the north. But you are a man. " — " Yes. We are going to tell you what we did with Wind. Wind old woman said to us, ' What are you doing round here, boys ? My husband will eat you up.' When we saw him, he was very mad, fire was coming from his mouth. We hid beside a big stone. He asked his wife, ' Who has been hunting my rabbits ? ' — ' Towa'e, they have come hunting for their grandmother.' — ' Well, they are not going to take rabbits from here, I am going to eat them up.' Then we went with him to his kiva. He said that we had to smoke like a man. I took my pipe out first. " — " I thought you did not take it. " — " Yes, I did. We gave it to him. He smoked only twice and he fell down from his *po'tsuno'*. Then we came out and took our rabbits and brought them to you. " — " Next time do not go that way, Towa'e. Next time they will eat you up. " — " All right, grandmother, we ought to obey you. We got scared ourselves. He was a very tall man. We wont go that way any more. Tomorrow we will go to the east and get some more rabbits. You ought to make some more arrows for us, grandmother, so we can get a lot more rabbits. " — " You have enough rabbits, you don't need them. " — " Well, why don't we need more ? " — " Because you are too small yet, Towa'e. She might get mad, Blue corn woman, that you need so many arrows. So you better not have so many. " — " Grandmother, I am going to ask you why you don't want us to go to the sky (*opakare*) ? " — " Towa'e, you are very mean. You want to go wherever I don't want you to go. Why do you want to go to the sky ? " — " We want to see the

1. White stone bead, made by Navaho.

sky and what they are doing there. " — " You do not need to go up
there, it would be very hard for you to go up. You are too small,
Towa'e, to go there. When you get old, you can go. Then you will
know what stones ¹ to bring from there, and what Okuwahse will say
to you. Now you are too small. " — " What do you say, younger
brother? Let's go, as we went the first time. " — " No, elder brother,
I don't know if we would be doing right. It would be hard for us.
We do not know how to climb up to the sky. " — " If you don't
agree, I will whip you. You ought to go where I say. " — " No, if
you whip me, I will tell grandmother you want to go to the sky. "
— " Don't tell her we are going. " — " Yes, I am going to tell her
if you whip me. " — " Don't. Let's go and see him, so we can know
what kind of man he is, as the first time. " — " No, let's go get
rabbits for grandmother. " — They went and got rabbits for their
grandmother, in every direction. Next morning they got up and
said, " We are going hunting again. " Grandmother said not to go to
the sky. "If you go, Okuwahse will prevent you. He might not let
you come [? return]. " — " What do you say, younger brother? I am
thinking about going again. Don't be afraid, I will do the best I can.
We might kill him with a pipe, as we did the other one. " — " No,
I do not think we can do it. " . . . That far I remember.

Variant (from Tesuque).

Eo' (once) Tsabaiyo' old man lived on *toyụ* (Black Mesa). Those two
boys, Towa'e, lived on Sandia Moutain. They came here and fought
with Tsabaiyó. He took them and put them in the oven ; but they
did not burn. At night they came out and ran away. Tsabaiyó caught
them again. This time they killed him.

White corn girl was the mother of those Towa'e. After they grew
up they went to live on Sandia Mountain, where they were always hunting deer.

29. TOWA'E VISIT SUN. ²

There were two little Towa'e. They had round things (rings?);
when they threw one down, they shot at it. Playing thus, they came to
the house of Sun old man (T'a sendo). Towa'e were *pinan*. They had a
little stone pipe they smoked. So they came to Sun old man. Sun old
man did not let anybody come into his house. These boys came there.
"I do not know what Sun old man is going to do to us. " — " Why
have you come, Towa'e ? " said Sun old man. " Come in, " he said.

Now we are going to smoke like a man." They sat down. They smoked. Sun old man smoked a long pipe. He did not let smoke come out. He gave it to the boys. "You must not let smoke come out." (He wanted to kill the little boys.) So he gave the pipe to one of them. He smoked, he swallowed the smoke, it did not hurt him. He gave the pipe to the other. He smoked and swallowed the smoke, and it did not hurt him. "Maybe you have something," said Sun old man. "Now we will smoke with our pipe." Sun old man was laughing at the little one. The elder one smoked and gave the pipe to Sun old man. "In one pull I will smoke it all." When he smoked, he coughed. "It goes into my heart," he said. "I wanted to cough, that's why I did that," said Sun old man. [1]

30. THE SUN'S CHILD : ASH BOYS. [2]

At San Juan they lived, Shrivelled corn old woman, Olivella Flower, and Prayer-stick old man and Yellow corn girl. Yellow corn girl was every day grinding corn. The San Juan boys asked her to marry them, but she would not. The Santa Clara boys came and asked her, but she would not marry them. The Nambé boys came, the Tesuque, the Pojoaque. She would not marry them. At one time she was grinding corn, in front of her was a little window. Sun old man came in, and from him she got a baby. So there in the ash pile she had the baby. She left it there. An old woman and an old man lived alone. The old man could not get wood, so the old woman went out to the wood pile after kindling. She heard that baby crying. She went where that baby was crying. She got the baby and brought him home and bathed him. Then she went to bed with the baby for four days (*jönita*). [3] She got up in four days. The old man made something to eat for the old woman. She got up, and named the baby, Pategee'nu, Ash boy. Then that little boy grew up and went to the pueblo. The boys were playing with bows and arrows. "This arrow my uncle made," one would say. "My father made this," the boys were saying. He heard them. That evening he went to his grandmother and asked her, "Who is my uncle? Who is my father?" — "We are your father and mother, we are your uncle, too." So he said, "Grandmother, make me a bow and arrows." So they made them. They took the poker and made a bow. They made arrows. Next morning the boy went into the town with bow and arrows and played with the boys. He beat all day. The little boys said they were killing rabbits, jack-rabbits, deer, turkey, they were killing them. So

---

1. "Nice story, but only to there I know it."
2. Informant 3 of Santa Clara.
3. This is the regular confinement period, at the end of which the infant is named.

the little boy went and told his grandmother, "Some little boys said, 'I have killed a rabbit,' other boys said, 'I have killed a jack-rabbit, a deer, a turkey.' I want to know what kind of animal a rabbit is, what kind a jack-rabbit, a turkey, a deer. To-morrow I am going hunting, too." So next morning his grandmother put down a rabbit track in the ashes, a jack-rabbit track, a turkey track, a deer track. Then she put up a lunch. He went, that evening he brought in a rabbit. The next morning, he went, and brought in a jack-rabbit. So the next day he wanted to go up to the mountains. He went, he brought some turkey. The next morning he was going back to the mountains, he asked grandmother to make lunch for him. So he took the lunch. He went to the mountains. At a certain place he met a man. He asked him, "Where are you going?" — "I am going hunting." — "Let us have our dinner before you go." So they had dinner. The little boy was ashamed of the lunch he had. That man had a good lunch of wafer-bread. The little boy had only *tsakewe* (corn bread like mush). He was ashamed to put it out. The man said, "Why don't you put out your lunch?" So he put it out. They had their dinner. They got up. He asked him who was his father, who was his uncle, who was his mother? "When you return you ask who your father is, your uncle, your mother. To-morrow you come back, we will meet right here again. You tell me who is your father, your uncle, your mother. To-morrow come and let me know. Go on that side in the brush, there is a deer. You shoot him." The little boy went and shot him and killed him. Then he did not know how to bring him home, he was too heavy. The man came and helped him. He came home, on top of the roof. "Grandmother," he said, "I bring a deer." So they would take it inside. His grandmother did not know how to pick it up, it was too heavy. The little boy picked it up and told her where to put it. They laid it down and took off the hide. They got through, they had supper. When they were through supper, he asked his grandmother, "Who is my father? Who is my uncle, my mother? Who is my grandfather and grandmother? A man came and told me to ask who is my father, my uncle, my mother." So grandmother told him, "Prayer-stick old man is your grandfather, Shrivelled corn old woman is your grandmother, Yellow corn girl is your mother, Olivella Flower is your uncle, Sun old man is your father." Then next morning he went, he met the man in the same place, they had dinner. After dinner he asked him, "Who did grandmother tell you were your grandfather and grandmother?" So he said, "Sun old man is my father, Yellow corn girl is my mother, Olivella Flower is my uncle, Shrivelled corn old woman is my grandmother, Prayer-stick old man is my grandfather." The man told him, "I am your father." Then he came back with another deer for his grandmother and grandfather again. Next morning he went back, he met the man again, Sun old man. With him he had dinner again. After they had dinner, his father told him, "Now you go, when you come home tell grandmother to cover you with a white blanket, and to get a stick to hit you hard on the head." He went, when he came home he told grandmother after supper to cover him with a blanket and to hit him with a stick, to hit him hard. They hit him, she hit as hard as she could, she thought they had killed him. He never moved. In a little while, they talked to the little boy, they were frightened, they cried. In a little while, grandmother told him to take off the blanket. Then there were two little boys under the blanket. So they went hunting the next morning. Sun old man came, they met again. They came there, they had dinner. After dinner, he brought them to where a spring was. He told the elder to take off his clothes. He took off his clothes. He told him to go into the spring. He went in. Sun old man bathed him. When he got through bathing him, he went out. When he came out he put a white blanket over him. He rubbed him under the blanket. Then he began to grow up like his father. Then he measured with him, he was not quite as big. He put the blanket over him, he grew a little more. He put the blanket over him again. That time he was as big as his father. So he put on his clothes — parrot tail feathers (*taiyiwœ*), pink quartz beads (*g'upikwa*), turquoise (*k'unœ*), he got them all. Then Sun old man told the other little boy to bathe. He got through. He did the same for him. He put the same blanket over him and did the same. So he got up and measured with Sun old man. He was nòt quite as big as his father. He put the blanket over him again. Then they measured again. He put on parrot tail feathers, moccasins, turquoise, pink quartz beads, and clothes. He finished. [1] He said to the elder, "Now do what I tell you." He went eastward to a place where he was told to come, like Sun old man. So he came slowly. He took a long time to go. Then the younger went, fast. First the elder came slowly, then the younger fast. So they got through. He told them, "Tell your mother goodby, your uncle, your grandmother, your grandfather. Tell them, 'I am going with my father.'" So they went home to Grandmother. "Grandmother, grandfather, goodby. We are going with our father, goodby (*sœngiriho*), we are going." So they went. Then they came to where their mother lived. They told their mother goodby and their uncle, and grandmother and grandfather. "We are going with our father. Do not cry for us. We are going with our father." Then the grandfather and grandmother and mother were crying for the little boys. But they went to where their father was. He told the elder, "Now you go in summer. Younger one, you go in winter. In winter the days are very short, you go fast. You in summer,

---

1. Cp. for this incident of Sun arraying his sons, Zuñi, Cushing 1 : 453, 454.

elder one, go slowly, the days are longer. " He told them what to do. From this the elder was to be the summer sun, and the younger, the winter sun. That's all.

31. IMPREGNATION BY PIÑON [1] : THE SUN'S CHILD CARRIES OFF HIS MOTHER. [2]

Owewehambaiya at Tekeowinge Yellow corn girl was living and she was not married. So lots of boys came to her house to ask her to marry. There was once lots of piñon on the hills, so Yellow corn girl went out over the hills. Up on the hill was a tree. The piñon fell down the hill on the ground. As she was picking up piñon, a boy on another hill talked to her. " Good morning, Yellow corn girl, are you picking up piñon ? " he said to her. She turned quickly and saw the boy. She did not know who he was, he did not belong to that place. Then he said, " Yellow corn girl, here I bring some piñon. Open your mouth and I will throw one into your mouth, " said this boy to Yellow corn girl. " When I throw it into your mouth and you catch it, do not eat it. " Then he threw piñon into her mouth, a big one down her throat. Then the boy said to her, " Go down to your house. " There piñons will grow and make lots of piñon in your house. " Then she came. Then her mother said to her, " Why have you come so early ? It is very early yet. " — " I got tired, that is why I came. " She opened the room and threw the piñon into the room. Then her mother said to her, " Why do you throw that piñon inside ? You ought to put them in a particular place. " In a little while her mother went into the place where she threw the piñon. Her mother tried to open the door. She could not open the door. Yellow corn girl stood up and came to the door and tried to open it. She pushed open the door, the room was full of piñon and piñon were pouring down alongside the door. Yellow corn girl said, " *Hubaharahia* ! that boy has lots of *pinang*, he spoke the truth. He said that the piñon would increase. The house is full of piñon. Thank you, boy. " The others came down, with lots of piñon ; but not like what Yellow corn girl had. Afterwards, in a few days she was sick to have a baby. So they said, " Every good boy who has asked her to marry she would not marry. Wonder why she is pregnant, " said the men and boys. They were talking a lot about Yellow corn girl. She got her baby. She had a little boy. He began to move about on the ground, that little boy. At that time all the men asked, " Whose baby is this ? " They wanted to know who was the little boy's father. So they called all the men into the kiva, young men and old men. Then they searched for the father of the

1. Cp. Cochiti, Dumarest, 228.
2. Informant I of San Juan.

baby. Every man came in there. They sent one of the boys to the house of Yellow corn girl's father for the father to take the baby to the kiva. So his grandfather took him to the kiva. So every man and boy had a flower in their hand. So they took the baby in and put him in the middle. The baby moved about, they moved the flowers: [1] Wherever the baby went there would be the father of the baby. There was a little hole. Sun came in through that little hole. So Sun was in there and the little boy was just playing on that spot, with the Sun. They moved the flowers, but the baby paid no attention, he was playing only with the tail of the Sun. The baby went to no other place, except where the Sun was standing. They did not know to whom the baby belonged. So they treated Yellow corn girl badly. They said, "If you do not put any heart to this baby, she must always do that," they said. The men did not know it was the Sun's baby, but it was the Sun's baby. So they said to the man he must go home. So he put the baby on his back and went home. After the old man went up with his little baby, those old men began to think of a plan. "We have not found the father of the baby. We do not know who the father of the baby is," they said. "Some of those boys must tell Yellow corn girl to get ready and in four days carry the baby to T'an̨ pokwi̧, Sun Lake (a blue lake), and throw it in." Yellow corn girl said, "*Hu̧baharahai*! I am having a hard time! They treat me badly, the people here. I don't know how I got this baby," said Yellow corn girl. In four days she bathed the baby well and dried him and she carried him to the lake to throw him in. When she was on one side of the lake, she suckled him, and she had no heart to throw him. She was sitting on the side to the north. Then she stood up and started to throw him, but she sat down to the west and suckled him again. Then she stood up and started to throw him, but she sat down again to the south and suckled him. She stood up, she started to throw him, but she sat down to the east and suckled him. Then she said, "What shall I do? It hurts me so much. Our rulers told me to do this." She turned her face and threw the baby back, without looking, [2] and the Sun picked the baby up before it touched the water. She looked. She did not see the baby. She cried, she went back to her house. One day they were getting ready a dance, *puwǫ́re* [3] they had not used for a long time. It was a four days dance, a big dance. There were no white people there, no Mexicans, only Indians. They called out for the four girls they needed, Yellow corn girl and three

---

1. Narrator showed how the flower was held in the right hand, which was moved by the left hand. This incident is Spanish. Cp. Parsons 4 : Pt. I, 104. Cp. also Russell, p. 239.
2. Acted out by the narrator.
3. The initiation war dance which was danced at Santa Clara in 1923, after a long interval. See p. 61.

other girls. The first day they were to dance, from every place the people came there. Sun old man told the little boy, " You must go to Tekeowinge, to the big dance. To-morrow you must go and bathe in Sun Lake, to wash your face. Your mother will come there for water. Do you say to your mother, 'Hello! mother, how are you?'" So when she went for water the boy was there. He said, " Hello! mother, how are you?" Yellow corn girl said, " I wonder why this boy is talking to me?" The boy said to her, " Mother, don't you remember that time you threw me in the water?" So then his mother said, " Are you my son?" She cried and held him. " Don't cry, mother, lest the people hear. " So he said, " Mother, ask the men who are managing to let you be the last of the women to dance. " His mother said, " Whatever you tell me I will do, " said his mother. So Yellow corn girl went and asked the caciques to let her be the last one. So they said, " All right, you may be the last one. " And they began to dance. And the next day another woman danced, and the third day, the third woman and the last day was the turn of Yellow corn girl. And those women, whoever they needed to dance with, they asked those boys, and Yellow corn girl's son said to her, " Don't ask another boy. I will dance with you, " said the boy. When they took Yellow corn girl out, she said, " I want to dance with that boy sitting up on the roof. He is a good-looking boy with parrot feathers coming up behind his head, fastened with a band of turquoise stones " [i.e. as a banda]. So he came down and went where they were going to dance. Blue corn girl, White corn girl, Red corn girl, Dark corn girl, Speckled corn girl, all said, " That boy does not belong here, we do not know who he is, " they said. They began to sing, they began to dance. They gave the last song. When they were through with the last song, they began to go up from the ground. [1] The boy reached down and took up the drum. They tried to catch it. He was high up, they could not reach it. He said, " At Tekeowinge people do not want to have babies. You threw Yellow corn girl's baby into the water. You made Yellow corn girl do that, and she did it, and maybe you people here do not want to have many people. Maybe you will all die. That's what you need and you will have it, so goodbye (*tsęngiriho'*). " And they went up high in the sky where Sun old man lived. That is why all the people died off from Powhaki.

Variant : The Sun's Child carries off his Mother. [2]

Owewehąmba at Po'suwage (Pojoaque) they lived. This old man and old woman had a girl, Yellow corn girl. She used to grind all day. She

1. Cp. Zuñi, Cushing 1 : 469-473.
2. Informant 4 of Santa Clara.

did not want to marry any of the boys. They came from everywhere to ask her to marry. She was grinding all day. The Sun came in through the high window. Then she was going to have a baby. That baby belonged to the Sun. The old man asked, " To whom does this baby belong? We might put all the boys in the kiva and bring up the girl and the baby. " So they did this and put the girl and the baby in the middle. All the boys said they did not know anything about it. Each boy had flowers, and offered them to the baby, and he would not take the flowers from any one of them. Then the Outside chief told her she could not raise the baby because it did not belong to the pueblo. So they picked up the baby and carried it to the river, into the water. They thought the baby fell into the water ; but the Sun came down and picked him up. The Sun brought him up. When he was a big boy he came down to find his mother. That time they were dancing *ti'ishare* (the so-called Butterfly dance). So this boy came into the house of his mother and grandfather. He said, " Grandfather, I have come. " So the old man said, " Yes. Why do you come? From where ? " The boy said, " I come from above (*k'ewepǫgere*). I heard they were going to have a dance to-morrow and I wondered if the governor (*tunjo*) would want me to dance. I would like to dance. " So grandfather said, " My child, I do not know if they will let you dance or not, but I will go and see the governor. " So he went to the *sharewǫgi*, and asked the governor. The governor said, " I do not know if he knows how to dance or not. These boys and girls have been practising a long time. I do not know if this new boy knows or not. " Grandfather said, " I do not know, but I will ask him if he wants to dance. I will come with him. " The governor said, " They are going to practise to-night and the dance is going to be to-morrow. " The boy said, " Yes. I don't know how to dance very well, grandfather, but if I can dance, I will. It is better for me to dance. Let me dance. " — " But I want to know from what pueblo you came before you go. The governor asked me to ask you. Tell me the truth, from where do you come? " — " I will tell you, Grandfather, why I have come. I have come for my mother. You remember that time Mother had a baby, and the Outside chief threw me away in the river? Do you remember ? I am the baby they threw away. My father sent me down. My father is Sun old man. So I have come for my mother. And I want to dance with my mother. " His grandfather told him not to dance at first, not until after dinner, [1] " then dance with your mother. " So those two danced, after dinner. They danced more prettily than all the others. Then they went up into the sky, that boy and his mother, to the Sun. The boy had told his grandfather, " I think you people do not want families. After this the pueblo will

---

1. They dance twice before dinner, twice after dinner.

all go, there will be no pueblo. " That is why they do not raise people in Po'suwage. [1]

32. IMPREGNATION BY PIÑON :
FOX MOTHER : THE TAOS PROPHET FORETELLS FLOOD. [2]

It was before the god was born. At Taos they had lots of piñon in the hills, and all the people would go out for piñon. There was a girl and she was going to have a child. She said to her mother, "I want to go out for piñon, too. " Her mother said, " Do not go. If you go you will be sick and have your baby. " — " I guess I better go, " said the girl. "I don't feel bad. " So her mother let her go. On top of the hill stood a piñon tree and the nuts fell down. As she was picking them up, she began to have her baby. She bore it, a boy baby. She left the child there wrapped in her drawers. When she went home she did not tell her mother. Then came a deer to the baby, close, and put its horn very gently under the baby and lifted it. Close by lived a fox [3] (*de'*) with cubs. There the deer carried the baby, and the fox gave the baby milk, and the baby became a brother to the little foxes. He would go out with them and the little deer. Once the Taos boys went deer hunting. One of them saw the little boy with the fox and the deer. He did not care about the deer, he wanted the little boy. The little boy was frightened. They ran home, the fox cubs and the little boy ahead. The hunter ran after them and saw where they went, how the little boy went into the fox house. Then the man stopped hunting, he was thinking only of that little boy. He went home, and when he got home he called all the men to his house and told them how he had seen a little boy with the foxes. " I don't know if you will believe what I say to you, but it is the truth. " Then they said, " We will go and make a round-up to find the little boy. " So they went up into the mountains and made a round-up. They did not find anything. The man who had found the little boy was thinking about him only. " Let us make another round-up and I am sure that we shall find him, " he said. " I better go where he went in, because I saw where it was. " So they made a round-up, and the man hid himself. Then they saw the deer and the fox and the little boy. They did not try to get the deer, they tried only to get the little boy. But nobody caught him. The man who had seen him was lying in wait for him. As the

1. Variant from Tesuque : They were living at Posǫa owinge, Uroto seno, Uroto kwiya, Kǫntsaianyo. White corn girl never went out... They were dancing *t'anshare* (Sun dance)... As the boy was dancing with his mother Sun took them up... Sun said, " Now they will see that they needed you. " After four days all the people died. There are no more people in that village.
2. Informant 1 of San Juan.
3. Coyote, but fox was the word used in translating.

little boy came on ahead the man caught him and held him in his arms. He let the fox cubs go in, but the little boy he held. As he was holding him, the others assembled and the man took the little boy to where they were in camp. And they took care of him as well as they could. They fried some meat; but he would not eat the cooked meat. The next day they gave it to him raw, and he ate it. So they all went home with the little boy. They took him to their house. Then they called all the men and women into the kiva and they asked them where that little boy came from. They were asking the women and girls. "Not from me, " "Not from me, " they said. Then the boy's mother said, "I guess he is mine, " said she, "because six years ago when there were lots of piñon, although my mother did not want me to go, I went and I got sick and on the side of the hill I had my baby and I left it there. " At this time the girl was married. All the men in the kiva asked the girl's husband if he would treat the little boy like his own son. He said yes. The man who caught the little boy said, "I do not relinquish the boy. I caught him. I do not give him up, because I caught him. He belongs to my mother's brother (*meme*) [1] because I caught him. " So the little boy stayed with his uncle. They kept the little boy in the kiva for one year. He was the first of boys like that ["*Pai'u*?" — "Yes"] [2]. He knew lots of words in his heart, he did not need to learn from anybody. He was a good boy. He understood the Coyote language. He knew when snow was coming and when rain was coming, and he let them know, and whatever he said, that way it would happen. So they believed that little boy. Whatever the number of days he said it would snow or rain, they believed. Whatever he said, happened. Then the little boy said to them all, "It is going to rain every day and every night and the water will rise. We should go to a big hill where the water wont reach us. " Thus the little boy spoke to them. "Whatever this boy says is so, " they said, "still this thing may not be so, " they said. " Maybe he is going crazy. " Some believed, some did not. They said, "From to-morrow on it will rain. " Those who believed said, " We will go out and find a place. " So all the believers went up on *mǫwolo*, [3] and those who did not believe stayed home. And that day and night it rained, and the water was rising over the houses, up on the hills. And they were up on the mountain [in concentric circles [4]], in the middle the buffalo, then the elk, then the deer, then white tail deer, then mountain sheep (*t'o*), then turkeys, and the water was all over the hills. The wind stirred up the water into foam. And the foam wet the tails

1. A characteristic reference to the maternal family.
2. Taos boys are sequestered at initiation a year or more. Initiates are called *pai'u*.
3. Mountain at Taos.
4. These were drawn by narrator, circle within circle.

of the turkeys. That is why the tails of turkeys are white, like the foam. ¹ Then the rain stopped, and the water went down, down, down. The wind came and blew hard over the earth, and the earth dried up. And they went to see if it was good. There were lots of mud, and the wind was blowing and blowing. One of them went down to see if it was no longer muddy. Then they all went down. And when they went home they found no people, they had all died. Then they believed in whatever he said, the little boy who was now a man. ² So they had a good man at Taos. And what he thought would happen, he told, and it would come out that way. He would say, " Some warriors (*hǫmbi*) are coming, Kiowa, Comanche. " Then no white people were here, nor Mexicans. So that man told the day they would come. They were to go into their town. So he said, " They will come into the town, they will kill just one man from here, " and he called him by name. Then he said, " We are going to beat them. " So they got ready and waited for them. This man he called by name they hid in the third room to the rear. The day he said they would come, they came into the town. And they ran after them, and when they came back they went to look at that man in the rear room. They found him dead with an arrow through the middle of his body. They did not know where it came from. The man's people said that little boy was a witch and his (the dead man's) people treated him badly. They killed him. So today those Taos people go into *pinang* [i.e. retreat for ceremonial]; but they will never have another boy like that.

33. IMPREGNATION BY PIÑON : POSEYEMU. ³

They used to live at Posé, ⁴ some people. And there was one woman lived there with her daughter. The people living there did not like them. When they went out they would throw refuse in front of their house, and the old woman would sweep it away. They were getting lots of piñon at that time in the mountains, the people were getting lots of piñon. The girl wanted to get piñon, too. The mother said, " If you want to go, you may go ; but don't go where those people

1. See p. 185.
2. Cp. Cheyenne prophet myth, Dorsey, 41-46.
3. Informant 1 of San Juan. For Poseyemu in other towns (Sia, Poshaiyänne, Stevenson, 1, 65-7; Laguna, Ts'itschinaku ; Poshean or Poshaiani also familiar ; Zuñi, Poshaiyanki, Parsons, 5: 261-3. Also under name of Montezuma, Cochiti, Dumarest, 228-231). When I spoke of Montezuma to my Tesuque informant, Poseyuma was at once mentioned by him. He said, " Poseyuma came and helped the Indians and Americans. To the Americans he gave money, to the Indians, the deer and mountain animals. When Jesus came down he took Poseyuma away. "
4. See Harrington, 1 : 162-6. There are hot springs here, which according to Harrington, are associated with Poseyemu. His grandmother lives within the pool and " Poseyemu comes from the south to visit her one day each year. "

are, because you know those people don't like us. " So she went. She
did not go where the people were, she went to another place. When
she was picking up piñon, a man came. That man was Opa'ochitse.
World Man. Then he said, " You are picking piñons ? " She said,
" Yes. " The man said, " Do not pick much piñon, little girl. You
better go home. " That man said to her, " When you go into your
house, tell your mother she must sweep the rooms and throw the
piñon in, and the piñon will know how to increase. Open your mouth.
I will throw this piñon in your mouth. " He threw a piñon into her
mouth. [1] He said, " Do not chew it. " Then she went home. So her
mother said, " Why do you come ? You did not pick up many. You
ought to have stayed longer. " She said, " Yes. A man came to
where I was and that man told me to come. " — " And you knew
that man ? " said her mother. " I do not know who that man is. He
is a good man. Then that man told me, ' When you go home, tell
your mother to sweep and throw in the piñon and the piñon will
increase. ' Then he threw a piñon into my mouth and told me not to
chew it. The piñon will know how to make lots of itself. " So they
got lots of water and sprinkled the rooms and swept up nicely and
threw the piñon into the room. In a little while the girl went and
opened the door. She could not open the door, the piñon was packed
up close to the door. [2] She said, " Come, Mother! Look how we have
got piñon in the house. That man was speaking the truth. " So they
were glad. Then that girl was sick to have her baby. Those people
said to them, " Look at that girl going to have a baby. Nobody likes
them. Wonder how she got a baby. " It was born, a baby boy. He
was growing. He had no name. They gave him no name. So he was
bigger, went down and began to walk around. His mother was poor
and he was not well dressed, that little boy. He went where those
other boys played and they made him cry. The little boys said to him,
" You have no name. " Thus they called him, No-name. When he
was a little bit bigger his grandfather made him arrows. He began to
go out and kill rats and he took them to his grandmother and mother.
His grandmother would said, " My poor little boy ! " He would bring
rats and say, " I bring you rabbits. " He said, " I have killed rabbits
and bring them to you. Cook them ; but I guess they are not rabbits.
Where are the rabbits, grandmother ? " She took some ashes and in
them made rabbit tracks, cotton-tails and jack-rabbits, and told him
how they looked. " All right, " he said. He went out and saw some
rabbits. " I guess these are rabbits. " So he shot and killed three or
four and brought them back. He was very glad because he was coming

1. P'ashaya·'nyi of Laguna is also associated with piñon. Out of his chest he takes
four piñon nuts and four grains of corn. Boas 1.
2. The belief expressed here, and on p. 88 of how much can come from little,
magically, is a common Pueblo habit of mind or faith.

with rabbits. They took them in and they were glad, his mother and grandmother. " Now you know how to hunt rabbits, my child, " they said to him. " I guess we won't have hard times now. " They skinned the rabbits, opened the stomachs, put salt in, stirred them with a stick [1] and cooked and ate them. He went out hunting, he killed more and brought them. And they did not have a hard time any longer. As he grew bigger, he began to kill deer. Now he was nearly a big boy. When they called, those people, they called all the men, and called him, too. So when he went there they told him to pass on, but he would not pass on, he stayed by the side of the ladder. They were talking about what they needed, and they told him to talk, too. When he talked, he talked well, using big words. So they said, " Wonder about this boy. He talks well. He has no father, no grandfather ; how does he know how to talk, using hard words? " They said, Winter chief and Summer chief, " This little boy talks good things. When you sweep out your houses, do not throw refuse in front of his house. He talks well. We do not need to treat him badly. " But the people did not believe this. They went on, some of them, throwing dust and ashes. He was a big boy now, but still he used only the arrows made by his grandmother. So he went out to the mountains. He was hunting deer. Then came his father, Opa'ochutse. He said, " *Tsǽngitsamu*, boy. What are you doing ? " He said, "I am hunting deer around here, to take to my mother and grandmother. " — " What is your name? " He said, " I do not know what my name is. I guess my mother and grandmother gave me no name. " — " How do they call you, those people who belong there ? " He said, " Those people, they call me Kąwc̜ebi (No-name). " That man laughed. He said, " You will like the name I will give you. " He was a good (noble-looking) man and he (the boy) was ashamed before the man. " You will give me a name ? " — " Yes, I will give you a name. " So he gave him a name, Posew'e'bi poseyemu (*pose*, dew [2], *w'é'bi*, kick ball [3] *pose*, dew, *yemu*, falls down). So he gave him this name. " This name I give you, do not forget it. Next time when they call all the men, go over and tell what your name is. Here I bring you some clothes. " He brought shirt and trousers, good clothes of buckskin. Those people did not use clothes like that. He got nice clothes. Also he gave him a quiver and a nice bow and arrows, all fixed up with feathers. He was glad. " I

1. Moving hand in anti-sunrise circuit.
2. In the Oraibi origin myth there is reference to the " god of dew, " father to his people to whom he gives corn and the power by magic words to ripen it in a day. Cushing 2 : 168.
3. Translated kick stick by a San Ildefonso man. But neither kick stick nor kick ball is played by the Tewa today. As kick ball is played by the Hopi, and kick stick at Zuñi, it is played for rain or moisture, and this the Tewa personal name also suggests.

shall have good times. " — " You are going to rule all the Indians.
When you grow up to be a man you are going to be the father to
them all. " He told him to go home. He did not know who that man
was. He came into his house. His grandmother and mother did not
know him. His mother saw him and ran inside and said, " Mother, a
man is coming. I don't know from where. " He came and went in,
and they did not know him. He said, " Mother and grandmother,
why do you act this way ; are you angry ? " His mother and grandmother said, " *Hewemboharihạ*' ! My child, we did not know you. Is
it you ? " — " Of course it is I. " Those people saw him and they did
not know who he was. He said, " *Harihạ*' ! Grandmother, my mother,
I am coming now ; but now I have a name. " His grandmother said,
" What kind of a name have you ? " He said, " My name is Posew'e'bi
poseyemu. " They said, " *Harihạ* ! my child, you have a nice name.
Nobody in this place has a name like yours. " So he went downstairs
and went out. They called every man into their house. They called
him, too. So he went. They did not treat him as they used to treat
him. They talked nicely to him. They began to talk. They said to
him, " You have to talk now. " Winter chief and Summer chief got
through their talk, those old ones, and they threw it to him to talk.
So he said, " Now I am going to say something. Nobody likes us
here. You treat us badly. You throw ashes and dust. You call us ' No-
name '. Because we are very poor you treat us as you please. Now I
am going to tell you something. All the men are here. Now you will
hear my name. My name is Posew'e'bi poseyemu. That is my name, "
he said to them. They just looked at each other, all those people. " He
looks so nice, so fine, like a chief, " they said. " *Harihạ* ! this boy has
a nice name, " thus said Winter chief and Summer chief. All the
people were their children. " I heard from their own mouth, not to
throw dust at us. But they did not believe, only some whose thoughts
were good. Those whose thoughts were bad always did that. You do
not know from whom you are getting along well. You do not think
anything good about who is working for the people to live well. "
They said to him, " You are talking the truth. We need what is
good. " They said, " Now we need to tell all in the town to sweep up
nicely. " They went to the house of the Crier (*tokạndi*) to tell him
to call out to all to sweep the town. So they swept. Some of the men
sweeping said, " Let us not sweep in front of Posew'e'bi poseyemu's
house. " Some of them said, " We have to sweep, because he is a good
man. " But some of them were angry with him and wanted to treat
him badly. Some said, " This boy wants to rule this place, this people.
If we sweep in front of his house, he will do what he pleases with us.
We don't know who his father is. " Some came and swept in front
of his house, others would not sweep and went away from there.
Some of those who swept went to the house of Summer chief and

Winter chief (they were together in one house) and said the others did not want to sweep, and what Summer chief and Winter chief ordered for them they did not believe in. So Winter chief and Summer chief and the Governor said, " Guess these people do not want to do what their Mother and the Governor tell them. They want to do what they please. This evening we might call them here and tell them to do what their Mother and Father tell. " So they called them and they counted how many there were who did not mind them. They began to talk. Summer chief said, " Whatever I order you, you should believe. Even Winter Mother's words you do not believe, even those Outside chiefs you do not believe. You have to say why you have acted that way. You have to say if you will mind your Mother and the Outside chiefs. " They said, " We did not mind your order to sweep for Posew'e'bi poseyemu. " They said, " Is it because Posew'e'bi poseyemu does not belong here that you treat him badly ? " So they asked them, " Why don't you want Posew'e'bi poseyemu to stay here? Did he treat you badly ? You have to say why you do not like him. Do you find something bad in him ? " And they did not find anything to say. They said, " We did not find anything bad in him. Just because we did not want to, that is why we did not sweep in front of his house. " Summer chief and Winter chief said, " Now the word belongs to you, " they said to Posew'e'bi poseyemu, " You have to talk. " He said, " Yes. Now I am going to talk to you boys here. I am going to talk about what is good, what is needed. I have no grandfather, no father, I just grew up; but I am going to talk. " He talked. He just talked hard words, good words. How they could move from that place, what they were to do, how they could live. He talked well, so nobody should hurt him. Those old men said, " *Harahi'* ! this boy talks well. Wonder who gave him so good a head, he talks so well. " The old men said, " What do you think about this boy ? This boy knows everything. " They said, " We must give all the things [1] to him. He has to be Mother and Father and rule us. " They said to him, " You rule us, all this place. " He said, " No, I do not want to. " But everybody wanted him. At that time there were only Indians, no White people, no Mexicans. So some Indians from a little distance went over to see that boy and hear him talk. So he told them what would come about the next year or in three years. At that time the Indians did not know about the Mexicans or White people and Posew'e'bi poseyemu said to them, " From the south they are going to come in, Mexicans. Next will come the White people from the north. " That is the way he talked, that man. He said, " Those Mexicans coming from the south are going to rule us. We are going to stand under the flag they are going to raise up. Next the White people

1. Presumably, the sacred things.

are going to take us and we are going to stay under their flag (*tso okuna*). " That is the way he used to talk. " And those people are going to come in. Clothes we have not seen here are going to be brought in and you are going to wear them. " At that time they wore only hides of deer, elk, and buffalo. He was talking so, and the people came and looked at him and listened to him. He said, " Wherever it runs water (i.e., springs), White people are going to live. " He said, " At Yungeowinge they are going to have a feast which I am going over to see. I am going to dress up just as I said the people coming would dress and then I am going to the feast. " He got two elk in a buggy to carry him, and he made shoes and trousers and a hat. At Yungeowinge they were dancing, lots of people, and they saw him, those Outside chiefs. So the Outside chiefs came and told the people, saying, " There, the men with shoes are coming. " So they hid their Oxuwah and they sat as if there was going to be nothing in that place. So he came into the middle of the place. He saw nothing. He said, " You have this kind of *oxuwahhi* [danced on the outside], but you do not want it. If you want to dance below [i.e., in kiva], that same way you are going to follow all your life. You have to keep on this way until I come back. [1] Now I am going to leave you who are living here. No more people will be born. Next time I come back I will find you just the same, no fewer, no more, when I come back. You are not going to grow like White people and like Mexicans. " That is why we do not increase. We are just the same as he left us a long time ago. Thus we stay. Only White people and Mexicans increase. We do not increase, because he said we would not. He said that some time he was going to come back, and when he comes back all the White people and the Mexicans will have to go away from here. I do not know when that time will be. That will be our rich time. That is the way I know the story. That Montezuma went south, and I do not know when he will come back. *Hu*[2]!.

34. THE WOMAN STEALER. [3]

Owewehǫdita, a long time ago they lived at Peraowinge, [4] Prayer-stick old man, Shrivelled corn old woman, Yellow corn girl, Olivella

1. The Arizona Tewa version of why, among them and at Zuñi, the Okuwa are hidden from the Mexicans is different. The early Spaniards asked where the Okuwa came from, and were told they came from a mountain spring. They said they did not believe it, and so, to see, they cut off the head of a kachina and found a human head. " Americans may see kachina because Americans wear masks too. "
2. The narrative closed, but comment continued. " Long time ago lots of people did not believe in him. People only got scared [when Montezuma predicted]. He told all about wagons and buggies and automobiles. But now we believe. "
3. Informant 3 of Santa Clara. See p. 217.
4. Across the river from San Ildefonso, a ruin. See Harrington, 263.

Flower boy. Yellow corn girl was the wife of Olivella Flower boy.
For some time that Tsihkue'nu (Arrow-point boy) had been taking
the wives of men to his house. Olivella Flower boy went hunting
every day, and every day brought back a deer. Yellow corn girl went
after water. They had a little baby. She left the baby with his grandmother and grandfather. When she went to the river for water, came
that Arrow-point boy. He said, " Yellow corn girl, don't you want
to go with me to my home ? " — " No, I can't go. I can't leave my
baby. " — " His grandmother will take care of the baby. I will take
you with me. " She did not want to go, but he took her. That time
the baby was crying. They were waiting for his mother to come. She
did not come. The baby was crying, and Olivella Flower boy came.
He brought a deer. They brought it in. When he came in, he asked
grandmother and grandfather where was Yellow corn girl. So grandmother and grandfather said to Olivella Flower boy, " She went
after water, she has not come back. Maybe Arrow-point boy took
her. " So Olivella Flower boy was sad. He went out and sat in the
sunshine. Then Olivella Flower boy told his mother to fix a lunch,
he was going after Yellow corn girl. So he went after Yellow corn girl.
He went far away. A *saiya* called him. So he went to her house. She
asked him, " Olivella Flower boy, where are you going ? " — " I am
going after Yellow corn girl. " She told Olivella Flower boy that
Arrow-point boy was very mean. " But if you are a man, you will
bring back your wife. " He said, " I am not a man, but I am going to
bring back my wife. " — " If you go, I will give you some root medicine. When you come there where Arrow-point boy is, chew the
root I have given you, and spit all around him. " She gave him a
pipe, too, and some tobacco. " When you come in his house, they
will give you a smoke. Give this pipe to him, and he will smoke, too.
He will fall down. You cut him open down the front, take out what
he has inside and put in good ones. You bring your wife before he
comes to life. So the other women may go home. " So Olivella Flower
boy left Grandmother (Awæwijo, Spider old woman). When he came
there where Arrow-point boy lived, he spit out the root grandmother
gave him. All those women that Arrow-point boy had taken were
grinding corn, all of them. His wife said to Olivella Flower boy,
" Why have you come? Arrow-point boy is an awful man. " He said,
" I have come after you. " She said, " If you are a man, you will take
me home. " So Arrow-point boy came from somewhere. He came
awful mad. Arrow-point boy said to Yellow corn girl, " Somebody
is here. " So Yellow corn girl said, " Nobody has come here. Who
do you think is here ? " Arrow-point boy said, " Somebody is
here. " Olivella Flower boy was hiding under the bed. Then
Arrow-point boy found him and got him out. He took Olivella
Flower boy to the kiva, he said to Olivella Flower boy, " Inside the

kiva we will talk with you. " So they went. They came into the kiva, they put out a seat (*puere*) for Olivella Flower boy, they talked together. They were smoking. Arrow-point boy put some tobacco in his pipe. Then he smoked. He said, " Don't throw out any smoke. Swallow it like me. " So Olivella Flower boy smoked Arrow-point boy's pipe. It did nothing to him. So he took his pipe and filled it with tobacco and gave it to Arrow-point boy and told Arrow-point boy to swallow the smoke like him. So he gave the pipe to Arrow-point boy. He smoked and he coughed. He smoked again, he coughed more. When he smoked again, he fell down. So Olivella Flower boy took out a knife and cut open his belly. He took out what he had inside — cactus points (*jo*) and points like cactus (*sæpa*). He put in some pink quartz and turquoise. Then Olivella Flower boy went out from the kiva. He got his wife, and all those women Arrow-point boy had taken went back to their homes. Olivella Flower boy took his wife. When Olivella Flower boy came close to where grandmother lived, Arrow-point boy got alive again, and came after Olivella Flower boy again. Olivella Flower boy and his wife went into the house of grandmother and she hid them. Arrow-point boy could not find them, he went back again. Olivella Flower boy brought his wife home. His mother and father cried. So he brought back his wife. That is all.

Variant (from Tesuque.)

Once were living at Kǫuchute Uroto seno and Uroto kwiyo and White corn girl. The boys would come to court the girl. Uroto seno had a large field of corn. He sent White corn girl to get some. Sefaenu (Cactus boy) saw the girl and came down from the mountain to get her. He said to her, " Come with me to my house. " She said, " No, my mother will scold me." — " It is not far. You will come back again. Come just to see my house. I will bring you back. " She went with him. He did not live nearby, but far away on the top of the mountain. In his house this boy had lots of girls whom he had brought from their homes, Blue corn girl, Yellow corn girl, Red corn girl, All Colors corn girl. When he got White corn girl into his house, he said to her, " Now you have to stay and work. " Her father went out to look for her in the corn field, but he did not find her. She had a husband, Olivella Flower, and he said, " I am going to look for my wife. Who will be a man, Cactus boy or I? " He said, " Mother, make me some bread. It is far. " Early in the morning he went to the spring on the mountain. White corn girl saw him coming. They went into Cactus boy's house where they were grinding corn. They told Cactus boy that Olivella Flower had come. " Tell him to come and talk to me, " said Cactus boy. Olivella Flower went to him. " What do you want?"

asked Cactus boy. "I have come for my wife," said Olivella Flower. "Let us play shinny (*punabe*)," said Cactus boy, "whoever wins will get the girl." Each boy had his own ball. First they played with Cactus boy's ball. Then they put down Olivella Flower's ball, and Olivella Flower won. "Now you have beaten me; you have to take the girl," said Cactus boy. Then Olivella Flower killed Cactus boy, and took away all the girls. As they came near where they lived, Olivella Flower said, "You know where you live. You have to go to your houses." All the girls went to their houses. But their mothers did not know them. Nor did the mother of White corn girl know her; it was so long since Cactus boy had taken her away. Cactus boy lived on Kųnyapin, Turquoise Mountain. and Olivella Flower went back to Turquoise Mountain and said to Cactus boy, "What shall I make of you?" — "Make of me a metate." — "No, for then the girls would be touching you. I will turn you into *tsekǫ kwiyo* and throw you to the east." That is the star that comes out now in the evening in the west.

35. ESCAPE UP THE TREES. [1]

There was an Apache girl and that Apache girl went after water every day. And every day in one place she would see a buffalo head (skull). And she said, "Maybe when this buffalo was alive he had good meat." Every day the buffalo head (*k'opo*) would talk to her. And the girl said, "Whoever killed you, maybe had a good time with your meat." Then the head talked to the girl, and became a good looking boy. The girl said to the boy, "I wish you were my sweetheart. Wherever you live, I will go with you," said the girl to the boy. This boy was *pinaṇ*, he had died and he had no heart. Then he took the girl, down to a lake which was dried up, to where the buffalo were, lots of them. They were glad to see their *sai'*. She wore a deerskin dress, with fringes. The buffalo took off the hoofs of their hind legs and fastened them to her deerskin dress, so when she moved it rattled. The buffalo had a round place and there in the middle of it they stayed.

Now the husband of Apache girl went after her and came to the lake, and he asked everywhere, but nobody let him know where she was. Then the boy went to the house of the chief (*toyo*) and said his wife was lost and asked that anybody who might have seen her should say so. Then everybody said, "We have not seen her anywhere." And Apache boy said, "What shall I do to find my wife?" And so he was searching everywhere. Then Vulture old man (*okąwe ⁺ sendo*)

---

1. Informant 1 of San Juan. See for bibliography, Parsons 1; compare also Taos, Parsons 2.
2. Cp. Henderson and Harrington, 36.

told him, " Buffalo Head took your wife, and she stays in the midst of the buffalo. " Vulture old man told him he had to make a bow and lots of arrows and a knife, and to sharpen it well. Then the Vultures said they would help him. In the middle of the day the buffaloes used to sleep. Vulture old man said to him, " I will wait for you here and take you over to where your wife is. " Then he got all his things together and went to where that Vulture was sitting and said, " Here I am come, friend. I am ready. " Vulture said, " I will carry you over to those buffalo, and if you kill the buffalo, all I want is their eyes. " Then Vulture spread his wings, and the boy got on top of him. And Vulture flew away, around and around, until he got down to those buffalo. The girl was in their midst, sleeping next to the buffalo chief. When his eyes were open he was asleep, and when his eyes were shut he was awake. [1] He slept with his leg over her dress, so if she moved he could hear. Then Vulture put Apache boy down, and Apache boy took his knife and cut her dress around and cut off the hoofs. Then he and the girl got on top of Vulture and he wheeled and wheeled and flew up. Vulture said to them, " Buffalo Head has no heart (since he had died) and he will chase us and not tire. " When Buffalo Head woke up he could not see his wife and he called her. Then all those Buffalo boys ran, with Buffalo Head in the lead. When he came near them he called her again. And Apache boy and Apache girl heard him and they ran fast, he was near them. They came to three big trees in a row, and they climbed up the biggest. As the buffalo came on they raised dust, like smoke. They were at the top of the tree and they saw Buffalo Head coming first and the others behind. They came close to the tree, rushing past. As they rushed past, at the rear came an old buffalo man. As he was passing by the three trees he said, " Oh how tired I am getting! He wont catch our *sai'i*, " said the old buffalo, and he rubbed himself against the tree. Then Apache girl said, " I want to urinate. " — " Do not urinate, " said Apache boy to his wife. " He will see us if you do. Wait a while. " She could not hold it. So she gathered up her dress and urinated into it, but drops fell down on the old buffalo. " *Harạhi'* ! it is raining, " said Old Buffalo. " The sky is clear. " And he looked up and saw them. " Here I have found them ! " called the old man. Then the rear ones heard, and called on to Buffalo Head. And they came back. " Just look at them coming, " said Apache boy and Apache girl. Then they came after them in lots of dust. And the old buffalo said, " Here they are ! " Then all of them butted at the tree. He took out his arrows and shot at them and he was killing them. When the tree was near falling, they jumped to the next tree, and he went on killing them. They butted at this tree. Just as it was falling, they jumped to the third tree. Now

1. This is a definitely European particular.

all the buffalo were killed, Buffalo Head only was left. Then Vulture told Apache boy where Buffalo Head had his heart. " When he turns around shoot him in the rectum, there he has his heart. " And he shot and Buffalo Head fell down. Now Apache girl began to cry, and her husband said to her, " I think you like him better than me. You weep for him. " Then they climbed down. They called the black-birds and the vultures, and told them to take what they wanted of the meat and eyes. So the birds came from every direction. Then Apache boy said to Apache girl, " You cared for him more than for me. " So he shot her and laid her on top of Buffalo Head. That is what happened to Apache boy.

36. THE TURKEY GIRL. [1]

At San Juan they lived, Shrivelled corn old woman, and Prayer-stick old man. They had a girl, Yellow corn girl, and another girl, Full-kernel corn girl (k'ǫke-anyǫ).

The elder was Yellow corn girl, the younger was Full kernel corn girl. When they went to the feast they took with them only Yellow corn girl. Full-kernel corn girl had lots of turkeys to take care of. She watched the turkeys all the time. They had a feast at Pe'sehre (west of San Juan). They went — Shrivelled corn old woman, Prayer-stick old man, Yellow corn girl. They left the younger one at home. She had no clothes, no moccasins, no beads to wear. So they went, before the feast in the evening. Full-kernel corn girl stayed home with the turkeys. The turkeys told her that if she wanted to go, she could go. She said, " I have no clothes to wear. " Pindi se (Turkey man) said, " I will get some clothes for you. " Turkey man shook his wing and there fell down a black shawl. Another turkey shook his wing and there fell down a belt, another turkey shook his wing and there fell down moccasins, another turkey shook his wing and there fell down a white blanket. This one shook his nose, and there fell down some beads. So everything was ready for her to wear — all her clothes. She got ready to go. She went. She came to Pe'sehre that morning before the dancers came out. She was standing in a corner. Her sister saw her and went to tell her mother. " Younger sister has come, too, she has got some clothes somewhere. " Elder sister scolded younger sister and her mother scolded her. She got mad. She saw just one dance, and went home, crying. The turkeys asked her why she came crying. She said because her mother and elder sister scolded her. " Now I am going somewhere they will keep me. I am going away, I will take you all, my children. " So they went, and came to where there was a

1. Informant 3 of Santa Clara.

lake. When she came to the lake, she called all her children, " From here go up to the mountains. Have your children in the mountains. I am going into the lake. I am going to live here. " So all her children flew away, to the north, to the west, to the south, to the east. So they flew away, all her children. "There in the mountains have your little ones, " she told them. She went into the lake. Then her mother and elder sister came and did not find her in the house. They did not know where Full-kernel corn girl had gone. That is all.

37. THE DEER TALKS TO HIM :
DUCK GIRLS ; DIVIDING THE HEIRLOOM. [1]

Owewehamba there was a boy, his name was Powitsire (flower bird). He was always killing deer. He had a little house of the big sticks they use. He killed deer and brought them to his door. He got the soft meat from the back ; the rest of the meat he threw to the wild animals (*tsiwinu*). Once he went hunting and the deer talked to him: " Flower bird, do not throw me away. " [2] And he said, " Flower bird, you always kill lots of deer and you eat only the meat of the back. You need a woman. Maybe when you find a woman, you will eat the rest of the meat. " — " Yes, where shall I find a girl ? " — " I will tell you where, " he said. " There are three Duck girls (*owįanyo*). They fly past here and go on into the water in the big lake. So two of them will come first, and then another last. That one will belong to you. They always come and bathe at *tawiriteipi'i* (12.30 p.m.). So you come and hide there, so the two wont see you. Do not let them see you. Hide, and don't do anything to them. Then this last one will come, and undress and go into this lake, and you take her clothes and hide them. " Then those two Duck girls came to the big lake, and took off their clothes and their skins, and they were nice girls. And Flower bird was just looking at them. They were laughing and running after each other. So they came out and dressed. Then came the last one. When she took off all her clothes she stood up a nice girl and jumped into the lake. And the other two flew away and left her there. Then Flower bird saw her in the water, and she went into the middle of the water. So Flower bird ran and took her clothes and hid them. Then the girl said, " Flower bird, why do you take my clothes ? Give me my clothes. Don't be mean to me. " Thus the girl spoke to him. " Flower bird, give me my clothes. Don't hide them. I belong to you now. You are my husband, " said the girl. " Are you surely going to be my wife ? " said Flower bird to the girl. " I want you to

<hr/>

1. Informant 1 of San Juan. Heard from his grandfather of Nambé.
2. At San Juan deer and rabbit bones are deposited in some shrine with meal, " so more deer and rabbits will come. "

be my wife, " Flower bird said to her. " Yes. Surely I am going to be your wife. " So she came out of the water and took her clothes. Then they went to the house of Flower bird and they came there. And that girl said to Flower bird, " I will tell you my name, Powitse'i (flower white). " Then the girl said to Flower bird, " Treat me like your daughter. " So Flower bird said yes. So that night they stayed in his house. They got in bed. White flower had *pinang*, so she made him sleep. So when Flower bird went to sleep, she got up and plastered the house. Lots of men and woman came to bring wood and to plaster. When Flower bird woke up, he woke up in a nice house, with lots of wood and lots of work done. " Don't think of it too much [Don't worry about it], " said the girl, " I did it. You are in your own house, don't get ashamed, " said the girl. " This is not my house, of sticks. " — " Yes, this is your house, " said the girl. So they had a good time there. One night they were in bed. He said to her, " Move closer. " — " I am your daughter, " she said. Then he made a big mistake ("lots of mistakes.") The next morning when he woke up, he woke up in his same old house. So he was sorry. He said, " What did I do ? I made a mistake, [1] because I had said to my wife she would be my daughter. And now I am in my old house. *Hubaharahia* ! I wonder where White flower went ? I wonder if I can find her? I am going to look for her. I am not coming back without her. "

So Flower bird went out to where the sun came up. He went after White flower. He went into another town, he saw three men. These three boys were angry. They had a pair of shoes and a head *banda*, and a walking-stick. Each of them wanted that stick. He came there and he said, " What are you doing ? " They said, " We are quarreling over a pair of shoes and a *banda* and a stick. Our father died and he left them to us. " They said, " Now you have come here. You must leave us satisfied and then go on. " So Flower bird said to them, " Why are you quarreling over a pair of shoes, a *banda* and a stick ? They do not cost so much. Why do you think they are so valuable ? " So they said, " We will tell you the truth. This pair of shoes, wherever they want to walk, go anywhere, don't get tired. Tie the *banda* round your head and you can't be seen, you are invisible. As for this stick, if somebody dies, and is put under ground, if you hit the ground with the stick, the ground will open ; hit again, it will open wider, the dead will live again, sit up; another hit, the dead will stand up living again. " Flower bird said, " I wish I had the shoes. " Flower bird said, " I will satisfy you, about the quarrel. You must go way up there in the court and I will stay here with the *banda* and shoes and stick. " So they went way up, and from there they started to run a race, first to come was to have the stick, next to come, the *banda,* and last, the shoes. Flower

---

1. For continence as a test, see Parsons 3 : 253.

bird said, "When I raise my hand, you start to run." They were coming running and Flower bird put the *banda* on his head, and he put on the shoes and he took the stick in his hand. When they came up, they did not see him. So they said, "You are the one who wanted that man to settle for us!" — "You are the one!" — "You are the one!" And as they quarreled Flower bird went away with all their things. He was walking far, far away. He saw a little hill and there were two little babies crying on that hill. They were wind babies (*wæ enyæ*). Their hair was all ruffled up. "Oh you are crying," he said to them, "Why are you crying, babies?" — "We are crying because our father died." — "Who is your father?" — "Wind old man (*wæ sendo*)." — "And who is your mother?" — "Wind old woman (*wæ kwiyo*)." — "Where is your mother?" — "She is away, making wind. She has not come, that's why we cry." He saw a dust far off. "Our mother is coming," they said. Then she came. Wind old woman said to him, "Flower bird, where are you going?" — "I go hunting for my wife. My wife is White flower. Where can I find her?" So Wind old woman said, "White flower is very far from here. I am Wind and go far, but White flower is still farther." Then she said, "I do not go where White flower lives, but maybe our father went there. They call that place Siraape' (*sira*, big mountains, Sp. *serra. Ape'*, up). But our father died." Flower bird said, "Do you think he knows about it?" — "We think our father knew that place. He walked everywhere." So he said, "If you think your father knows the place where my wife stays, I will make him live again." — "Yes." — "All right." — "Our father was always mad. Sometimes he went very far away." — "Only show me where he is," Flower bird said to them. So they took him where he was. "Right here in the earth." So he took the stick and struck once and the ground opened. He hit again, the ground opened wider. He hit again, he [Wind] sat up. He hit again, this was four times. He was alive and stood up and began to turn around and around. His wife said, "Don't be angry. Flower bird made you live. Don't be angry. Flower bird is going after White flower." So the Wind stopped. Then he said, "I made you live, Wind old man. I have come here because your wife told me you knew where my wife lives." — "*Hubaharabia*! Are you going after White flower? It is very far from here," he said. "Maybe I came close, but I did not go into the town. That is what I recall." Then he put Flower bird in a round basket and covered it up. "Get ready," said Wind old man, "I will take you up." So Wind old man carried Flower bird up. Then they arrived at *teipi'i* (3.30 p.m.). They did not go into the town. Wind old man stopped at a distance away from here to our house [in San Juan, from two to three miles away]. "Maybe she is in that place," said Wind old man. "You stay here. I will blow a little, and go over to see if she is here." They were washing clothes, some of them, and the clothes were hanging up, and Wind old man came and blew, and the clothes flew up. So they said, " Did you ever know of the wind coming here to Siraape'? We never heard of it, wonder what is going to happen. " So Wind old man blew again. So he said to Flower bird, " Here is the place. They were washing clothes and I blew and the clothes flew around, and they said, ' The wind is blowing, we never heard of the wind blowing here'. Here is the place. " So Wind took him up and set him down close to Siraape'. " Now you go into the town. When you get your wife, come here. I will wait for you here and take you up. " So he put the *banda* on his head, and the people passed him by and did not see him. There were lots of houses, so he said, " I wonder where she lives, my wife. I will find her. " He went into the first court and went into one house and did not find her, and went into another house and did not find her, and went into another row of houses and went in, and in the fifth house he found her in the middle of the house. His wife was making bread. He sat near her. She did not see him. She had a pile of bread (*kapwenu*). Flower bird took some off the pile and ate it. And she did not see him and she said, " I wonder why I can't get through with my bread ? I have been making it for a long time. " Then Flower bird finished eating and got up and went to another place. So White flower's brother and two sisters came in. So Flower bird went out and took off the *banda* and knocked at the door and said, " Father and Mother, how are you getting along ? " White flower saw him. " *Hubaharahia*! Where do you come from? " And she held him *tight*. " Now you may treat me as sweetheart and wife, now you may have me. " Then her mother and father and sister were wondering. White flower said, " This is my husband. " Then White flower's mother got up from where she was making bread and said, " You are my son. " They said, " The father of White flower died four days ago, now we are getting bread ready, so tonight we are going to have lots of people. This is the last time we are going to give him food. [1] So he wont come back again, even when we sleep, and we wont dream of him. " So White flower got food ready for Flower bird. He was full and did not eat much. " Why don't you eat, Flower bird ? Are you ashamed ? You ought to be glad because you see me. Eat ! " — " But I am full, " said Flower bird. The mother said, " Don't be ashamed, Flower bird. You are in a new house, eat well. " But he was full. White flower said, " Maybe you are ashamed because I do not eat with you. " She began to eat with him. He was full, but he tried to eat. Then came the people into the house and everybody shook hands with him and were glad to know their new *soyingi*. So they passed the night. In four days and nights they said to

---

1. People take out a bowl of food, any kind of cooked food, for the deceased.

the dead, " You are not of this place. You are a kind of wind. You
have no heart. " Then everybody said to him, " You are not of here.
You died, you have no heart. I never heard of you moving again. You
belong to Oxuwah and to Kaye, to the blue, the yellow, the red, the
white, the dark, the spotted. There you belong, do not think of us." So
Flower bird said to them, " I will make him live, my father, if you wish. "
They thought a lot about it. " Show me where he is, I will make
him live again. " So the next day, they went with all their relatives.
" Stand right here. " They were all standing away. Flower bird
took his stick, he hit the ground with it. The ground opened. He hit
again, the ground opened wider. He hit again. The dead sat up. Again,
four times, he was alive again. So they rejoiced. Then the relatives
said, " We want our people to live again. " So they carried Flower bird
to where their people were in the ground. " Here's my father! Here's
my aunt ! There's my sister ! " And he made them live. Then the
day following they wanted to go home. They left, they came to Wind
old man and went into the basket, both of them. He blew it up, he
took them to Wind old woman, and from there he blew them to their
house. And that is what happened to Flower bird. Hu' !

38. SEVEN HEADS. [1]

Shiete Cabeza, Seven Heads, was eating all the girls. A man was
going along. It was very hot, he lay down. Above him the doves
(tortolla) were singing, " If this man could trap and catch me and take
out my heart, and give it to that animal, he could kill that animal,
and Rei's daughter he could marry. " This the man did. He killed
Seven Heads and took out his tongues. [2] He showed the tongues to
Rei, and married the girl.

39. Variant, SEVEN HEADS : TEST OF SHIRT-MAKING. [3]

An Apache chief (sabe toyo) used to stay to the eastward. He had
two big girls. They used to stay up where now they go for wood.
There was a popowendi (yellow fox with white on the tip of its tail
like a flower). The Apache chief said, " Whoever catches that popowendi with a tail white like a flower shall marry my daughter. " No
boys could catch it. An Apache boy was living with his grandmother.
The people did not like them, they treated them badly. They threw

1. Informant 3 of Santa Clara. He did not remember this story well, he said.
Cp. Powhati, Parsons and Boas, 52-3 ; Zuñi, Parsons, 3, 240-2.
2. The incident of the false claimants and of producing the tongues as evidence is
entirely forgotten.
3. Informant 1 of San Juan. For the suitor tests, and producing the game animals
after famine, see, Taos, Parsons 2.

dust and ashes before their house. This Apache boy said, "I better
go to my grandmother's way up there on the river and hunt some
ducks so we can make arrows." His grandmother had *pinang*. She
made some nice arrows. "Now you get ready," she said, "that *popowendi* will come again." Those other boys took his bow and arrows
and spat on them and threw them away. One man said, "Don't do
that! He is a man, too." Then they circled out (as they do in the
rabbit hunt) to shoot the *popowendi*. The boy shot and killed it. But
the other boys took the *popowendi* away from him. The boy said,
"I killed it, but the other boys were stronger and took it away."
The other boys took the *popowendi* to the Apache chief and threw it
down, and said, "This is what you want." That *popowendi* did not
have a good coat of hair. "This is not the one," said Apache chief.
Apache boy said to his grandmother, "I killed it, but the others took
it away from me." — "When they were pulling it from you, did
hair fall off?" — "Yes." — "Go get that hair." The boy brought it.
She laid down a deer skin and on it put the hairs. She covered them
with another deer skin. She took off the cover, a *popowendi* with a
flower on its tail was lying there. The boy took it to the Apache
chief. "Here is what you want." — "This is a nice one. This is
what I need. There lacks something yet, a *powotse*, on that same big
tree. When you bring it, you may marry my daughter." The boys
went, also the little boy. The other boys took his arrows and spat on
them and threw them away. "Don't do that!" said the man. "Let
him shoot." He shot, close to where he sat at first. He shot four
times. On the fourth shot he killed the *powotse* which fell down, and
rolled over and over. The boy jumped up and said, "I have killed
it!" Another boy took out the arrow in the *powotse* and stuck in his
own. He took the *powotse* to the Apache chief. "Here I bring you
what you want." He threw it inside. "This is not the one, take it
home, the feathers are not good." The little boy took the feather
that had fallen out and went with it to his grandmother's house. She
put it down on the deer skin and covered it over with another skin.
She took off the cover and there was that *powotse* with nice feathers.
He took it to the Apache chief. "This is the one I need. Come on,
girls," he said. "Here is your husband." The younger said, "I don't
want him." The elder said "I have to do what my father says. Besides
he is chief." The chief said, "My words cost much. You have to
mind." He gave the girls to the boy. The younger did not want to
go, she went along mad. The Apache boys were just looking at him,
going with the two girls. They went to his house, he put down a
buffalo skin as bed. The girls had dresses made up nicely from a big
deer skin. That night they slept. In the middle of the night the boy
urinated (much laughter) and the younger (girl) grew still more angry
and next day went home and left the elder behind. (He had urinated

for fun to see if they liked him.) He said, " Now the Apache people
will see who their mother is. They treat us badly. I am going to shut
up the buffalo, deer, and all the birds. " The Apache got hungry,
they had nothing to eat, they cooked cow hide and ate it. The Apache
girl and boy had a good time. The girl went to her father's house.
" *Hewemboharạhiʻ* ! child, how well you look. Look at us, thin and
poor. " — " *Hewemboharạhiʻ* ! my father, we do not have good times.
Don't you see how the people do not like us? How they throw dust
and ashes? We do not have good times. " — " But you eat well. "

They got very hungry. The boy and his grandmother made *pinan*
(worked magic). They said to the girl, " You must get a piece of meat
and go to your father's house and sleep there. " (That night they
were going to have *pinan.*) She went, she said, " Here I bring a piece
of meat. See that you have a good time. " The younger sister ate too.
Her elder sister said, " Don't eat ! You did not want to marry him. "
Their father said also, " Don't eat ! You did not mind. " She tried to
get a piece. They gave her only a little (laughter). The next night
the girl came with a larger piece. Four days and nights they worked
pinan. Then the boy went into the father's house and told him to call
all the Apaches to get ready. " Early in the morning I am going to
come with turkeys, chichen', deer and buffalo. " So they called them.
They could not find strings for their bows. Early in the morning
they heard those buffalo. U-----u ! They did not sleep that night.
That night the girl went to her father's house to sleep, and his grandmother fixed the boy up nice. In the morning it was misty, they
could see nothing. The boy was covered with a buffalo hide, the hair
inside ; he had a little stick in his hand, and a rattle with the nails of
buffalo tied to the stick ; he had feathers in his hair. He came first,
then followed buffalo, elk, deer, *odụ,* white-tailed deer, goats, and
turkeys. The mist was lifting, the Apache could see. " Here I bring
these. You may kill them and have them, all but one buffalo without
hair ; do not kill him ; that is for me. " After they killed them, they
began to eat, without cooking, they were so hungry. The girl went,
and she could not find her house. " Some place here we live. I can
not find it. " Grandmother said, " Come on, daughter, here is the
place we live. " Her husband was lying down in his house. She was
ashamed before her husband, he looked so nice ; she looked sidewise.
That is why Apache look sidewise. The younger sister, she just stood
there ; they did not want her. Her father said (to the elder sister),
" You have to go your husband. " So she stood around, and stood
around, then she went. Her husband gave her twelve deer skins.
" You have to make twelve shirts from breakfast to dinner time. If
you make them, you will belong to me ; if you do not make them,
you will not belong to me. " So she called in all her relatives, and
they made them, trousers, shirts. She belonged to him. That is the
way it passed.

40. THE KING'S SON BECOMES A DEER; MAGIC MIRROR; THE GRATEFUL
SPIRIT; WHISTLING BACK THE RABBITS; RAT DETECTIVES. [1]

They were hunting deer at Taos (Tawi), Rei and his boy. They
carried water with them hunting. This time Rei's boy did not take
any water when he went hunting. There was a spring in the mountains where the deer drank. This boy left his friend, he was going on
one side and his friend on the other side. Rei's boy was very parched.
He asked for some water of the man with him. He told him about
the spring there. The boy drank some water, and became a deer.
After a while when they stopped to eat, his friend asked the hunter
where his friend was gone. " He was dry, he asked for some water,
I showed him the spring. He drank and became a deer. " In the evening they returned to Taos. Rei went over to his friend's house to
ask where he left his son. He said, " I did not see him anywhere. "
Rei was angry, he thought that people had killed him in the mountains. He said to the friend, " If you don't bring my boy, I will kill
all the people of Taos. " This boy had a grandmother, she was *pinandi*,
she made *pinan* to catch that deer. On the fourth day the boy went to
catch his friend. Grandmother gave a piece of *posu* (river reed [2]) to the
boy. He had lots of arrows, too, and a bow. He went early in the
morning to the spring. (Grandmother told him that his friend would
come along early in the morning. " You dig a hole and wait for him.
When he comes, shoot him. ") He went to the spring, he dug a hole,
he waited for his friend to come. After a little while, he was coming,
he would stop and look around, he came a little way, and he stopped
and looked around, he came again a little way, he stopped and looked
around, he came again a little way, he stopped and looked around.
He saw nothing, he came up to drink. While he was drinking, the
boy shot him. He fell down, then got up and ran away. (Grandmother
had put water in the reed.) When he overtook him, he gave him water
from the reed to become a man again. He took off the hide, [3] he
became a man again. He went to Taos. He put him in a place where
they never made a fire, where there was no smell of smoke. He stayed
four days. Then the boy who became a deer said to his friend, " Go
to my father's house and say, ' I found my friend. ' He will say, ' If
you bring my boy, I will pay you all the money you want. ' Take no
money, ask for a little looking-glass hanging by the door. That will
give you everything you want. It is *pinan*. " So he went and said,
" I found my friend. " Rei said, " If you bring my boy I will pay you

1. Informant 3 of Santa Clara. Heard in Tesuque, where he visits his wife's family
for a month or so at a time. They tell many stories.
2. See Robbins, Harrington, Freire-Marreco, 66.
3. Here a listener might say, " I wish I had that hide ! "

all the money you want. " He said, " I don't want money, give me
something I want and I will bring your son. " So the boy went back
to get his friend, and brought him to Rei's house. When he brought
him, Rei asked what he wanted. "I don't want anything but that
looking-glass by the door. " — " Why do you want that ? If I give
you money, you can buy anything you want. " — " I want that
looking-glass. I am young yet. I could carry it in my pocket, to see
how I look. " Rei did not want to give it, but he gave it. Rei's boy
told his friend, " You can ask that looking-glass for anything you
want. " The boy went away to work. He found a man dead on the
road, having lain there three or four days. He picked him up and took
him into a Mexican's house. He asked the Mexican where the priest
lived. That night they watched and took care of the dead man. Next
morning they took the dead man to the church. The priest was along,
the Indian boy paid for the mass. They buried him there. After that
he went to another place, looking for work. There lived another rei.
Men were working for him. The boy went to the house of an old
woman. He asked, " Grandmother, do you know anybody who wants
a man to work ? " — " Yes. Rei needs lots of men to work. " He
went over to Rei's house. Rei asked grandmother, " What kind of
work can he do ? " — " Any kind of work — feeding chickens, cows,
burros. Whatever you say. " Rei said to take the boy to his house.
Rei gave him work. He was a very good worker. The other men got
jealous, got mad. They told Rei, to make trouble, that he was the
very best rider, and he could break horses and mules. He said nothing.
Rei told him to break a wild horse. He went to the barn, he got a
rope, he caught the wildest horse there, he put on the saddle, and
rode him. He went away at midday, when he got back the horse was
tired, sweating all over, and tamed. That night other workmen told
Rei to take some jack-rabbits out in the hill, so he could herd them.
If he lost any one to kill him. So Rei told him to take out some jack-
rabbits. The man went and caught jack-rabbits, twelve of them. The
man took the boy and rabbits out to the hills. He turned the jack-
rabbits loose. Another man went out to test the boy herding them, to
ask him to sell one. He said, " No, they are not mine. " He asked
again and again. So he sold him one, for a bag of money. The man
took the rabbit in the buggy. The boy had a whistle. He blew; the
jack-rabbit jumped out of the buggy, and went back again to the boy.
That evening he brought back all the rabbits and put them in the
corral for Rei. Rei went over to count them and found them all there.
Next day [another task, but this was forgotten]. So Rei took good care
of him, because he was a very good worker. He gave him one of his
daughters to marry. So they were married. They were living in one
house. Another man was a former sweetheart of his wife. His wife
asked him how was he able to do everything Rei told him, did he have

some *pinan* of his own ? The boy did not think that his wife would do anything against him, so he showed that looking-glass to his wife. She said, " Why don't you let me keep that looking-glass in my trunk. " — " No. I got it from my friend. I will give it to nobody. " The wife told her friend about the looking-glass. She said that he better go to the store and buy one just like it. He went to the store and bought one. She asked her husband to let her have the glass for a little while. Then they changed the glasses. That night they went to sleep. When her husband slept, her sweetheart came and knocked at the door. She said, " I am ready, whenever you are ready, I will go with you. " They asked the looking-glass to take them somewhere and to leave the husband out in a desert place in the hills. So they went. Next day he was by himself when he awoke. Rei came there, to ask where was his daughter. Rei said, " If you don't bring my daughter in four days, I will hang you. " That night a cat came around where he was. The cat asked, " What is the trouble you have had ? " — " I was married to one of Rei's daughters. My wife asked me for my looking-glass, she changed it and went away with another man. " — " All right, I will get your glass and your wife. " (The cat was the dead man lying in the road. He had come down to help him.) Cat went where there were lots of rats (*wį*). Cat told the rats to all come out. So they came out. He told them, " A man has lost his looking-glass. If anybody finds it, he will be chief (*tunjo*). " First the four oldest rats went out to look. Cat had told them where the looking-glass was. The next night three or four more went. The next night more went. The fourth night when his wife and her sweetheart were having a big dance and feast, four little rats went and got into the place where the trunk was. From underneath, in the floor, they made a hole, then they made a hole in the trunk and got the glass and carried it to the cat. Cat took it to the man. He asked the looking-glass to bring his wife. Next morning his wife was there again, and her sweetheart was left far away where nobody lived. Next morning Rei came to see them again. They were both there. They all had breakfast together, Rei and his girl and his son-in-law. In four days they wanted to go to the man's house, to see all his family. Rei told them to get his buggy and train of horses, and Rei told his soldiers to go with him to guard him on the road. So he came to Taos, with his wife. And he saw his friend again, Rei's son. That is all I remember.

41. WHITE PIGEON (PALOMA BLANCA). [1]

At Tetsuge (Tesuque) lived a man. He played shinny (*po'nabe*) everywhere and he never lost, he won all the time. One time the

---

1. Informant 3 of Santa Clara. Heard at Tesuque.

devil (*penisen*, dead horn, or *penisendi*, dead with horns) knew about it and came and told him to play with him. So they played. Dead-with-horns said to the man, " We are going to play and you bet your life (*woatsi*) [1] and I bet my daughter. " So they played and the man beat, and Dead-with-horns lost. So they went to the house of Dead-with-horns. Then they came where he lived. He said, " You beat me. Now you will marry my daughter. But it is not all yet. " First they told him to cut some brush. So he went out, that night, and sat down. He told the man to get an ax that could not cut anything. So he got the ax that could not cut anything. So he told him where to cut the brush. He could do nothing with the ax. The girl came, she took the ax from the man. The man went to bed, and she cut all the brush, leaving just one or two pieces. She said, " When my father comes, you will be cutting these two pieces. When he comes, you say, ' I am through, just these two to cut. ' When you are through, there will be something else for you to do. " He was through. Next morning he told him to put a bridge over the river. So she came back, that girl. All the things he had, hammer, saw, he could do nothing with them. He told him where to put the bridge. He was working on the bridge, but could do nothing. So she came back, the girl, and told him again to lie down. Then she was working at the bridge. She left one pole for him to work. So Dead-with-horns came to see the bridge. That man was working on the pole, everything else was finished. So he was through with the bridge. The girl told him, " We are going tonight. " That night they went to bed, all of them. She told the man to go and find the horses. " You take out the poorest horse you find in the barn, and an old saddle, so father will not catch us anywhere. " Then that man went into the barn. When he came into the barn, he said, " That poor horse can't take us, he will get tired too quickly. " So he took out a fat horse, and picked up a new saddle. So he brought the horse to where the girl was. The girl picked up three pease (*tutsǫbe*) and put them on top of the table. She told the three little pease, " When mother calls you, say yes. " So the girl went with the man. Dead-with-horns had three girls named Paloma Blanca, Flora, and Maria. She told the man, " I told you to bring the poor horse, but you did not bring it. My father will come after us and catch us. " They went, they were gone a long way. Then the mother called the girl, " Paloma Blanca ! " and one of the pease said yes. They called the other girl, " Flora ! " they called, " Maria ! " All the pease said yes. In a little while they called again. The pease said yes. At daylight they called again, and all said yes. The oldest said yes softly. At daylight they called again and Paloma Blanca did not say yes, only the other two. The old woman called to the old man, she said, " Paloma Blanca

1. *woa*, medicine ; *tsii*, somebody walking or travelling.

9

has gone away. " He got up to get the old, poor horse. He went after
Paloma Blanca. When they were gone a long way Paloma Blanca
heard her father coming after them. She told the man, "Now I am
going to make you an old man and I will be the land and this horse
I will make into a watermelon. When my father comes, he will ask
you, ' Did Paloma Blanca pass by ? ' You tell him, ' I sell the melon
for a quarter. ' If he ask again, say, ' I sell the melon for a quarter. '
Every time answer the same way. He will get tired and turn back. "
Then Dead-with-horns came and asked him, " Did Paloma Blanca
pass here ? " — " I sell the melons for a quarter. " So he got tired.
He said, " I can't ask you any more, I am tired. " So he turned back.
Then Paloma Blanca and the man went on and Dead-with-horns came
home. The old woman asked him, " Did you find them ? " — " At
one place I found an old man and asked him, ' Did Paloma Blanca
pass by ? ' and every time I asked him he said, ' I sell melons for a
quarter. ' So I turned back. " She told the old man, " That old man
was the one who took Paloma Blanca. You go back. " He went back.
He overtook them. Paloma Blanca heard her father coming. She told
the man, " My father is coming again. I am going to made you an old
man, this horse, a burro, and myself, an apple box. When my father
comes, you tell him, ' I sell one apple for a nickel, ' and he will turn
back. " So Dead-with-horns came. He asked the old man, " Did a
man and woman pass by ? " He said, " I sell apples for five cents. "
Every time he asked, " Did a man and woman pass by ? " he said, " I
sell apples for five cents. " So the old man went back. When Dead-
with-horns came home, the old woman asked him, " Did you catch
him ? " — " I met a man a long way off. He was selling apples. Every
time I asked him, ' Did a man and a woman pass by ? ' he said, ' I sell
apples for five cents. ' That's all he told me. " — " They were those
you went after ! " She told him again to go back. So he went, and
caught up with them again. Paloma Blanca told the man, " Father is
coming again. Now I will become a church, the horses, the bells, and
you be the man to ring the bells. When my father comes, and asks
you, you say, ' Everybody is coming to mass. This is the last bell. '
Every time you say that, so he will turn back. " He came, he asked,
" Did a man and woman pass by ? " — " Everybody is coming to mass.
This is the last bell. " He went home. The old lady said, " Tomorrow
I am going myself. " She put some wheat in a sack. She went with the
sack. They were far away. She told the man, " My mother is coming
after us. When she comes, she will give you some wheat, but don't
eat it. " Then the horses became a lake, and Paloma Blanca and the
man became ducks and swam on the lake. Dead-with-horns woman
came and threw the wheat into the lake. The girl told the man,
" Don't eat the wheat that mother throws us. " So the man did not
eat it. Then Dead-with-horns woman threw in all the wheat. Then

she said to Paloma Blanca, " So you are going with him, but you are not going to get to where he lives, he will leave you somewhere. " Then she went back. Then Paloma Blanca and the man went on to where the man lived. " What did I tell you ? Had you chosen the poor horse they would never have overtaken us. " So they went. They almost reached the place where the man lived. He said, " I can't take you on horseback. I will go and get a buggy. " Paloma Blanca said, " You go now. Tell your elder brothers and sisters and your younger brothers and sisters and your mother and your father not to touch you. ". . . . So the man was tired and went to sleep. Then in came his aunt (*ki'i*). She said to the man, " *Sægipoa,* " and shook hands with him. He had told his father he came for a buggy. So when his aunt shook hands he forgot everything. He left Paloma Blanca in that place and did not go back for her. Then his father said to him, " You came after a buggy. Aren't you going ? " He said no. He had forgotten. So Paloma Blanca made a house. After that two boys became friends with the man. Then after a time Paloma Blanca made a dance. The man and his two friends went to the dance. They danced that night. They saw Paloma Blanca. They wanted to marry Paloma Blanca. Next night one friend said to the man, " We want to see her. " So the boy came and asked her if she would marry him. She said yes. At bedtime they took off their clothes. She said, " When I go to bed, I shut the window. " The man said, " I will shut the window. " All that night he kept on shutting the window, till daylight. Next morning he met his friend again. He asked him how he had passed the night. He said, " All right. " The other boy said, " I am going tonight. " So that night the other boy went to see her. The other boy asked if she would marry him. She said yes. That night, at bedtime, she said, " When I go to bed, I throw out the water. " The man said, " I will throw it out. " That man was throwing out the water all night. Next morning he went home. That evening he met his two friends who asked him how he passed the night. He said, " All right. " Next night the husband of Paloma Blanca went. (He had forgotten she was his wife.) He went to see her and asked if she would marry him. She said yes. At bedtime they took off their clothes. She said, " When I go to bed, I play the drum first. " So that night he was playing all night, till daylight. So Paloma Blanca made another dance. She made a nigger boy. (*Pendi e'nu,* black boy). She brought a whip of green willows. She got ready for the dance. First to dance was that nigger boy. Paloma Blanca asked that nigger boy, " Don't you remember when my father asked you to cut brush and I did it for you ? " and she whipped the little nigger. " Don't you remember when my father told you to build a bridge and I built it for you ? When we left I told you to take out the poor horse, but you took the good one, don't you remember ? " Then she whipped the little nigger. " Don't you remember that time our father came after us, I told you I would make you an old man, and myself, the ground, and the horse, a watermelon ? " Then she whipped the nigger boy. She asked him again, " Don't you remember, Father came after us again and I became an apple box and you an old man, and the horse, a burro ? " And she beat the little boy. " Don't you remember our father was coming after us and I became a church, and you an old man standing up, and the horses, bells ? " And she beat Black boy. She asked him again, " Don't you remember when Mother came, I made the horses into a lake and we turned to ducks and Mother gave us some wheat and I told you not eat it ? " And she beat Black boy. " Don't you remember, Mother said, ' Paloma Blanca you are going with that man, but he is not going to take you into his house, he will leave you somewhere ? ' You remember when we went on and came near your house. You said, ' I can't take you on my horse. I am going after a buggy.' " She beat Black boy and that time it hurt more. (Whenever she beat Black boy her husband (*seh*, man), felt it.) So that man went to where Paloma Blanca was and said to her, " *Sængiæ*, my wife. " And then they married again and they made a feast — one whole day for the rich people, and next day they had a feast for the poor people. They had a good time, all the people. So he took his wife (*kwi*) home. That time, he brought his wife home to where his father and mother lived. That is all. From that game of *po'nabe* he got his wife.

42. THE THREE BEARS. [1]

One woman and one man were living, they had three boys. The man would go and get wood and sell the wood in town. The three boys wanted to go where their father was getting wood, but their mother would not let them go. One boy was little, another a little bigger, another still bigger. They started to where their father was getting wood. The smallest boy got tired. The other boys said, " Younger brother, you stay here. We will go where father is getting wood, and we will come back here quickly. " So the two boys went on to where their father was getting wood. He asked them if they had come by themselves. They said yes, they did not tell him that they had left their younger brother way back. When they did not come back their younger brother looked for a place to hide. Bear Woman lived there and two little bears. They had gone out to look for berries. They had lots of berries, their bowls were full. The little boy went in to their house, he found nobody. Their table was laid with their bowls of berries. The little boy ate from one bowl and then from another. Then he lay down in the bed of one of the little bears. At dinner time the bears came back. The little boy was asleep. The bears went

1. Informant 1 of San Juan, who stated that it was a Mexican story.

up to the table. One said, "Who was eating in my bowl?" Another said, "Who was eating in my bowl? Just look at it!" They said, "Who came in here?" One little bear said, "Somebody is lying in my bed." They saw the little boy lying down. They woke him up. He sat up, he got scared and started to scratch his head. Bear Woman said to him, "Don't be scared. Who brought you here?" He said, "I was looking for my father and I came here." — "So!" said she. "Now you must stay and live with us." Meanwhile his mother was crying because her little boy was lost, and she scolded the other boys..... Bear Woman asked the little boy to eat. "Eat!" she said. He did not want to eat. Bear Woman talked nicely to him so he would not be afraid. She said to the two little bears, "This is your younger brother. That night he stayed there, that little boy. The next day Bear Woman went out to get some more berries. She said to the little bears, "You must stay here with your younger brother. Don't make him cry." So she left them. The little boy and the little bears played out-doors. While they were playing the little boy hid from the little bears, then he ran off to look for his house. In his house his father and mother were crying. The little boy could not find his house and he began to cry. A man heard him crying and went up to him and took him home. His mother was crying because they could not find him. They asked him where he had slept. He said, "I went to the house of Bear Woman. They treated me well, and I slept there." His mother was frightened. "When I came there, nobody was there. The table was set and I ate from the bowls. I lay down to sleep. The bears came in and woke me up. Bear Woman asked me to eat, she told the little bears I was their younger brother. Next day she went hunting berries and left me with my bear brothers. I was frightened and ran away from them." His mother was glad that Bear Woman had treated him well. So she said to her husband, "Whenever you see a bear, do not kill it because Bear Woman was good to our child." That is the way it happened to the little boy, (*Hawage*, thus; *ubo*, it happened or passed; *ienoke, i?* little boy.)

43. THE CLEVER HELPERS. [1]

At Tsuira [2] they lived. Crow put some eggs in a nest and went away. And another crow came around and she saw the eggs. So she hatched the eggs. The layer came, and fought for the baby crows. A *rei* (Spanish, king) lived there. They told him about the cotton wood tree where the baby crows were and how they were fighting for the babies. The layer wanted the eggs because she laid them. The other

1. Informant 3 of Santa Clara. Heard from a San Juan man in Colorado.
2. Mexican place-name.

wanted the eggs because she hatched them. They told that king about
it and asked him which had the right. They came every day, but the
king did not know why they had come. Rei asked everybody why they
came. He told them what day to come. All the people came. Rei had
some daughters. If anybody could guess why the birds came every day
he could marry his daughters. All the boys were guessing, but none could
find out. Three men met in the road *Eleposo* (with sores [of leprosy] all
over his body.) Everybody was afraid of him. The three men met him
and said, "Elepo, do you want to marry the king's daughter?" — "Poor
me! they don't want me. Everybody is afraid of me, I can't marry."
The three men said, "No. You marry her. You have some trouble; I
will take it away." — "If that is so, I will marry her." — "Now
you go. Stand in the king's house, where they are, so they see you.
They will ask you, 'Do you know what those birds fight for?'" The
three men told Lepros what the birds were fighting about. Those
three men were Santiago, San Pedro, San Paul. Then Lepros came to
Rei's house, so Rei asked him, "Tell me why those birds come every
day to fight?" — "The bird put eggs in the nest and the other bird
came and hatched the eggs. The first wants to take the babies away
and the other does not want to give them. For that they come to ask
Rei every day which one is right." Thus Lepros told Rei why the
birds came. Rei said, "The hatcher has the right." So the other bird
went away angry. Then he told Lepros, "You may marry my
daughter to-morrow." Rei had a witch woman (*chuge kwijo*). She told
him what to do. She gave him mixed seeds for Lepros to sort. They
told him that during the night he had to sort them all. So that night
Lepros was crying, he did not know what to do. He said, "Those
three men got me into trouble and do not come to help me." That
is what he said, and he prayed for them. Somebody knocked on the
door. It was Santiago. He told him to come in. He asked him what
had he prayed for. He said, "You men got me into trouble, and
nobody came to help." So Santiago said, "Go to sleep, we will help
you." He went to bed. "You call, 'Soplin and soplum.'" He went
out, Santiago. Lepros said, "Soplin, soplum, come, help me!" They
came in, they told him to go to bed. So he went to bed. He could
not sleep. So they sorted all that night. So he saw all separated. They
called Rei. He saw all the grain and seeds separated. He took Lepros
to breakfast. He breakfasted. Rei asked Witch Woman how they might
kill him. Witch Woman told Rei to tell him to go get water in
Powipoge, Flower River. So that evening they gave him a bottle. Rei
told Lepros to get the water which smelled very nice. It was the same
kind Witch Woman was to get. [1] Lepros did not know what to do

---

1. Told obscurely. That he was to race Witch Woman we may infer from the
parallels.

that night. He prayed. He asked God what to do, to help him. "Those three men are to blame for this." Somebody knocked at the door, San Pedro came. He told him to come in. "What are you saying, Lepros?" — "They told me to get some water in Flower River." San Pedro told him to call, "Korin korium wenkoredor." So he called, "Korin korium wenkoredor. You come here!" So he came in. "What do you want, Lepros?" — "They told me to go get some water in Flower River. You go and get it for me." He gave him the bottle. So he went. It took a person one hundred years to get to Flower River. Then he went and was returning from Flower River in the middle of the same night. He got the water, he rested for a while in the middle of the road. That Witch Woman came there. She had a ring. She put the ring on the middle finger of Korin Korium wenkoredor, so he would not wake up. Lepros was worrying that korin korium wenkoredor did not bring the water. He could not sleep, he prayed to God. "Those three men! I am in trouble. They never come to help me!" Then San Paul came and knocked on the door. He told him to come in. He said, "You three men put me in trouble, and you never come! That Korin korium wenkoredor is not back yet with the water." —- "You call for Miring mirung w'em mirador." So he called him. So he came. "What is the trouble?" Lepros said, "Korin, korium wen koredor has not come yet, you go and look for him." So Miring mirung w'em mirador took his looking-glass [spy glass] and saw him. He said, "He is at a place in the middle of the road, Witch Woman put a ring on him and he has not waked up. You call for Tering terong w'en tirador. So Lepros called for Tering terong w'en tirador. Then he came, he knocked. "Come in." So he came in. Then Tering terong w'en tirador shot off that ring. So Korin korium wer koredor woke up, and he came and brought the water. So early in the morning Rei came in and saw the water. When Rei came inside the door, it smelled sweet, and Rei was happy. He told him, "Now you may marry my daughter." So he told all the people working for him to make a big pile of wood. He told the men to catch Witch Woman and put ropes around her. "You put her on top of the wood and build the fire." So Witch Woman was burned, and Lepros married the king's daughter. They put water to heat, and put him into the water. The water boiled. They brought the water in to the bedroom of Lepros. He took off all his clothes and they put him into the water. They rubbed him with a brush. When he was through bathing, they washed him with the water from Flower River. You could see no man as handsome as he. All the sores were gone. So he married Rei's daughter.

44. *Variant* : WARRIOR WOMAN. [1]

At Suida (? Sp. ciudad, city) Rei wrote to every place that if the boys could guess something (*adivinhar*), they could marry his daughter. From everywhere boys came. If they did not guess, they were to be hung. At another place another king lived. He had a son. He heard about it. He wanted to go, too. Rei said to his son, "My child, saddle a mule, put some money on the mule. Take it along." So he went along. He came to a town. He met a man outside the town. This man was living with his mother. She was a very poor old woman and had only the one son. He brought wood and every thing they needed. Rei's son met this man, and asked if he wanted to work with Rei's son. "I want to work, but I can't leave my mother. I am poor. There is nobody to take care of my mother." — "If you want, I will take you along, and leave you money to buy for your mother what she needs." So they went to this man's house and let his mother know about it. She said, "Yes, you can go." They went towards a town. They met another man outside town. Rei's son asked if he wanted work. "I want to work, but I can't leave my mother. I am poor. There is nobody to take care of my mother." — "If you want, I will take you along, and leave you money to buy for your mother what she needs. It will last until we return." So they went to this man's house and let his mother know about it. She said, "Yes, you can go." They went along, they came to a town, they met another man. They asked him if he wanted to work with Rei's son. The man said, "I want to work, but I can't leave my mother. I am poor. There is nobody to take care of my mother. I have to take care of her." — "If you want, I will take you along, and leave you money to buy for your mother what she needs." So they went to this man's house and let his mother know about it. She said, "Yes, you can go." So he left money in all those places, for the men's mothers. They went and had dinner at a place far away. Of the first man he met he asked what kind of work did he know? He said, "I know how to cook." He asked the second man what kind of work did he know? "I will tell you what I know. I can carry in one night what you would take ten days to carry." Of the third man he asked what kind of work did he know? "I will tell you. When people travel for ten days [i.e. a ten days' journey] that far I can hear." — "All right, you first man be the cook; you next, carry us where we are going; you last man, you listen to what they are talking about." Then they stopped there, they slept there that night. That night as they slept, he picked up the three men and the mules and everything, and he carried them a distance

1. Informant 3 of Santa Clara. Heard in Tewa.

of ten days in one night. The next day they stayed there, and that night they lay down, and when they went asleep, he carried them a ten days' distance again. The next day they stayed there. The first man cooked, and the third man listened to what was being said. The next night he carried them a distance of ten days. Then Rei's son asked the last man, " Did you hear anything ? " He said no. So they went on again, that night. They came near to where that Rei lived. Rei's son said, " You go to the town and rent a house for three men. We will go there. " So he found a house and they went there that evening. When they came, the house was all ready to go in. So Listener said to Rei's son, "To-morrow you go into the town and buy a saddle, a bridle and boots and big hat and silk handkerchief and spurs and leggings. " So he bought all that and came to where the three men were. "You saddle the mule that is broken and ride to Rei. " So he dressed up like a cowboy, riding that mule. When he went into the street the mule began to balk. He reached Rei's house about noon to tell Rei he was going to guess, to let him have four days to think, and to let him have his house, to dance in. He went into town to look for musicians. He found two of them. He invited his friends to the dance that night. He took lots of money, filled his pocket. Every time they danced, when they stopped that man gave a dollar to every woman who danced. [1] They danced again, he gave a dollar to every woman. And so on, until they finished. He went back to the others. He asked Listener what he had heard. He said he had heard nothing yet. The next night they danced again. Lots of money. The king's daughter said that he must be crazy. That night he went to Listener. He had heard nothing yet. He went back again, till midnight. The next morning he asked Listener had he heard anything? He had heard nothing yet. He went back to dance, the third night. Rei's son was getting frightened because they had heard nothing about the riddle. He was dancing, but he did not feel like it. He danced only once or twice, he went to Listener. He had heard nothing. In a little while, he asked him again. He had heard nothing yet. They stopped dancing at midnight. The next morning he was thinking about running away. Listener advised him not to run away. This last night he went into the same house, he was dancing, although he did not feel like it. Still he danced. Every once in a while he went to Listener and asked had he heard anything. Listener would say he had heard nothing. They stopped dancing at midnight. He asked Listener again. In a little while they began to talk, Rei and his wife. " The people must be crazy, they will never guess what our girl has on her body. " Rei's wife said, " When our girl was a baby a gold hair came out from her and now she is tall, that gold hair is blossoming like a flower. Nobody

1. Perhaps a reminiscence of the Navaho woman's dance.

will guess what our girl has. " Listener heard this and told Rei's son. "I have heard what they are saying. " — " Tell me. " — " Not till morning will I tell you. " Rei's son was thinking of running away. When Rei's son lay down to go to sleep Listener told him. " When the girl was born a gold hair came out on her body, as the girl grew, the gold hair grew and blossomed, now there is a flower on the end of the hair. Nobody will guess this. All are trying to guess, but they can't guess. " The next morning Listener told King's son, " Go and saddle that same mule, and wear the clothes you have. Go to Rei's house, tie the mule outside, ask the man outside on guard where Rei is. " So he went, he asked the guard where Rei was. The soldier told Rei. Rei said to bring him in. He went in, he took off his hat, he said, " I have come to guess the riddle. " So Rei asked, " What do you guess ? " He stood up as if thinking about it. Then Rei told him to guess. So he said, " I am going to guess now. Your girl was born with one gold hair in the middle of her head. Every day she grew, the hair Grew too. Now she is a big girl (*anyo he'e*) that hair is blossoming like a flower. That is what I guess. " Rei said, " Yes, that is it. So you may marry my girl. " Then they called all the people. She is going to marry the king's son. So he had guessed. Next evening they were married. The first day they made a feast for the rich people. The second day they made a feast for the poor people. The boy went after those three men. Those three men had a good time, too. So they lived there where Rei lived. Everything Rei had, they gave to their son-in-law. Those three men they stayed there, too. His son-in-law told Rei, " All the wagons you have, hitch up and go after lumber. " So they all went. They built a corral. Everything Rei had, all his animals they brought into the corral and counted them. That night they went to bed. He told the man who could carry a distance of ten days to come in and bring them down. So they took away all their animals, a distance of ten days. They stayed there that day, the next night they packed up again. They stayed one day, the next night they packed up again, and went the same distance. He came to where he had met Listener. He gave one third of the animals to that man. He started to go to where Carrier had been, he gave one third of the animals to him. He went to where he had met the last man. He gave the last third of the animals to him, the cook. This man told Rei's son and his wife, " You go now and stop in the middle of the road. Take the right hand road. " They went on, they did not see where the right hand road led. They took the left hand road. They went on, they came to another town. In that town there lived a king whose son had been killed because he had not guessed the riddle. The king was angry. He told them to catch Rei's son and his wife. They caught them, they took them upstairs. The man went in first, his wife behind him. The guard who had all the keys pulled her back. He told her to go out where the mules were. She went out, and got the mules. The king's son was locked up. That man and Rei's daughter went on out of the town. Rei's daughter said she never slept outside, he must find a house. So he went to look for a house. He took her there, they slept there that night. They had locked up the man [husband]. He saw a rope hanging down from his window. He got out, he went on the road, he found the mule track, he followed the track. About the time they started from the house, the husband got there. The wife and the other man came to a place with cotton trees. Then after dinner the woman said, " I would like something to eat. " — " What ? " — " The green plume on the cotton tree. " He climbed up the tree. She was thinking that " as soon as he goes up the tree, I will put on the bridle and run away. " — " Which do you like, this one ? " — " No, one farther up. " He climbed up. She said, " I am going to put on the bridle ready to leave here. " — " Which do you like, this one ? " — " Yes. " She bridled the mule, she started. The man came down in a hurry, he slipped and fell down and broke one of his legs. Soon her husband came there. The man on the ground asked Rei's son to pick him up. Rei's son had a pistol. Then Rei's son recognized him. He took out the pistol and shot him, he killed him. He followed his wife's track. It was dark, he lost it. The woman went on and came to a place where an old woman (*saya*) lived. Next morning the woman asked Grandmother if there was any work for her. Grandmother said she would go over to Rei's house and ask for a job. She went, Rei said, " I would like a man for a soldier. " Grandmother came back and told the woman that Rei wanted a man for a soldier. The woman said, " All right, I'll go. Find some men's clothes for me. " Grandmother got some clothes. The woman put on the clothes. She went to Rei's house. Rei said, " All right, I will give him the position of Captain. " They were marching on horseback that morning on the road about nine o'clock. There were some people, Mutes (*t'umpi'i*), they were fighting with. Rei's soldiers were killed every time they fought with them. This time the woman captain led the soldiers against the Mutes. The Mutes ran away when they saw the captain and threw themselves off the mesa and were killed. They told this to Rei. After this he noticed the captain and took good care of him. After this the husband came to Grandmother's house and asked what had happened. Grandmother told about the woman captain. The husband got a job under the captain. This Rei had three daughters. One wanted to marry the captain. He would not agree to it. Grandmother went to Rei's house to ask for a job for the husband. Rei said, " Ask the captain. " Grandmother asked him. The captain said to bring him over. He was poor and ragged. He did not look like her husband. But she knew at once it was her husband. He asked for a job. " All right, I will give you one. First come into my office. I am going to eat dinner. We will eat together with Rei and Rei's wife. " He was ashamed, he had no good clothes. " No, " he said. " You have to, " she said, " if not, you have got to be hanged. " Supper was on the table. The captain wrote what had passed on the road. She was writing about what had happened. They gave her letter to Rei. Rei said, " All right. " He was reading it. They had their dinner, all of them. Rei and his wife, the captain and the man. Afterwards, they went into Rei's office. Rei asked, " Do you know this man (i.e. his wife)? " He said no. Rei said, " That is your wife. You have got to stay with us now. " He told his wife to get some new clothes and bathe him. Next day they were married again. They made a big *fiesta*. There they stayed for some time. Then they told Rei they were going home. Rei told them to choose a buggy and he appointed three, four soldiers to take them to their house. Next day they started. In the evening they came to their home. That is all.

ANIMAL TALES.

45. OLIVELLA FLOWER BOY JILTS THE GOOSE GIRLS. [1]

At Chunge[2] lived Olivella Flower boy. Every day he killed[3] blue birds. Sometime before Olivella Flower boy wanted to marry the Goose girls (kạgianyo). They said they would not marry Olivella Flower boy, but later they married him. Then the Blue birds took some blue wafer-bread and came to where Olivella Flower boy was. Then they said to Olivella Flower boy, " Olivella Flower boy, I want to marry you. We bring some corn bread with us. " Then they ate all together. Then, they went to where lived Olivella Flower boy's father and mother. Then they went in. Then they [children inside] said to their father and mother, " Some girls are standing there. Tell them to come in. " Those Goose girls were grinding corn, and they heard. They wanted to go home. They brought in those Blue bird girls. Father said, " You have some [women], you bring more. " Those Goose girls did not like it. They went to Chama and to Chikomo (Mt. Tsikomo). Then Olivella Flower boy went after those Goose girls. He went up Chikomo. He came where they lived, those two Goose girls. So he came, and they told him to come in. And they put white blankets down and told him to sit down on them. So

1. Informant 3 of Santa Clara.
2. Near Chamita.
3. By trap made .of stalk of sunflower, horse hair, and a bent stick. There is another kind of trap for snow birds (*ko'i*), grey birds, with black striped yellow neck, flocking in winter. These two types are the only traps in use.

he sat down. Then they turned him into a yellow ¹ snake (*panio-tse'yi*). So they went. Then they went where the snakes lived, all together, the Goose girls and Olivella Flower boy. All the snakes came to see him. He did not know how to walk, but they showed him how to move. He learned how in a little while. The Goose girls made him into a snake because he ran away from them for those two Blue birds. That is all.

(*Variant.*) ²

Kægianyo (Goose girls) used to live down by the river and Oli-vella Flower boy found them and asked the Goose girls, " Don't you want to stay with me ? " — " All right. " So he stayed with them. Then he went out hunting rabbits and turkeys, and they had a good living. One day he stayed out all day. Then these Goose girls said, " He stays out all day. He says he likes us ; but maybe he does not like us. Sister, let's grind meal and go home. " So they ground meal and made ready to go away. And they got their goose skins and they said to Olivella Flower boy when he came back, " We are going away. " They said it once, twice, three, four times. And they flew out so high (two feet up). He said, " Why do you go ? " They said, " *Henaho* ! " and they flew away to the north. "Why do you go ? " he said too late. As they flew they called :

Awiwiku   tuwak'u
name of hill (awipi)   talk stone

So Olivella Flower boy was left there, just looking up at them.

46. YELLOW CORN GIRLS MARRY FISH-HAWK BOY AND LEAVE HIM. ³

They were living at Kuochute'e, Yellow corn girls, Fish-hawk boy (Pokepeenu), and Olivella Flower boy. Olivella flower boy wanted to marry them, but they would not marry him, and they married Fish-hawk boy. He took them to his mother's house. He said, " Mother, I am bringing two girls. Tell them to come in. " His mother said, " I do not believe you are bringing two girls. They would not have you. Nobody likes you. What will they think of me ? Nobody like you, brown as you are. " — " Shut up, Mother. " — " Come down ", she said to them. When they put down their foot she went *hit! hit!* She was startled because she had not believed they were there. " Sit down, " she said to them. " Have you nothing

1. Yellow, the color of the west, is associated with Chikomo, the mountain of the West.
2. Informant 2 of San Juan.
3. Informant 2 of San Juan.

cooked? " said Fish-hawk boy. " Give it to them. " His mother said,
" I have nothing. " So she built a fire, and made a little bowl of *aga*
(Mex., *atole*). [1] She took a little stick and stirred it and sang :

> Poranka poranka poraka
> Kiru' kiru' wentu wen'tu
> painted painted

" How can we fill our stomachs from that little bowl ? " said the
girls. They began to eat. There was enough *atole* and meat for them.
They stayed four days. Fish-hawk boy went out hunting. He had been
out all day. The two girls said, " We do not like to stay here. He is
away all the time. We better go home. " So they went. Fish-hawk
boy came back and asked his mother, " Where are they gone ? " —
" I do not know, " said his mother. Fish-hawk boy just cried and
cried. He went after them; he found the two girls, he said, " Let's go
home. " — " No. Why do you leave us all day ? We do not want to
stay with your mother. Besides you are a brown boy. We are nice
white girls. We do not want to be with you. " So they left him and
came back home. *Hu* !

47. JEALOUS OF FROG. [2]

Oweweham'baiyo there lived two Koyi enu [3], one Koyi e'nu (*koyi*
youth) and one Koyi anyo (*koyi* girl). And one side of those there
lived one Pemp'owi (Frog). And once Koyi anyo went after water
and Koyi enu was in the house. Frog saw her going after water, and
she went to their house and said, " Sængitsamu. " — " Sit down. "
And Koyi anyo was a long time down at the ditch and when she
came back, she saw Frog going out from her house. Then when she
came in she asked if Frog had been there. " Yes. She came for salt, "
said Koyi enu. " No, I do not believe she came for salt. She came to
stay here with you. " So Koyi anyo got mad. And she got a little
basket of corn and put it in the grinding room, and she went in there
and began to sing :

> Koyi enu enu enu
> tsæ wiri tsæ wiri
> æ hi æ hi

" What's the matter with you singing that way ? " asked Koyi enu.

---

1. Corn meal gruel. Robbins, Harrington, Freire-Marreco, 93.
2. Informant 2 of San Juan.
3. Little brown bird. Possibly here and p. 143, n. 7, the Mourning Dove is
referred to. Henderson and Harrington, 35.

" You stay with that Long-leg girl. ¹ I do not want to stay with you. I better go to my mother and you stay with that girl Long-leg. " That's why you like her. " She went on grinding. When she got through, she went out with her basket of meal and went home. And she went to the west and she went crying with her basket. And when she came near the big lake, she threw out in front of her the meal, ² and she saw a ladder. She stepped on it and went down under the water. And Koyi enu ran after her and saw her go under the water and he just cried for her : " Koyi anyo, why are you going away? " Then he came back to his house. That is all. *Hu'* !

48. RABBIT FLEES THE SONG. ³

At A'a'pena ⁴ lived Puh (Rabbit) and W'æ (Rat). They lived close together. So one day Rabbit went and invited Rat to grind corn. She said yes. So Rat went to Rabbit's house to grind corn. Rat sang. [The song was forgotten.] Next morning Rat went to Rabbit's house to invite her to come to grind corn. She came and Rat sang,

W'æ mami ⁵ w'æ mami
rat   rat
Shukwaiye   sinyo   sinyo
nose on top of wrinkles wrinkles

Rabbit got mad, because Rat sang that song. She got mad and ran away. People say, " If you sing that song, I will run away " [referring to this story]. That is all.

49. BAT PRETENDS TO BE A BIRD. ⁶

There were some little birds, *hoyé*, ⁷ cleaning seeds from *tsuta* ⁸ and singing :

atsiningki apu
together   it blows
kah pu   pu   pu   pu
leaf blows blows   blows   blows

---

1. *Pempokwinanyo* (from *p'olaęsoyo*, sticking out legs, according to narrator).
2. This is a reference to the common Pueblo rite of making the road by sprinkling meal ahead.
3. Informant 3 of Santa Clara.
4. Name of a hill, near Tesuque.
5. No meaning.
6. Informant 1 of San Juan.
7. Brown birds, flocking together.
8. A red, seed-bearing grass.

Bat (*tsipi*) heard that those birds were cleaning. So he went too
" What are you doing, *hoyé*? " — " We are cleaning seeds. " —
" Let's see. " They flew down and sang :

atsiningki apu
together   it blows
kah pu̧   pu̧   pu̧   pu̧
leaf blows blows blows blows [1]

" I know it just the same, too, " said Bat. The birds said, " When
he says some words, let's fly away from here, and leave him. " —
" I know the same song, " he said. He sang the same song, and the
birds flew away and left him there. He stayed there and he cried and
he went away and he sang :

tsirebaomu̧wæ̧
I was a bird
nawaowæ̧ tsibemu
my teeth are open
nawaoye ti'mu
my ears are round
hoye hoye tsiwiwi tsiwiwi

He went to the church and on one side a crack opened and he
went in there and stayed there. And that is what happened to that Bat.

50. COYOTE STEALS FIRE. [2]

Long time ago (*ḥ*ạo) they always took care of the fire ; they did
not let them blow it out, they always kept it up. At Yungeowinge,
some people were living, and their fire went out. Down at Tekeowinge they were having a big dance, *pokwashare*. [3] They said, " Where
can we get fire ? Ours is all gone. Let's go and tell Coyote to go with
us. Maybe he can get fire. " They made up a bundle of chips and rags,
to burn well, to tie on his tail. They said, " Let's not let him know
it, so he will bring the fire. " They went down to Tekeowinge and
the dance began, man and woman, man and woman, man and woman
all around. One of those people was watching his fire, sitting near the
fire place. [4] So Coyote old man began to dance with them. The man
keeping the fire was watching the dancing. Coyote was turning round,
turning round ; he put his tail into the fire, it caught on fire. He began

1. The reference is to the winnowing breeze.
2. Informant 1 of San Juan.
3. Informant had never seen this dance. Knows of it only by name.
4. *Bahbuge*, fire in. The word first given was stove (Sp., estufa ; Tewa, *pasuwabe*,
fire warm round).

to run and they ran after him. He was coming to Kosowe. [1] They were pretty nearly catching him. There was *Sawe*. [2] Coyote said, "*Tiupare*, help me! They are nearly catching me." So *Sawe* put the fire on the back of its neck, and flew up the tree. Just then they overtook Coyote. Then they went back home, and when they went back, *Sawe* brought down the fire to Coyote. So Coyote brought the fire. He wanted to cross the river to Yungeowinge. He could not cross. He said, "If I cross, the fire will yo out." He did not know what to do with the fire. He saw some *poteyi*. [3] He said, "Wont you help me?" They said, "All right." They took the fire. They began to burn their hands and they said, "r--r rehrö." Just the same they still say in just the same way, "r--r rehrö." Thus Coyote took the fire to Yungeowinge. They said, "Thank you," and they paid him well. And after that they did not let the fire go out. Thus it passed at Chamita.

51. COYOTE IS TORMENTED. [4]

Coyote old man was going along. He had nothing to eat and he said, "I better go down to San Juan to every house to find bread," said Coyote old man. So he made a big sack and went to San Juan, and he came into a house and began to dance. His tail was up. He turned round and round, and the people just laughed, and gave him bread. And he went out from there and into another house [5] until he went through all the houses in Akongeinge. And at the end house [southwest] there lived Yellow corn girls, and he went in there and began to dance. Those two girls said, "*Harahi!* Coyote old man, maybe you are hungry. We will give you something to eat." They began to cook chili and gave him to eat. He burned his mouth with the dish and began to cry. He drank water but could not get rid of the burn. So the two girls said, "Let's go to the ditch, to get rid of the burn." So they went and gave him water, but he could not get rid of the burn. He scolded them. So they said, "Let's push him into the water." So they pushed him in. The water turned him and turned him and he called, "Yellow corn girls, take me out!" And then the crows heard Coyote old man cry. They said, "Who is crying? Coyote old man. Poor man! Let's take him out." So they took him out. He was all wet. They put him in the sunshine. He got warm and went to sleep. And the crows said, "Let's eat his eyes." They began to bite him

---

1. Related to Kosoge, a wash. This one is south of Santa Cruz.
2. Brown bird with yellow on back.
3. Brown birds that run very fast, along the water edge. (Cf. Henderson and Harrington, 46.)
4. Informant 2 of San Juan.
5. Such dancing from house to house, and largess of bread occur on Kings' Day (January 6) at San Juan, and is a common dance pattern everywhere.

and took out his eyes. When Coyote old man woke up, he had no
eyes and he could not move. He stayed there with nobody to give him
water or food and so he died, when they left him.

52. COYOTE MARRIES AND CANNOT BUILD A HOUSE. [1]

Prayer-stick old man and Shrivelled corn old woman had two
girls, and the girls said they did not want to marry any of the boys in
town. The boys came to see them, bringing women's clothes and
belts and moccasins and a water jar. One time these girls went to the
river for water. They heard singing :

> Kotįti [2] lenaho! [3] lenaho!
> Kotįti   lenaho!   lenaho!
> Aya   lenaho!   lenaho!

Coyote old man was coming in the water, with cedar berries around
his head. They did not know who was singing. Then he came up
close to the girls. He took the berries off and put them in the water,
and those girls picked up the berries and ate them. And they said,
" I wish somebody would bring berries like these to give to us. " So
he came close to them. He heard what they said. Then he sang again
for the two girls :

> Kotįti   lenahɔ!   lenaho!
> Kotįti   lenaho!   lenaho!
> Aya   lenaho!   lenaho!

The girls said, "Somebody is singing an awfully pretty song. "
Now he had taken the berries off and the girls had eaten them.
They said, " They are sweet, these berries somebody put in the water.
I wish they would give some to us. " And Coyote old man said,
" Somebody is talking about me. " He came up to look at the two
girls and ask what they were doing. They said, " We have come after
water. " Coyote old man knew that that night they were going to have
a dance. He came to the pueblo, he brought with him some women's
clothes and belts and moccasins and a water jar. He said to those
two girls, " Will you take me into your house tonight ? I heard that
they are going to have a dance. " The old man was mean to the
boys, he did not want them to come into the house. The girls had
some wafer bread, they brought in Coyote old man. He said, " Try
on the clothes. " The girls put on the clothes. They said, " They fit

1. Informant 4 of Santa Clara.
2. Medicine man's stones, two or them, used "like a drum" [i.e. clashed together ?].
3. A recurrent song word, meaning unknown.

us well, only we do not want this water jar. But for this jar we would marry you. " The elder said, " If you take back this jar, we will marry you. " [1] The old man said, " I do not want you to marry, because Coyote old man has no house for you to go to; but if you want to marry him, marry him ! " So she married him. They had trouble and they said, " Now you must go and build a house, we wont give you room any more. " He did not know how to build a house. So he went and dug a hole. The girl said, " What are we going to do here ? We are going to freeze to death. " Coyote old man said, " I don't know how to built a house, and this is my home. " Then he took his clothes off, to his hide. The girl said, " I do not want to live with you. You bring me nothing. I thought you were an Indian. You have not built me a house. [2] I can't stay here; I am not used to living in a hole. "

53. YELLOW CORN GIRLS MARRY COYOTE. [3]

Yellow corn girls long ago used to live at San Juan in Green corn kiva [4] and Coyote old man went over to ask them if they wanted to marry him. They went after water. Coyote was at the water. Then Coyote said, " *Hu!* *hu!* *hu!* If you do not marry Coyote to-morrow, they will kill you. " The older one said, "Younger sister, somebody in the ditch said we must marry Coyote. " The younger one said, " No, I am speaking from the nose. " Then she said, " Oh yes, it is true what you said, elder sister, I guess we must marry Coyote. " And they went home with their water. So they came and they said, " Grandfather, we are going to tell you something we heard at the ditch. From the ditch somebody said we must marry Coyote, and I guess you better go and tell Coyote to marry us. " Then their grandfather went over and told Coyote, and Coyote said, " Thanks. That is what I want. " And Coyote came and married the two girls.

Variant (from Tesuque).

Coyote was living in the mountain. The White corn girls were going along and met Coyote. He had plum tree twigs around his head and he was singing,

Kǫtsaianyo (White corn girl).
Kǫtsaianyo (White corn girl).

1. This jar incident is obviously fragmentary or undeveloped. It appears with more significance in the tales of First Mesa.
2. As Tewa men often do, after marriage, unless one is given to them, or their wife happens to own one.
3. Informant 2 of San Juan. Heard from Informant 1.
4. *Kǫtseanyo owewe' hæmba data oke k'unochute'e.*

They went together to the White corn girls' house, Coyote between the girls. Coyote would go hunting deer in the mountain, and the White corn girls would grind blue corn and make wafer bread. Coyote came back with the two deer he had killed and the girls went out to take the deer. The other boys were angry with the girls because they had not married them. So when Coyote went to the mountain the boys followed him and killed him. He did not return, so the two girls stayed by themselves.

54. COYOTE PLOTS TO BECOME SUMMER CHIEF.[1]

This Coyote old man wanted to be Summer chief. He was just thinking about what he could do, how he could cheat all those people in Santo Domingo. He said, "I wonder how I can become Summer man and rule over everybody here. " Then he said, "I am going to make a tunnel from here to the river. " Near the river there were lots of grasses and lots of trees. He made a hole through the grass. The people from Santo Domingo would go early in the morning to the river to wash their faces. Now when Coyote old man woke up he went to the river and waited for the people to come and wash their faces. He had made a flute (*tempe*). He said, "I wonder who will come. " A boy who was Outside chief came. He heard Coyote old man blowing. He blew *hu...u...u*! So Coyote old man said, "*Hu*! if you don't make Coyote old man your Summer man, the water is going to kill you. " Outside chief was scared. He thought that maybe it was Avanyo, under the water. So he went to the house of the head Outside chief and he said, "Avanyo said under the water that if we don't make Coyote old man Summer man, the water is going to kill us. Let us go so you can hear what he says. " Coyote was lying down. He heard the two coming. He began to blow again. "*Hu...u...u*! "Then he said, "*Hu*! if you don't make Coyote old man Summer man, the water is going to kill you. " They heard him. "What is going to happen? This evening we shall have to call every man and if they do not believe us to-morrow morning, some other boys will have to come and listen ". So they called all the men. Then they said, "This is what we heard in the river when we went to wash our face. Avanyo said, ' If you don't make Coyote old man Summer man, the water is going to kill you. ' I guess we have to do it. If you don't believe us, go three or four of you, and listen for yourselves. " Now Coyote old man was thinking to himself, " Maybe they have called all the men to make me Summer man. " The people were saying, "How could he lie, this Outside chief? Still, perhaps we had better listen for ourselves. " So they went, five or six. Coyote old man went early in the morning

---

1. Informant 1 of San Juan.

to wait for them. "Lots of them have come," he said. He blew, " *Hu . . . u . . . u!* " — " Just hear it, " they said. He blew again, " *Hu . . . u . . . u!* " Then he said, "If you do not make Coyote old man your Summer man, the water is going to kill you: " So they believed. They said, " We have to do it because Avanyo sendo said it; we have to do it in order that the water will not flood us. " Then Coyote old man went to his house. There he was sitting and looking about. "From which direction will they call me, " he said. He saw two of them. "They are coming after me, " he said. He sat down in his house. They reached his house and they stood there tapping with their feet. He acted as if he did not hear. " Guess he is not here, " they said. They tapped again. "I wonder who is tapping, " he said. "We are tapping, " they said, " let us come in; we want to say a few words to you. " So he said, " Come in. " The two Outside chiefs stood up in front of Coyote old man who was sitting there. [1] They said, " Here we have come, our old man (*nabi sendo*). We have come here to call you because in the river we heard that Avanyo say, 'If you don't make Coyote old man your Summer man, the water is going to kill you. ' So we called all the men and all the boys and they have sent us to call you. We are going to make you Summer man. That is why we have come. " Then he said, "I am very poor, nobody will mind me. Somebody will say, ' Let us not mind this old fox.' They won't mind me. I do not want to be Summer man. Go and tell this to the men. " So they went, these Outside chiefs, to tell the men. When they left him Coyote old man said, "That is the way I want it to be. " The Outside chiefs reached San Juan. [2] "What happened to you?" they asked them. "Coyote old man said that nobody would mind him ; he is a very poor man ; he does not want to be Summer man ; that is what he told us." So these men said, "You have to go and bring him, and we *have* to mind him because Avanyo told us to make him Summer man. We will help him ; he has to come." Now Coyote old man went up and looked around. "They will come back for me pretty soon, " he said. He went down and sat down. They came again; they tapped very softly. "Come in, " he said. " Ah, old man, we have come after you. They told us that if anybody does not mind you, they will help you." So he said, "All right, I may go with you, boys, just wait awhile. Let me paint my face and put on red spots. " He put red paint on the parting of his hair [3] and under his eyes. So they took him. He went up. They told him to come down. " Come down, our old man, Coyote old man. " So he went in. Then they cleared a way for him to pass. He

---

1. Narrator dramatized both Coyote and the messengers.
2. From lapse of memory the scene shifts from San Domingo to San Juan.
3. I observed red paint on the parting of one of the Winter men of San Juan.

did not want to pass. He sat down near the ladder. Then they let him know why they had called him. They said, "From to-day you are Summer man. You have to rule your children and we have to do whatever you order. From now on you are to rule this place where we live. Here are lots of men to help you if anybody does not mind you. " He said, "I am very poor, nobody will mind me; it is too hard. " They said, " Do not speak that way. You *have* to be our Father ; you are our Father and our Mother. " So he said, " All right. " So they made him Summer man. From now on they had Coyote old man as Summer man. That is the way it happened.

55. HOW COYOTE BECAME GOVERNOR.[1]

At Wange (Jemez, in Tewa, *Hemi*) lived Coyote old man. He wanted to be governor (*tujo*). He went to the *capitan* (*akonotujo,* Outside chief). He said, " Outside chief, I have come. If all want me, make me the governor. " So Outside chief called all the men to ask if they wanted Coyote old man as governor. So they all came to Outside chief's house. He told them all what Coyote old man said. They said. " We don't want him for governor. We have a governor. We don't want Coyote old man. " The next morning Outside chief went to tell him, "No, they don't want you. " So Coyote old man was thinking what he would do. The people from there went to a lake every morning to wash their faces. So Coyote old man made a hole from where he was to that lake. Then he got a stick. He made a flute, but it was not right. So he went after another one. Then he made that. He said, "That is better than the other. " He went after another stick. He made that. He said, "That is still better. " At daylight he came down into the lake where he had a hole. In the hole he was playing on that flute. He heard one of the men. He said, "In four days if they do not make Coyote old man governor, lots of water will come and kill all the people. " That same morning the man who heard this went to the Outside chief and told what he had heard. Outside chief called a meeting, and told what Coyote old man had said. They heard what was said from inside the lake. Outside chief sent the boy who had heard first and another man to the lake. They went the next morning and heard what was said. They went and told Outside chief. " That is true ! The water is coming in four days unless Coyote old man is made governor. " In four days, at daylight, they heard lots of water coming down from the mountain. So Outside chief called another meeting of all the men. Then they went after Coyote old man and made him governor. So where Coyote old man

1. Informant 3 of Santa Clara. Cp. San Juan, De Huff, 65-69.

lived they cleaned up everything outside. [1] So Coyote old man was the governor. That is all.

56. COYOTE GOES FOR SALT. [2]

At Puambu they used to live, Coyote old woman and Coyote old man. Coyote old woman said to Coyote old man, "I have no salt. You go after salt." So he went and came where the salt was. He was very tired; he lay down on one side. He said, "I will sleep and when I wake up I will put salt in my bag and go home." As he slept the Butterflies came and played around him and picked him up and carried him to his house. When he woke up he thought, "Why am I here? What did I do? I was by the side of the lake where the salt was; now where am I? I guess I am home. But who brought me?" Then he went in. Coyote old woman said to him, "*Hewemboharqhi*! You don't take long to get salt. You came quickly." He said, "I lay down on one side of the salt lake. I was very tired; I slept. When I woke up, I was beside my house. I do not know who brought me." — "I do not believe you," said Coyote old woman. "You are very lazy. You did not go at all for salt. Now you must eat this hot soup without salt." — "Surely, I went," he said. She did not believe him. "Lazy man! lazy man!" she said. "To-morrow morning I am going very early." He said, "If I get tired I will lie down to one side and when I get up I will fill up my sack." So he went early in the morning. He got there. He had some little sticks. He said, "Guess I had better sleep a little bit to get strong. When I get up I will get salt." He was very tired and he slept soundly. Again the Butterflies came and picked him up and laid him in the upper room of his house. Then he woke up to pick up his sticks and begin to dig for salt. He was in a hurry to get it. He made a lot of noise. [3] Coyote old woman heard him and went up. "My old Coyote man, are you crazy? What are you doing?" — "I thought I was lying on the top of the salt and began to dig for salt. Who brought me here?" — "You lazy old man. I do not believe you." — "Sure, I went for salt, but I do not know who brought me here." Coyote old woman was very angry. She made her bread without salt. He said to her, "Don't scold me! See how tired I am!" She said, "You can't get tired lying down up here." — "But surely I went for salt; I wonder who brought me here? When I was sound asleep, maybe somebody carried me. My wife, don't scold me," he said. "I am going again. Even if I get

1. Before that they had thrown ashes and dirt around the house of Coyote old man.
2. Informant 1 of San Juan.
3. Narrator acted out Coyote digging in his own house floor in a very lively way and there was much laughter.

very tired I won't sleep; I won't lie down. Don't scold me, " he said. "I am going to-morrow and I won't lie down. " She got angry. " Well, go to-morrow, but don't come back to my house with your story. If you don't have salt, don't come back. " So he went. He arrived and dug up salt and put it in his sack. He was sleepy, but he did not lie down. He was going along over the salt, very sleepy. The Butterflies were just laughing at him. He got so sleepy he could not walk. He put the sack of salt down for his pillow and lay down. "Whoever has carried me ought to come now and carry me with my salt to my door. " But the Butterflies said, "Poor Coyote old man. His wife scolds him. We had better pick him up with his salt and lay him near his house. " So they picked him up and carried him near his house. When he woke up he said, "Whoever took me home is mean. Maybe they took my salt and put it into my sack. I had better look at it. " He looked and he found the salt. "Thank you, " he said. "Whoever carried me, thank you for carrying me. The salt was too heavy. " He went in his house. "Here I come with the salt, " he said to Coyote old woman. She smiled at him. "Now I believe you, " she said. "The other two times I did not believe you, but now that you come with the salt I believe you. " She was glad. "I was not lying, " said Coyote old man. "I went for the salt, but I do not know who carried me back without it. " Thus it happened to Coyote old man.

57. THE WAGON SINGS FOR COYOTE.[1]

There was a black beetle (*pegapusade'e*).[2] He went for wood. He was coming with the wood, and the wagon was crying, full of wood. Wagon cried, "*Ai! ai! tsehanono.*" He came to a little hill, the wagon could not carry up the wood, it tried and tried, but it could not pull it put. He went to the house of Coyote old man. He said to Coyote old man, "I can't pull my wagon up, wont you come and help me pull it up?" — "If you bring me wood, I will go, " said Coyote old man. So he said, "Of course I will. I'm not lazy about bringing wood. I will bring you all you need. " So Coyote old man said to Black beetle, "Pull it! " and the wagon began to cry. "*Huba-harahia!* this wagon sings nicely, " said Coyote old man. "Pull it again so I can hear the song and learn it. " He pulled, it sang,

> ai ai ai tsine tsine
> tsin tsehanono te

So they did not pull up the wagon, they just learned the song. Coyote old man said, "I guess we will just take the wagon to my house. "

1. Informant 2 of San Juan.
2. Henderson and Harrington, 60.

So Black beetle did not take it to his wife's house. They pulled it and pulled it and Coyote old man's mother said, " What a nice song ! " So Black beetle said, " I will go and cut some more wood. " So he went after wood. Then he brought it again. And he came to the same hill and he could not climb it. So he went over to Coyote old man's house. " Come and help me, " he said. So they went. " Pull it, " said Coyote old man. And the wagon began to cry,

> ai ai ai tsine tsine
> tsin tsehanono te

Four times he went for wood. " What a nice song ! " So they took the wagon to the house of Coyote old man. Four times he did this and Black beetle old woman did not cook, did not eat, she had no wood. When Black beetle went home she said, " *Hŭbaharahia !* You are so slow in bringing wood. " He said, " You will see how nicely the wagon cries. " So he pulled it and pulled it, and it sung :

> ai ai ai tsine tsine
> tsin tsehanono te

" It's nice to learn that song, " said the woman. So he said, " We must not make fire, nor cook anything. Just let us learn the song. " — " All right, I wont go for wood. " — " I wonder why our wagon knows how to sing so nicely. " They were asking the wagon if it knew another song. So Black beetle said to the woman, " Don't you wish you had a little baby to sing the song and make her sleep ? " — " Yes, I would like to have one. Let's make a doll of rags so we can sing to it and make it sleep. " Then they began to laugh. So they made the doll and sang for it. And then they all went to sleep. And they did not know who came and killed them and stole the doll (*hŭ'ŭ*). They did not wake up again.

58. SLIDING ON THE ICE (TESUQUE).

They were living at Tabaungi. Pehbeh seno (Mexican, cajon) would go to the river when it was frozen over to play and slide on the ice. Two birds came, they were sliding, too. They had red on their shoulders. Pehbeh seno said to them, " You look so nice with red on your shoulders, and I have no red on mine. " He wanted to be red, too. So they took a stone to cut him on the shoulders. As they cut him, he cried ŭi ! ŭi ! As they cut him, they told him he was nice and red. They stood to one side to slide, and Pehbeh seno on the other. The birds sang,

> We have red shoulders.
> We are going to slide.

They said to Pehbeh seno, " Now you sing ! " Pehbeh seno sang in a deep voice,

I have nice red shoulders.
I am going to slide.

The birds said, " Pehbeh seno will eat us up. When we slide again, let us fly away. " The birds slid and flew away to the east. Pehbeh seno went away, cutting his nails.

59. THE BEST MEAT : HOW SKUNK FIGHTS. [1]

Coyote old man was married to Humatoge (another kind of fox). This fox lived at Tsingwake [2] (*tsin*, sheer cliff ; *gwake*, hill). This Coyote was a good boy, not lazy. This Fox was a nice girl. " Nobody can beat my wife, " said Coyote old man. So Coyote went out hunting rabbits. Fox said, "How good they are, these little rabbits ! But my grandfather and grandmother used to say that the meat of big rabbits is better." So he went to hunt rabbits and brought a big one. So she ate the big rabbit meat. Then she said, " This is very good meat, this big rabbit. But grandfather used to say that antelope meat (*t'ǫpiwi*) is still better. " So Coyote went and got a mountain lion. " *Harahi'* ! this is good meat. But my grandfather used to say that white-tailed deer meat (*ohǔ piwi* is still better. " So Coyote brought some white tailed deer meat. She ate it and said, " *Harihi*c ! this is good meat. But my grandfather used to say that *pink'uwa* (mountain sheep) meat is still better. " So he went to hunt mountain sheep. He was trying to be a good boy. He said, " I am trying to get what she wants, but she is not satisfied yet. " — " *Harahi*c! mountain sheep is so good and tender ; but my grandfather used to say that elk meat is still better. " So he went after elk and brought it. So she ate the elk meat. " *Harahi*c ! this is good meat. But my grandfather used to say that buffalo meat is better." So he went after buffalo. He was hunting buffalo and the buffalo broke his lower arm. So he came. So he said, " Those fighting people fought with me, and here in my arm they shot me. " He said, " Those fighting people are coming. I have to call all my friends (*nabi kemaį*). " So he called. And they came. " Wonder what has happened to Coyote old man, " they said. So they came, bear (*ke*), lion (*kæ*), mountain eagle (*tse*), hawk (*chuga*), porcupine (*sǫ*), skunk (*tsą*), and Coyote old man was talking to them. " I was after buffalo and those fighting people were fighting me, and they broke my arm. And they are coming here and I called you. We have to get ready now. So when those fighting peoples come we can go out. I will let you know what we need so those fighting peoples

---

1. Informant, of San Juan.
2. To the west, across the river and the railroad.

cannot do what they want with us. " So he asked that bear, " How are you going to fight? You have to let me know, " said Coyote old man. He got a big piece of wood, and beat on it. " I am going to beat with my paws. " — " That's good, I like that, " he said. " Now you, Lion, how are you going to fight ? " He wrapped his tail around the log of wood. " This way I am going to catch them and pull them out. " — " That's good, I like that. And you, Porcupine, how are you going. to fight ? " — " I am going to make holes everywhere. When they come on horseback, the horses will step into the holes and fall down. "[1] — " That's good, I like that. And you, Hawk, how are you going to fight ? " —" I am going to fly way up high and swoop down, and beat with my wings. " — " That's good, I like that. And you, Skunk, how are you going to fight ? " — " I am going to help you from the back. " Coyote old man did not like that. (It meant he was going to run away.) " You will run away ?"—" No, I am not going to run away That is the way I am used to fight. " — " Now we shall see how you are to fight, if you are a man and a woman, we shall see, we will look at you. " — " All right, " said Skunk. So he went to the door as it he was going out, and he turned and threw it (his stink). They coughed and choked. " That's enough ! that's more than enough ! " they said. He threw it, and he killed them all. That is why even the dogs do not fight with Skunk.

60. HOW THE DEER GOT THEIR SPOTS. [2]

Posew'a kwiyo[3] (Coyote old woman) had four little coyotes and Deer old woman, Pǫe kwiyo, had two little deer. They were living close. So Wolf woman said to Deer woman, " Harąhiᶜ ! Deer woman, your little deer have nice spots. How do you give them those nice spots ? " So Deer said, " I make a great big fire inside and big smoke and I leave no place open and I leave them inside, and they come out spotted. " So Wolf said, " I want to do that the same way, so my children will have nice spots, too. " So she said, " My children, wouldn't you like to be like those little deer ? I will make a big fire inside and when it gets full of smoke I will shut you in there and when you come out, you will come out spotted. " So they said, " All right, Mother, we would like it. " Inside she made a fire in the middle and put in every kind of grass and wet wood, so flames would not come up, and left all closed up tight. She went outside and sat down. The house was full of smoke. They said, " Mother, open for us. We are full of

---

1. This would be an appropriate performance for badger, and *so* had been translated badger, but see Henderson and Harrington, 18.
2. Informant, of San Juan.
3. Informant said, " I made a mistake, not Coyote old woman but Kụyo kwiyo, Wolf old woman."

spots. " — " Don't be in a hurry. Don't you want to be spotted all
over nicely ? Wait a while. " Then after a while she opened, the smoke
came out. " Now I will find my children, " she said. She picked one
up ; it was dead. She picked up another, it was dead. All were dead.
" *Heweharạhi*ᶜ ! My little children ! I killed them all myself, " she said.
" But Deer woman, she told me that. I know what I will do. I am going
to tell Deer woman to come and sit in the sunshine and I will look
her head over. " She went to Deer woman's house. Those little deer
were out walking. She said, " I have come to see you to look your
head over for bugs. " She said, "I have no bugs in my head. You don't
need to look. " — " Of course you have bugs, " she said. " All right,
if you want to hunt, sit down. " So she sat behind her and bit into
her neck and killed her. So she took her away to her house. The little
deer came home and did not find their mother. Wolf cut a piece of
meat from Deer and took it out. The little deer were going along
asking for their mother and they met Wolf going with the meat. " Your
mother has gone walking, " she said. " She told me to take care of
you boys. So here is a piece of meat. You must cook it. " So they took
the meat and went in and got fire. They got a long pointed stick . They
put the meat on it and when they were going to put it on the fire,
the meat spoke to them . " My little children, don't put me in the fire.
Wolf killed me and she may plan to kill you; too. You must go way
from here, go way over to Poyegi ¹ where Oyoseno, Beaver
old man, is living. " So they came to Poyegi. They asked Beaver
old man to carry them across the river, to Tạtsạwapokwinge
(sun blue lake). There lives Pọẹtoyo (deer chief), your father. "
They went and left the meat. Wolf looked at her dead children and got mad again. " I am going to kill Deer children. I
am going in when they are eating their supper. " The little deer left
the meat and went out and came to where Beaver old man was working. They said, " Beaver old man, good evening, wont you pass us
across ? We are going to visit our father. " So he said, " All right,
children, I will pass you across. That Wolf woman is mean. When
she comes here, I will detain her a while. " So he swam in the water
and carried them and set them on the other side of the river. Then
they ran. And Wolf woman, when she went after them, did not find
them. She followed them and came to where Beaver old man was
living. She said, " Good evening, Beaver old man. " Beaver pretended
he did not hear her. He was singing, " I am going to clean on this
side, " he said while Wolf was talking to him. " I am asking you if
Deer children came this way. " — " It needs cleaning on this side,
too. " — " *Hewẹharạhi*ᶜ ! Don't you hear what I am saying ? " —
" Maybe tomorrow I shall get through. " — " Beaver old man, don't

---

1. Between San Juan and Santa Clara, on the east side of the Rio Grande.

you hear me ? " — " Maybe this is going to come out all right now. "
So she caught him and shook him. " Don't you hear me ? " —
" *Hewęharạhi*ᶜ ! I did not hear you. " — " Pass me across. " —
" Yes. What are you saying ? " — " Pass me across this river. " He
just went on talking about something else and kept her waiting a long
time. Finally he said, " All right, I will pass you across. Lie on top
of me and hold me tight. If you don't hold me tight, I will throw you
into the water. " He jumped into the water. They were going over
the river. Beaver old man said, " *Ta ha* ! ¹ *tanbume* " and turned her
over into the water. In the middle she went down. So Wolf said to
Beaver, " Why don't you want to cross me over to the other side ? "
— " I tried to, but I could not, " said Beaver. Then Beaver took her
way down, very far down. She got across, way up opposite where
Beaver lived. She said, " I better follow them from here. *Hewęharạhi*ᶜ !
that Beaver old man was mean to me. The little deer he took right
across, me he carried way down. " The little deer were running along.
The younger got a sore foot. The older one was carrying him. They
went along crying and singing. ² Wolf woman was pretty nearly catching
them. They came to Sand Lake and went in, and there was their
father. They were trembling, they were scared. He said, " Don't be
scared, my little children. Wolf wont do anything to you. You have
come to your father. " Wolf came then, she came up and was calling and
asking if the deer had come there. " Yes, they came, " they said. The
little deer were just shaking. Their father said, " Don't be afraid, my
children. " Wolf woman said to send them out. Their father said to
Wolf, " When people need something, they come in themselves and
get it. " He told two deer youths (*pæ enu*) to stand, one on one side of
the ladder, one on the other side. When she came down she stepped
down, she drew back, she stepped down, she drew back. She went in.
The two deer youths caught her in the middle on their horns. She fell
down and was killed. They opened her and cooked her. When they
cooked her, they told all the deer to come and eat, and Deer chief said, " I
have called you all to eat Wolf. Be careful not to let any drop of Wolf
fall to the ground. " They all began to eat of the soup. Somebody made
a slip and dropped a bit and from that all the bones stood up. ³ And
that's why Wolf always kills Deer, and that is the way it passed. *Hu*ᶜ !

61. TELL-TALE GREASE : STORM COMING : HOLDING-UP THE MESA. ⁴

Coyote old man killed a gopher, he took it where it was warm. " I

1. No meaning.
2. This song was forgotten.
3. Cp. the conclusion given to Tar Baby at Taos. Parsons 2.
4. Informant, of San Juan. Cp. San Juan, De Wulf, 3-4, 5-6.

am going to eat good, " he said. He made a big fire and put the gopher on
the fire. He made a little hole and put the gopher in the hole and
covered it over with ashes. He lay down and went to sleep. Came
along Grey Fox and found Coyote old man sound asleep. He saw the
little gopher and took it out from the fire. It was well cooked, he ate
it. It was fat; he took the grease and smeared it around the mouth of
Coyote old man. He took the little nails of the gopher and stuck them
up in the ashes. Then he ran away. When Coyote old man woke up,
he said, " I am going to eat good. " He laid hold of the nails, pulled
them up, only the nails came up. " Perhaps it was very well cooked, "
he said, " that is why the nails came out. " He stirred up the ashes, he
found nothing. He felt his mouth. I have grease on my mouth, " he
said, " but my belly is hungry. I don't know when I ate it, but just
look at my mouth ! " said he. He began to jump up and down. " I can
jump, " he said. " I did not eat it. If I ate it, I could not jump, I would
be too heavy. " He looked about, he saw the tracks of Grey Fox.
" When I was sleeping Grey Fox came and ate it all up and smeared
me, " he said.

He started after Grey Fox. He followed the tracks to the carcass of
a cow, there he found Grey Fox. " *Hewemboharqhi* ! Grey Fox, you stole
my gopher, I am going to kill you and eat you. " — " *Hewemboharqhi,*
Coyote old man, don't kill me. This evening snow and hail are coming.
I am going to take off this cowhide and make a sack and cover us over
so we wont be killed.... I will put you in the sack and take it up in a
tree and hide you, " said Grey Fox. The sky was dark, as if snow were
coming. So Grey Fox made the sack and put Coyote old man into it.
" Right here is a good place, " he said, " here I will hang you up. "
So he hung up the sack. Then he gathered up some stones, little ones
and big ones. He picked up a stick and threw it at the sack. Then he
threw the little stones. " Little hail stones are coming ! " he
said. Then he threw bigger ones, and bigger ones. Coyote old man
said, " I am in the sack, but I am hurt ! " — " You are hurt ! "
— " Yes, it hurts ! " Grey Fox kept on throwing stones. Coyote
old man was almost dead. " Maybe he will die, " said Grey
Fox. " I will run away. " So off he ran. Then Coyote old man bit a
hole in the sack and came out and fell down. He saw all the stones.
He was very angry. " He said to me big hail stones were coming and
look at these stones he was throwing ! When I find him I am going to
kill him. " So he followed him to the east.

Grey Fox saw him coming. Grey Fox was under a mesa. He began
to lean against the wall as if holding it up. Mist was blowing across
the sky. It made the mesa look as if it were moving. Up came Coyote
old man. Grey Fox said to him, " If this wall falls down, it will kill
us. Look up at the sky, the mesa is moving. Come and help me. " So
Coyote old man leaned against the wall. Grey Fox said, " Hold that

wall so it wont fall down, while I look for others to help us. " Then
Grey Fox ran off. Coyote old man began to get tired. " I am so tired
and Grey Fox is away so long! He brings nobody to help me. I am very
tired holding up this wall. I am going to jump away. I guess I better
jump four times, so the mesa wont catch me. " So he jumped, he
jumped to the north, to the west, to the south, to the east. He looked
back, the wall was standing just as he left it. He said, " *Hewemboharahi* ! that Grey Fox is forever cheating me. " That is what happened
to Coyote old man and that is the way Grey Fox cheated him.

62. MOON CHEESE : STORM COMING (*Variant Tesuque*).

Once at Potsew'aie, Pohunge (blue fox) was sitting by the river
and Coyote old man was hunting rabbits. Coyote went and spoke to
Blue fox. " What are you doing here ? I am going to eat you up. "
Blue fox said, " What do you mean ? I am working here, fixing this
river. At dinner time the girls from Potsew'aie are coming to bring
me dinner. " Coyote said, " All right, I will help you. " Blue fox
said, " If I see the girls coming, I will tell you. " He was fooling him.
He said, " Unless you work well, I will throw you into the water. "
He went up on the hill to see if the girls were coming. Then he ran
away. Coyote was working all day. Nobody brought him anything
to eat.

Blue fox ran up to Tsakona where there was a pond. As he sat
there, the moon showed big in the water. Blue fox thought it was a
cheese. Along came Coyote and saw Blue fox sitting there. Coyote
said, " Now I am going to eat you up. " — " No, don't eat me, help
me get this big cheese. " Coyote looked down into the water. Blue
fox said, " Let us take out that cheese and both of us eat it. You put
your hand first into the water. " Coyote put in his hand and Blue fox
held him by the foot. Blue fox threw him down into the water. He
was scratching away in the water and Blue fox ran away from him
again, fooling him again.

Coyote came out from the water. Blue fox was over at Potsew'aie.
Coyote went there and said, " I am going to eat you up. " Blue fox
was making a bow and arrows. He said, " The soldiers are coming to
kill me. Don't eat me up ! " — " All right ", said Coyote, " I will
make a bow and arrows, too, and a big bag to cover us up when the
soldiers come. " They made a big bag. Blue fox said, "I will put you
in first. " Coyote went into the bag. Blue fox threw stones at him,
first little ones, then big ones. Then he killed that Coyote. He skinned him and cut off his hands and head, and cut out his stomach, and
threw them all away. He washed it all out and he took some meat to
Tsakona and sold it for corn and bread, to a man who had lots of
children.

63. WATER CARRIER.[1]

At Nanghuu (Sand hill) Coyote old woman lived. She had three little ones. She went after water down to the river. From the river she carried water to her children. Coyote old woman would always laugh at everything. One day as she went that bird Oguyá [2] said, " I am going to make her stay and laugh. " She got lots of water in her mouth. As she came near the bird began to sing:

poo	henge		henge
water	spit it out		spit it out
kina	oguyá	tee	kewena
this is the way		tree	up
tu̧	aaaa		
it says			

Coyote laughed and dropped the water. She scolded the bird, " You make me laugh and I drop the water. " She went after water again. As she came near the birds, she said, " I am not going to laugh. " The bird began to sing again,

poo	henge		henge
water	spit it out		spit it out
kina	oguyá	tee	kewena
this is the way,		tree	up
tu̧	aaaa		
it says.			

She laughed, she dropped the water again. She said, " I guess I better go after water again. I am going to paint my mouth with piñon gum (*tokwæn*). " So she came again. As she came near the bird, the bird began to sing,

poo	henge		henge
water	spit it out		spit it out
kina	oguyá	tee	kewena
this is the way		tree	up
tu̧	aaaa		
it says			

She began to laugh, her mouth opened again, she dropped the water. She scolded the bird, " Maybe my children are nearly dying, you make me drop the water. " So she said she was going to sew her mouth

1. Informant, of San Juan.
2. Breast, yellow; back, brown; black across throat.

with jucca. So she filled up her mouth with water. She sewed her mouth. She came again, the bird sang,

poo	henge		henge
water	spit it out		spit it out
kina	oguyá	tee	kewena
this is the way		tree	up
tʉ	aaaa		
it says			

She laughed, it hurt her badly. She dropped the water, and began to cry. Then when she came to her house all her children were dead. That is what happened to Coyote.

(*Variant.*) [1]

At Kombuge (some place in an arroyo) lived Coyote old man. Coyote old woman had four babies. She went to Sąwemange [2] to get some water for her babies, She came with water to a place in the brush where sat a bird. The bird was singing for Coyote old woman. She laughed, and dropped the water. She turned back for more water, she came near where the bird was. She was tickled again and laughed and dropped the water. She turned back for more water, she came near where the bird was. She was tickled again and laughed and dropped the water. So she said, "I am not going to laugh any more. " She went after some jucca. She said, " I am going to sew up my mouth and not laugh any more. " She went after water and sewed up her mouth. She came again to the bird. She got tickled again and she broke the stitches and dropped the water. Then she got mad at the bird singing. When she came home all her babies were dead because they were so thirsty. That is all.

64. BORROWED FEATHERS. [3]

The birds were picking up wheat and Coyote old man, Posewᶜa sendo, came and said, " What are you doing ? " — " We are picking up wheat to take it home. " — " Will you let me pick it up ? " — " Yes, if you can. " So he tried to pick it up with his mouth and he could not. And he said, " How do you pick it up ? " He talked hard (roughly) to them. They said, "How roughly he speaks to us ! Next time he speaks, we will fly away. " Coyote could not pick up the wheat. He said, " Little birds, show me how you

1. Informant 3 of Santa Clara. Heard at Tesuque.
2. *Sąwe*, cloud figure ; *mąnge*, flat stone used in making wafer-bread.
3. Informant 2 of San Juan. Heard from Informant 1, also from her husband's brother.

pick that up. " The little birds got scared and flew away. Coyote said, " Little birds, I will not talk so roughly to you. Show me. " Then they came back again. Then Coyote said, " Little birds, show me how to fly like you. I want to be a bird and fly like you. " — " All right, we will show you. " And they took each of them a feather and gave to him. He took them in his hand and he tried to fly and he could not and just fell down. And the birds told him to stand up and he could not. And the birds said, " Did you ever see a coyote fly ? " — " No, ve never saw a coyote fly. Wonder what this coyote is going to do to us ? Let us make him sleep, so we can eat his eyes, " said those birds. So he tried to fly and fly and he got very tired. He said, "*Hewemboharahi*ᶜ! Birds, I am so tired, let me sleep a little. " So he went to sleep. Then they said, " Let us eat his eyes. " Then when he woke up he could not see, he had no eyes, and when they came back they saw him dying. That's why when somebody wants to fly and he can not do it, they say to him, " Maybe you want to die. "

65. FALSE MESSAGE. [1]

At K'uwhanoge [2] was living Coyote old man with Coyote old woman. A little snow fell about this high [indicating half foot.] Coyote old man said, "I better go hunting rabbits, those big ones and small ones. " He went up to the east. He went very far and he met Pindi sendo (Turkey old man). He was going westward, and he met him. He said, " I am fortunate. I am not yet tired and here I find a turkey. I am going to kill it and eat it for supper. " Turkey said, " Yes. I will go to your house that they may cook me. " — " All right. Where I come from there is snow and you can follow my tracks, to Coyote old woman. Tell her to cook you. I will go on hunting for breakfast. " So Turkey went. Coyote said, " I am going on to where there is nice sunshine, and lie down. I don't need to hunt another. " So Turkey was coming. He came to where Coyote old woman lived. So he said, " *Sægitàmu*, Coyote old woman. " She said, " Yes. " Then Turkey said, " Coyote old man told me you had hanging up some sinew (*tsa*); you must take it down and cook it, when he comes back for supper. " So Coyote old woman said, " I wonder why he wants me to cook it ? What will he make moccasins with ? But whoever came here has maybe minded him. I better cook it so when he comes he wont be mad. " So Turkey flew far away, to Shunpikwaiye. [3] Coyote old man was sleeping soundly in the sunshine. In the evening he got up. " I am very hungry, " he said, " I am going to have a good time,

1. Informant 1 of San Juan.
2. A little to the south of San Juan on the east side of the river.
3. In western range, north of Tsikomó.

with lots to eat. " So he went straight to his house, following the tracks. " *Harǫhi*ᶜ ! that turkey was a good turkey. He told me the truth that he would go to my house to be cooked. " He saw the tracks up to the door, and he thought Turkey had gone in. He went in, he said, "I am tired from running after a big rabbit. I could not catch it. " So he got ready to eat. She put out the stew of sinew. He began to eat it. It was very hard. " *Hewemboharǫhi*ᶜ! this turkey is as tough as sinew!" He asked, " Did the old turkey come here to be cooked ?" Coyote old woman said, "Yes, he came, I did not see who it was. He said you said to cook the sinew. "So he said, " *Hewembohara hiʔ*! He cheated me a lot! " That is the way Turkey cheated him.

66. MOCK PLEA. [1]

There were two little rabbits. They went out hunting for something to eat and they came to where Coyote old man was sleeping. " This is my grandfather. Mother (*yiya*) used to tell us Coyote old man was our grandfather. "They said to him, " *Sǫngitsamu*, Grandfather. "— " Where do you come from, Little Rabbits ? *Hewemboharǫhi*ᶜ ! I am so hungry. You have just come in good time for me to eat you. " — "Don't kill us, Grandfather. Don't you know we are your grandchildren (*iʔeteʔe*), and our mother said you were our grandfather, and you want to eat us ! " And they were talking and talking and they ran away, and Coyote old man did not see where they went. Then when they were coming in the evening Coyote saw them. " *Hewemboharǫhi*ᶜ ! here they come. I am going to eat them now. I am going to build a great big fire. " — " *Sǫngitsamu*, grandchildren. You have come at a good time. I am going to cook you. " — " Don't cook us, Grandfather. We will go out hunting and bring you big ones. On that side there are some big ones. "So Coyote caught them and threw them on that side, into some woods. They said, " Thank you where you threw us. This is where we live. Come now, you can't find us. " Coyote cried and cried. " What shall I have to eat ? " he said. " *Hewemboharǫhi*ᶜ! I never make good. They are so little and yet they do whatever they want with me. But next time I see you, I will eat you. I will eat you whenever you come this side again. " That is all.

67. RELAY RACE. [2]

Oweweham'baiyo Little Rabbit came and said to Turtle (*oku*), " Let's run a race and bet on it. I wonder who will beat. " — " I can't run, " said Turtle. " Of course you can, " said Little Rabbit. So they said,

1. Informant 2 of San Juan.
2. Informant 2 of San Juan.

" In four days we must be ready. "On the day they were going to run the race, they went up there. There were two turtles, one went to run on one side, one on the other side. Now those turtles can't run. They said, "One, two, three, four! " And they ran. And Little Rabbit ran as fast as he could and Turtle went quietly along and Little Rabbit said, " Surely I can beat, that Turtle can not run. " Little Rabbit sat down and began to eat cactus fruit. And Turtle went along and he got tired, and another turtle was waiting on the other side. So Rabbit, when he got full of cactus, ran again. That turtle was waiting for him. " I beat you! I beat you ! " said Turtle. " When did you pass ? I did not see you pass. " — " When you were eating cactus fruit. " And Little Rabbit believed him. Turtle killed him and ate him.

68. THE GIVE-AWAY. [1]

Oweweham'baiyo lived a little rabbit (*pu'e*) and he was always going out to hunt for something to eat. So he went out and found some cactus (*tsape*, red on top) and was eating. Then came Coyote old man and said, " I am going to eat you. " — " All right, if you find me to-morrow, you may eat me. " He went away. He said, " I guess I better go after dinner, then Coyote old man will come home. " Coyote was lying down in the sun, asleep. Rabbit said, "*Hewemboharahi*' ! here is Coyote old man, maybe he is waiting for me. Those Coyote when they are dying they move and move, and when they are alive, they don't move. " Then Coyote said, " I guess I better move so he will think I am dying and I can catch him. " So he moved and moved. " That's the thing I want, " said Little Rabbit. " I guess I better go away. Did you ever hear of anybody dying and moving ? I never heard of it, " said Little Rabbit. " Whoever dies doesn't move, doesn't laugh, doesn't smile or do anything. I never saw any dead one do those things. " He ran away. Then Coyote old man got up and ran after him. Then Coyote came into Snake's house and wanted Snake to catch Rabbit for him, he was so tired. Little Rabbit was running and running and wanted to hide here, too. He said, " *Sængitsamu*! Little Hole. If Coyote old man is here, you will say he is not here. If he is not here, you will say he is here. "And then the little hole said, " He is not here, " and he was there. " Did you ever hear the little hole say when Coyote is here that he is not here. I guess Coyote is here. I guess I better run away. " And then Coyote old man went again to a chicken's house, just to ask if the Rabbit had passed by. When Little Rabbit came, he said, "*Sængitsamu* ! Little Chicken, did you see Coyote old man pass ? If he passes, say *kakaa*. If he does not pass, say nothing. " Coyote said to the chicken, " Say nothing. " And he said nothing.

1. Informant 2 of San Juan.

" Did you ever hear when Coyote passes that a chicken says nothing.
I guess I better go away. *Hewembohaṛạhi*[c] ! Coyote runs after me ! "
So he went in the Snake's house, and said again, " *Sǫngitsamu* ! Little
Hole. " And the hole said nothing. So he went in there and hid. And
Coyote came to the same place. " Has my little rabbit come, Little
Hole ? " Little Hole said nothing. And then came the snake and tried
to go in ; and Little Rabbit piled up stones in the door and the snake
could not go in. Then the snake got mad and bit Coyote, and then the
snake went to look for another house, and Coyote old man swelled up
and died. That is all. *Hu*[‘] !

69. GUM IMAGE. [1]

Owewehǫdita, long ago lived a man. He planted a melon patch.
Somebody was stealing from it, he did not know who. After some
time he began to think how he could catch the one who came to steal.
He went up to the hills and got some piñon gum. He brought the
gum and melted it well and put it on a piece of wood, and put that
at the entrance to the melon patch. That night Rabbit came to where
that gum was. So Rabbit asked him, " What are you doing, my
friend ?"It never said anything. He asked again. It never said anything. Rabbit said, " If you don't say anything, I am going to hit you. "
He asked again, it never said anything. He hit him with his right hand.
It stuck. He said, " Turn me loose. If you don't turn me loose, I
will hit you with my left hand. " He hit him with his left hand. It
stuck. "Turn me loose! If you don't turn me loose, I will hit you with
my foot. " He hit him with his right foot. It stuck. "Turn me loose.
If you don't, I will hit you with my left foot. " It stuck. So he was
stuck all over. So next morning came that man, the rabbit was sticking
to that *po*. That man took the rabbit, he told him, "You are the one
come to steal the melons. I am going to eat you now. " From then
on we never steal melons. That is all.

70. STONE FIGURES NEAR TAOS. [2]

The people were a little way from Taos, they said, " It does not
matter if God does not want it, we are going to Taos today. " They
were turned to stone, sitting in a circle they were turned to stone, with
their babies on their back. Those who believed were all right and
later went on. If stones were taken from those stone figures, the stones

1. Informant 3 of Santa Clara.
2. Informant 3 of Santa Clara. Heard from his adoptive mother, a Taos woman
married into Santa Clara.

would leave the house, or would make rain fall on the house and flood them and make them leak.

71. AN APACHE VISION. [1]

This Apache was hunting up in the mountains. He heard somebody singing. He thought it might be some kind of Ute or Kaiowa. He went there. He found somebody lying down with his arms crossed above his head. It was Ohụ (white tailed deer) that Apache told my father. He sang the song to my father and I heard it. I was a little boy then, and I have forgotten the song. " White tailed deer are people, " said that Apache. That is why Apache do not eat white tailed deer, they are people.

72. NAVAHO HIDE HORSE TRACKS. [2]

One year Navaho stole some horses in the mountains. The snow was so high [indicating half foot]. They stole lots of horses, and the Tewa started after them. They went into the big moutains where there were lots of big trees. There they lost the tracks. They searched for them, they said, " Wonder where they took the horses, underground or up into the sky flying ? " The Navaho had driven the horses on top of the fallen trees, jumping them from one fallen tree to another, so on the ground there were no tracks... After they stole horses Navaho would make wind and snow, through their *pinang*. They had arrow-points, large ones, and they made wind by waving these arrow-points around this way [sunwise circuit]. That is the way they did, long ago, the old men said.

73. NAVAHO PARACHUTE. [3]

The Navaho used to steal cattle and horses and boys [4] out herding. The Navaho had lots of *pinang*. [5] One time after a raid San Juan men

1. Informant 1 of San Juan. This is a very interesting reference to the vision and supernatural helper of Plains type.
2. Informant 7 of San Juan.
3. Informant 1 of San Juan. Cp. the Acoma story of the parachutic escape of the Franciscan friars at the time of the Great Rebellion.
4. The Tewa also took captives. The father of the narrator had a Navaho boy captive. " He was a good boy. We treated him like a brother. "
5. I had been telling of the Navaho method of finding lost articles known to certain men at Zuñi. See Parsons 14. This was unfamiliar ; but that the Navaho were efficient in magic was familiar.

I happened to go from San Juan to Zuñi the day after, and there I heard that a string of beads had been lost and was being looked for by the Navaho method of detection.

went in pursuit of the Navaho. They saw their tracks. The chief chose three good strong boys to go up on the mesa to hunt the Navaho. The boys went up in the single place they could go up. They saw fresh tracks. Except the place they went up all the other sides were sheer. The Navaho were on top, the Tewa behind them at the only place of ascent or descent. There were three Navaho and three Tewa. The Navaho were running, and after them the Tewa. The Tewa said, " If they go to the edge of the mesa, they will have to fall off. " The Navaho had blankets, tied around their middle. At the edge of the mesa, each man spread out his blanket, his arms stretched out like wings, and they went down the side of the mesa very slowly and softly, and got away. They had lots of *pinang*, but the wind buoyed them up, too.

74. EXPERIENCE WITH A SKUNK. [1]

When I was a big boy, I was taking care of cows with five other boys. A skunk came out. We did not know it was one. We ran after it. " I am going to catch it first, " said one boy. " I am going to catch it, " said another boy. There was lots of jucca, and the skunk went in there. They ran after it. Skunk turned. The boys passed, but the last boy saw where Skunk had turned and caught Skunk by the tail. Then Skunk *threw it.* The boy cried out he could not walk, he could not open his eyes, he was covered with yellow. The boys were holding him by the hand, leading him. They all smelled of skunk. They picked up chips and rags and set them on fire and told us to stand up and be smoked. That one boy was pretty nearly blinded. He shut his eyes just in time not to be blinded altogether. When my father came, he scolded all of us. When we came to the house our mother would not let us come in. That's the way it passed.

75. SNAKE STORY. [2]

We went up north, herding cattle. A little Mexican boy was with us. He saw a snake eating a *kolohe'.* [3] He called, we ran up, we saw the legs of the *kolohe'* going down the snake. We got stones to kill the snake. One of the bigger boys said, " Don't kill him yet, until he eats it all. Then we will kill it. " The snake got big in the middle. We stood around looking at it. The snake was turning on one side, it

1. Informant 1 of San Juan.
2. Informant 1 of San Juan.
3. In Mexican, *molendeira*, grinder, from the way it moves its head back and forward as if grinding, when hit on the head. It is brown-yellow, the size of a match box, with horns. It is the horned lizard. (Henderson and Harrington, 48.)

burst open, the snake, and that *korohe* came out still living, almost living, and slapping its horns. Then the snake died.

76. ABOUT THE PENITENTES. [1]

The *penitente major* was Cata sendo, a pure Indian of San Juan. [2] He had a large house at San Juan... They made a *penita* (skeleton) of an old woman, from sticks, and placed it in a little wagon. And they had a skull. That skeleton has arrows in her hands. In Cata's lifetime that skeleton was kept in his own big house where they met. After he died the skeleton was taken up here to Alcalde to the *morada*. [3]

When a *penitente* is in hard times, if he is out of wood, etc., he tells them, and they help him. When Cata was going to cut his wheat and get in his corn, lots of them (Mexicans) would go over and help him. When somebody dies who belongs to them, they get money from the *major* and buy meal and meat to eat that night. When Cata died, in the night when they were going to bury him, they took him in the church and then around San Juan four times, carrying him on a ladder. Four men carried him, the others prayed. Then they took him into his house again. Cata's children did nothing, those *penitente* cared for him. Next day they carried him to the graveyard.

Easter day, San Juan people come to see the *penitente* procession. *Penita kwiyo* is sitting outside the *morada*. They carry crosses, two men, two crosses, just one man behind, whipping himself. They do not hang anybody to their crosses. They say they lay a man down on the cross on the ground; but they do not hang him nor raise the cross.

1. Informant 1 of San Juan.
2. He died before the informant, a man of sixty, was born.
3. The meeting house and sanctuary of the organization.

PART II. TEWA OF ARIZONA.

Emergence and Migration Tales.

I. THE EMERGENCE. [1]

When they were way underneath they were ants. Then they came to another place and turned into other creatures. At another place they became like people but with long tails. They knew they had tails and were ashamed about it.

They had a flood there and they were crazy. The flood kept on coming and they tried to reach the sky, and they built a tower, but it fell down. Then the women said they would build a tower to reach the sky. They were very crazy, the women would not mind their husbands. They said, "We are not living because we are married. (We are not dependent on marriage to live)." There was a river and they divided, and the men went across the river, and the women stayed where they had been before, at their village. In springtime the women planted their corn and melons by themselves, and the men planted, too. The men raised lots of crops, and the women, too. But next year the women raised only half of what they raised before. That flood was coming from every direction, they knew the flood would kill them. Yet they carried on their work. In the third year, the women got very little corn and melons, but the men got more than before. In the fourth year the women had no crops, but the men had large crops. They were calling from the women's side to the men's, "Throw us some corn, some watermelons," the women said. "We can't throw anything to you," the men said. About that time the flood was coming closer and closer, and the women began to build a tower. They built and built, but they never reached the sky. The women thought they were braver than the men, smarter than the men; but the men thought women could not do much. The tower fell down again. Then the men began to think about it, the flood kept on coming. They were thinking about what would reach the sky. First they planted pine, it grew and reached the sky, but could not go through. Next they planted reeds.

1. The narrator was aware of the Hopi origin of this tale. He was ignorant of any corresponding Tewa tale.

They planted reeds, and sang a song to make the reeds grow. Then they began to grow. They sang and sang, and they grew and grew and the reeds reached the sky and went through. It was Badger they sent first, [1] and he stepped on the reeds and went up and up and up. Pretty soon Badger went through and was looking around. But there was not enough light to see. Then Badger went back. " What did you see ? " said the men. "Did you find the earth ? " said the men. " I could not see much up there. It was dark. " Under there where they were living, there was only a little light, and so they did not know yet that they had long tails. " From today in four days we go up, " said the head man. Then just when the flood was close to their village, they went up, they all went up. Then when they came up, it was dark. While they were coming out, Mocking bird was sitting right close to the hole where the people were coming out. He gave them a language. That is how they got their language. The women went to the place where the men went up, and they followed the men, so the women came out last, but not all of them, only about half went up on the reeds before the flood came and drowned the other half.

When they came out, that time they came out with no tails. There was no light. So they thought about it by the hole where they came out. Now they could talk. They said, " How can we get a light ? " One said, " We will make stars. " So they made stars. Coyote was sitting with them (different kinds of animals came out with them), he could understand them, but he could not talk. They sent two boys and said to them " When you go to a certain place, put these stars in a good shape. " Coyote said, " I will go with the two boys. " When they came to the stars, they put the seven together (*tsubauta'kama*), the Pleiades, in good shape, and those six (*hutu̧-kama*) [2], they put them together, and the biggest one they put towards the east, and one they put on the south side, and one on the west side, and one on the north side. Then they put up *sopöchkoho* (Dipper). Just when they had put all these up, Coyote said to himself, " It is a great big work." He said to the boys, " We never will finish this work, we will all die, why can't we do this? " Then he took the stars and threw them in every direction, in a bad shape. So they came back, the boys and Coyote. Next night they were watching and they saw the Big Star come out, before daylight. That will be *talesoyö* (Dawn Star : in Tewa, *agoyosoyu*). Soon another star came out from the south. Then they said, " We will call that star *ponu'chona* (in Tewa also *agoyosoyu*). " Then there were two came up, but did not give much light. When they were going down in the west, another big star was going ahead of them. " We will give him a

1. Cp. the Northern Tewa account of first sending Wildcat.
2. Orion.

name, " they said. " We will call him *tasupi*, " [1] they said. About that
time a north star came out. " We give him a name in Tewa *wöku'soyu.*"
About that time the Pleiades came out from the east, then the six came
out, it began to get cold. They did not give much light. Then they
saw stars scattered all over the sky. Then the people said, " Bad
Coyote, you did that ? " — " Yes, " he said. " If you had not gone
with them, all the stars would be in good shape. But you are bad
Coyote, you scattered them all over the sky. " They were very
angry. But Coyote said, " That's all right. It's lots of work to put
them all in good shape, better to scatter them around. " Well, those
stars did not give much light, so they thought about what they could do
for more light. So one of them said, " We will make Moon. " They
asked him what they could make it of. Then he said, " We will make
it of the wedding blanket. " So they sent those same boys who put
up the stars. They took that wedding blanket, and put it up in
some way, and went back home. They were watching it. Then they
saw a light coming out and it was Moon and they gave it a name,
möyawö. It gave them some light, but not enough, they said. Then they
thought about it again. One man found a way. " We will make
something else for a better light, " he said. He took a blanket and a
buckskin and a white foxskin and a parrot tail, and he sent the same
two boys (they did not know who those boys were — they were
brave boys), and they took the things to the east and they put them
up in some way, somehow. Well, when the moon came out and
went down, about the time daylight would first come, out came the
foxskin for daylight, next out came the parrot tail, making it yellow.
Then the sun came out, but it could not move. Then the people were
talking, " Something is wrong. Why can it not move ? " Then
they asked each other, " What can make it go ? " At last Coyote said,
" Nothing wrong with it. All is fixed as it should be. Nothing
wrong, but if somebody should die right now, then it would
move. " Then just there a girl died and the sun began to move.
When it got to the middle of the sky, it stopped again. " Well, what
is the matter ? " they asked again. Coyote said, " Nothing is the matter, nothing is wrong. If somebody die right now, it will move. "
Then the son of one of the head men died, and that made the sun go
again. " It is only by somebody dying every day, — morning, noon
and evening, — that will make the sun move every day, " said
Coyote. — Coyote thinks more than anybody. Smart fellow ! —
Then everything was fixed.

First a girl died, then a boy, then a woman died. After four days
she came back again. Well, if somebody dies, in four days they will
come back again. Then Coyote said, " I don't think that will be right

1. Equated with the Tewa star called Gray haired old woman. Cp. pp. 23, 116.

for us. If we die and come back in four days, we won't be afraid to die, " said Coyote. " That wont do any good. We will be living all the time. That wont do any good, " said Coyote. " I will die and never come back."Then he over-ate and died, and after four days he did not come back. He never came back. About that time another woman died and they counted four days, but she did not come back again, just because Coyote died and did not come back. This made the people feel very bad. The husband of the woman was very unhappy and he went back to the place where they came out ; they had put a round cactus over the hole they had come out. He pulled away the cactus and looked down into the hole. His wife was way down underneath, she was combing her hair. [1] And there was Coyote there too, he heard something and he raised up his head and said, " You know I am dead and your wife was dead too, but we came back here. And after this when anybody dies hew ill come back here and live forever. So do not feel so bad about your wife, "said Coyote to that man. Then the man closed the hole and told them how his wife was down there and he went back to the people and also Coyote.

Well, those two boys, they did not know who they were. Underneath, while they were living separate, the men and the women, a man killed a deer and cut the neck, and the blood came out, and they poured it into a gourd. Two men were brothers. Younger brother told older brother, " Well, you do the business while the blood is still warm. " They made a baby inside of the gourd cup and then they put the cup by the fire and kept it warm. And after a time two babies came out, two boys. And so those are the ones who were making the stars and moon and sun. So the people found out who they were. " Who is your father and who is your mother ? " the people asked. The first one said, " I am *Pöökong.* " The other said, " I am *Palüngawiya, "* he said. And *Pöökong* said, "I am the son of the Sun. I am Sunbeam's son, " he said. The second one said, " I am Water dripping's son, " he said ? " That is my father," he said, " and so my name is *Palüngawiya.* "

(15. *Variant.*)[2]

The people had been living way down underneath. There were black ants living down there. Those were the people then. Afterwards they came up on the earth. Then they turned into another kind of creatures. They had tails. From there they went up to a third world. Here they began to turn into people.

They were living there, but they had no light. That is the way

1. Cp. p. 22.
2. Recorded by Ruth Bunzel a few months before the preceding tale was recorded from the same informant.

they were living. They were all crazy. They had only a little light like moonlight. The first world was all dark and the second world a little bit light. The third world was like moonlight. When they were in the third world they were all crazy. They took their wives away from one another. A man married one woman one day and after a few days left the woman and married another. They were all like that. Finally the women said, " We can get along without men. We are not living just because the men are living. We can do our work and get along without any man, " said the women. They were fighting there and they separated, the men and the women. There was a river and the men crossed the river and the women stayed where they were. The men lived on one side and the women on the other side. They were close together but on opposite sides of the river. The first year the women raised good crops. The second year they only raised about half of this crop. The third year they raised about a third and the fourth year they did not raise anything. Then the women got tired. The men raised good crops, corn and peaches and everything. They got along without the women. They were used to it and did not care about the women. They cooked for themselves and did all things for themselves. About that time the women said, " Let us erect a tower. We have sense enough to build a tower and go up to the other earth. " They began to build it, but they never reached the sky. The tower fell down. Then they got tired and needed the men. They needed children. They had to have children. They could not get along without men. " How can we get children, " said the women, " if we go on living alone without men ? We need children. The men are living by themselves. They have no women or girls, but they are getting along all right. " After that a flood came. The flood came to destroy the whole village. The whole earth was flooded. Then the people began to think how they could save themselves. Then they planted a reed. Then they sang a song. They kept on singing and soon it began to grow. It grew up and up and up and up until it reached the sky. Then Badger said, " Let us go. " He climbed first. When the reed reached the sky it kept on growing up until it came through the earth to this world. The people kept on coming up inside of the reed. They came up to this earth. They came out. They all came out. Soon they were all out. But there were no women. Then they shut up the reed to stop the people from coming up. Then the Bear came and separated the people and gave them languages. The Bear separated one people from another and gave each one their language. That is the way they got their different languages.

They were up on this earth. It was not very light. They began to make stars to make it lighter. Then the head man put them on something and put the stars in a row. They arranged the stars in the constellations and fixed them in good shape. While they were doing this,

Coyote came along. " What are you doing this for ? It is a hard job.
You will never finish this. You can never finish it. I will do it for
you. " So he took them and threw them up and scattered them all
around. That is the way they finished it. That is why the stars are
not all in good shape. If Coyote had not done that, the stars would
have looked better in the sky. After they were finished with the stars,
they did not give much light. Then they thought, " What will give
us good light ? " Then they made a moon. They made a wedding
blanket (*kwatckiappa*). They made it into a moon. It was made ot
cotton and was all white. Then they sent up the moon and put it in
the sky to give them light. They finished. The moon came out, but
it did not give good light for the whole world. Then they thought,
" What next ? " Then they made the sun. In the morning it came
out. It just came above the horizon but it never came all the way.
Only a little of the sun came out and never any more. Then the
people and the birds and the animals were through making it. All
the creatures were tired of working together. The sun came out but
it never got far. Then a smart fellow (Mocking Bird) said, " If
someone should die this morning, the sun would move on. You must
do that for the sun to go on. " The daughter of the head man was
there. The head man's daughter died and they all felt sorry. Then the
sun began to rise. That is the way the sun goes. Then they said,
" Every day, every morning or afternoon or night, a person will have
to die, and that will make the sun go, " said the Mocking Bird. The
head man was sorry on account of his daughter and someone told
him, " You just look right down back into the hole where we came
out. " So the head man looked in the ground where they had come
out and way down in the bottom of the earth was the daughter of the
head man combing her hair. " Now after this whenever a person dies
he has to go down there where we came out and live there forever. "
One man said this. Then after that the head man did not feel so sorry.

After a time the people separated. The Navahos got their language
and went to the Navaho country. All the different Indians got their
languages. They put up the kind of houses they were going to live
in. The Hopi Indians and the Pueblo Indians put up their houses in
villages the way they were going to live. The Navahos put together
sticks and made a hogan. The Pimas and Supais and Mohaves put up
a few sticks and lived that way. All the different kinds of Indians put
up the kind of buildings they were going to live in.

The people were not afraid to die. They knew that when they died
they would go back to where they had come from and come back
after a time. Then Coyote said, " I am going to die, and I won't come
back. " Then he ate and ate and ate until he was sick and he died
and he never came back any more. After that the people did not
come back after they died. Before that they used to come back, but after
Coyote died they never came back any more.

After many years they began to move from where they had come out in the east. For many years they lived there. Then they started and went. They do not say where they stopped for many years, until they came to this place. The Bear people came from the east. They came to Walpi in the morning and the Coyote clan came in the afternoon. That is the way the Coyote clan and the Bear clan came here. They were the first ones to come. They came and looked around and saw a track. Someone [1] had been living here. They saw only one track. Next day the Snake clan came. Therefore the head man always belongs to the Bear clan. The Coyote clan has the next head man and Snake clan the next head man. That is all I know about it.

2. THE MIGRATION OF THE TEWA FROM THE EAST.

I

Bear [2], Snake, and Coyote chiefs were talking about their enemies, many enemies. One said, " I heard that Tewa people are living in the East, who are good fighters. Could we get them to fight for us ? " The two others said that would be good. Next day they made prayer-sticks, and Snake clan boy and Bear clan boy were sent to look for the Tewa, at Ch'æwage. They reached Ch'æwage and asked for their chief. They went to his house. He was very much surprised. " Who are you ? " he said. " We are from Walpi, " they said. " We have come to get the Tewa people to come and fight our enemies. " — " No, I do not want my children to be killed. I cannot let you have them. " The boys said, " Bear clan chief sent us, also Snake clan chief, also Coyote clan chief. " — " Yes, but I cannot let you have my children, " he said. After that they went home and told those chiefs. They sent them again. They reached Ch'æwage and asked for their chief. They went to his house. He was very much surprised. " Who are you ? " he said. " We are from Walpi, " they said. " We have come to get the Tewa people to come and fight our enemies. All the Hopi are getting killed. We want you to come and help. " — " No, I don't want my children to be killed. I cannot let you have them. " The boys said, " Bear clan chief sent us, also Snake clan chief, also Coyote clan chief. " — " Yes, but I can't let you have my children, " he said. When they got back home, the chief asked what the Tewa chief had said. " I can't let you have my children. " They sent them again. They asked the chief again, and he said the same thing again. The third time they went back and reported the same thing. The fourth time the three chiefs made prayer-sticks again,

1. No doubt Skeleton is referred to. Cp. Cushing 2 : 165.
2. Cp. Fewkes 3 : 614.

eight prayer-sticks. " Now, " they said to the boys, " go and give those prayers-sticks to the Tewa chief, and ask for his children. This will be the last time. " They went to Ch'ǽwage and asked for their chief. They went to his house. He was very much surprised. " Who are you ? " he said. " We are from Walpi, " they said. " We have come to get the Tewa people to come and fight our enemies. " — " No, I don't want my children to be killed. I can't let you have them. " The boys said, " Bear clan chief sent us, also Snake clan chief, also Coyote. " — " Yes, but I can't let you have my children. What have you brought ? " and there were eight prayer-sticks. " All right, half of my people I will send to you, " he said. " We wont do any harm to your people, " they said. So next morning he called out, " Who wants to go to Kosoówinge, may go, in four days. " So they talked it over among themselves. The fourth day he called again. " Who wants to go may go, but not *all*. " But all wanted to go. So they started, and went a long time, and finally they got to the foot of the mesa. Then the three chiefs came out to meet them. " Have you come ? " — " Yes. " — " We wanted you to come to help us, but you cannot go up on the mesa, but stay right here. " They felt bad over this. Then the three men went back onto the mesa. At the foot they lived many days. Then some enemies were coming, and the three chiefs came and told them enemies were coming. Then they dressed up. Lots of Utes were coming. " You have to fight with those Utes, " said the three chiefs. " If you drive them back, there from the gap east, all this land we will let you have. " They made them say this four times. They went and fought with the Utes and drove them back. At Sikwi'töyoka [1] (Tewa, Tochyoowidi chyoo), they drove them back, then they left their food and their women. Their food was all meat. So they called that point Tochyoowidi. From there they drove them back, killing them and driving them to Wipo canyon. There was a place where there was a rock fence. By there they killed all but one boy. [2] The Tewa told him to go back and tell his people all were killed but him. The Ute boy said, " I do not want to go back alone. No use for me to go. I want to be killed. " Four times he said this. The fourth time he said, " I will never fight against you again, " he said. He said this four times. Then he gave his bow and arrows to the Tewa. " If ever Utes fight with you again, use my bow and arrow. You are the best fighters, " he said. " Utes are the best fighters, but you beat them, " he said. Then he went on. They made a stone fence there to show that so far they had driven the Utes. They came back. The three chiefs met them and said, " Thank you, you fought for us, " they said. " Yes, we killed all the Utes but one boy, but he will

1. Cp. Fewkes 3 : 616.
2. Cp. Harrington : 257.

never fight against you again. " Then the three chiefs pointed out the land. " This will be your land, " they said. After that they brought them up on top of the mesa, and gave them the place they are now living in. Here they were to be watchers for the Hopi. This is a real talk that they handed to each other, the old people say.

II

At Ch'ǽwage Tewa people were living. They had a big village. They had lots of game. They had troubles together through their games. One kiva (*te'e*) was a witch kiva and they beat all the others in the games. Everybody was getting crazy about it. Spider woman was living close to the village with her grandson, Pati'e'enu. Witch kiva was going to have a dance at night and called it out for eight days, a dance or tricks of some kind. Spider woman heard about it and she was very unhappy about it. They called it in the morning, in the evening she was very unhappy. Her grandson asked, " Grandmother, what makes you unhappy ? " He asked four times. " Yes, my grandson, in eight days the Witch people are going to do tricks in their kiva and there will be no more people ; I love my children and there will be no way to save them. The Witch people are very smart, and they will kill all the people. " Next morning Pati'e'enu went out to trap mice, on which they were living. He found some green grass growing under a rock, and it was *elu poye* (hidden ball moon, i. e. January). " Now I will be ahead of those Witch people. There are no other green things at this time of year. " Then he pulled up the grass and with the clay took it to his grandmother. " Grandmother, I will beat those Witch people. There wont be any green things at this time of year. " Grandmother just laughed. " Poor grandson, " she said, " poor grandson, that is nothing for those Witch people. They are not going to do any little thing, they are going to do the biggest thing. No way to save the people. " (The Witch people were going to have the plants grow just as Pati'e'enu did. Then they were going to call Avaiyu, [1] they had him under the floor, and he was going to bring the flood.) Next morning Pati'e'enu went out to look over his traps. Then he saw a yellow butterfly sitting on his trap. " That is a wonderful thing. I must catch it and show it to those Witch people. There wont be any butterflies at this time of year, " he said to himself. So he spoke to the butterfly, " Sit still there, sit still there, I will catch you and take you to my house, so I will beat those Witch people. " But the butterfly flew off to a rock. He went up to it and tried to catch it again.

---

1. Horned water serpent. " We ask Avaiyu for rain, just as we ask Oku'wa. Maybe there are four Avaiyu, red, white, black (no yellow).

Butterfly flew away again. That way Butterfly led Pati'e'enu on, flying a little way, alighting, then flying a little way again. Pati'e'enu did not know he was going so far. Butterfly looked as if it were growing tired. Pretty soon Butterfly came to a big jucca plant (*pahla*) and Butterfly went inside. Pati'e'enu looked, but he could not see Butterfly. He pulled up the jucca plant and there were a hole and a kiva. He was surprised and frightened. He looked in, there were people in there. " Come in, " they said. He was afraid. " Come in, " they said. So he went in, and they gave him a seat. There was a girl sitting on one side of the room. She was making a fan of cloth to cool herself, the sweat was running down her face. There were lots of good-looking people in there, girls and women and men. They all looked alike, they looked yellow. There was a big man sitting by the fireplace. " My son, " he said, " I sent this girl to you because a big trouble is coming, in six days from today. Those Witch people are going to kill all in the village. They have been having lots of games and now there is going to be a big flood. That is why I sent the girl after you. Now we are going to tell you what to tell your grandmother so you can do it that night in the kiva. " Then they gave him good food, watermelon and muskmelon and wafer-bread (*piki*). And they told him what to do and gave him melons and wafer-bread. So he went back home, pleased to have seen the people he had never seen before. They told him when he went back not to show the melons outdoors, but if somebody came and smelled the melons, if it was a woman and she asked if they had melons, not to tell her. " In six days in the morning you have to come back here. " In the evening, when he got back, he told his grandmother to come out and get something. But she did not believe him, there was nothing anywhere for him to get. He called her four times. Then she went out and got the watermelons and the muskmelons and the Hopi wafer-bread roll (*ma'kano*). She was surprised, but she knew where he got it. Still she asked, " Where did you get it ? " Then Pati'e'enu told it all. " That was at *pokwinge* (lake) and those *Oku'wa* people were living under the lake. " He told his grandmother, " In six more days in the afternoon they want me to come there and we will make some prayer-feathers (*pehlechidi*). Of course we have no turkey feathers or other feathers. In the morning we will wash our heads and bathe ourselves. Then I will go and ask the Witch peoples for turkey feathers, but they will not give me any. " After six days in the morning they were washing their heads, and then an old woman came in and asked them why they were washing their heads. Then the grandmother said to the old woman, " They are going to have a trial (*ibiye'yętoh*) tonight and we have to go over to witch kiva (*kyugete*). " — " I will go with you, " said the old woman. " If anything happens, we shall be all together. " Spider woman said, " Go back to your house and wash your head and come back here. "

(This old woman was one of the Spider people, too.) So she went and washed her head and bathed and came back. Spider Woman said to Pati'e'enu, " Go over to the Witch kiva and ask them for turkey feathers. " So he went. He called down, " Have you any extra turkey feathers ? " So the old man called back, " No, we have no extra turkey feathers, we are using them all, " they said. Then he went back to his grandmother. Grandmother said to him again, " Go and ask them there for some yellow bird feathers (*chidepo'*). " So he went and asked again. But they said again they had no extra feathers. So he went back to his house. Finally his grandmother said, " I think I still have some feathers. " So she looked in the back room, she went and found some turkey feathers. " I think I have some yellow bird feathers. " She went and looked and found some. Then they began to make prayer-feathers, and when they finished them they smoked over them. " Now it is time for you to take those prayer-fathers where you were before, " she said. So he took the prayer-fathers where he had been. Then he removed the jucca plant, and went in. They gave him a place to sit and then the large man gave him a smoke. After he finished smoking, they gave him something to eat. After he finished eating, he untied the prayer-fathers. He picked out one and gave it to the large man first and then one to each in the house. He had enough and more. " What is left is for our altar (*owing*), " said the the large man. He gave them to him. " Thank you, " he said. " Now you must go back, and get ready. Then you must go to every house and ask for dance kilts (*wage*), " he said. " But they wont let you have them ; but it's all right if they wont let you have them. " He went back. Grandmother said, " It is about time for us to get ready. " — " Yes, and we must go around the houses to ask for a dance kilt for me, " he said. So he and his grandmother went to every house, asking for a kilt ; but nobody let them have one. These Witch people were living on one side of the village. Spider Grandmother went into a house, a boy was living there. " My grandson, " she said, " you go around to every house on this side, to those who do not belong to the Witch people, and tell them not to go to the Witch people's kiva. Mind me, something is going to happen, and I want you to be safe. Let only the Witch people go to their kiva. " So they went back home, and Pati'e'enu had nothing to wear. So they put some whitening in a bowl and made a design on Pati'e'enu instead of a kilt. Then they went to the Witch kiva and the people laughed at them, and they got sticks to kill Spider woman and her grandson and the other old woman. They were in there, kiva chief (*te'e toyu'*) said it was time for them to dance. " I guess you are coming to dance. " — " We have nothing to dance, " said Spider Grandmother, " but I guess we can see something. " So she took ashes in her hand and threw them (with a slicing motion) and said, " *Tubahai !* it is too dark, I don't see

anything. You try, grandson, " she said. So Pati'e'enu took some
ashes and threw them and said, " *Tubahai !* There is a fog (*sobakua*), "
he said. " Now your turn, grandmother. " She took out ashes. " You
saw nothing but fog, but a tiny thing is under the fog. " Now the
other grandmother took up ashes. " Two of them are walking. "
Pati'e'enu said, " Lots of them are walking. " " Try again, " said
Pati'e'enu to the other grandmother. " Let's kill them, " said the
people. They were very angry. " They wont see anybody. " But the
Kiva chief said, " Let them finish it. " So they threw the ashes
again. Pretty soon on top of the kiva there was a noise. " Well, come
in, " said Spider, and the boy said, " Come in, " and the other grandmother and the Kiva chief said, " Come in. " So the Oku'wa came
in and spread out some sand on the floor and planted some seeds, and
made some rain. Then they began to dance, and as they danced the
plants grew. Pretty soon the watermelon was ripe. They cut it up and
gave it to Spider, " You eat this, " they said. " Thank you, " said Spider.
Pretty soon everything was ripe, watermelons and corn and beans,
and the dance was over and the Oku'wa went out. And Spider and
Pati'e'enu and the other grandmother gathered up all the melons and
beans and corn, and went out of the kiva. Then the Oku'wa sent
lightning into the kiva and killed all the Witch people in there. Then
they got cacti and closed the kiva with it, and Pati'e'enu blew on the
cacti and froze it tight so they could not come out. Next day Tokei-
toyo, Crier chief, called out to get ready in four days. " We have to
move away from this place, " he said. So they all heard and got ready.
In four days in the morning he called out again, " Today we are
going to move, so whatever you have, you take along. " So from there
they started out to go to Kosoo'winge. [1]

At the time they killed the witches, a witch woman was at her house
with a baby, and she did not get killed. That is the reason there are
witches now. That baby grew up and became a witch, and taught
others to be witches.

They went on their way till they got to Gawai'ka (Laguna). They
left some people there. The others kept on going. Then they got to
Koshawae [2] po'o [3] (Rock spring). About that time they saw something
going ahead of them. It looked white. So they sent a boy to overtake
it and see what it was. The boy went and overtook the big white
thing. It was a house that two mice (*chet'awin*) were pulling. He looked at that house and there was somebody looking out of the window. It was a girl, Yoopobiayo (cactus flower girl). " I am going on

1. Hopi town, Tewa for Walpi. The mesa as a whole is called Tsihtokwi
(Flower Mountain) by the Hopi; Pobiping by the Tewa.
2. Obsolete.
3. Some place between Fort Defiance and Keam's Canyon.

my way to Kosoo'winge, " she said. She had started after the people, but now she was on ahead. The boy went back to the people. " What was that white thing ? " — " It was a house and two mice were draging it, " he said. " And who in it ? " — " Cactus flower girl. " Some said she was at home when they started. They overtook the white house, and Cactus flower girl was ahead as their chief woman (*toyo'-kwiyo*). So they went till they got to Kosoo'winge and they left the house at Tewa to be her home. Then she got ready for *tantai'*. [1] This is the reason they have *tantai'*, because Cactus flower girl brought it for the people. She sang the songs they still have. [2]

3. THE MIGRATION OF THE HOPI FROM PALATKWABI. [3]

The Hopi people were living at Palatkwabi. There were lots of Hopi living there, there were Sand clan (*tewanyamu*), Rabbit clan (*tap-nyamu*) and *patkinyamu*. They were very crazy in everything. They gambled a lot, that made them crazy, and also they danced a great deal at night, the girls were dancing most of the time. In *pamuye* (February) they were going to have a girls' dance, and the wife of the Town chief (*gigmungi*) went to the kiva without asking him. He went every night to his mother's house to smoke. While he was gone, his wife went to the kiva where they were practising. When he left his own house, he came back to his wife's house and she was not there, but he did not think to look for her, he just let her go, he knew she was crazy like the other people. He knew that the people were crazy. So he was thinking about what he could do with his children (the people). They were doing lots of bad things. Whenever they met an old man, they just spit on him. When · they met anybody carrying water, they would spill the water. And the men were crazy about the girls and women. These things Town chief was thinking about, he did not sleep for thinking about them. Next night he went to his house again and his wife went to the kiva where they were practising. When he came back to his wife's house, his wife was gone again. He thought he must go to bed then, and so he did. While he was lying down, his wife came ; she was very happy, and she told her husband what a good time they had. That was all right, he said, that she should go and make herself happy where they were dancing. So four nights she went. The fifth morning Town chief got up and got his corn meal and went out and prayed to the Sun. When he came back, his son was there. He told his son, " After we eat our breakfast, you go over to your aunt's house. I will be there. " So after

---

1. Winter solstice ceremony.
2. Because they got the ceremony from a woman, formerly girls of the Bear, Corn, and Tobacco clans used to go into Mona kiva the night the men made prayer-feathers.
3. Cp. Cushing, 165.

they ate their breakfast, the boy went over to his father's house. His father was there smoking. Then the boy went in and sat down by his father, and his father gave the pipe to him and he smoked and passed it back to his son. " My son, " he said, " tomorrow morning do you run around the big mountain south of Palatkwabi. Do your best. You cannot go around the mountain at first, but go as far as you can. " So, early in the morning the boy went and ran down south of the village, but he could not reach that mountain. He was very tired when he came back. " I can not reach that mountain, " he said to his father. " You keep on trying, " his father said. " Some day you will be able to go around that mountain. " So, next morning early he got up and ran down from the village again and went south, as fast as he could, and this time he reached the mountain, then he got tired and came back home. When he came back, his father asked him, " How far did you go? " The boy said, "I got just to the foot of the mountain. " — " You did pretty well, keep on trying, " said the father to the boy. Next morning he ran again, as fast as he could, and this time he got way around the mountain; then he got tired and went back home. " How far did you go? " asked the man. "I went part way around the mountain, but then I got tired, " said the boy. Next morning he got up and ran down again and ran as fast as he could and did not tire and came back home — that was the fourth morning. His father asked him, " How did you make it? " — " Yes, I went all round the mountain and did not get tired. " — " You did well, my son, " said the father. "Tomorrow morning you go out to the west and look for antelopes, " he said, "The antelopes (*chōbiwō*) live always in the flat land, not up in the mountains. That is why you have been practising running, " he said. " When you find the antelopes, look for one with two prongs, and chase that one. " So next morning the boy went out and before sunrise he found some antelopes, and they all stood and looked at the boy, and then they started to run. The one that had two prongs he chased him. This antelope separated from the others and ran towards the big mountain. The boy ran after him and near the big mountain he caught the antelope. When he caught him, the antelope cried. "Never mind crying, " said the boy. Then he took out his knife and while the antelope was alive, he cut off the horn. Then he took four prayer-feathers and tied them around the antelope's neck, and two beads, one turquoise and one white, were tied to the string. Then the boy ran back home as fast as he could. Soon after sunrise he came back with the horn. His father was very glad. " This is what I want, " said his father. " I am very glad you got the horn, " he said. His father was smoking. (The boy's mother was gone again.) " Let's go over to your aunt's house, " said his father. When they got there, his father said, " My boy, tonight when the sun goes down, you come over here. I will be here all day, keeping that horn. " In the evening the boy

went to his father's house, and his father had something by him.
It was a mask, painted green. There were four masks lying there.
The other three looked very ugly. When the boy came in, he began
to tell him what he was to do. " You go out to the north from the
village, then go to the west. I will go out by the south, and then
west. " They went by different directions, and then west and they met
and there his father fixed up the boy; he put an old antelope skin on
his back. The good mask was at the bottom and the others on top,
and then these four he put on his boy's head. " Now you go near the
village, and the people will know about it, " said the father. And he
gave him some kind of fire. When he came close to the village somebody saw the fire coming, and it was coming closer, and the man got
afraid and ran off. So the boy went around the village four times
and then went off. So that man told them in the kiva that he
had seen somebody with fire in his eyes and in his mouth. But the
people did not believe it. At night the boy came again, and that
man and two others were standing outside the village and watching for
him. They watched the fire coming closer, and then they all ran
off, up to the house where some other men were watching. He was
coming, but they were all frightened and ran away. When he got into
the village, he went around four times again and they did not catch
him. Next morning those men who saw him told about him. But the
other men said, " We will go tonight and we will catch him. " So at
night they went into the empty house. The man who first saw him
went with some others to watch for him. Soon he was coming, and
they went and told the others in the house. They saw him and they
all ran away, they did not catch him. He went round the village again.
Next morning they were all in the kiva talking about it, " Well, we
have all to go and we will catch the boy, " they said. Then the father
said to the boy, " This will be the fourth night and they are going
to catch you. Let them catch you. My son, I love you. You are supposed to be my leg and my hand and my heart. But I let you go
and let the people kill you. We will all go after you. And I will not
cry when they kill you. Nor do you cry when they kill you. I will
tell them where to bury you. " Then the father told his wife to make
soap weed suds and wash the boy's head. So in the evening the father
put his beads around his neck and he told his boy, " Now you go a
little earlier tonight. " So he dressed himself and went. All those men
of that kiva went into the empty house, waiting for what was to come.
They were watching for him. Then he came again. The other men
who watched before were watching. " He is coming, " they said to the
men in the empty house. " Why did you not catch him? " they asked.
" We were afraid of him. " — " Well, let us be brave men, " they
said. When he went into the dance plaza they caught him and took
him into the kiva. Then they made a big fire, for light. Then they

took off the top mask and under it was another mask and they took it off and under it was another mask, and then they took off that third mask and there was that good mask, and that was Soyal kachina, Ahulani. He was dressed just as he is today, with a foxskin collar. Then they pulled it off, and there was that boy, Town chief's son. And they felt pretty bad about him. " Well, you kill me! " said the boy. " Do as you wish. If you cut my head off, that will be all right, " said the boy. Some of them did not want to kill him, but some said, " Why do we not kill him ? " But the oldest man said, " Don't kill him, but just let him go. " So they let him go ; but they kept the mask in the kiva. Well, the older men were crying because they knew something was going to happen. When they let him go, he went to his father's house and his father said, " Thank you, they did not kill you. But you have to go, " said his father. At that time of night they were still practising in one of those kivas. Then the father gave him a smoke, and when he finished smoking then his father gave him something to eat. While he was eating, his mother came back, very happy. They had been having a good time. " Why did you not go ? " — " Well, I did not want to go. Everybody was in there except you and your father, " she said. " Just because we did not want to go, we did not go. " She was tired from dancing, and went to sleep. But the father and son were sitting there. Soon all the people went to sleep. " My son, take off your moccasins, all your leggings, also your shirt. " Then he tied a prayer-feather on his son's head, and he tied two prayer-feathers on each horn. " Now let's go, " he said. Then they went to the dance plaza, where was the shrine (*pahoki*). He put his son inside of the shrine and he told his son, " You hold the horns down like this (pointing them to the ground), and then you will go down into the earth, " he said. The boy just pushed the horns down into the ground, and soon he was sinking into the ground. His father had said, " When all your head goes into the ground, hold up your hand and leave out four fingers and leave them all day. Next morning you put down one finger, next morning another finger, next morning another, fourth morning the last finger. " So the boy sank down and held up his hand with four fingers up. In the morning somebody was passing by and he saw the hand sticking out of the ground inside the shrine with four fingers up. He looked at it closely. He went into the kiva and he said he had seen something. They asked him what it was. He said in the shrine a hand was sticking out and four fingers were up. Then the older men went to the shrine and saw it. And when they came back into the kiva they were talking about it. And some of them said, " You know last night you caught somebody and brought him here and that is he, " they said. Next morning they went to look at the hand. Only three fingers were up. They went into the kiva and talked about it. " Only three fingers are up; surely something is going to happen." The third morning only two fingers were up. The fourth morning only one finger was up. The fifth morning the last finger was gone. This morning the water began to come up from all the fireplaces. In the afternoon the water was coming out everywhere. In the dance plaza something was making a big noise. They said they were going to have a flood. Before evening something was coming from that place where the hand had been. It was Palülü-kon. [1] That boy had turned into Palülükon. Before night the people were transporting their things to a height on the east side of the village. In the morning when they woke up a big Palülükon was coming out from the dance place. Some houses were falling, water was everywhere. There were two old men living close together. One old man went into the house of the other old man. They could not come down. The water kept on rising. They went to a corner of the house and up on the beam where people used to keep things. They got up there and sat there together. In the morning Palülükon was growing bigger and bigger, water was everywhere. One man said, " We have to give two children to that Palülükon so he will go back. If we don't give the children, he will never go back, " said the old man. " The boy will be the son of Crier chief and the little girl, the daughter of War chief. " Then they all began to make prayer-sticks and put them in a flat basket. Then in the afternoon they gave the basket to the little boy and said to him, " Take these prayer-sticks and give them to Palülükon. When you meet him, don't be afraid, put your arms around him. " These two little children were brave enough to go, they went into the water and reached Palülükon and put their basket of prayer-sticks close to him and their arms around him. Then Palülükon sank right down into the water; he was going back and with him the boy and girl. Crier chief told the people, " We can move from here to some other place. We were too crazy, that is why this happened. So we have to go off and leave our village. " And so they started off towards Walpi. Well, they were going many days. Those old men sitting up on the house beam became turkeys and their tails were hanging down and the suds of the water touched their tails and they became white, and that is why the tips of turkey tails are white. After all the people went off, two little boys were left behind, and they were living way up in the fourth story, and while they were asleep, they were forgotten and left behind. Four days later the boys looked out and the water was going back into the hole Palülükon went into. Then the boys went down and around in all the houses and up in one house they went into two turkeys were sitting. " Somebody has forgotten his turkeys, " said the older boy ; the younger was just beginning to walk. While the boys were going about, the older carrying the other on his

1. Horned water snake, or, in Tewa, Avaiyu.

back, Palülükon said, " I guess I better come up and see where my people have gone. " He came up and saw the people way off. They were by now far away. Those little boys were looking around and they went into the dance plaza and saw that big thing there. That big thing said, " Poor little boys, they left you. " And they were very much afraid of him. Palülükon told them not to be afraid of him. "I am your uncle, " said Palülükon and he said again, " Don't be afraid of me, I am your uncle. Two old men have been left and they have turned into turkeys. You go into that room and pull out some feathers from each of them. " So they did. Then Palülükon said, " Go and follow the tracks of your people. They are far away, but you will overtake them some day, " said Palülükon. So they took some food along, and the turkey feathers and followed the people. They went on many days. They found two men staying under a tree; one was lame and he could not walk, and one man had legs, but he was blind. The little boys were frightened. The man with eyes told him not to be afraid. " We are people, " he said. " We will go all together. " So the blind man carried the lame man, and the little boy carried his younger brother. They came to the forest and a deer was standing close to them, and the lame man had a bow and arrow in his hand and he saw the deer standing close to them. He said to the blind man, " Wait! " he said. " Why ? " — " There is a deer standing close to us. Let me shoot him. We have nothing to eat tonight. " So the man with eyes shot the deer and killed him. And they stopped right there and made fire and skinned the deer and cooked the meat. That man said, "We will stop here all night and go on tomorrow morning. " At night they put the deer-head by the fire. The eyes exploded with a noise and scared them. The man who could not walk jumped up and ran off and the blind man was so scared he opened his eyes and could see. He said, "I am very glad my eyes are open and I can see, " he said, and the other said, "I am very glad I can walk. " The man who had been blind said, " I must not go to sleep, if I sleep I will get blind again, " he said. " I must stay awake all night. " And the man who had been lame said, " I must not go to sleep. If I sleep, I will get stiff again. I must walk about all night, " he said. And so the blind man did not sleep, but kept his eyes open all night, and the other man walked all night. At sunrise the blind man said, " I guess I will not be blind again, " and the lame man said, " I will walk always. " Then after they ate their breakfast, each man took a boy on his back, and went on following their people. It was a long time before they caught up with their people, at a place called Humulobi. Those people on their way from Palatkwabi took a rest every afternoon and before they rested they danced, they danced *lakunti*.[1] They did that every day. At Humulobi they made a home and lived

1. A woman's harvest dance.

there a long time. But there were a lot of mosquitoes there and they were killing the babies. So they thought they would move again. So they started again, and every afternoon when they stopped, again they danced *lakunti*. That's the way they came to Walpi. That is why the *patki wungwe* clan owns *lakunti*, and that is how they first got turkeys.

4. THE MIGRATION OF THE MUSTARD CLAN.

After the Asa wungwe, Mustard clan, left Zuñi (where they left one mask), they came to Yöbökpö', Sink. There they lived a long time. (Big ruin there.) They were moving away. A woman having a baby was left behind. After they left, the head man sent a boy back to see if the woman had yet had her baby and how she was feeling. He got there and looked around. He went to the house where the woman had lived. Nobody was there. He looked in every house. He went to the east side and there by the side of the cliff she was sitting, and close by were two little animals, instead of a baby. The woman heard something above her, she looked up and saw somebody standing. She tried to hide the two little animals, they were little deer, but the boy standing up there had already seen them. Then the boy asked the woman, " How are you feeling this morning ? " — " Pretty well. Do not think about me any more. Tell the people I am alive and I have my babies. But I am not a real person, to live outside. I am going to hide myself in some hole. You will never see me again. But when you reach Walpi, if you think of me, make a prayer-stick for me, and bring it here. If you want rain or crops, ask for them, and I will do what you want, " said the woman. And so that boy went back and overtook his people. At night he told them all about the woman and how she had two little deer and what she said. So they say the woman lives there underneath somewhere. There is a crack in the wall, and designs and tracks of two little deer, and they called that place Chakwena [1] e'ke' (there).

5. THE MIGRATION OF THE SNAKE CLAN. [2]

It was a long time ago the Snake clan peoples were living away off where they call. — A boy was living at another place right close to the river, and every day he would go to the bank of the river and watch the river. And one day he said to himself, " I wonder where this water is running. I wish I could follow it. " And then he thought to

1. The kachina belonging to the Mustard clan.
2. Written by the narrator of the other tales from First Mesa, with grammatical corrections by the editor, and in a few cases substitution of a word more expressive of the writer's meaning than the one he used.

make a little box out of cotton wood. And so next day he went
to the river and found a big cotton wood, and so he cut it down. And
then he began to work at it. He finished it in three days, he cut a
hole to be his door. Well, the next day he told his father and
mother that he wanted to follow the river, he was thinking about
the river, how the water was running and, " I wonder where it is
running to, and so now think I must follow it and see where it is
running. " He said he had a box ready to go with. His father and
mother and also his sister were very surprised, but his father said he
thought it would be all right for the boy to go. So next morning after
they ate their breakfast, his mother washed the boy's head and also his
father washed his head, too. Then they began to make prayer-sticks
for the boy to take along, and then the mother of the boy said, " We
have forgotten our uncle. " So she sent her daughter to their uncle.
When she got in her uncle's house, she told him, " Go over to our
house. Father and mother want you to come over. " Her uncle said, "All
right, I will go. " Then he went over to the house. When he went he
saw that the boy and his father were making prayer-sticks. As soon as
he got in the room, he asked them quietly, " What do you want me
for ? " — " Yes, said the father and mother, " the boy wants to go
off. " — " To where ? " said the uncle. The boy answered, " Yes, I
want to follow the river. I have been thinking of it all the time. And
so now I want to go and see it, see just where the river is running to. "
Their uncle said all right. Then he made prayer-sticks. Well, they stayed
right there together all day till night came. So after they ate their
supper they began to talk to the boy. " If you reach anybody anywhere or if you meet somebody, give them all these prayer-sticks [1] and
also if you find somebody somewhere you must look out and watch
yourself. " They stayed up all night till daylight, then they ate their
breakfast, and after they ate their breakfast then the boy got ready.
All the folks went with the boy to the river, and when they got to the
river, the box was there. So they put the boy inside of the box. Then
they put the prayer-sticks in, and then they put in his bottle of water and
his lunch, and they shut the box and put gum on the side of the door,
so the water would not get inside, and there was a little place where
the boy could see out. Just as the sun rose the father and uncle rolled
the box into the river. The mother of the boy was very sorry, and
his sister, too. They all said good bye. They watched the box
till they could no longer see it. Now the boy had left his folks.
He was going for many days and nights. Every day he would open the
place and look out, and he was still going, then he shut it again.
One day at dawn the box was so still, the boy thought something

1. The Keres say that the prayer-sticks given to the dead are for them to take to
their Mother.

was the matter, so he opened the place and looked out, and it was just daylight, and he was out on the side of the river, but he stayed in the box till the sun came out. The boy came out and he saw a very big mountain right close to him. He walked around it, then he saw there was someone near, close to him ; it was a girl. He looked at her and said, " Who are you ? " The girl began to laugh, and said, " I am the one that made you come down. " The boy went to his box and took out the prayer-sticks, and he went with the girl. They came to the mountain and they climbed up till they came to a place where there was a house. The girl opened the door and went in. All the people in there said come in ; they were all glad that the boy had come. They gave the boy something to eat right away. They gave him some yellow round bread. The boy was so suprised for the girls looked all the same. The boy could not tell which girl brought him. After he finished eating, he gave a little bag to the man sitting by the fire. That was the father of the family. Then the man said, " Thank you! " Then he began to untie the bag, and there were some prayer-sticks for them. Then he gave the folks all the prayer-sticks. The prayer-sticks were just enough to go around to every one of them. Well, then he found that these were snakes. When they went outside, they were real snakes, but when they were inside, they were people. Just as soon as he gave the prayer-sticks the mother fixed soapweed to wash the boy's head. Then she said, " Come, my son–in–law, I will wash your head. " Then the boy moved over to the bowl. Then the mother washed the boy's head. The boy was to marry the girl. He stayed there for many days. Then the Snake people were going to show him the snake dance. Four days they had a snake dance. He was so suprised that the dancers carried the snakes in their mouths. They taught the boy all about it, also they sang him the songs. He learned all the songs, also he learned everything they did. Then next day the father said, " It is about time for you to go back home. Your father and mother and also your sister are now all home-sick for you, so I think you can go back home tomorrow. And my daughter will go with you. " So early next morning they ate their breakfast and they started off. The rainbow took them home in one day. The boy got back home and also he brought a girl. She was a very good-looking girl, very pretty. There was no girl pretty like her. She was a yellow snake girl, that was the reason she was so nice a girl. After she was there a long time, she had babies, two boys. The mother and father and sister also were so happy to have them. Just in four days they began to move around inside of the house. And in four more days they began to go outside. Their grandfather followed them when they went out. And in four more days they began to go around the village and play with the children. One day one of the snake boys bit a child and the child's leg began to swell. Then the next day he bit another.

Then the father and mother of the child were mad and they told the
Snake folks or family to go off and not to live there with them. So
the Snake woman and her husband and the two little children left
the place. Their grandmother and grandfather were very sorry to
have them go away. They started out to the south. They were sorry to go. Some of the people followed them in the evening. They
overtook them and they said they wanted to go with them. They
asked the Snake woman where was she going ? She answered, " I am
going out south to the place which they call Follow Mountain. " The
people were anxious to go, so they started out the next day. They got
to a place where some peoples were living. The people asked them
where they were going. The Snake woman said she was going to
Follow Mountain. The people said, " We were going to that place,
but we are still here. " The Snake woman asked them what clan they
were. They answered, "We are the Sand clan. " — " Well, you are
my people then, "said the Snake woman. " I live on the ground and
sand. You belong to my clan. I am a snake, " said she. That is where
they made a clan together. From there they started off, they came to
a place where there were lots of cactus, and a child was crying, and
the mother gave the child a piece of cactus, and that is where they
made that clan. And while they were going on their way they saw
a lizard and they said, " Let this be in our clan, too. " This is the way
they got their clan. When they got to this place, they saw the track
of only one man. [1] They did not come up to the mesa, but they
stopped on the west side of the mesa, and while they were staying
there, a very tall man came up to them who looked very dangerous.
This tall man tried to kill the people, but the Snakes he did not kill for
they bit. So the tall man told them to come up on the mesa and
live with him, they were very brave like him. Just then the Bear
people were there, too. The Bear clan and Snake clan came at the
same time, but the Snake clan people stopped at the side of the
Mesa and the Bear clan people did not stop till they came up the
Mesa. This is the way they came after this. Thus the people came.
By this time the Snake woman had some more babies, but she went
down the side of the Mesa to have the babies. This time they were
real little snakes, so she left the little snakes there. And after two
years then the Snake woman said, " Let us have a dance. " So her
husband went in the kiva and one of her sons went in the other kiva
for Antelope chief and the other boy went in with his father. Next day
they stayed alone, but next morning a few men appeared, Tobacco clan
and Coyote clan man went into the Antelopes. The Coyote clan
man made fire for the chiefs and the Tobacco clan man put tobacco
in the pipe. They stayed seven days and then they went to get the

1. Cp. p. 175.

snakes. The snakes were still at one place. So they did not hunt them. In the evening of the seventh day they danced for the Antelopes, and then next day was the Snake dance. The peoples were much surprised to see that wonderful dance. This is the way the Hopi got their Snake dance. This is the reason the snakes are around here.

NOVELISTIC TALES.

6. WARRIOR GIRL. [1]

Where they were living lived Pohaha, a girl who would not mind her mother or father or uncle. They were telling her to be a good, girl, but she got angry quickly. Then they got tired telling her to be good so they just let her go. One time she was grinding corn, and many enemies were coming, very close to the village. Her uncle came to her house and asked her mother where she was. Her mother said she was grinding corn. He went to where she was grinding and caught her arm and said, " Take your bow and arrows and go and fight with the enemies who are coming. You would not mind us and behaved like a boy. Now is the time for you to go and fight and be brave, " said the uncle to the girl. She laughed ha! ha! " I am very glad to go, " she said. " I am very anxious to go and fight the enemies. I am not afraid. I will do all I can. " — " That is why I tell you. Come out ! " said the uncle. " I will, " she said. She stood up and her uncle gave her bow and arrows and hung the bandolier around her. Then she looked around and there was a rattle hanging on the wall. She stepped up and got it. Then she started to sing. As soon as she stopped singing, she laughed ha ! ha ! She sang four times in the room. Then she went out and sang outdoors four times. Whenever she paused in singing she laughed ha ! ha ! because she was not afraid to fight. Then she started, and the men followed her. People were saying, " The Cottonwood People (clan) girl (*te' towa*) is going to fight. " Some of them laughed at her. But she just went on, singing and laughing ha! ha ! happy she was going to fight. Before she met the enemies, she pulled her dress up, four times, to show the enemies that she was a girl.

1. Chakwena *mui su'amö* (their grandmother) was similarly a girl, sent to war by her uncles, and also, while she was fighting, her face turned into a mask. Her mother was combing her hair, and had only one side whorled, and the stick she used was still in the whorl. Then her uncle came in. (The scene between Pohaha and her uncle is repeated.) In this case the uncle also gives a quiver of mountain lion skin and the mask is different, too, black, with yellow eyes, and tongue hanging out. The same story is told of He''e'e', whose mask is also black with yellow round eyes. Hair like that of Chakwena their grandmother, but crow tail feathers are at the back of the head. He''e'e' belongs to Powamu chief. (See Fewkes 2 : Pls. IV, XI.)

Then she fought. She killed all the enemies that same day. After that the fighting was over and she turned back. The men fighting with her saw she had turned *okuwa*, she was wearing a mask, one side was blue, and one side was yellow, and she had long teeth. They were afraid of her, she looked strange, she no longer looked like a girl. But she kept on singing her song, ending with ha! ha! She kept on going home, and the men followed her. When they got to the village, all the people came out and watched the girl, how she had become some sort of a person. When she went to war, she did not look like that. She went to her house and went in, and then she took off her mask and hung it on the wall, and she hung her rattle in the same place and the bow and arrow close, too. That is the way that girl became *pohaha*! [1] Her uncles came to the house at night. They had been talking about her. All day they had been thinking that she must be a man. So they went in there, all gathered together, the oldest uncle [2] said they would put her in as Pota'i (war chief). Even if she was a girl, she was a man, too. So they said that whenever enemies came she was to be the leader in war. " You have to watch for the people, " they told her. " If any sickness comes, you have to drive the sickness away from the people. And consider that the people are all your children. Treat them right, " they told her. After that she became a good girl, she no longer acted as she used to. When war came, she went first and dressed as she did before in war. After she died, she left her mask and said that it would represent her. She would always be with the people, even if dead. "I will be with you all the time, " she said, " the mask is me, " she said. That is why those Cottonwood People keep that mask.

7. WATER JAR BOY.

They were living at Sikyat'ki. There was a girl living there, a fine girl, and she did not want to marry any of the boys living there. After a while boys in the other villages heard there was a fine girl living at Sikyat'ki but she did not want any boy. Her mother was all the time making water jars. One day when her mother was mixing clay and using one foot, she was watching her mother. Her mother said she wanted to go for some water. " You can keep on doing this for me, " said her mother. So she stepped on the mud and began to mix it with her foot on top of a flat stone. So she was trying to mix

---

1. Named from her call and *po*, meaning wet. While she was fighting she was very wet between her legs. But compare term *powaka*.

2. The characteristic Hopi-Tewa maternal family is being referred to, the English term " uncle" always meaning in the mouth of a Pueblo Indian (Taos alone excepted) mother's brother or mother's mother's brother. The influence of the " uncle " comes out clearly in this tale, as well as the relation between maternal family and clan.

the mud for her mother. Somehow that mud got into the girl, it flew up. She felt it on her leg, but not higher up inside. Then her mother came back and asked her if she finished the mud. " Yes, " she said. So her mother went on making the water jars. After some days the girl felt something was moving in her belly, but she did not think anything about going to have a baby. She did not tell her mother. But it was growing and growing. One day in the morning she was very sick. In the afternoon she got the baby. Then her mother knew (for the first time) that her daughter was going to have a baby. The mother was very angry about it; but after she looked at the baby, she saw it was not like a baby, she saw it was a round thing with two things sticking out, it was a little jar. " Where did you get this ? " said her mother. The girl was just crying. About that time the father came in. " Never mind, I am very glad she had a baby, " he said. " But it is not a baby, " said her mother. Then the father went to look at it and saw it was a little water jar. After that he was very fond of that little jar. " It is moving, " he said. Pretty soon that little water jar was growing. In twenty days it was big. It was able to go around with the children, and it could talk. " Grandfather, take me outdoors, so I can look around, " he said. So every morning the grandfather would take him out and he would look at the children, and they were very fond of him and they found out he was a boy, Sipe'geenu (Tewa), Water jar boy. They found out from his talking. About this time of year (December) it began to snow, and the men were going out to hunt rabbits, and Water jar boy wanted to go. " Grandfather, could you take me down to the foot of the mesa, I want to hunt rabbits. " — " Poor grandson, you can't hunt rabbits, you have no legs nor arms, " said the grandfather. But Water Jar boy was very anxious to go. " Well, grandfather, " he said, " I am very anxious to go. Take me anyway. You are too old and you can't kill anything. " His mother was crying because her boy had no legs or arms or eyes. But they used to feed him, in his mouth (i. e. in the mouth of the jar). So next morning his grandfather took him down to the south on the flat. Then he rolled along, and pretty soon he saw a rabbit track and he followed the track. Pretty soon the rabbit ran out, and he began to chase it. Just before he got to the marsh there was a rock, and he hit himself against it and broke, and a boy jumped up. He was very glad his skin had been broken and that he was a boy, a big boy. He was wearing lots of beads around his neck and turquoise earrings, and a dance kilt and moccasins, and a buckskin shirt. Then he chased the rabbit, he picked up a stick and ran. Pretty soon he killed it. Then he found another rabbit and chased again. He was a good runner. So he killed four rabbits, jackrabbits. About that time the sun was setting, so he went home, carrying the rabbits on his back. His grandfather went down to the place where he had carried him and waited for him. While his grandfather was waiting there, somebody was coming. Then came a fine looking boy, but his grandfather did not know who it was. " Did you see my grandson anywhere ? " said the grandfather to that boy. He said, " No, I did not see your grandson anywhere. " — " Well, I am sorry he is late. " — Well, I did not see anybody anywhere, " said the boy. His grandfather was looking so bad, the boy said, " I am your grandson. " — "No, you are not my grandson. " — " Yes, I am your grandson. " — " No, you are just teasing me, my grandson is a round jar, without arms or legs, " said the grandfather. He did not believe it was his grandson. But the boy said, " I am your grandson. I am telling you the truth. This morning you carried me down here. I went to look for rabbits near here. I found one and chased him just rolling along. Pretty soon I hit myself on a rock and my skin was broken and I came out of it and I am the very one who is your grandson, and you must believe me. " So he believed, and they went home. When they came back and the grandfather was bringing in a good-looking boy, the girl was ashamed. The grandfather said, " This is my grandson, this is Water jar boy, " and the grandmother asked how he became a boy, and he told them how it had happened to him, and they believed it. Then after that he went around with the boys. One time he said to his mother, "Who is my father ? " he said. " I don't know, " she said. He asked her again, " Who is my father ? " But she just kept on crying and did not answer. " Where is my father's home ? " he asked. She could not tell him. " Tomorrow I am going to find my father. " — " You cannot find your father, " she said. " I never go with any boy, so there is no place where you can look for your father. " But the boy said, " I have a father, I know where he is living, I am going to see him. " The mother did not want him to go, but he wanted to go. So early next morning she fixed a lunch for him, and he went off to the southeast where they call the spring Waiyu powidi, Horse mesa point. He was coming close to that spring, he saw somebody walking a little way from the spring. He went up to him. It was a man. He asked the boy, " Where are you going ? " — " I am going to this spring. " — " Why are you going ? " — " I am going there to see my father, " he said. " Who is your father ? " said the man. " Well, my father is living in this spring. " — " You will never find your father. " — " Well, I want to go into the spring, he is living inside it. " — " Who is your father ? " said the man again. " Well, I think you are my father, " said the boy. " How do you know I am your father ? " said the man. " Well, I know you are my father. " Then the man just looked at him, to scare him. The boy kept saying, " You are my father. " Pretty soon the man said, " Yes, I am your father. I came out of that spring to meet you, " and he put his arm around the boy's neck. His father was very glad his boy had come, and he took him down inside of the spring. A lot of people were living down inside of the spring, women and girls. They all ran to the

boy and put their arms around him because they were glad
their child had come to their house. Thus the boy found his
father and his aunts, too. Well, the boy stayed there one night and
next day he went back home and told his mother he had found his
father. Then his mother got sick and she died. Then the boy said to
himself, " No use for me to live with these people. " So he left them
and went to the spring. And there was his mother. That was the way
he and his mother went to live with his father. His father was Avaiyo′
pi'i (water snake red). He said he could not live with them over at
Sikyat′ki. That was the reason he made the boy's mother sick so she
died and " came over here to live with me, " said his father." Now
we will live here together, " said Avaiyo′ to his son. That's the way
that boy and his mother went to the spring to live there.

8. HANDMARK BOY.

Owęheyamba (far away there) at Kuņluokyut'e'e [1] there lived Cactus
Flower girl. She had a mother and father. She had no older brother nor
younger brother, no older sister nor younger sister. She was a grown
girl. Her mother and father loved her very much. Her father, when
he came back at night from work, would tell her that it was time for
her to marry, he was getting old, he was tired of working so much by
himself, he was tired of going for wood or going alone to the fields
to work. " You must get married, " he said to the girl, " so that I
may have somebody to help me in going for wood · or in working in
the fields. " Every night he would say this to his child. Her mother,
too, would talk to her about getting married. All winter long they
talked thus to their child. During *elu poye* [2] the girl's father would stay
in the kiva to which his clan belonged, [3] *k'eeht'e'e.* [4] There he spun and
wove, weaving dresses and belts, for his child and his wife. There he
worked all the time.

During the *elu* moon they were to have a girls' dance. Cactus
Flower girl had never joined in a dance. They would go to her house
and try to get her to dance ; [5] but she did not want to dance, she

1. This place was underground, where the Tewa lived before they came up into
this world. Cp. p. 19, n. 2
2. *Poye*, moon, *elu*, the hidden ball game (Zuñi, *iyankoli'we*), which is played in
January and so gives its name to this month.
3. During the Winter solstice ceremony, men must go to the kiva which is associated with their clan ; at other times they frequent the kiva which is most conve-
nient, often the kiva near their wife's house.
4. *K'eehti* means " on top of ", and so *k'eeht'e'e* means hill top kiva. Such a kiva
there was once at Tewa " because such a kiva there was at Kuņluokyut'e'e. "
5. As girls are now invited to take part in the so-called girls' dances. A man charg-
ed with assembling the girls goes about from house to house early in the evening
they are to practice the dance in the kiva.

never would dance. They were going to have the *kohea* [1] dance. The kiva chief [2] asked the father of Cactus Flower girl, if she would dance. " I don't know if she will dance, " said the girl's father, " I want her to dance; but I don't know if she will dance. " He went home to supper and told his child about the dance. " My child (*nabi e'*), will you join in the dance with the other girls ? " he asked her. She said nothing. He asked her again, " My child, will you join in the dance with the other girls ? " Again she said nothing. He asked her four times. She said nothing, she said neither yes nor no. He waited for her to speak ; [3] but she said nothing. After supper he went to the kiva. The man asked him, " Did your child say if she would join in the dance ? " — " She did not say. I would like her to dance; but she said nothing. "

Cactus Flower girl used to grind corn every night, half the night, then she would eat and go to sleep. These people lived down in the *koye'*, [4] and Cactus Flower girl ground corn in the room above (*kwa-k'eibi*). Her father came back from the kiva after they were through practicing the dance. Next morning he took his spinner (*tili-lipeh*) and wool and went to the kiva to spin. Soon his child came and called him. [5] " Father, come ! We are going to have breakfast, " she said to him. He went to breakfast. He said to his child, " We had a good dance last night. I wish you would be in that dance. " She said that she did not care to go to a dance nor to look on at a game, she never went out. They were going to dance again that night. The boys came into the kiva to practice their songs and to make new songs to dance to. Then everybody went back home to supper. Cactus Flower girl's father asked her again, " My child, will you go into the dance ? " She said nothing. Then her father put his buffalo pelt [6] around him and went to the kiva. They brought in the girls. They began to practice their songs. They began to dance. [7] There were

1. A dance like that the Hopi call the Butterfly dance (*politih*) and the Tewa, the *kwatikih*, Line-up dance. *Kohea* proper is no longer danced.

2. Among both Tewa and Hopi he is of the clan the kiva is associated with, the clan is said to have built it. Succession as kiva chief passes from uncle to nephew exactly as succession in the proprietorship of any ceremony or office.

3. As she should have done after the fourth question. Asking a question four times, or making a request, before getting an answer or compliance is a convention of Pueblo Indian society. For Navaho, see Matthews 1 : 127.

4. The ground room which was entered by ladder or steps from the room above.

5. As a regular thing, girls will go to the kiva to call their father or grandfather to come to meals. Cp. Voth. 1 : 148.

6. *Koh.* Formely buffalo pelts were worn as blankets.

7. In just the order I have observed followed in the Buffalo dance, which is also a girls' dance where the young men practise their songs an hour or so before the dance begins. See Parsons 11. Since the Buffalo dance had been performed at Sichumovi only a few days before this tale of Handmark boy was told, it is quite likely

four girls dancing and four boys, all together. They practised their dance all night. After they finished practicing, the dance leader told the people not to leave as he had something to say. They remained quiet. He smoked and smoked, and after he finished smoking, he said, " Well, in five days from tonight we will have this dance so that everybody will be happy and we shall give pleasure to the children of our Father and Mother. " [1] Everybody was glad that they were going to dance in five days. When the father of Cactus Flower girl, went home, he told his wife that in five days they were going to dance. His daughter he did not tell since she was asleep. The following morning he took his spinner and went to the kiva. His daughter went to call him to breakfast. . . . In three days the men went after wood (*songede*). [2] The next day the women baked wafer-bread (Tewa, *mowa*; Hopi, *piki*). They boiled meat also for the next day. Everybody was busy that day. The *kohea* chief [i. e. the dance chief] was busy, too, borrowing the things for the dancers to wear — moccasins, dresses, beads. Every evening the men had gone into the kiva and the men in charge of the girls had collected them and taken them into the kiva. There they practised their songs all night till daylight. The *kohea* chief told the people to tell the girls to make ready their wafer bread, and the boys to make ready their cooked rabbits (*pukoh*). [3] — At the end of the last night of practice they watched for the sun. At sunrise they came out of the kiva and all went to *moñekwaa'* [4] to dance. They danced there, and the chorus, too, danced. They finished dancing that morning. The dance chief told the girls to go and wash their heads. All, girls and boys, went to wash their heads. Then they ate breakfast. The *kohea* chief went into the kiva and staid there. The man in charge of the girls brought the girls in and dressed them up. The boys dressed themselves. After they finished dressing they went out [5] and danced all day till evening. But Cactus Flower girl did not go out to look at the dance. [6]

Spring came, and the people were glad spring had come. They took their hoes ready to work in their fields. The first planting-

---

that the narrator amplified the references to the dance in the tale, knowing my interest in all the dance particulars.

1. The *poant'oyo*, Town chief. All the people are called his children.

2. Hopi, *komoktotokya*. This is always the third day before the conclusion of a ceremony, and in every ceremony, this day is always named *songede* and the following wafer-bread or food-preparing day is *mowakoko iti'* (Hopi, *totokya*).

3. These were presents from the boys to their dance partners. The wafer-bread the girls baked each day was for all in the kiva.

4. Hopi, *kisuñabi*. It is the middle or dance place, the *kakati* of the Keres.

5. In successive sets of eight.

6. For this recurrent theme of the girl who would stay home, cp. Zuñi, Cushing, 429 sq.

time ¹ came. Cactus Flower girl planted her father's early planting. Soon the next planting-time came, the planting of watermelons, pumpkins, squashes, and, last of all, corn. The field the girl's father had was big. He was getting old, too old to work this big field. Soon the plants came up. They were glad they were up. Of cotton-wood branches they made a little shade there at the field for him to eat his lunch under. They cut the weeds. (There is a plant they eat called *kwęo'*, ² which the women gather.) The mother of the girl told her that she was going with a lot of women to gather *kwęo'*. The girl said to her mother, " Well, go! " So her mother went with the women, and the girl stayed behind in the house alone. There was an old man living next door. The girl wanted to build a fire; her fire was out. She took a potsherd and went into the house where the old man was. He was weaving a dress. She asked him if the fire was in. The old man told her that the fire was in. So she put some embers out of the fireplace into her potsherd. As she was going out, she stepped up to the old man weaving. " Whom are you weaving for ? " she asked the old man. " I am weaving for my spouse, " ³ said the old man. She went on talking to the old man, and the old man talked to her. She began to play with the old man. There she stayed playing with him all day. She never went back to build her fire. The wife of the old man came back from the fields, and saw the girl lying by the side of the old man. She stepped up to her, and seized her arm. The old woman was very angry. She went to the girl's house. The mother of the girl had come in and found the fire out. She was surprised, since her child never went out. The old woman came in and said, " Your child was lying with my husband. " She went to the old woman's house where the girl was still lying with the old man. Her mother grabbed her up and whipped her, whipped her hard. She took her home and whipped her again. The girl picked up her blanket and left. She went to the east. She came to a road, and she follow-ed that road all day. She came to a place where somebody called her, saying *shö*' ! ⁴ And again *shö*' ! She looked around, but she saw nobody. Again she heard *shö*' ! The voice said, " My grandchild (*nabi sayae'*), where are you going ? Here I am. " She looked around, and

---

1. On First Mesa a series of plantings are regulated according to solar observations which have been correlated in some way with our calendar, the first of the nine plantings being on April 15th and the last on June 16th.

2. *Sporobolus strictus (Scribu) Merill.* In Hopi *kwahkwi*, used in prayer-sticks in the Soyal ceremony. (Voth 2 : 20.) Used also in prayer-sticks on the Rio Grande (Robbins, Harrington, Freire Marreco, 49, n. 1).

3. *Nabi soŋ*, applied to either wife or husband. A woman may also call her hus-band *nabi seŋa*, my old man. See, too, Freire Marreco, 280. The Tewa, like the people of Zuñi, call their Town chief *nabi seŋa*, a term of reference not used by the Hopi.

4. This is the call at Zuñi, too, for anyone passing by.

she saw a little spider sitting by a bush. " I am your grandmother, "
(*saya'*) Spider Grandmother (*yowelu saya* [1]) said to her, " I was waiting
for you to stop you. You are going away never to return to your
mother and father. " Spider Grandmother thought that maybe a
giant [2] had made her go away because she never danced or went to a
game. And Spider Grandmother grieved to have her grandchild go
away and leave her mother and father. She said to her, " I am very
unhappy to have you go away. I think the best thing is for me to go
with you. If anything happens to you, I will protect you, " she said
to her. — " How can you go with me ? " the girl asked. " I will go, "
said Spider Grandmother, " I can climb up back of your ear. " So
Spider Grandmother said to her, " Well, I will get ready my medicine
(*wo·lo*). " She wrapped up her medicine in a cloth and put it on her
back. The girl picked up her grandmother and put her back of her ear.
Then they started on.

The girl was crying as she went along. She cried, cried, cried,
crying in this song :

> Owe we wee
> Way away
> Owe we wee
> Way away
> Pogwinge omengneng
> Big Lake I am going.

She kept on crying until they came to a place where there was a big
lake. Spider Grandmother said to her, " Here is the place you are
bound for. " The girl was frightened. She did not know how she was
going to stay here, there were no houses here to sleep in. Soon they
reached the edge of the lake. In the middle of the lake were two poles
coming out of the water. As they watched, the poles grew higher and
higher, soon there was a big ladder coming out of the water. They
heard a sound, someone was talking under the ladder. They saw the
head of somebody coming out of the water. This was a kiva, and
coming out of it was a good-looking woman. It was Pokekwiya
(Pour-water Woman). [3] She politely addressed them, asking them to

1. Cp. Voth 1 : 30.
2. *Pęnatoyĕ* (Hopi, *suyuku*) would kill and eat a person, or could make a person do
something bad or go crazy. This concept of inspiring evil I have never heard expressed elsewhere among Pueblo Indians. But compare Voth 1 : 56. *Suyuku* (*suuke*)
figures at Zuñi and among the Keres, but always as a giant, or as a child- or body-
snatcher (See too p. 50), but not as a devil. In this case I suspect school influence.
3. Hopi, Hahaaiyi. She carries a gourd bottle (Fewkes 2 : Pl. VII) and pours from
it on everybody. She is the mother of all the kachina (Tewa, k'atsina.) She is also a
wöye or clan kachina of the Kachina clan. According to Fewkes (2 : 68) she appears
in the *palülükonti* (Fewkes 2 : 42) when she offers her breasts to the snake effigies.

go to her house. The girl said to her, " There is no way to go to you. " Pour-water woman had a ball of corn meal in a placque basket. She picked the meal ball out of the basket and threw it across the lake. ¹ The water spread away, there was a road for the girl to go on. The ball reached the girl. Pour-water woman told the girl to go on and follow the track. She followed the track and reached the kiva. When she reached the kiva she looked back, she saw that the water had closed in and there was no road. Pour-water woman said to her, " My daughter, I have been waiting for you all day. I am glad that you have come. I have been expecting you many days. I am your mother. I will care for you like your mother and father. I am your mother. Follow me. " They went down into the kiva. Pour-water woman said to her, " My child, be happy. Your older sister is here, your younger sister is here. " Everybody said, " Come in. " Everybody said, " Here is a place to sit. " She saw lots of people inside. They were good people, they shook hands with her. They said, " My older sister, I am glad you have come. My younger sister, I am glad you have come. " There was a big fat man sitting by the fireplace. He was called their father, he was Möyingwĕ. ² He said he was glad that his daughter had come. They gave her something to eat, watermelon, muskmelon, also *maka'no*. ³ She ate. After she finished eating, Möyingwĕ filled his pipe with tobacco. It was a big pipe. He lit it, he smoked four times and he passed the pipe to the girl. " After you smoke, " he said to her, " we will talk about how you came here. " The girl had never smoked. She was frightened. Spider Grandmother said to her that it was all right for her to smoke, she would help her. She smoked and blew the smoke from her mouth. Möyingwĕ told her that she must swallow the smoke. Kyungi (pocket gopher) was the girl's grandfather. He dug out under the lake, he dug a tunnel to where the girl was sitting. The girl felt something poking her and she thought she should move; but Spider Grandmother said to her, " Under you there is a hole for the smoke to pass through. The smoke will pass through

This might equate her with Hemokatsiki of Zuñi who performs a like rite in the initiation of the children. At the corresponding Hopi ceremony, the *powamuye*, Hahaiyi also appears. Cp. Voth 3 : 119. Voth refers to another kachina, Hããã, as the mother of the kachina. (ib., 117.)

1. Cp. Hopi, Voth 1 : 36 ; Zuñi, Parsons 3 : 237. The ritual meal-road is ubiquitous in Pueblo ceremonial.

2. The name is Hopi, the Tewa borrowed it. Möyingwĕ is not a *k'atsina*. He is dressed in grains of corn, all of different colors, and the grains are all over his body, and over his face and head and hands. (Cp. Voth 1 : 39 ; Voth 3, Pl. LVII.) He is the corn supernatural, corresponding, with a change of sex, to Iyatiku' of the Keresans. This narrator betrayed the same reluctance about naming him as would a Keres about naming Iyatiku', saying at first that he had forgotten his name.

3. Hopi, *mŏpi*, wafer-bread in long, narrow rolls — a common way of serving this bread.

you and into the hole and through the tunnel a long way (perhaps four miles) beyond the lake. " The girl smoked, smoked, she never got sick from the smoke. She handed the pipe back to the fat man. " You are a man, " (*she*ŋ *umu*ŋ) he said to her, " nobody before you has been able to smoke out this pipe. You are a man. You are safe. " So Cactus Flower girl was to live with them, with these *k'atsɩna.*

Well, after a while, Pour-water woman said to her, " I am going to give you some work. Grind our corn and you will be safe. " She led her into another room. She took a big chunk of ice and put it into the mortar. " If you grind this corn before dark, " Pour-water woman said to her, " you will be safe. " She picked up the grinding stone. There was no way, she saw, to grind the ice. She tried to grind, she began to cry. Her grandmother told her not to cry, but to keep on grinding. Then Spider Grandmother came down from her ear, she got out her medicine, put it into her mouth, and spat it on the ice. The ice began to melt. It melted, melted, melted. Before dark it was all melted and they poured the water into four jars (*pomele*). Before dark Pour-water woman came in, only a little ice was left. She said, " I am so happy you have been grinding. The water you have ground is for you and for all the people on the earth. It is rain. " She told the girl to come out and she gave her supper. After supper Pour-water woman told the girl to go with her into another room to sleep. " There is a bed for you, " she said to her. She closed the door. It was dark there. Cactus Flower girl put her hand on the bed. It was not a bed, it was a cake of ice. She wept, she said to herself, " This time there is no help, I shall be frozen to death. " Spider Grandmother said to her, " It is all right. I will help you, " she said to her. Spider Grandmother came down from her ear, and untied her bundle of medicine. In the bundle were two turkey feathers. " Put this feather on top of the ice, " Spider Grandmother said to her grandchild, " you will be able to lie on it. And this other turkey feather put on your chest, for your blanket. " [1] She put one turkey feather on the ice, and the other turkey feather on her chest. [2] She became warm, and she slept well all night. Early in the morning Spider Grandmother told her to look down from where she had been asleep. She looked and saw that she was on the edge of a cliff, outdoors. " Look down again, " said Spider Grandmother. She looked and she saw a lot of bones lying below. They had been killing the girls who slept there. " You might have died, " said Spider Grandmother to her, " but you are still safe. " Now somebody said, " I guess I had better go now and throw her away ; she must be dead. " Pour-

---

1. The single turkey feather at the back of Hopi, Keresan and Jemez prayer-sticks is called the blanket or mantle.
2. Cp. Voth 1 : 162, 164.

water woman went to her and said, " Why are you not dead? You
are a man. Nobody could sleep on that ice and not die. " The girl got
up; she hid the turkey feathers from Pour-water woman who did
not know that she had had anything for her bed and blanket. Pour-
water woman said to her, " Come. " She followed Pour-water woman
to the room where the people were. They gave her breakfast. After she
finished eating, they said to her, " You may work now. You cannot
sit here all day without work. Work to make yourself happy. " Pour-
water woman took her back to the same room, where again there was
a pile of ice. " Grind this, " she said to her, " if you grind it before
evening, you will continue to be safe. " Again there was no way to
grind the ice until Spider Grandmother put her medicine on it when
it began to melt. Towards evening in came Pour-water woman again.
There was left only a little piece of ice. Pour-water woman said to
her, " I am so glad you have ground this. " They poured the water
into four jars. That is rain, " said Pour-water woman. She told her to
come out and she gave her supper—watermelon, fresh corn, fresh wafer-
bread. They finished eating, they talked, it was bedtime, the girl was
tired. Pour-water woman said to her, " Come, go to sleep. " She took
her into the same room. " That is your bed, " said Pour-water woman to her, and she went out. The girl was no longer afraid. She laid
one of the turkey feathers on the bed, and the other on her chest. She
slept warm and well. Next morning Spider Grandmother said to her,
" Wake up. " She sat up on top of the ice. Soon she heard a voice
saying, " Well, I think by now she must be dead. The wind was blowing all night. Everything was frozen. I better go in there and throw
her away. " Pour-water woman went in, there the girl was sitting,
looking happy. " Come, follow me, " she said to the girl. She followed Pour-water woman to the same room where they gave her breakfast. She ate, she finished eating. They said to her, " You may go to
work now that you may not feel lonesome. " Pour-water woman
took her into the same room. There was a pile of ice. " Grind this
corn, " said Pour-water woman, " that you may be safe. " And she
left. The girl was no longer afraid. Spider Grandmother came down
from her ear, she took out her medicine, she put it into her mouth,
she spat it on the ice, the ice melted. Before evening in came Pour-
water woman, she saw that the ice was ground up. She said to her,
" You are a man. I am very glad you have ground all this ice. This
you have done for the whole world. It is rain. " Again she gave her
supper. She ate her supper. Now this was the third night. It became
bedtime. " You may go to bed now, " said Pour-water woman to
her. She took her into the same room. No longer was she afraid. One
turkey feather she lay down on, the other she covered herself with.
Soon she heard sounds. It was a heavy wind storm, a heavy snow
storm. It snowed all night. All night the wind blew. The girl was

covered by the snow; but she did not freeze. In the morning she heard a sound, a voice saying, " I better go in and throw her away before she rots and stinks. " The door opened and in came Pour-water woman. The girl did not move. Pour-water woman said to her, " Wake up, my child. " She stirred, she got up, she was covered all over with snow. " Well, you are a man, " said Pour-water woman. " I do not know why you did not freeze. You must be some kind of a person (*kevidahe leumuŋ*)," [1] she said to her. "Well, follow me, my child. " She led her into the same room where the people were. She gave her breakfast — watermelon, muskmelon, corn. That was the fourth day. " Well, this is the last day, " said Pour-water woman. " You may go to work. " They went into the same room. There was a basket there with corn in it, real corn. " If you grind all this before evening, you will be safe, " said Pour-water woman to her. She ground all day; before dark she had ground it all. She heard a sound. " I better go in, " Pour-water woman was saying. Pour-water woman came in. She saw that all the corn was ground. " I am so glad, my child, that you have ground all the corn, " she said to her. She led her back to the room where the people were. They gave her supper.

" Well, " said Pour-water woman to her, " now you are safe. You are going to get a husband. You will remain here for a boy, for my child. " She left the room, she returned, a boy followed her. " Well, here is your husband, " said Pour-water woman, " his name is Mantaenu (Handmark Boy). [2] That is your husband, " Pour-water woman said to her. " This is the last time you will have to do anything. " The boy went back to the room he came out of. In that room she heard a noise. *K'atsina* in there were making a noise. Out came Pour-water woman at the head of the *k'atsina*, lots of *k'atsina*. They put a buffalo skin around the fire to make it dark. Then they drew the buffalo away [3] and it was light again. There were Avayun (water-

1. If anyone fell off a cliff, without hurt, this would be said of him ; but if a man with a fetish (*tiponi*) made rain or if he raised more corn than anyone else, they would say of him *ku'tawiŋataping'anke'le*, which was translated " his heart is strong, " how literally, I do not know.
2. On his mask there is a hand print. Cp. Fewkes 2 : Pl. XLI. Possibly the girl in the picture is Cactus Flower girl. At Zuñi this girl kachina is known as Wolekwenon and she appears among the Wotempla dancers.
3. In this kachina dance water snake images project through apertures in a piece of canvas stretched on a frame with yucca twisted ropes. While they are getting this property ready they will cover the kiva fire..... Anyone may call for this water snake (Tewa, *avaiyun*, Hopi, *palōkün*) dance. They plant corn in the kiva for *palōkün* four days in advance ; the men must stay in the kiva fasting from salt and meat and keeping away from women, i. e. they *nabwala*, (Zuñi, *teshkwi*). There are six or more images, each dancer carrying one. The night of the dance they carry the images from kiva to kiva. Koyemshi sing. Cp. Fewkes 3 : 40-2. The performance seen by Fewkes in 1900 was held in *kisunbi* kiva in Tewa, and he states that the snake images were owned in that town. These images are permanent. A Snake clansman is their custo-

snakes), coming out of the holes (screen apertures), and dancing. On
them Pour-waterwoman sprinkled corn meal. Some of them were big,
some were small. Spider Grandmother said to her grandchild, " My
grandchild, look closely at them. Which is your husband ? " The girl
said, " That large one is my husband. " — " You are mistaken, "
said Spider Grandmother, " the smallest is your husband, he is inside
of that water-snake. " Pour-water woman stepped up to the girl and
said to her, " Well, my child, which is your husband? If the one you
say is the right one, he will become your husband. Stand up and
walk to the right one and say, ' My husband, come out ! ' " She stood
up, she looked at them, still she did not believe that the smallest
was her husband ; but Spider Grandmother said to her, " Indeed, the
smallest is your husband. " She walked up to the smallest, she said,
" My husband ! You are my husband. " She seized the horn of the
water-snake and pulled, and her husband came out. Pour-water
woman said to her, " Well, I am glad that you chose your husband."
The dance was over, they all went into the other room. Soon, on
the north side she heard a noise. Out came Pour-water woman again.
There were some *tameh'gehin k'atsina*, [1] lots of them. They began to
dance. They danced, danced, danced. Pour-water woman stepped up
to the girl and told her to guess which *k'atsina* was her husband. If
she guessed right, she was to have him for her husband. Spider
Grandmother said to her, " My grandchild, do you know which is
your husband ? " — " Yes, " said the girl, " that one is my husband. " — " No, " said Spider Grandmother, " that is not your husband. Your husband is the little boy at the very end. " That was
Fire maker (Poteke). [2] At first she would not believe that was her
husband. Pour-water woman said to her, " Well, show me your husband. " She walked around them, she said, " Here is my husband. "
And she pulled off his mask. That was her husband. Pour-water
woman said to her, " I am glad you guessed your husband. " The
dance was over. Then on the west side she heard sounds. They were
tempeh k'atsina. [3] They came out and began to dance. Spider Grandmother said to her, " Look closely and see which is your husband. "

dian, but they are kept in his wife's house, a Tobaccohouse. The images are fed and
cared for like any fetish. At Zuñi this water snake (*kolowisi*) ritual is found in the
kachina initiation ceremony. There is also a water-snake priesthood set of *ashiuanni*.
   1. Hopi, *suyun* kachina, " all kinds ; " Zuñi, *wotempla*.
   2. Hopi, Avatshoya. See Fewkes 2 : Pl. XXI. I was told that Abachewe or
Avachwia, as I got the name, looks like Zuñi Shulawitsi, he is white all over spotted
with black. The spots represent grains of corn, and he carries corn in his sack. The
comparison is somewhat corroboratory of the suggestion that Shulawitsi as well as
Shuraiya of Laguna is a Corn being, his spots also representing corn. (Parsons 12 :
222, n. 7) Shulawitsi and Shuraiya are firemakers, and Shulawitsi, like Avatshoya, a
little boy. See pp. 91, 94, 95.
   3. Hopi, *lehna* (flute) kachina. Fewkes 2 : Pl. XXXXIX.

She looked at them, they all looked alike to her, she did not know which was her husband. But she guessed. " Well, that one is my husband. " — " No, you are mistaken, " said Spider Grandmother, " none of them is your husband. Your husband is inside of the flute which the dancer in the middle [1] is carrying. " Pour-water woman stepped up to her and said, " Tell me which is your husband, and you will have him. Walk up to him. " The girl did not believe that her husband was in the flute ; but Spider Grandmother repeated, " There is your husband in that flute. " — " Show me your husband, " said Pour-water woman. So the girl walked to the dancer in the middle and took the flute from him, holding it in her hand. " Blow it, " said Spider Grandmother, " and he will come out. " She blew it, out dropped her husband from the flute. " I am glad you found your husband, " Pour-water woman said to her. " Once more you have to guess, " said Pour-water woman. The dancers withdrew into their room. Soon, she heard sounds in the room to the south. Out came Pour-water woman, and more *k'atsina*, lots of them, *pon k'atsina.* [2] They began to dance. " Well, my grandchild, " said Spider Grandmother, " which is your husband ? " She looked at them, at one of them she looked closely. " That is my husband, " she said. " No, my grandchild, your husband is not in this dance at all. But the next song in the dance will be about you. If you cry over it, you will lose your husband. So you must not cry, " said Spider Grandmother. They finished their song, they started on the next song. Pour-water woman said to her, " This song is to be about you. If you cry over it, you may not marry my son ; if you do not cry, you may marry him and take him home. " They began to sing of Cactus Flower girl, why she came there, and how she had left her father and mother. Soon a tear began to trickle down her face, but Spider Grandmother was sitting on Cactus Flower girl's cheek and she swallowed the tear. Everybody was watching the girl to see if she would cry. She did cry ; but there was Spider Grandmother drinking the tears as they came. Pour-water woman stepped up to her. " Thank you, my child, " she said to her. " You are a man. You never cried. You may marry my son. " The dance was over. All the *k'atsina* brought presents for her, for their female connection by marriage (*sa'i*) — corn, watermelons and muskmelons.

The sun was about to rise, and at this time they were to wash Cactus Flower girl's head. Pour-water woman started by untying her hair wheels. She put water to her head with the *pochtsele,* [3] telling

---

1. The position, as at Zuñi or Jemez, of the dance chief or director. He is the one to carry or wear the significant paraphernalia of the dance.

2. Hopi, *növak* (snow) kachina. Cp. Fewkes 2 : Pl. XXII. Said to be a Tewa kachina (Ib., p. 83).

3. The completely kerneled ear of corn which is given to a child or adult on receiv-

her to live long. Everybody, including Möyingwĕ, washed her head, dipping four times with the *pochtsele*. They washed the boy's head too. That day she again ground corn. Then she finished grinding and began to cook for them. She cooked *muwashing*. ¹ After she finished cooking, Pour-water woman said to her, " It is dinner time. You had better get ready some food for the man who is at work. " She did not see any man at work ; but they piled up *maka'no*, and prepared *kĕnshi*. ² They opened the door on the south. Cactus Flower girl did not go in with them, Pour-water woman and the girls carried in the food. Before evening Cactus Flower girl cooked some more *muwashing*. They had supper. All the people there were glad they had their *sa'i* with them. It grew dark. Pour-water woman said, " It is bedtime, we did not sleep last night, we are tired. " She opened a door. "Well, come in, " said Pour-water woman to Cactus Flower girl and to her son. She made a buffalo skin bed for them. They slept together. It was daylight ; she was safe. That day Cactus Flower girl ground corn again and made *muwashing*. Pour-water woman took some *maka'no* and *kĕnshi* into where the men were working. Cactus Flower girl did not see the men at work. They said the men were working for her. After dinner she began to grind again. She made *muwashing* again for supper. They had supper. At night they went to bed. That was the second night. The next day they did as before. At night they went to bed, that was the third night. The next day, right after breakfast, in came a big black man they called Nepokwa'i'. ³ He brought in a big buckskin on his shoulders. They gave him breakfast. " *Sa'i*, " he said to her, " come over here, and I will cut you moccasins. " He had some buffalo skin to make soles. On the right side of the room he sat, making the moccasins. Before dinner he had made one moccasin. He started on the other. A boy came in. He was Mukwanteenu. ⁴ He stood by Nepokwa' i'. He picked up the finished moccasin, and began to crush it. " What are you doing ? " said Nepokwa'i'. " You are a bad boy. That moccasin is still damp. " Mukwanteenu took a stick and tried to reshape the moccasin to look

ing a name, after it has been used, as in the tale, as a dipper, and which as a person's " mother " figures frequently in ceremonial.

1. Corn meal cooked in corn leaf and with ashes and sugar. See Robbins, Harrington, Freire-Marreco, 91.

2. Parched sweet corn flour in water. It is associated with the kachina. (Robbins, Harrington, Freire Marreco, 92.)

3. Hopi, Kopopölö (See Fewkes 2 : Pl. XXV.). He has a gourd penis and is perhaps to be equated with the chief personage in the *ilolowishkya* ceremonial of Zuñi. (See Parsons 13 : 195-199.) The ceremonial at Laguna corresponding to the *ilolowishkya* of Zuñi opens the deer hunting season. Kopopölö is a hunting kachina. (Cp. Fewkes and Stephen, 211, n. 1.)

4. Hopi, He'he'a. Fewkes 2 : pp. 13-14, Pl. XI ; Stevenson 2 : Pl. LII, LIII ; Dumarest, 177-178.

like the other; but he could not do so. ¹ Nepokwa'i' was very angry.
He said, " After this whoever makes moccasins will not be able to
make them look alike. " He stood up, he whipped Mukwanteenu
with the stick he had. Mukwanteenu moved his mouth like this
[twisting down a corner], and his mouth has been crooked ever since,
and he began to cry, and ever since his eyes have been dropping tears.
If all that had not happened then he would not look now as he does.

That evening two men brought in a *shehka*, ² an *ayu*, ³ a *malap'ai*, ⁴
and a *k'oa*. ⁵ To Cactus Flower girl they gave the *k'oa* and the *malap'ai*.
Then Pour-water woman cut her hair as Tewa women now wear it
cut, and she tied it as Tewa women now wear it tied. ⁶ " Well, "
said Pour-water woman to Cactus Flower girl, " I think your mother
and father must be homesick for you. They are lying down. ⁷ They
neither eat nor drink, they are very sick. We had better take you
home to your father and mother, " she said to her. So all the *k'atsina*
who lived there came in, filling up the room. They dressed up Cactus
Flower girl, in the *k'oa* and *malap'ai* and *shehka* and moccasins. " We
must all go, " said Pour-water woman. They all started out from the
kiva. Pour-water woman threw out a ball of corn meal, and all walked
over the track it made. They all went on, each *k'atsina* carrying a present for his *sa'i* — corn or watermelon or muskmelon. They reached
the place the girl came from. Cactus Flower girl called, " Mother !
Father ! " She heard no voice in answer. She called again, " Mother!
Father ! " She called four times. Then she heard a voice saying,
" You are a naughty girl to call ' Mother! Father! ' Our child went
away long ago. There is none to call us Mother, Father. You are a
naughty girl. " — " Well, my mother, I am here. My father, I am
here. " They did not believe her. She said it four times. Then she
stepped down inside. They sat up, they put their arms around her,
they wept. They were very much surprised that their daughter had
come back. Pour-water woman said to her child, " My child, you

1. At Zuñi anyone who is a hasty, incompetent worker is said to work like He'he' a.
2. Large white, cotton embroidered blanket, made for a bride.
3. White blanket with red and dark blue border.
4. Large cotton belt, with large knots and long fringe. Made for a bride, used also
as a dance belt.
5. Black and dark blue woolen dress, the native dress which is worn over the
right shoulder and under the left arm.
6. Banged to reach to the tip of the nose but drawn accross the forehead and
tucked under the longer locks which are left hanging on either side of the head. They
are rolled loosely, not wrapped with grease stiffened yarn, in the Hopi fashion.
7. Unless she is sick or " homesick " a Pueblo Indian woman would not think of
lying down in the day. I recall how once a Hopi girl, seeing me lying down, —
I was resting from taking down one of these lengthy tales, — remarked to her mother,
" She is lying down, she must be homesick. " Cp. Voth 1 : 72. (" They were no
longer sitting up because they were so homesick. ")

must stay here and work for your old man [1] and your old woman. Do not return home. Do not be lazy ; work well for them. " Everybody said the same thing to the boy. They brought their presents in and filled the house up. And the houses of all in the town they filled up with watermelons and muskmelons, while the people slept. [2] When the people woke up, they wondered who had brought them the melons. The old man who had the trouble with the girl was dead, and his wife was dead. Another old woman who lived next door saw Cactus Flower girl and told the people that Cactus Flower girl had returned home, bringing with her a boy. All the people were glad to see her. They went to see her and shake hands with her.

That year the boy staid there. One night there was a call, announcing that they were going to hunt rabbits. The boys of the village were all angry that Cactus Flower girl had brought home a boy, they had all wanted to marry her, all had asked to have her. Now they were planning to take his wife away from Handmark boy. [3] The man who killed most rabbits was to take her. [4] Everybody was happy, thinking he was going to get her. In the morning Handmark boy picked up the four rabbit sticks he had brought with him from home. His father-in-law got out his rope [to tie the rabbits] for him and they got some food for their son-in-law (*soyingi*, male connection through marriage). He came to the place where the men assembled. They started out, all day they killed rabbits, all but Handmark boy who killed only one little rabbit. But when they started home Handmark boy began to kill rabbits and jack-rabbits, and he killed more than all the others. So they could not take away from him his wife.

The next night they called out for a race, the winner was to take Handmark boy's wife. Some of the boys were good runners, they expected to take her. The race leader [5] came and told them to go below, on the flat. Everybody went below, including Handmark boy and his wife. The runners took off their clothes, to run a long distance. The race leader said, " The man who comes in first will take Handmark boy's wife. " The mountain they were to run to was a long way off. They were good runners, Handmark boy was behind them all. He reached a hill where a bird was sitting, a swallow (*avamiu*). Swallow said to him, " My nephew (*memee'*), my poor boy, you will never beat those runners. They are a long way ahead now. Get on my back, " Swallow said to Handmark boy. " How can I get on your back ? You are so small, " said Handmark boy. " Well then, stay here. I will go

1. *Obia sena*, Englished as father-in-law, and *obia kwia*, mother-in-law.
2. Cp. Voth 1: 73. See also 91 I may recall the fact that the kachina are preeminently bringers of gifts, gifts of crops and of rain.
3. Cp. Voth 1 : 149.
4. For the idea at Zuñi of competing for a man's wife, see Parsons 3 : 243.
5. *Uneluhkena* > *eluh*, race, *kena*, leader.

for you, " said Swallow. Soon he overtook one of the runners. He
looked like Handmark boy. He went on and he overtook another
until he overtook them all. He reached the mountain, he circled around
it and returned. He met the runners and he said to them, " You
boys must run harder to get me. " They thought it was Handmark
boy, but it was Swallow. He reached Handmark boy. " Well, my
nephew, " he said to him, " I will go on with you; but they will
overtake you. " He went on. He looked back. " They are catching up
with us now, " he said. They ran on. Swallow said, " I guess you
had better hold on to my wings. " Now they were close to the line
where the people were. Everybody called out, "Handmark boy, come
on ! Come on ! " They had no more than reached the line when
the other runners came in. But Handmark boy won, and he kept his
wife. The people said, " He is a good runner. It is well that he keeps
his wife. "

Next day in the evening he heard another call, tomorrow they
were to hunt mountain sheep. Handmark boy did not know where
the mountain sheep were. His father-in-law told him that they were
far out in the moutains. Only four men were going hunting. They
went south to a big canyon. Handmark boy saw a mountain sheep
and followed it into a canyon. The others were hunting somewhere
else. The sheep went into a very narrow place. Handmark boy came
close up to him. The sheep turned back. Handmark boy took his
medicine into his mouth, and spat it on the sheep. The sheep turned and ran at him to toss him. He pulled his bow, shot and killed
the sheep. That was a man in that mountain sheep. That was the
way they planned to kill Handmark boy. [1] He did not go down to
get that sheep, but looked for another sheep. He did not go after the
sheep because the mountain lion [2] he carried in his wallet [3] said to
him, " That is not a real mountain sheep. It was a man to kill you.
We had better look for a real sheep. " Handmark boy took off his
wallet, and placed the mountain lion on the ground. The little mountain lion turned into a big lion and chased a real mountain sheep and
killed it. Handmark boy took the sheep home. (The lion turned back
into stone.) They were witch people [4] trying to kill him. The boy
who had turned into a sheep went home.

The next day, in the evening, Handmark boy heard a voice calling out that they were going out to hunt down a certain bear with
cubs, that was killing people. That bear, too, was a man changed to a

1. Cp. Navaho, Matthews 1 : 186-187 ; See p. 68.
2. Tewa, *kenhepii* ; but here, the term used is *kenhepiipung*, referring to the fetish
of mountain lion as in Hopi the suffix *poko* indicates the fetish animal, *tohoe*, mountain lion, *tohopoko*, fetish of mountain lion.
3. Tewa, *patikimu* ; Hopi, *pilamuki*.
4. Tewa, *kyuge'*, Hopi, *powaka*.

bear. This time they were sure to kill Handmark boy. A call came to hurry. Handmark boy got his arrows and bow, and went out with the men. They found the track of a bear. They said to Handmark boy, " Follow the track, If you kill the bear, you may keep your wife. If the bear kills you, somebody will take your wife. " Handmark boy followed the track. He came to a place overgrown with bushes, it was the only place for the bear to go. He followed the track. His mountain lion said to him, " My father, stop here. That bear is asleep. Soon he will wake up and attack you. Take me out. " Handmark boy took him out. " I will lie here, " said Mountain Lion. " If the bear is strong enough to kill you, run to me. Shoot him in his paw when he wakes up and stands up and raises up his arms. " Handmark boy came up to where the bear was, he shuffled his feet. The bear jumped up, and held out his arms. Handmark boy shot him in the paw. The bear fell down dead. Handmark boy cut out his heart. (He was not really a bear.) He dragged him along to Mountain Lion. Mountain Lion put him on his back and carried him until they came near where the people were, then Mountain Lion went back into the wallet. The people said to Handmark boy, " Did you find a bear ? " — " Yes. " — " What did he do ? Did he fight ? " — " He stood up and held out his arms, and I killed him. " — " Where is he ? " — " Over there, " he said. Everybody with him was happy. This was the last thing they did to Handmark boy.

After this they lived on to the time of planting corn, to June, when it was very hot. Handmark boy went to the fields to cut weeds. His wife said to him, " I will bring you your lunch. " She started out to take his lunch to him. When she reached the field, she found him sitting under the shade. They ate together and then she said to her husband, " You better go now and cut the weeds. " — " It is too hot, " he said to her. " Nevertheless, you better go and cut the weeds. " She said so four times. He went to cut the weeds. He felt weak and he stopped working. His wife came up to him and asked, " Why did you stop working ? " He said nothing. She took him by the arm. He was dead. She came back and she found grass growing there where he lay. His bones had become grass. He was an ice-boy, and he had melted away. In this way she had killed him for what they did to her in his home.

Naheimoʻtʼoʼpitʼai, thus far I know.

9. THE BROKEN WATER JAR: [1] WATER SNAKE BOY. [2]

Long ago the people were living at Walpi. The Tca'akamuni (Crier

1. This tale is known also at Zuni where it was outlined by Nick on showing him Fewkes 2 : Pl. XXVI.
2. Recorded by Ruth Bunzel, four years after the preceeding tale was recorded, from the same informant.

chief) had a daughter. She was a Cactus clan girl. She was a fine looking girl. The War chief had a good looking son and he wanted to marry the girl. The girl also wanted it. Both of them wanted to marry. In the evenings the girls went down to the spring to get water. They carried water jars on their heads and went down to the spring. She never went with the other girls. She never went outside to any of the houses. She stayed at home all the time and did her work. She did not go around like the other girls. One day a young girl came there and said, "Let us go down to get water," she said. " No, I don't want to go down to get water with you, " said the girl. " You ought to go, "said the younger girl. All the girls wanted the War chief's son to marry one of them, but the Cactus girl got the boy and they were angry about it. So they sent the little girl to tell the Cactus girl to go down to get water with them that evening. She persuaded her to go with them, and soon she said, " All right, I will go with you. " So in the evening when it got cool the young girl came again ready to go down. Then she took her jar and both of them started down the trail. When they came there the girls were already going back, carrying their water. " Are you going now ? " — " Yes, "they said. " We will wait here for you, " said the girls. Then the two girls went on. They went to the spring and filled their jars with water and went back home. When they came up they came to the place where the other girls were playing. They put down their jars and began to play. While they were playing the girl who had come to ask her to go down kicked her jar and the jar was broken. When the jar was broken the little girl said, " Your jar is broken. " She said she was sorry and cried. She did not know how the jar had been broken. She cried and went home without water. When she came home her mother asked her, " What is the matter ? " — " I have broken my jar. " — " You have broken your jar ? You are a naughty girl. You should know enough not to break jars. " She took up a stick and began to hit the girl. She was angry that her mother whipped her. She took her blanket and went out.

It was nightfall and she went down the trail. While she was going southeast she stopped to pass water. Then someone said something to her. " Move back. " She heard the voice and looked around, but it was dark and she could not see anyone. She looked around but she just heard the voice. Soon the voice said, " Here I am, granddaughter. " She looked closer and there was a spider. " Here I am, granddaughter. You are going where your life is in danger. You would never come back home. I am sorry for you and I was just watching for you to come along. Come in, " said her grandmother. " How can I come in ? It is a tiny hole, " said the girl. " You just step in and it will be a big place, " said the Spider. She did so and it became a big door. She went in and it was a nice room. She had lots of things there.

" Now this will be your home. You will stay here forever and never go home, " said the Spider. " You are the daughter of the Tca'aka-muni, and you are the mother of all the people, " Spider-woman said. " You stay right here. I have the same kind of jar as the one you broke. You need not feel sorry. Whenever you go home you can take one of these jars with you. " Next day she washed her hair. She lived with Spider-woman for many days.

The boy who was going to marry the girl lay on the top of the house and waited for the girl. He wondered what had happened to her. Every evening when it got cool he went to the top of the house and watched for the girl to see what had happened and where she had gone. He did not see her for a long time. He was lonesome for the girl, because he wanted her for his wife. It was about the time she should have become his wife and he was very lonesome for her. Her mother and father and brother felt the same as the boy. They did not know what had happened to her. They did not know where to look for her. They asked from house to house to see if anyone had seen her, but no one had seen her. No one knew where she had gone and what had happened to her. Her father and brother did not know where to look for her and they gave up. They did not look for her any more. They were all sick in bed because they felt so badly. Her father and brother and mother were all in bed because they were lonesome for the girl. They were thinking and thinking of the girl all the time, but she never returned.

At that time Spider-woman told the girl, " Well, my granddaughter, I will wash your hair early in the morning. " As soon as she got up in the morning her grandmother was ready and she washed her hair. She washed it and dried it and after it was dry she put it up in whorls, and she dressed her. Her grandmother gave her a new dress and a new belt and new mocassins and a new blanket. Then she said, " Well, my granddaughter, it is about time for you to go back to your home. Your mother and father and brother are sick in bed. They are lonesome for you and they are sick in bed for many days now. You must go back home. Here is a water jar to take back with you. " The water jars were all in a row. " Now, my granddaughter, you pick out the one that suits you best. " She looked at all the water jars. She looked and looked and the best one in the row was just like the one she had broken. So she pointed to that jar. " This is the one I want to take, " said the girl. " Oh dear, " she said, " do you want the best pottery ? Why don't you take a new jar. You ought to pick out a new jar. " — " No, grandmother, I want to have this one. You told me to pick out the one I want, and this jar suits me, so I will take this one. " — " All right then, " she said. " But never put your finger into the jar. Use the dipper. Remember, do not use your fingers or hands, or put your hands into the jar when there is water in it. Remember this,

my granddaughter, " said her grandmother. " When you go down
to the spring the boy will come down to meet you. The boy is watching for you. While you are inside the spring and your jar is full of
water, if the boy comes and asks you where you have been, do not
tell him. Watch the boy. Don't let him put his hand or his finger in
this jar. Remember this. Then when you fill this jar it will last forever, "
said the grandmother, " it will never get dry. There will be water in it
forever. That is the reason why I was wishing that you would not
pick out this jar, but you did. So be careful and watch everybody.
If anyone comes into the house for a drink of water they should
not use their hands or put their fingers in this water jar, " said her
grandmother. Then she said, " Well, it is about time for you to go. "
Then she said goodbye and the girl went home. The boy was still looking for her. He thought that the girl was coming to the spring. About
the time the girl went into the spring he sat up and ran down to the
spring. When he got there, there was the girl just about filling her
water jar. " Where have you been ? " said the boy. " Oh, just visiting
around, " said the girl. " At what place have you been ? I have been
looking for you many days. I am lonesome and I am sick. I am anxious
to see you, and I saw you down here and came down to look for you.
Give me a drink of water, " said the boy. " Get it yourself, " said the
girl. " No, give it to me. " The girl looked around and just then the
boy put his hand into the jar and took a drink. Then right away there
was a water snake standing there at the edge of the water. Then she
ran to the water snake. " My love, " she said, " I love you. I am
anxious to see you. I was glad to meet you, and now you have been
turned into a water snake and I must leave you here. I am sorry to
leave you. " Then she left the boy and he went into the water and she
went back home. She got home about nightfall. Her father and mother
were lying in bed. " Mother ! " said the girl. It was a long time before
she heard an answer. " Who is that ? You are a bad woman. You are
teasing me. There is no one to say 'mother' to me. My dear daughter
has been gone a long time and we are lonesome for her. " Then she
said, " Father ! " After a long time he answered, " You are a naughty
girl. You are just teasing us. There is no one to say that. Our dear
kind daughter has been gone a long time. There is no one to say that
to us. We have lost our daughter, " they said. Then she said
again, " Brother ! " He said the same thing to the girl. At last she said,
" I am your daughter. Here I am. I am your daughter, " she said to
her father. " I am your sister, " she said to her brother. " I have gone
and left you for many days and here I am returning. " At last they
all jumped out of their beds and ran to the door to meet her. There she
was standing at the door. So they reached out their hands and brought
her inside of the house. That is the way she came home. They were
all glad of it. After four days, about the time they went to bed, she

did not go to bed. Her father and mother had gone to bed, but she was still sitting there washing her head. After she had washed her head she put up cornmeal to take along. " I am going down to the spring to marry the boy, " she said. She put up meal to take. At last she said, "I have to make prayer sticks to take along. " She began to make them but she did not know how to make them. At last she went to her father and waked him. "Father, " she said, "wake up. " — "What has happened ? " said her father. " I want you to get up." He looked at his daughter. He was surprised to see her doing something. There was a basket full of feathers and sticks there. He was surprised to see her making prayer sticks. "Father, I am going down to the spring to marry the boy. Four or five days ago when I came home I went to the spring and filled the jar my grandmother gave me. While I was filling the jar the boy came and put his hand into the jar and turned into a water snake and went down into the spring. I am going into the spring to marry that boy. But I do not know how to make prayer sticks. I want you to make them for me. " Then her father said, " My dear daughter, why should you go there ? There is none of our kind of people there. You do not know where you are going. I do not want you to go down there. You will never come back. But you want to go, so I will let you. " Then her father began to make prayer sticks. After he finished, then he smoked tobacco. Then he woke up her mother, and her mother cried because her daughter was going away. Then her father took her cornmeal and put the prayer sticks in a basket and took them along. They went. They went to the spring Tawapa (Sun spring). When they got there inside the spring he said, " Let us in, " he called out. " Let us in, " said the father. " Let us in, "said the father again. " Let us in, " said the father the fourth time. Then they heard a sound coming from way down. There was a voice saying, "Come in, come in. " Soon a stick came up out of the water. It was a ladder. Then someone came out and said, " Come in, come in. " Soon a woman came out. She was Ahai'iwuxti, the mother of the katcinas. She said, "Come in, come in, my daughter. "Her father took his daughter's hand and said, " Be a good girl and do your work well. Whatever comes to you, do your best, " he said to his daughter. Then he left her and went back home. She went into the water. There were a hole and a ladder. They went in, way down into a cellar like a cave. When she got down there were lots of people there. A big man was sitting by the fire. He was the chief of the katcinas, the people who were living there. M..... wa (? Möyingwĕ) was the name of the man sitting by the fire. There were many people there. They all said, " We are glad that you came." They put away the cornmeal and gave her something to eat. As soon as she finished eating they said, " We are going to bed now. " She went to bed. They put her in a bed in back of the house. She looked around. There was no bed. Then the mother of the katcinas told her,

" You will sleep there. There is a place for you to sleep. " She looked around and there was no bed and nothing to sleep on, only ice. Then the grandmother said, "This is your bed. Just put this on top of the ice. " The grandmother took out a turkey feather and put it on top of the ice. " Just lie on that, and put this one on top of you to cover yourself. " She put it on top of her blanket. She went to sleep. She was warm in bed. Early in the morning she woke up. Ahai'iwuxti called her, " Daughter, come out. " She went out. She was very surprised that she was alive. She thought she would freeze to death. She did not say anything. She took her to the place where they ground corn. She began to grind. She put her hand on it, but it was ice. Just big chunks of ice were lying there. Then she took up the grinding stone and mashed the ice and began to grind. She put the turkey feathers on the stone she was going to grind on and held them with her hand. It was warm and the ice began to melt. The ice all melted and in half a day she had finished it. Ahai'iwuxti was very surprised that she had melted all the ice. " Thank you, " said the mother of the katcinas. She stopped. In the evening after they had eaten their evening meal they all went to bed. She went into the same bed she had used the night before. She went to sleep and had a good sleep. Early in the morning she called to her to come out and grind the same ice. In three days she had ground it all. On the fourth morning early in the morning the mother of the katcinas said again, " Come out, my dear daughter. " She came out. The room was full of women and girls ready to wash the girl's head. Then the mother of the katcinas untied her hair and washed her hair. Then every one of the women and girls in the room washed her hair, and she became their daughter-in-law and their sister-in-law. They were glad the girl was there. All day she ground corn and cooked whatever she could. In the evening the mother said, " We are going to have a dance. " In the evening the dancers came out for the Balilukan dance. The mother of the katcinas was there. When the dancers came out the other katcinas brought presents for their sister-in-law. The mother of the katcinas said, " Your sweetheart is in one of the Balilukan. If you guess the right one you can take him home. " Grandmother-Spider was sitting behind the girl's ear. Then her grandmother asked her, "Did you guess ? " She said, " No. " She looked at one Balilukan and pointed to it and said, " This one. He is inside this one. " Then her grandmother said, " No, that is not the one. He is in the little Balilukan. " Then the mother of the katcinas said, " Have you guessed which one the boy is in ? If so, take it by the horn and pull him out. " She walked up to the dancers and put her hand on the horn of one and pulled him out. " Here you are ! " said the girl, and her sweetheart jumped out of it. Then the mother of the katcinas said, " I am very much surprised. What kind of a girl are you ? You guessed the right one ! " Then

the dancers went into the kiva. Next, other dancers came out of the
west. They were called the Neva (snow) katcinas. They came out
and began to dance. Then Old-Woman-Spider asked her granddaughter,
" Have you guessed which is the boy ? " She looked them over and
said, " That is the one, " and pointed to him. " No, that is not the
one. The very small boy is the one, " said the grandmother. " Do
you want to guess now ? " said the mother of the katcinas. The girl
went over to the dancer and said, " Come out ! " Then he came out.
She kissed him again. Then the mother of the katcinas said, " What
kind of girl are you ? You guessed right again ! " Now another dance
came from the south. They are called the Lena (flute) katcinas. They
all had flutes. They came out and danced. When they were dancing
the mother of the katcinas said, " Just guess which is the boy. You
have two more times to guess. If you guess the right one you can take
him home. " Then the grandmother asked her, " Have you any idea
which is the one ? " Then she pointed to one and said, " That is the
one." — " No, " said the grandmother, "That is not the one. None
of them is the boy. He is inside the flute. The small one who
leads the dance, he is inside his flute. " Then the mother of the
katcinas stood up and said, " Have you any idea which is the
boy ? If you have guessed the one, just say so. " She walked over to
the dancers while they were dancing and went to the small one who
led the dance and said, " Here you are! Come out ! " said the girl and
pulled at the feather hanging from the flute. Then the boy dropped out.
That is the way she got him the third time. " Well, you have only
one more time. If you guess him this time I will let you have him, "
said the mother of the katcinas. Soon they came out from the east. They
were the Seyuin (mixed) katcinas who came out. She looked around
and could not see which was the one. They were all different. They
did not look alike, but she could not tell which he was. At last her
grandmother asked her, " Have you any idea where the boy is ? " She
said, " I cannot tell. " — " All right, " she said. " That man sitting
by the fire is about to join the dance. The middle one who leads the
dance will have all different kinds of grain covering him. Well, now
you will find the boy. Watch the middle leader of the dance. He has
a white grain of corn over his heart. He is in there. " Then the mother
of the katcinas asked her, " Have you any idea where the boy is ? "
She went up to them and put her finger on the white grain of corn and
pushed it off. " Here you are ! Come out ! " Then the boy came out.
" Well, that is the last time. You have beaten me. I will let you have
the boy. He came to be my husband, but I will give him back to you.
Now you can take him home. You have beaten four times," she said.
Early in the morning they dressed her up and said to the girl, " You
have beaten us in everything. First you did not die when you slept on
the ice. Next you melted the chunks of ice and you beat us there.

Next you guessed the boy and you beat us there, and so I am returning to you your husband. Now when you go home you take this corn and put it in your house, " said the mother of the katcinas, and she gave her an ear of corn. " Whenever you think of having this Balilukan dance, make clothes like those you have seen here and dance. Then plant the corn in the kiva and when it comes up you will be ready for the dance. But you have to eat inside of the kiva, " said the mother of the katcinas, " and don't go outside of the house, but stay in there for four days. When they dance you will be their mother and you will dress like me. " So she came home to the spring Tawapa. They took her up to the top. When she got to the top of the mesa it began to rain and it rained all day. Then the girl came home and she brought the boy home with her. The people asked her where she found the boy, but she never told anyone where she had been. She never told the people where she got the boy. In the winter, about February, she planted the corn in the kiva with her husband and the youngest of the boys. When the corn began to come up they went into the kiva and stayed for four days and made a Balilukan, and then after four days they went into all the kivas and danced. That is the way they got the Balilukan dance. They still have it the same way.
That is the end.

10. THE WOMAN STEALER. [1]

Far away there at Kunluokyut'e'e a girl was living. She was a fine girl. She had a father and mother. At her town they played games in the *elu* moon and the girls danced. But this girl never danced with the others. Her father said to her, "You never go out with the other girls. They are happy, but you are not happy. " In the evening the girls would get their jars and go to the spring for water. She would not go for water. Her mother told her to go with the other girls for water. The boys would have the girls to dance. " If you go to the dance, you might find a boy and get married. I am getting too old to do all the work, " said her father. The boys of the village would come in the evening as she was grinding corn and look in through the window and try to talk to the girl. But she would not talk with any boy.

Soon Okuah ch'ee enu, Cloud yellow boy, heard about the girl and said, " I think I had better go and see that girl. " At night he went and looked through the window. She looked at him as she was grinding the corn. She stopped grinding and asked the boy, " Who are you ? " — " It's me, " said the boy. " Where do you live ? " — " Not in this village, out to the north. [2] Why do you ask

1. See pp. 113-116.
2. Yellow is the color of the north.

me where I live ? " said the boy. " I just wanted to know where you live, " said the girl. Soon he said, " I guess it is time for me to go home. " — " All right, " said the girl, "Come tomorrow evening. " — " Well, I am going. " — " Wait, " said the girl. She went into her *koye'*, took out some *makáno* and put it into her *ayú* and wrapped it up for him. She gave it to him. " Take this to your house. " — " Thank you, " said the boy. He was happy he had talked to the girl. A little way out of the village he put up his rainbow and on it went back to his house. When he reached his house, his people were not yet asleep and he gave his bundle to his mother. She opened it and found some *makáno.* She was pleased. " Where did you get this ? " asked his mother. " I went over at Kuṇluokyut'e'e to see that girl who would not talk to anybody, but she talked to me. " They were all happy over it. Next day he put up his rainbow again and travelled back on it. He carried some meat for the girl. He looked in at the window. " Is that you who came here last night ? " — " Yes, " said the boy. " Well, come in, " said the girl. He went in and handed his load to her. She opened it and found the meat. She took it down to her mother and father who were surprised by it. " Where did you get this meat ? " asked her father and mother. " There is a boy who brought it for me. He came here last night and I gave him some *makáno* in my *ayú* and today he brought back the *ayú* with this meat. " — " Well, that is what I want for you, " said her father. " You must talk with him. But you must not sleep with him. When you have talked enough, let him go back to his own house, " said her father. So she talked with him, and they ate their supper and she told him that he must go home. She gave him some more *makáno*, more than she first gave. He was glad to have it. Then he went out, and he went outside the village and put down his rainbow and on it he travelled home. His mother and father and sisters were pleased with what he got. Next day he went hunting; he killed a deer and carried it back with him. In the evening his mother told him to take the whole deer to the girl. So he put the deer on his back and put up his rainbow and travelled to the girl. That time he did not look in through the window, but went straight up to her room. " Here is a deer I have brought for you, " he said. She was surprised, she had never seen a deer before. She ran down and told her mother and father that there was a big animal the boy had brought. They went up and there was a big deer. They were very glad about it. They picked it up and took it down into the *koyé*. They skinned the deer. Her father and mother told the girl, " You must tell the boy that tomorrow you will go with him. " So they talked together. They had supper and then the girl said, " Tomorrow is the day I will go with you, so tell your father and mother about it. " — " All right, " said the boy. She gave him more *makáno.* So he put his rainbow outside of the village and went home on it. His father and mother were pleased with what he got. " Tomorrow the girl is coming with me, " he told them. They were glad. Next morning his father said, " Go hunt deer, so there will be some food for the girl. " He went out and killed a very large deer. He brought it home, they skinned it and cut it up and boiled it. In the evening he put up his rainbow and travelled to the girl. It was dark when he got to the girl's house. His father and mother told him, " When you get to her house, say, ' Let us go to my house for supper.' She will come out and you bring her to us. " He went to the *koyé*. He said, " *Hau*. Let us go to my house for supper. " — " All right, " said the girl. Her corn meal¹ was all ready. Then her father came out first and then her mother and then the girl, and the boy went ahead. They went through the village. They said, " We will go back to our house. You go with the boy. He lives a long way off. We can't go. " So they said good bye and went back. The girl went on with the boy until she got tired. " I am tired, " she said to the boy, " I can not go any farther. " — " Let me carry your load, " said the boy. She went on again ; but again she got tired. " I can not go any farther. " — " My house is a long way off. Close your eyes and don't open them until I tell you. " So he put up his rainbow and they went on the rainbow until they got to his home. " Well, all right, " said the boy. She opened her eyes and there was a beautiful place of grass and flowers. She was very glad. They walked and came to a place where there was a kiva. " We have reached my house.... I am not alone, " said the boy. " Well, come in, " said the people inside. They got her load. They found that it was a very good-looking girl the boy had brought and they were pleased. They gave her supper, meat ball and watermelon and muskmelon. After supper, the father said, " Well, we will go to bed. " And the girl slept with the boy's mother. Early in the morning she began to grind corn. ² After breakfast she ground corn again. By this time the boy's aunts began to come to fight with his family. They put mud on one another and poured water on them. They had a big fight. They nearly killed the boy's father, his own sisters. He said to his sisters that he had a very good *sa'i*, " better looking than you, " he said. They dragged him to the ground, put some mud on him and threw mud on the walls of the kiva... ³ The girl went on grinding all day,

1. The meal which the bride takes to the bridegroom's house. See pp. 224, 248. Also for Zuñi, see Parsons 8 : 314.
2. Cp. Parsons 8 : 325.
3. This incident of the " women's fight " was inserted, I surmise, because a day or two before we had witnessed a like attack on a neighbor's house. Sikaiyauusi, the sister of the Town chief of Walpi and Sichumovi, was remarrying. Two women, the groom's " aunts, " i.e., father's sisters or father's sisters' daughters, made a raid on the groom's house. In this case no man figured in the fight. There is some evidence here for cross-cousin marriage.

until they made her stop and eat supper. All went to bed. Early in the morning she began to grind corn, they had breakfast, she ground again. In the evening the boy's mother made the girl stop grinding. They ate supper, they sat up a while, they all went to bed. Early in the morning she began to grind corn, they had breakfast, she ground again. She ground till evening. Then the mother of the boy told the girl to stop grinding corn. She ate supper with them. Next morning early in the morning, that was the fourth day, the boy's mother fixed some soap-weed ; and untied the hair wheels of the girl. First she washed the girl, then the father of the boy, then his sisters; then his aunts came in and washed the girl's hair. After breakfast the men began to spin in one kiva. They finished in one day. Next day they began to weave. Bow snake (Na'la) made the *malap'ai*. Runner snake (Pisuh) made the *shehkah* and *ayú*. They finished the *shehkah*, *malap'ai* and *ayú* in one day. The next day Nepokwa'i' came in and he was the one to make moccasins for her. He finished in one day. That evening the father and mother of the boy said, " Well, tonight we take our *sa'i* back to her house, " said they to their people who were living in another kiva. So they all came in and they dressed their *sa'i*. As they were all starting, they told the boy he must not be lazy at the girl's house, must plant corn and watermelon and do other work. Every-one said the same thing to the boy. The father said, " Take some watermelons and muskmelons and squash and corn for our *sa'i*. " They went for a while afoot, then they put up a rainbow and travelled with clouds and rainbow. They spread the *shehka* for the clouds and the *malap'ai* they put on each side of the *shehka* — that was for the *sa'i*. — That is the reason they make the *shehka* and the *malap'ai* for a mar-ried woman. — They travelled on the clouds and rainbow to Kun-luohkyut'e'e. It was raining when they got there. They went into the girl's house. Her father and mother were glad to see her and to get the presents they brought for her. The room was full of corn, water-melons, muskmelons. Also all the houses of the town they filled up. Next morning when the people woke up, they found their houses full of corn, watermelons and muskmelons. They found that the girl who had gone with the boy had come home. " We must be kind to the boy," said all the people of the town. They washed the boy's head that morning.

They lived there many days until spring time when the boy went to his field to plant. The girl had a baby by that time. She left the baby with her mother and took her jar and went down to get some water. Just as she had filled her jar, somebody was standing there. She looked at him. He said to her, " Give me a cup of water " (*k'ehde*, gourd cup). She thought she would not talk to him. " Take it yourself, " she said. " Don't talk that way to me. Give it to me. " — " Get it yourself. " — " Give it to me. " So she gave it to him. He left a little water in the cup and sprinkled it on her. She sprinkled water on him. And so they played all day. He had a flute in his left hand and he blew the flute and he put the girl inside of the flute and carried her away. Her husband came back and found the baby crying. He asked the mother of the young woman (*kwia k'ele*) where she was. " She went after water this morning, but she never came back. " He went down to the spring and saw her water jar. There was her track and there was the track of another, and then the tracks disappeared. So he knew somebody had carried her away. He took the water jar to the house and he said to the mother that somebody had carried her daughter away. She was very sorry. The baby was crying. " Well, tomorrow I am going after your mother, " he said to the baby. " I know who took her away. " Next morning he started out. He came to a place where he heard a sound. That was Spider grandmother. She said, " My poor grandchild, you are looking for your wife. I think I will go with you. " [1] — " How could you go with me ? " — " Put me back of your ear and I will sit there, " said Spider. So he put her back of his ear, and they went on. He put up his rainbow and they travelled to a mountain, Chikumup'ing. [2] That was the place where the man had taken his wife. They left the rainbow, and went up the mountain, they went in. Lots of women were grinding in the room, and in the middle his wife was grinding. He did not know who the women were. As soon as he came in his wife looked at him and cried, " Why did you come up here ? " said he to his wife. She said nothing. She just kept on crying. The man who had taken his wife came in. That was T'ai'owa. [3] " Why have you come to my house ? " said T'ai'owa. " I have come for my wife, " said Yellow cloud boy. " If you beat me, you can take her, " said T'ai'owa. He got his bag of tobacco and his pipe, and it was a great big pipe. He filled his pipe, and lighted it and handed it to Yellow cloud boy and said, " Do not blow out the smoke, but swallow it. " There was Pocket gopher who made a hole through the mountain to Yellow cloud boy and the smoke came out from him and went through that hole. All day he smoked and the tobacco was all out and Yellow cloud boy handed the pipe back to T'ai'owa. " You are a man, " said T'ai'owa. Yellow cloud boy had beaten him. " Well, you have beaten me, " said T'ai'owa, " but there is one more thing to do. If you beat me in that, you may take your wife, " said T'ai'owa. " Well, all right, " said Yellow cloud boy. " We will race. " So they came to

1. Cp. Voth 1 : 144.
2. It is in the lower world ; but there is at Santa Cler (Clara) such a mountain called after the lower world mountain. (It is Tsikomo, see p. 40, n. 1).
3. Any handsome man may be called T'ai'owa. (See Fewkes 1 : 124) T'ai'owa is referred to as the inventor of the flute in the underworld and the founder of the *wŏwŏchimtu*, one of the phallic men's societies, and *mamsrautu*, the related phallic women's society.

the foot of the mountain and he made a line there. There was a mountain far off they were to race to. His grandmother said to Yellow cloud boy, " Leave me on this line, " and she gave him some medicine. " Before you start to run, " she said to Yellow cloud boy, " spit the medicine on T'ia′owa. " Then they went. T'ia′owa left a big knife on the line. " The first who gets here will cut off the head of the one who comes after, with his knife. If you beat me, cut off my head and take all those women. " They stood on the line and then they started to run. Yellow cloud boy was faster than T'ia′owa because he was a cloud boy. His grandmother was blowing medicine out before T'ai′owa so he could not run very fast. Yellow cloud boy ran faster than T'ai′owa and came in first. Then he took the knife and caught T'ai′owa by the forelock and cut off his head. He cut open his chest and took out his heart, and cut it into small pieces and mixed them with sand, and threw them in every direction. " We must hurry now, " he said to his grandmother and he went up to the house and told the women they were all to come out and go to their houses. He told the women to shut their eyes, and he put up his rainbow and they travelled on it. Then he told the women to open their eyes. They came to a place near the spring where his wife had been stolen. He told the women to go to their houses. Some were from Kuṇluokyut'e′e, others from other places. So they started home. At that time T'ai′owa came to life again. He went to his house and found that all the women had gone. He put up a rainbow and went to the place where he had taken the girl ; but all the women had already left that place. So he went back to his house.

After that they lived there for a time ; but Yellow cloud boy was thinking all the time how his wife had been taken away. So he thought as he was not a person like the others in the village but a cloud boy he would go back home. His wife had done a bad thing, and he was going home. One night when his wife was asleep he took the baby boy and went out of the village, put up his rainbow and went back home. [1] " Why did you come home ? " asked his father. He told how T'ai′owa had taken her to his house and he did not want to live with his wife. " It is all right for you to come back and stay with us, " said his father and mother, " since your wife did that bad thing. " So he stayed there and kept his boy with him, and he is living there yet.

11. WOLF BOY.

Far away there at Muchobekedih lived Koñlutseyaayu‘, Yellow corn girl. In the winter in the moons of *elu* and of *k'aut'o* (February ; Hopi, *powamu*) they danced ; but this girl never went out to dance. The people would go out now and then for wood, with the girls. (They called

1. Cp. Voth I : 99.

this work, *ti'chundisomeh* (*chundi,* lots of people, *disomeh,* go for wood) [1]. All the girls would go except Yellow corn girl who would never go. Her father told her she must go whenever the girls went. But she did not like to go. In spring time in cactus-flower moon (*yopovipoye,* March) the men had a foot-race (Tewa, *tibikwehebe*) every afternoon. One of their kivas had the best runners, they never were beaten. Members of the other kiva wanted to beat them, but they could not.

One time one of the men said they would go for wood with the girls. He called out that in four days they would go. After four days the men got their ropes and their stone axes (*k'owileh*) [2] and they went. They got to the trees and chopped enough to carry. They got two straight logs, laid their wood between and tied the wood on and carried on their backs. [3] In the afternoon the girls had to go to meet the men, carrying food along. This time Yellow corn girl told her father and mother she wanted to go. They were very much pleased. She got ready some food. They told her that the first man or boy she met she must ask to rest, and give him the food and go ahead of him. " That is the way the girls will do, " said her father and mother. They started, and a little girl was ahead of her. " Are you going to meet the men with wood ? " — " Yes, " said the little girl. So they went together. Then the men were coming, but the other girls had met them all. Then the men said there were still some men to come. They came to a place where somebody was coming. It was an old man. The little girl ran up to him and said, " Rest, " and she gave her food to him. That was the last man to come. The little girl asked the old man, " Is anybody coming behind you ? " — "I don't know if anybody is coming behind me or not. I guess I am the last. " Yellow corn girl was sad at that. Well, they saw somebody coming, so she waited for him. He came up to her, and she walked to him and said, " Rest, " and he sat down and she gave him her food. After he finished eating they went on. She did not know who he was, for she knew none of the boys or men. Well, she went on ahead of the man and she brought him to her house. Her father and mother were glad that she had brought a boy with a load of wood. They unloaded the wood and the boy said he was going back home. The mother of the girl asked him where he was from. " I am living in the East, [4] " said the boy. They gave him some food and he went home. Next day the men boiled some meat and they took it in bowls to the girls' houses, each man to the girl who had taken him

1. Hopi, *komukwehe.* The custom has passed out ; but a middle-aged woman remembers it as a girl.
2. Hopi, *wilige,* groove.
3. So packed, the wood looked like a ladder, it was dragged by a tump line across the forehead. An old man may still bring wood in this way (*k'aleqong*). For the same method at Zuñi, see Handy, 451.
4. The direction Wolf is always associated with.

home. In the evening there was the boy who had carried wood to the house of Yellow corn girl. Nobody knew who he was. He was a fine looking boy. Next day, while Yellow corn girl was grinding, somebody looked through her window. " Who is that ? " said Yellow corn girl. "It's me. " — " Where are you from ? " — " I am living in the East. " — " Are you he who brought wood ? " — " Yes, I am he. "She began to talk with him. " How far away is your house ? " — " Not very far away. " She gave him some *makáno.* The boy went home, the girl went to bed. In the morning the girl told her father and mother, " There was a boy came to me. " — " Who was he ? " — " The boy who brought me some wood. " — " What did you say to him ? " — " I asked him where he lived. He said in the East. I gave him some *makáno,* and I want to marry that boy. " — " All right, that is what we want for you, " said the father of the girl. " I am getting old, and I want some one to help me. " — " Tonight if he comes, I want to go with him, " said the girl. So they got ready some meal for the girl. In the evening the mother of the girl went to tell the girl's brother and her own brother to come to their house. When they came in, the mother of the girl said their daughter wanted to marry that boy. " It is all right, " said the brother and uncle. Night came and she went up to grind her corn. The boy came up to the window, and she told him to come in. The father of the girl said, " My daughter is ready to go with you to your house. " They put the corn meal on the girl's back, and they started off. They went outside the village and soon the girl said that she was tired. The boy took her load and put it on his back. Soon the girl got tired again. She asked the boy, " Where is your house ? " — " Soon we shall get there, " said the boy. Soon they came to a forest. " Here is my home, " said the boy. They came to a place where the ladder came out. He called out, "I am not coming alone. " — " Well, come in ! " They went in. There was a woman in the house and a man, the mother of the boy and the father of the boy. They were very glad he had brought the girl. They gave them food for supper. The mother of the boy said, " It is about bedtime. We shall all go to bed. " She told the boy to go and sleep outside, and she slept with the girl. Next morning she got up and said she wanted to grind corn. But the mother of the boy said they had no corn to grind. They ate breakfast. All day the girl did nothing. At night after supper they went to bed. The girl was there three days. On the fourth day she washed the girl's hair. The girl was sorry there was no work to do and she was unhappy. Nobody came in to wash her head, only the mother of the boy and his father washed her head. The mother of the boy said, "Tonight we will take you back home. " The girl was unhappy that there were no wedding garments for her. [1] At night somebody came in with a bundle. The mother of the boy

1. Cp. Voth 1 : 148.

said she was very glad he had come. That was the boy's uncle bringing a *shehka*, *malap'ai*, *ayu'*, and *k'oa*. Then the girl was happy. They dressed her up and said they would take her to her house. The mother of the boy, the father and uncle started with the girl to her house. At midnight they reached the girl's house. They called out that they had come. The girl's mother made a fire. They brought in the girl and she was glad. They left the boy and started home. Next morning she made soapweed and went around the village and called in her clanswomen and they all washed the boy's head. Then he went out, he came back, they ate their breakfast and he stayed there all day.

Next morning they called out that there was going to be a foot race. This young man said, " I guess I better go with them to the race. " There was a long line, everybody was ready to run. They saw somebody coming; they said, "Wait until he comes, then we will start to run. " Then he came, they saw him, the young man who was just married. All belonging to one kiva were together in a bunch, others of another kiva in a bunch. Every bunch invited him. " Come to us and be our partner, " they said to him. His father-in-law was standing in one bunch. He thought he had better join his bunch. They started, he was a very good runner. He kicked the ball and went ahead. This time they beat the best runners. These wondered how they could win again. So next day they called out for another race. Again the young man was the best runner. They did not know who he was. They were asking one another. Nobody knew what villlage he belonged to. One of the boys said, " In four days we will have a race, and the winner will cut off the heads of the others. " Some of them did not want to do this ; but they said that the young man who made this proposal could run with that other young man. So in four days they all went down to the line where they started. There the leader of the race said, " If this boy beats this young man, we will kill all the men of the young man's kiva. If this young man beats the boy, then the kiva of the young man will kill all the people of the town, " said the leader of the race. Before they started to run an old man came up and asked what they were going to do. They said, " If this boy beats this young man, we will kill all the men of the young man's kiva. If this young man beats the boy, then the kiva of the young man will kill all the people of the town. " The old man said he did not like that kind of a race. They listened to the old man, and they stopped that race and everybody went back home. Next day they were to have a race, a *k'atsina* race (Tewa, *wanaing*, Hopi, *wawash*), and the old man was to be the leader of the race. He belonged to the kiva the young man belonged to. In the afternoon all the members went into that kiva and they painted some masks to wear. The old man said to the young man that he would fix a mask for him. They called the mask P'otsáleh. [1] They went

---

1. Hopi, Hemisho. Cp. Fewkes 2 : Pl. L.

down to a place whence the *k'atsina* came in. They brought with them a ball of cooked sweet corn, the Huntamehlepong [1] carrying it in their blanket on their back. When these [the *k'atsina*] got to *monakwa* [plaza] these Huntamehlepong called out, " Boys, come down! [from the house tops] Come down ! We are going to have a race with you. " The good runners came down. They made a line for the *k'atsina* to stand, another line, for the boys to stand. These were to start at the same time and if the *k'atsina* caught the boy, they would whip the boy and then the boy would go and get some sweet corn. There stood P'otsáleh ; the best runners among the boys wanted to race with him. P'otsáleh caught one of the boys and took him by the hair and cut his hair. Then he caught another boy and cut his hair. The sweet corn was all gone, so they went back home. Next day, another man called out that they would have another *k'atsina* race. It was a man of the other kiva. They used the same kind of mask. When the *k'atsina* came in to *monakwa*, Huntamehlepong called out for the boys to come down. That young man came down and there was P'otsáleh. " That P'otsáleh. will run after me, " said the young man, but P'otsáleh did not catch the young man, he was the better runner. In the evening all went back into their kiva and all talked about how they could beat that boy. The leader of the last race said, " I am going over to Sumpáviwili [2] to tell them to come to race. " All the men said, " All right, you can go, the best runners live in that village, tell them to come and race for us. " So he went to Sumpáviwili and the people were not yet asleep and he went to the Town chief and said he wanted his children to come and race for them. " It is all right for them to go, "said the Town chief. So after four days they dressed and went to *monakwa*. These people of Sumpáviwili were witches. They were very good racers. One of them was dressed as P'otsáleh. The leader of the race said this Po'tsáleh would run with that young man and if he caught him he would cut off his head. They came to Muchobekedih. The Huntamehlepong called out for the young men to come to race. That young man came down and said, " That P'otsáleh will chase me. " So he chased him, but he did not catch him. He was the better runner. That night they talked about it. One man said, " We will go over to race the people of Sumpáviwili. " Next day he called out, " In four days we will go over to race the people of Sumpáviwili."Then the best runners invited this young man to go with them, and he dressed up as P'otsáleh. And they went to Sumpáviwili to have a race. When they got there, they went to *monakwa*. There came the boys to race with them. One boy said that P'otsáleh should race with him. So P'otsáleh ran after him and caught him. And he took his knife and cut off his head. Then all the runners

1. *Huntamehle*, ball, *pong*, head ; the *koyemshi* (Hopi, Zuñi) are so called.
2. *Sumpavi*, chopping wood, *wilige*, groove, gap. It is a ruin to the east.

got their bows and arrows and ran after that young man. They could not catch the young man. He went back to Muchobekedih. He took off his clothes as he ran, and he took off his mask. He reached Muchobekedih. He gave the head of the boy to his father-in-law, and he told his wife to get ready to go away with him. By this time all the people came back to the village and they started to run after this young man. But they could not catch him. As he and his wife ran he put up a ring ¹ and he jumped through it ² and he became a wolf, and his wife jumped through it and she became a wolf. The people running after them came to the wolf's track and they never caught the wolf. After this they lived in the woods. After that Sumpáviwili people came to Muchobekedih and began to fight. They fought and fought and they burned the town. ³ This happened because he who cut off the boy's head was a wolf.

12. COURTSHIP FEUD. ⁴

Once upon a time the people were living at Sikyatki. Lots of people were living right there. There were not many clans living in the village ; they called the clans the Coyote clan, the Corn clan, the Sun clan, the Rabbit clan, the Sand clan and the Cottonwood clan. That many clans were living together in the village. It was a big village where they were living together. The people were doing many things in order to enjoy themselves. There was a chief who had a daughter and a son. The boy's name was Sikyatciteyu (Yellow bird boy). This brother and sister were very kind to each other. The girl was sewing on a wedding garment. She did more of this sewing than any other kind of work. She enjoyed herself sewing on this wedding garment. In the winter time her brother went out to hunt rabbits. When her brother was going out to hunt rabbits his sister fixed his lunch. The boy carried it himself. He went out each day to hunt rabbits. He killed one or two or three in a day, and when he came back home, his sister was very glad to have the rabbits. This is the way they got their meat. Their father and mother were still living. Both of them were very kind to their father and mother and their father and mother were both of them very kind to their son and daughter. This is the way they lived. When springtime came her brother went over to the edge of the mesa to Polixti. He had a friend with him. They always went together everywhere they went. They were good friends and they called themselves partners (*senwa*), and they always went together.

1. For this common method of metamorphosis in Pueblo Indian witchcraft, see Parsons 3 : 244 ; also pp. 240-1, 274.
2. Witch-ring. Tewa, *kyugeh tẹmeli* ; Hopi, *pohoköla*.
3. Cp. Fewkes 2 : 115 ; Voth 1 : 244-246.
4. Recorded by Ruth Bunzel.

Well, one day they both went to Polixti just looking around. They were visiting around to see some girls. There was a house where there was one girl grinding corn at night. They both peeked in at the little window. The girl saw them. "Who are you?" she said. They did not answer the girl who they were. She said again, "Who are you?" but they never answered. Then she said, "What are you? Are you from this village or are you from the other village? Where are you from?" she said, but they never answered her. "Well, I don't know you. You had better go right back where you came from. I wouldn't think of marrying either one of you." Well, both the boys were cross about it. They were angry. They just walked away. Both of them carried their bows and their arrows on their backs. They had quivers on their backs. Both of them had their weapons on their backs. After they had gone a little ways from the house Yellow bird boy pulled an arrow out. "Partner, what do you think about this?" — "About what?" he said. "About the words the girl said to us." His partner said, "Well, her words hurt me. My heart is hurt now. I am going to say something about that girl," he said. "Well, you go ahead of me," he said. "All right," he said. "We will just go in and shoot her. We will both shoot at the same time so that one of us won't have to say, 'I shot the girl.'" Then they took their bows and arrows and went back. They stepped up to the window. The girl was still grinding. They looked right in and said, "Look out!" One of the boys said it. The girl looked up to the window and they shot her. As soon as they had shot her, they shot again twice. Then she was dead. She never cried out or said a word. They shot her in the right place. She lay right down in the place where she had been grinding corn. They went back to Sikyatki. They were going to have a dance at Sikyatki four days after they killed the girl. They went back. Next day the girl was found. She was dead. She had been shot with an arrow. She had a brother. They were the son and daugther of the Calling-out chief. He had a son and a daughter and now the daughter was shot. Her mother and father found out she had been killed. They told her brother that his sister had been killed by some man, by an enemy. They did not know what enemy he was. The boy thought that someone who came from Sikyatki had done it. He thought that himself, but he wanted to find the right man. He told his mother and father, "I am crying, but you must not cry for the girl for many days. Just four days," he said. "I am going to do something in return. I am going to kill the sister of Yellow bird boy." He had found it out in his own mind. Next day he went out to the northeast. He found tracks. He found the tracks of the two boys and he followed the tracks. Even where their tracks could not be seen on the stones he followed them. They went to Sikyatki. He found it out. The two villages did not like each other. He knew that some people from Sikyatki had done it. The boy knew just who had done it. He found it out some way.

Four days later there was going to be a dance at Sikyatki. The boy from Polixti went out early in the morning and went down to the spring Tawapa to bathe himself early in the morning. As soon as he had bathed himself, he ran to the east to the foot of the mesa. He ran as hard as he could and went to Sikyatki. He went around the east side of Sikyatki and went up on the sandhill near Sikyatki. He could not get to the top because he was tired. After a while he went back to Polixti. Next morning early in the morning he started out at the same time. He went to Tawapa spring and bathed himself again. As soon as he was finished bathing, he went out and ran in the same direction that he had gone the day before. Then he went out the same way and followed his tracks and went up the sandhill. He went a little farther but got tired before he got to the top. He went back home. On the third morning he got up again early in the morning and at the same time he went down to the spring at Tawapa and bathed himself. As soon as he finished, he went out and ran in the same direction that he had gone the other two mornings. He followed his tracks again and got to the sandhill and ran up. He got almost to the top of the mesa and then he got tired. Then he went back. On the fourth morning he got up again and went down to the spring and bathed himself and went out and ran again, went just the same way to the sandhill. He got up to the top this time. He did not get tired but went all the way up. Now he had run enough to climb that sandhill. He went back home. That was the fourth day, the day they were having the dance. The people of Sikyatki were having a katcina dance. They were dancing all day. After he had his breakfast the boy told his mother and father. " What do you think ? " said he to his father and mother. " Well, " they said, " we feel like paying them back and killing that girl. " — " That is what I am thinking. That is why every morning for the last four mornings I have run and climbed the sandhill. They are having a dance today and they are going to have it again tomorrow. Tomorrow is the best day, the biggest dance, so I am going to be there tomorrow. I am going to dress up today and put on my mask, my Hemsum katcina mask. " [1] He put on his mask and told his father, " I want a scissors and a knife. " He was dressing all day, the day the people were having the dance at Sikyatki. Lots of people were at Sikyatki to see the dance. They came from many villages, from Oraibi, Shongopovi, people came from all over to see the dance. The head man called for the dance for the next day and the katcina dancers went back into the kivas. The people said they were going to have it again. The boy stayed at his house. Early in the morning he

1. See Fewkes Pl. L.

didthe same thing again. He went down to the spring to bathe himselt, but he came right back home from the spring. He did not go where his tracks went. He just bathed and came back home. After they had had their morning meal his father told him, " What time are you going to Sikyatki ? " — " In the afternoon, "he said. So his father put on different kinds of clay, yellow clay and black. He painted his son on his body, and he wore a dancing kilt and a belt and a fox skin behind. He dressed up and put the scissors between his belt and his kilt. Then hesaid, " I am going now, " he said to his father and mother. "Watch for me at sunset. If I get the girl, I shall be back home before the sun goes down. But if I don'tget the girl before the sun goes down, I shall be killed. If I am not back home before the sun goes down, you will know I have been killed, so look for me before the sun goes down," said the boy. He went up on the mesa at Walpi. There was no one living at Walpi then. He hid behind the rocks on the top of the mesa so that no one would see him. He went on, on top of the mesa, until he came to the place where the two little ruins are now, to Kikotsima. There were people living in that village, but no one was in the village. They had all gone down to see the dance. He waited for a long time until late in the afternoon. Then he went down to Kikotsima spring. No one saw him go down. He went to the spring. He waited there a while and then he went to the village. He was carrying some baked sweet corn fot a present. He went to the plaza where theywere dancing. He went in there and no one knew who he was, or where he came from. He went into the dancing plaza. The people saw that some kind of katcina had come there. They were surprised. They did not know where he was from or who he was. He was wearing his mask and they did not know who he was. He stood there. There was an old man sitting by the house. He stood up and went to the katcina. He came up to him and he sprinkled some corn-meal on his head, he " fed him. " He said, "Where did you come from ? " He held out his hand towards the west, towards San Francisco Mountain (Nevatikiovi). He asked him again, " What did you come here for ? " He just showed him by holding out his finger that he had come to have a race. The old man said, " All right, " and said to the young men, " Come and race with this katcina. " The dance was over but the people were still watching. They had the clowns there. One of the clowns said to himself, " I will be in the race, " and stepped right up to him. They made a line about six feet from the katcina. The clowns stood on the line and the katcina had his line too. Then they went. They ran. They had only run a little ways when the katcina boy grabbed the clown's hair and cutit off with thescissors. He cut it and everybody laughed. Then the second clown started and the katcina boy caught him and cut his hair too and the people laughed again. All four clowns ran and they were all caught and had their hair cut off. Then the old man who had been standing there said, "Well, young men, let the best runner come down and race with this katcina." The boys knew that one of them was the best runner and he went down to race with him. This katcina boy raced with him and caught him again and cut his hair again. Then another boy went down, the best runner. They raced again. He caught him again and cut his hair off again. This was the second boy. Then his present of baked sweet corn was all gone. Everytime he caught a man he gave him a piece of the baked sweet corn, a present to make him happy. But now his present was all gone. He was just looking around. Soon he saw a girl standing away up on the top of the houses. This was Yellow bird boy's sister. He saw her and ran towards the girl. He climbed up to the top of the house. The girls all started to run away. They ran into the house, but the last one was the one he was looking for, Yellow bird boy's sister. Before she went into the house he caught her in the door. He caught the whorl of her hair. He took out his knife and cut off the girl's head and waved it on top of the house. Then he went down the steps of the ladder and the people all started to run after him, but not a single one caught him and he ran out of the village. He ran as fast as he could to the sand hill. All the people chased this katcina boy, but they never caught him. He went to the foot of the sandhill. He ran away up to the top of the sand hill. When he went up to the top of the mesa he was way ahead. He took off his mask and said, " Indeed, this is because Yellow bird boy killed my sister. I am paying back for it. If your heart hurts, or if you are angry, just chase me to Polixti, " he said, " and do whatever you like. Let us have a war between Sikyatki and Polixti, and ruin all the villages. So if you are brave enough to do it, go right to Polixti tonight, or four days from now. I am going to wait for you four days from now. And if you are not brave enough to fight four days from now, I will not fight with you after that, " he said and then he went. Everyone was sad because she was the daughter of the chief. The people all felt badly about it. They talked about the girl all night. The people who had come from other villages went home that evening because they were afraid something would happen. There was surely going to be a war between Sikyatki and Polixti, so the people from other villages just went back home. That evening they buried the girl. They were very sorry about it. They did not sleep. The men went into the houses and talked about the girl. Then the chief said, "All right, my children. Four days from now we will go and fight. I will go myself, " he said. " I am going to kill the boy myself instead of any of you. I want to do it myself. Let all the men and boys make arrows and bows and after four more days we will go. Not a single one shall be left in Polixti. " The katcina boy brought the head to Polixti. He brought it to his father. The father of the boy got down his pack of tobacco and a pipe and put the tobacco in the pipe and smoked. Then he said to his wife, "Go and call the War chief (*kaletaka*)." His wife went out and called for the War chief. She said, "The Calling-out chief wants you. " — " Wants me for what? " — "He wants you to come over and have a smoke with him. " — " All right, " he said. He took out his pack of tobacco and his pipe and went over to the Calling-out chief. The Calling-out chief was smoking there. He sat down and the Calling-out chief gave him his pipe to smoke. He smoked and after he had finished smoking he filled his own pipe and smoked and after he had finished, the War chief asked the Calling-out chief, "What did you want me to come over for ? " — " Yes, " he said, " my son brought this head from Sikyatki." — "Is that so ? " he said. "Yes," he said, " And that head is for you. " —" Thank you, " he said, and smoked again. "In four more days we are going to have a war. The Sikyatki people are going to come over to this village and fight, " he said. " All right, " he said. "I will take it and mind to do it [take charge of it]. " They finished their smoking and then the War chief took the girl's head and took it home and put it away in the inside of his house. Then it happened. After three more days in the evening at sunset the Calling-out chief (at Sikyatki) called out for all the men and boys to come to his house in the evening. He told them to come with their bows and arrows and whatever they had to fight with. They did it. They came there with their bows and arrows and knives and whatever they had to fight with. They stayed there half the night. Then the War chief said, " We will go right out and half of the men will stay in one place and the other half in another place. " (He meant where the trail goes down to the spring.) They stopped at the trail in the middle of the night. Half stopped on one spring trail and the other half on the trail to the other spring. They were there in the trail waiting for the people to come for their water in the morning. Early in the morning a couple of women were going for water. The two women came to the group of men. They shot the two women and killed them. Next a boy come running along. They shot at him but did not hit him and he went back to the village and called out that some enemies were hiding themselves on the trail on the side of the mesa. The people knew it. Then the people who were hiding on the trail stood up and went to the village. They fought. Some people were still in bed and they killed them all. They burned the whole village. That is the way they destroyed the village. Of course some of the men who came from Sikyatki got killed too. That is the way they destroyed the village of Polixti.

After that some of the people of Polixti were not killed. A few were left. They got away. A couple of them were safe and they went to Oraibi. One more was saved. He went to Samumpavi(?). They talked about the matter and what had happened. The people who had gone to

Oraibi talked about their troubles and how all the people had been killed, and the Oraibi people were very angry about it. After a few days the Samumpavi people came to Oraibi. The two villages were angry about how the Polıxti people were destroyed. They talked it over and they said they would fight for these three men, all the people of Samum-pavi and Oraibi. They called out for all the people at Oraibi to get ready to fight. After three more days the Oraibi people went over to Samumpavi. They stayed there overnight and the next day early in the morning all the Samumpavi and Oraibi people went together to Sikyatki. They fought and fought. They destroyed the village. They burned it. Some girls were caught and made slaves. The Oraibi people caught them and made them slave girls. That is why the Sikyatki people are now living at Oraibi. They were taken from Sikyatki. They are the Coyote clan at Oraibi. One of the girls was Coyote clan and one was Sand clan. The Oraibi people say that these two clans came from Sikyatki.

13. DOVE BOY AND COYOTE.

Far away there at Kuṇluokyut'e'e Blue corn girl (Kụlutsáyuayu$^{c\prime}$) and Yellow corn girl (Kụlutseyuayu$^{c\prime}$) were living. They had a father and a mother. They were two sisters. They had no older brother nor younger brother. They would grind corn all day and at night, too, they ground corn. They lived in the *koyé*, and up ladder in *kwak'eibi* they ground corn. Every morning they would cook for breakfast and in the afternoon they cooked for dinner. The girls did all the cooking and housekeeping. Their mother let them do all the work. Their mother loved them, and their father loved them. Their father fetched wood for them, and water he fetched for them every day. During the winter in the *elu* moon the people would dance, but these girls would never watch the dance. The boys who lived there tried to marry them, but they did not like the boys. From another village boys came to marry them; but they would not marry. In the daytime there were games and races, but they never went out to see them. They ground corn all day.

In summer their father went to work his field, planting pumpkin, watermelon and corn. When the corn was about ripe their father told them that it was ripening. They were happy. They said, "Tomorrow we will go to our field. " The next day they took some lunch for their father and they went to their field. They said to their father, " Father, you better go home. We will stay here to watch our corn. " In the evening it was time to go home. They started for home. They saw lots of flowers and grass on the way, and they picked the flowers. They reached home. Their mother cooked supper for them. They were happy, they talked about the corn and what they saw on the road, the flowers and grass. They said to their father, " Father, we will go tomorrow again to our field. " He said to them, " All right, you may go. Go and be happy. " The next day, before sunrise, they ook a lunch and they went to their field. They got some fresh corn and they began to cook it. They got some watermelon and they ate it. As they were sitting under the shade, somebody was coming along. The younger sister (Blue corn girl) saw him, she said to the elder sister, " My elder sister, somebody is coming. " Her elder sister paid no attention. She said again, " Elder sister, somebody is coming ". There was somebody standing there wearing a *tsaweětoh* [1] (*poncho*) and he had a *kyumta* [2] on his face. He was a goodlooking boy and he wore turquoise in his ears, and a string of beads around his neck. They were ashamed to talk to him. Younger sister said to Elder sister, " You better talk to him, learn where he comes from. " Elder sister said, " Never mind, don't talk to him. " Younger sister said, " He is a stranger, better talk to him. " Elder sister said, " Father might scold us if we talk to him. " Pretty soon Elder sister turned to him and said, " Where do you come from ? " He said to her, " A little way from here. " The girls said, "Let us eat our lunch. Have you eaten already ? " they asked him. " No, " he said, " I have not eaten yet. " So they ate together. As they ate, Elder sister sprinkled water on the boy. The boy sprinkled water on both the girls. They played together, sprinkling water. They played all day. The sun went down. Younger sister said, " The sun is down, we better go home. " — " All right, " said Elder sister. They went home and the boy went his way home. As they went home they were happier than they ever were before. The next morning they said to their father, " Father, we want to go to our cornfield again. " — " All right, " he said to them, " you may go. " They went to their corn field. One said to the other, " I wonder if that boy will come again. " It was about dinner-time. " Somebody is coming, " said Elder sister . It was the boy. " Have you come?" said Elder sister. " Yes. " — " Where do you live ? " asked Elder sister. " A little way from here, " the boy said. They ate their lunch together. Elder sister began to sprinkle water on the boy and he sprinkled water on the girls. They played together, they played all day. Pretty soon the sun set, before they knew it. Younger sister said, " The sun is down, we better go home. " They went home. The boy also went home. They were happy. That night again they ground corn. As they ground somebody looked into the window. " Who is that boy ? said Younger sister to Elder sister. " Don't watch him, " said Elder sister, " keep on grinding. " So they went on grinding.

---

1. Translated " blue woolen shirt, " but a picture showed the familiar *poncho* cut. It was woven by men for themselves. It is no longer worn.
2. Black line across each cheek, from nose to jaw.

Bedtime came, they went to bed, without looking at the window.
At breakfast they told their father that they wanted to go to their
field again. " All right, you may go, " he said to them. When they
reached their field, Younger sister said, " I wonder if he will come
again. " Elder sister said, " I don't know whether he will come or not. "
So they watched for him. Somebody was coming. It was the boy
who was there before. They turned around. " Did you come again ?
said the Elder sister. " Yes, " said the boy. They talked, talked.
Pretty soon Elder sister said, " We better eat our lunch. " They ate
together. Then they began to sprinkle water on one another. They
poured water on one another all day. Then the sun went down.
Younger sister said, " The sun is down, we better go home. " Elder
sister asked the boy, " Where are you living ? " — " A little way
from here, " said the boy. " Tomorrow we want to go with you to
your home, " they said to him. " All right, " said the boy. That
night they ground and they put the meal into a basket. The next
morning at breakfast they said to their father and mother, " Father
and mother, we want to go to the corn field again. There was a
boy came to us there three times and we played with him, we want
to go to his home today. " — " Who is the boy ? " they asked them.
" We don't know, he is not from this village. He is a good boy, we
want to go with him, " they said. Their father and mother said, " All
right, but you must be careful. Take care of yourselves. " They
dressed up in a new dress and belt and in new moccasins, and their
mother put up their hair in wheels. When they got to their corn field
they waited for the boy to come. " There is that boy coming now, "
said Younger sister. " Did you come? " said Elder sister. " Yes. " —
" Well, we said we would go with you to your house. " They started to go. Then they asked the boy, " Where is your house ? " —
" A little way off. " They kept on going. They got tired, they asked
him, " Where is your home ? " — " A little way farther. " By noon
they were very tired. They said to him, " Well, we can't go any
farther, we are so tired. Your home is too far away. " — " Soon we
are there, " said the boy. So they tried again. At sundown they
approached a mountain, and came close to it. " Here is my home, "
said the boy. He pulled up a yucca plant and there was a kiva
ladder coming out of the kiva. The boy said, " I am not coming
alone. " They heard voices, lots of people said, " Come in. " They
went into the kiva. They saw lots of people, lots of goodlooking
people. All the boys looked alike, they all looked like that boy. All
the women looked alike. They were kind people. The mother of
the boy took the corn meal and put it away. They gave them supper.
Night time came, the mother of the boy said, " We better go to bed,
you must be very tired. " So they went to bed in the other room.
They slept well. Next morning they began to grind corn, and they

ground until the sun went down. They stopped grinding. The mother of the boy came in and was glad that they had finished grinding. " Come out to the other room and we will have our supper, " she said to them. They went out and ate supper. Soon it was bedtime and they went into the same room as before and slept well. They woke up early in the morning before sunrise. A basket of corn was there and they began to grind. They kept on grinding until breakfast. Then the sister of the boy brought breakfast in to them. They continued to grind until the sun went down. Then the mother of the boy came in and told them to stop grinding. She took them in to the other room and they ate their supper. They went into the same room and slept well again. Next morning they began to grind again. They ground until breakfast and after breakfast they ground and kept on grinding until sundown. The mother of the boy came in. She said, " I am so glad you have finished your work. " They went with her to the other room. They ate supper. It was bedtime, they went into the same room to sleep and they slept well. It was daylight. Then the mother of the boy came in. She said to them, " My daughters, wake up and come in. " They went in and the room was ready for them to wash their heads. In there were lots of girls and women. They all looked alike. The mother of the boy first washed Elder sister, then in a separate bowl she washed Younger sister. While she was washing Younger sister, the boy's sister washed Elder sister. All the women washed them. When the sun came out, the mother of the boy took them out and they sprinkled corn meal to the Sun. They went back to the house and began to grind corn. Then they began to make *muwashing.* All the people in there ate the *muwashing.* The father of the boy said, " Your mother and father are lonesome, we better take you home. " The bridal garments were finished. Bow snake made the *malap'aiye,* Runner snake made the *shehka.* The moccasins were made by Nepokwa'ici. So they dressed the girls up. The mother of the boy said to him, " My son, these girls are going to take you to their home. You must not be lazy. You must help your father-in-law. If there is no wood, you must get wood for them. If there is no water, you must get water for them. " His father spoke the same way. His uncle spoke the same way. They said to him, " If you have trouble, you must not come back home, but if our *sa'i* want to marry another man, then come back home and stay here. But if nothing happens to you, live with them all the time. " Then they all started with the two *sa'i.* The *sa'i* never knew what kind of people they were. They were dove people (*k'owile t'owa*) who turned themselves into people. They all went bringing the *sa'i* home. They made the distance short, so that they soon got to the girls' home. The girls were glad. The girls said when they got to their *koye',* " Mother ! Father ! " — " There are our

children, " said their father. "Well, come in, " he said to them.
They all went in. The girls' mother gave the people something to
eat. " We brought this boy for you to work for you, " said the mother
of the boy. " If he is not lazy, he will help you, " — "That is what
we want, we want a son-in-law (*soyingi*), " said the father of the girls.
Then the other people all left. The father of the girls said, " It is
bedtime. " The boy brought in four buffalo skins for his bed. They
slept together. Next morning, the mother of the girls went to the
houses of her clan and told all the women to come to her house.
They all came, and were glad. They made ready to wash the boy's
head. They all washed the boy's head. They said they were glad to
have a *soyingi*.

After this he went out to work all day. He fetched the wood and
the water. In the springtime he said he wanted to go to plant. His
father-in-law (*wiaseno*) went with him and showed him his field.
He went to plant every day. He finished planting. Soon the ·first
plants came up. His wife, one of them, said to him, " How is the crop
doing ? " — " The crop looks pretty well, " he said. " Well, I want
to go with you today, " said Younger sister. " You don't need to go, "
he said to her. They prepared a lunch for him. He started. Then they
said they, too, would go. It was hot as they went. They came to a
dove sitting on a bush. He was saying something. Younger sister
said, " This dove is saying something, just as if he were calling us. "
— " We better go on, we are so thirsty, " said Elder sister. The dove
was singing :

> Kulutseyeayu ᶜ'
> Blue corn girl
> Kulutsáyuayu ᶜ'
> Yellow corn girl
> *Neeanaha napoko* ᶜ
> Here is a spring
> *ewiyu heh ewiyu heh*

Younger sister said, " Elder sister, that bird is calling us. He is
telling us that there is water. " They listened, he sang once more :

> Kulutseyeayu ᶜ'
> Blue corn girl
> Kulutsáyuayu ᶜ'
> Yellow corn girl
> *Neeanaha napoko* ᶜ
> Here is a spring
> *ewiyu heh ewiyu heh*

" There is water, " Younger sister said, " water right there. We
better go for it. I am so thirsty I can not reach our field, " she said

to her elder sister. So they went to him. " You must not fly away, "
said Elder sister, " for you are to tell us where there is water. " They
looked around. " Where is the water you talk of ? " He just did this
(poking head forward, as a dove does). They found the little spring and
they drank. " I wish you would not fly away, but let us take you to
our home and sing to us while we grind corn, " said Younger sister.
She walked up to the bird and she caught it. They carried the bird with
them to their field. They looked for their husband, but they could
not find him. They saw his tracks and they looked for him. They left
the dove under their shade. They walked around their field, but they
could not find their husband. They went back to their shade, and
there sat their husband. They were surprised to see him. " We were
looking for you all over this field, " they said to him. " How did you
come here. " They began to think that that was the dove. They
looked for his track to the shade. They could find no track. They
looked for the dove's track and it was still there. They said, " We
caught a bird and he sang to us about water. " — " What kind of a
bird? " asked their husband. " A dove, " they said. " Why didn't
you tie him here ? He may have flown away, " said their husband.
They kept thinking that he was the dove. They all came back home.
They ate their supper and at bedtime they went to bed. Early in the
morning he went out. He would always go out early in the morning.
This morning Younger sister thought she would go after him. She
followed her husband away from the village. As she went down a
hill, there was a dove sitting and singing, " Huh huh ! huh huh ! "
There was the dove, but her husband was gone, and there was no
track. She went up to the dove, closer and closer, and she said, " Is
that you, my husband ? " She went closer and said, " Is that you, my
husband ? " She went closer and asked again, " Is that you, my husband ? " He shook his head like this (poking head forward). " You
are the one who sang to us yesterday." He shook his head, he never
spoke. She caught the dove and carried him back. She put the dove
inside where they had slept. She did not tell her mother and father.
Soon after sunrise they went in and there was their husband. Thus
they found out that their husband was a dove. He said to them, " I
am going away to see my father and mother. " — " When are you
coming back ? " asked the girls. " Tomorrow. " The next day he left
and carried some *makáno* and some *keñshi* to his mother.

As soon as their husband had gone, they said, " Well, we want to
go to our field. " So they went to their field. As they were eating
their dinner, somebody came to them, a boy came to them. For a long
time they said nothing. Finally Younger sister said, " Who are you ? "
— "My name is, Pokwashé, Coyote." [1] — " Well, we don't know who

---

1. A folktale designation for Coyote. A related term, Poshekwaishing' (see
p. 245), is translated Water-drag man.

you are, " said Younger sister. " Where do you live ? " — My home is over yonder. " Soon they began to play with him. They did not notice that the sun had gone down. " We better go home, " said Younger sister. They went home. There they found their husband already back. " Why did you come back so late ? " asked their husband. " It was so far, " they said. He knew that they had been playing with Coyote. He was unhappy about it. At supper he looked unhappy. They kept talking to him to keep him from thinking bad things. At bedtime they went into another room. They lay down. Their husband lay down and was quiet. Younger sister said, " Why don't you talk to us. What makes you unhappy ? " — " I am so tired. I am not unhappy. " They knew they had done something, so they kept asking him why he was unhappy. About midnight he said, " Well, do you want me to tell you why I am unhappy ? " — " Of course, " said his wives. " Well, when I went home this morning, you went to our cornfield, you walked about the field and you went to the shade to rest, then Coyote came to you and you asked him, ' Who are you ? ' And he said, ' My name is Coyote.' He said some funny things and you began to play with him. " — " No, we did not play with him. " — " But I saw you. I was sitting on a post near by and I saw you. " So they cried and cried. " I am going back to my house," said Dove. So early in the morning he went home. They never saw him again. Their father and mother asked them where their *soyingi* had gone. " He went home, " said the girls, but they did not tell them why he went home. Well, they went to their field again. The same man stood close to them. " Who are you ? " they asked. " Well, I am Coyote. " He went on saying funny things and they began to play with him. He was a witch. Younger sister did not want to play with him. " You better go away, " said Younger sister. "No, I want to marry you both, " said Coyote. "No, we do not want to marry you, " said Younger sister. "Why don't you want to marry me ? " said Coyote " Because I don't like you for my husband. " — " Why don't you like me ?" he asked Younger sister, " Whom do you like for your husband ? " — " The man who dies four times and comes back, " said Younger sister. " Well, then, kill me, here is a stick. I will die and come back." She was angry and took up the stick and killed him. They dragged him away to the shade. There at the shade they found Coyote. " Well, I have come back, " said Coyote. " I said the man I wanted for my husband has to die four times. " — " Well, kill me again, " he said. So she took up a stick and killed him again. They went to their shade and sitting there was Coyote. "Well, I am alive again," said Coyote. They hit him on the head, threw him away in the grass. As soon as they reached their shade, there was Coyote. They were so angry they got a knife and cut Coyote into little pieces and threw them in every direction. " Now he can not get alive again," they said. As soon as they reached their shade, there was Coyote. They were angry. "Now it is four times that I have come to life," said Coyote. There was nothing more for them to say. They had to marry him right there. [1] Coyote was a witch who turned himself into a man. He sang a song to make them become his wives.

They took Coyote to their home. Their father said, "Who is this boy you have brought ? " They never spoke. Their father and mother kept on asking, " Who is this man ? " — " We have married this man, " they said. Their father and mother were angry. They said, " Well, if you want to be married to him, you must leave this house." At night they went upstairs and made their bed. Coyote slept between them. They played together and went to sleep. [2] In the morning there was a woman living near by whose fire was out. She went to the girls' house. She saw them sleeping and between them something sleeping. It was a coyote (*pañyena'*). She did not ask for the fire, but went back to her house. She said to her husband, " Blue corn girl and Yellow corn girl are sleeping with a coyote." He got up and looked and saw the coyote. He went up to the top of his house and called out, " Boys and men ! Here are Blue corn girl and Yellow corn girl sleeping with Coyote. You who are up get your rabbit sticks and we will kill him. " They got their sticks and joined the man. He said, " Now make a ring around the village." Some of them went to the house of Blue corn girl and Yellow corn girl. The man from next door went in and saw Coyote and started to hit him. Coyote opened his eyes and jumped out, away from the boys and men. The dogs chased him out of town. The men in the circle tried to hit him, but they never hit him. He escaped. The father and mother of Blue corn girl and Yellow corn girl were angry. They said, " You have done such bad things, you may not live with us, you must go away. "

So they started north. They went all day until they met a coyote and that was their husband. "I am Coyote, " said he. " Well, I will take you to my house, " he said. But he lived in the ground in a hole. They could not go into the hole. He went in and brought out for them to eat some cedar berries. That was all he had. They tried to eat them, but they did not like them. " You see how I have turned myself into a man, " he said to them. " I will show you how, " said he. He went into his hole and brought out a wheel. " Now watch me and see what I do. " He lowered his head and put it through the wheel, and he became a coyote. " This is how I become a coyote,

1. Cp. Navaho, MAFLS 5 : 93-94.
2. Cp. for the marriage of Coyote to two girls, in Ute folk-tales, Mason, JAFL 23 : 350; Taos, Parsons 2.

or, when I am a coyote, how I become a man. " Elder sister put her head through the wheel and she was a coyote. Younger sister put her head through the wheel and there was another coyote. There stood three coyotes. Off they went without turning themselves back into women again. They traveled and traveled. They had nothing to eat, they were starved. They cried, the tears ran down. They could go no farther, they were so poorly and so thin. Their husband coyote had left them. They lay on the grass (*tapewiñ*)[1] almost dead. There was no water, nothing to eat. They were crying. Up above, in the sky, the Eagle people (*che t'owa*) knew that they were about to die. The Eagle chief (*che t'oyo*) said to his people, " Well, my children, Blue corn girl and Yellow corn girl are about to die ; they have nothing to eat. You better go down and get them. " — " Well, " said two eagles, " we will go. " Two other eagles said, " We will go, too. When you carry them up you will get tired, then we will help you. " Two other eagles said this likewise. They went down to them. Blue corn girl and Yellow corn girl were lying down. The eagles shook their heads. Blue corn girl and Yellow corn girl opened their eyes, they wanted to say something to the eagles, but they could not say anything. The eagles said, " Poor girls ; that bad coyote took you away from your father and mother and left you and you are about to die." The coyotes shook their heads. " Put your arms around my neck and your legs around my tail, " said each eagle. Thus they flew up into the air. They were just about tired out when the other eagles came and took the coyotes. They kept on going. They got to a place where another pair of eagles carried them. Then another pair carried them and another pair until they had been carried by all the ten pairs of eagles. They were carried up into the sky (*opa*). There was a hole in the sky (*teh'pola*). Another world was there, a big white mountain, that was their home. They brought the coyotes into their house. Their father and mother said that they were glad that they had brought the girls. " We will work over these two girls, " they said. The fire was burning and the water boiling. The mother of Eagle boy said, " Go out and get your grandmother. He went and got Spider grandmother. The sweat was running down his face. " What has happened that you have come for me so fast ? "asked Spider grandmother. " Here are Blue corn girl and Yellow corn girl, " said Eagle boy, " our mother told me to go and get you. " " Is everything ready ? " asked Spider grandmother. "We must hurry, they are about to die. " They put the coyotes into the boiling water. She put a stick like a cross between the coyote's ears and began to twist it and pull, singing a song. She put medicine in her mouth, and spat it into the boiling water. Pretty soon the girl's leg came out, then

---

1. Used in making brushes.

the knee of the girl came out, then her body, her arms, chin and face. Then the girl's head came out. She threw the skin to one side. This was Younger sister. Then they put Elder sister into the boiling water. Spider grandmother put the stick between the ears and began to twist the stick. She sang and she spat her medicine into the water. Soon the girl began to come out of the skin. They threw the skin to one side and there was Elder sister. [1] There the sisters were, but they could not get up or speak. Spider grandmother said to Eagle People, " You better hurry and get something for them to eat. They are about to starve to death. " — " Everything is ready, " said the mother of the eagles. She gave them water and afterwards *keñsiboa*[2], then they ate some boiled meat. They became strong by night. They slept. Next morning they were still better. They stayed there many days, each day getting stronger. When they were strong, they said they wanted to grind corn. The mother of the eagles said it was all right for them to grind corn. They ground every day. The mother of the eagles said, " Your father and mother are homesick for you. They can not eat nor drink. You had better go home. " — " How shall we get there ? " they asked her. " These are your brothers now. They will take you down. " The father of the Eagle People gave to each a present, he gave them beads like those we wear now, strings of turquoise. Then the same twenty eagles brought them back to the earth, close to their home. The eagles went back to *opa*, and the girls started for home. At night they reached their house, their *koye'*. They called. Younger sister called, " Mother! " Elder sister called, " Father! " They heard no sound. They called four times. They went in and looked around. There was their father prostrate, there was their mother prostrate. They were dead. They were unhappy and cried for their father and mother. They went to the close relatives in their clan. They were all homesick for them. After that they lived with their relatives. Thus far I know.

14. CLOUD BOYS AND COYOTE. [3]

Far away at Kuṇluokyut'e'e there were living Blue corn girl and Yellow corn girl. They were the children of Crier chief (*tokei*[4]). They were fine looking girls. All the boys of the village wanted to marry them. Both girls would grind corn every night after supper. Two boys would go there together to look into the window where the

1. Cp. Voth I : 107; De Huff, 141-148.
2. Sweet corn flour in water.
3. Cp. Voth I : 157-159 ; Navaho, MAFLS 5 : 88.
4. Among the First Mesa Tewa there is no Crier chief. At San Juan there is a crier, *tokǫndi*.

girls ground. They tried to talk to them, but the girls would pay no attention to the boys looking through the window. When the time came they went to bed. Every night the girls ground and every night the boys came in couples. All the boys of the village had been to see the girls, but the girls cared for none of them. Then boys from another village would go to see the girls. All the boys of the different villages had been to persuade the girls to marry them. At last Yellow cloud boy heard that two good-looking girls were living at Kunluo-kyut'e'e. Yellow cloud boy said, "I will go and try to marry those girls".[1] He packed a *shehka* and *malap'ai, ayu',* and *k'oa.*[2] Then he took his bottle of water and started. He went on a cloud. It was a yellow cloud, he was Yellow cloud boy. He had a long journey to go. He got there at night. Blue corn girl and Yellow corn girl were grinding corn. He stopped near at the village. Soon the girls began to grind. Then he started on and looked through the window. He tried to make them stop grinding and look at him. But they would pay no attention to him. They were grinding in *kwak'eibe.* He went up there with his bag. They looked at him once and said nothing to him. He waited a long time until they stopped grinding to go to bed. "What have you come for," asked Blue corn girl and Yellow corn girl. "I have come to marry one of you," said Yellow cloud boy. The girls said, "What have you to give us for marrying us?" — "Here is my load," said the boy. Elder sister told Younger sister to go down to *koye'* to tell her father and mother to come up to see what they would say. She went down and told her father and mother that some one had come to marry them. Their father and mother went up to them. "Why did you want us to come up?" they said. "Here, Father and Mother, somebody has come to marry us. Here he has this to marry us with." — "We are not the ones to say," said the father and mother, "you are the ones to say." He opened the bundle and took out the *shehka* and the *malap'ai,* the *ayu'* and the dress.

They looked at the things. They were all yellow.[3] There was a gourd bottle in the bundle. They said, "The goods are very pretty; but there is a gourd bottle which we do not need. We think we cannot marry you." — "All right," said the boy, and started back home. Next day Okuahtsayuenu (Blue cloud boy) said he wanted to marry one of the girls. He packed up a marriage blanket and a marriage belt, the other blanket, and inside he put his bottle of water. He traveled a long way on a cloud. He stopped at a place near by until they began to grind corn. He started right up the *kwak'eibe*

1. Cp. Voth I : 143.
2. Formerly a Zuñi suitor, judging from the Zuñi tales, brought much the same gifts. See Parsons 8 : 302.
3. Cp. Voth I : 177.

and went into the room where the girls were grinding. " What do you want ?" asked the girls, " I want to see you," said the boy." Why ?" asked the girls. "To see about marrying one of you. " Elder sister sent Younger sister to their father and mother to tell them to come up. Their father and mother went up to them. " What do you want ?" asked their father and mother. " I wanted to see you, a boy came in here with his goods, to marry us, " said Elder sister. " We are not the ones to say, " said the father and mother. The boy untied his bundle. In it were the marriage blanket and marriage belt, the other blanket and the moccasins, together with a bottle of water. All the things were blue. " The things are very nice," said the girls, " but among them is a bottle of water which we do not need, we cannot marry you. " — "All right, " said the boy, "if you do not want to marry me." The girls went down to *koye'* to go to bed. There was a cloud in the south ; (Red cloud boy) *Okuahp'i'enu* he had heard about the girls. He packed up his goods and his bottle of water. " I am going to get those girls, " he said. He reached Kuṇluokyut'e'e. He stopped until they began to grind. He went on straight up to *kwak'eibi* where the girls were grinding. " What do you want ?" said the girls. " Yes, " said the boy, " I came here to see you. " — " About what ? " said the girls. " I want to marry one of you, " said the boy. Elder sister sent Younger sister down to tell their father and mother to come up. " What do you want ? " said their father and mother. " Here is a boy who wants to marry one of us, " said Elder sister. " We are not the ones to decide, " said their father and mother. Elder sister walked to the bundle ot goods. She untied it, she found the marriage blanket, and marriage belt, the other blanket and moccasins, and a bottle of water. The girl said, "It is all very pretty, but I do not care for this bottle of water. Had you not brought this bottle of water I would marry you. " — " All right, " said the boy, " I can go home. " Next morning Cloud in the East, White cloud boy (*okuahche'ixenu*), said, " I am the one to marry both of those girls. " He packed up a marriage blanket and a marriage belt, another blanket and moccasins, together with a bottle of water. He went to Kuṇluokyut'e'e. The girls were not yet grinding corn. So he waited near by. Then when they began to grind, he came and went on straight up to *kwak'eibe.* He walked inside the room. "Sit down, " said the girls. "What do you want ?" — " I want to see you. I want to marry you." Elder sister said to Younger sister, " Go down and tell our father and mother to come up. " Younger sister went down and told their father and mother to come up. " What do you want us for ? " asked their father and mother. "We wanted you to come up because here is a boy who wants to marry us. " — " We have nothing to say. " So Elder sister walked to the bundle. She opened it. She found the marriage blanket and the marriage belt, the other blanket and the moccasins and the bottle of water. The things were pretty. They were all white. She said, "I like these goods, but this bottle of water is not for me. I cannot take it." — "It is all right," said the boy, "if you do not want to marry me." He packed up the things, he started back. Next morning Cloud-above boy (*Okuah nǫkuenu*) [1] heard that all the Cloud boys (*tañepede*, from every direction, *okuah enung*) had gone to Blue corn girl and Yellow corn girl to marry them, but they failed to marry them. "I think I am surely the one to marry them," said Cloud-above. He packed up a marriage blanket and belt, another blanket and moccasins and a water bottle. He arrived before night and he stopped near the village and waited awhile. Soon the girls began to grind corn. He went into *kwak'eibe*, where they were grinding. "Sit down," they said to him. He sat down. They asked him, "What do you want?" — "I want to marry you," he said. "I have brought you these goods." Elder sister told Younger sister to go down and ask their father and mother to come up. She went down. "Why did you want us to come up?" they said to Younger sister. "There is a boy who wants to marry us." — "You are the one to say. If you want the boy, you can marry him," said their father and mother. Elder sister opened the bundle and looked at it. She found the marriage blanket and belt, the other blanket, the moccasins and the bottle of water. All the things were speckled (*toñluix*). "Well, this bottle of water we have no need of," she said. "But for it we would marry you," she said. So the boy said, "It is all right." He packed up his goods and started home next morning. Poshekwaishing [2] (Water-drag man) heard that the boys had been trying to marry Blue corn girl and Yellow corn girl. "They are lazy about it," said Water-drag man. "I will marry them," said Water-drag man. He went to look for something to give the girls. He found *po·be* (stalk of yucca), and he went to cedar trees and got some berries and put them into a sack and carried them in his arms. He made out that the yucca stalks were his beads. He started off. He arrived at their house. Their house was a solitary house. As he came near, Elder sister said to Younger sister, "Look out through the window." They saw Water-drag man, coming dancing with his song:

Enatoli...i
Enatoli..i
Enatoli, enatoli
Kųlutsayuayu'
Kųlutseyĕayu'
Enatoli, enatoli.

1. Literally, ? Dark cloud boy.
2. Thus Coyote may be referred to in the tales.

He was dancing with his song. Soon the girls stopped grinding corn and looked at him. They laughed at him, and laughed. They went outside of the room and came near to him. " You dance again for us, " said the girls. " All right, " said Water-drag man :

> Enatoli..i
> Enatoli ...i
> Enatoli, enatoli
> Kulutsayuayu′
> Kulutseyĕayu′
> Enatoli, enatoli.

They were so pleased, they laughed at him. Soon they told him to come up. " Come in, you dance so nicely, we want to have you live with us ; we want to marry you, " said the girls. " All right, " said Water-drag man. So they got the yucca stalks and the cedar berries. " You must wait here, " said the girls, and they went down to have their supper with their father and mother. They did not tell them about Water-drag man. They came up, bringing *makáno* and *keñsi*, and they ate together with Water-drag man. While they ate together, Elder sister put *keñsi* on some *makáno* and sprinkled it on Water-drag man. Younger sister sprinkled on Water-drag man, and Water-drag man sprinkled on both. They played together half the night. When they grew tired, Elder sister went down to get her buffalo cover (*koh poya*). They went to bed, Water-drag man, between the two girls. They played together. They slept late, they were so tired, they did not know when it was daylight. The woman next door went in to get some fire. She went up and saw a coyote sleeping between those girls. [1] She never asked for fire, but went and told her husband that there was a coyote sleeping with Blue corn girl and Yellow corn girl. The man was so angry that he went out of his house and called out that there was a coyote sleeping with Blue corn girl and Yellow corn girl. They should get their sticks and come and kill the coyote. Four boys came and he put them outside the house. He went in with his stick, but Coyote jumped out and passed the four boys. The dogs chased him past the men encircling the village. He jumped over them, he escaped. The people were so angry that they said that thereafter the boys could not marry those girls, so the girls never got married.

15. SU′MAKOLI; STUFFED BEAR.

Far away at Kunluokyut′e′e there was living a girl, the daughter of Crier chief (*tokiei pié*). She was a good-looking girl. She did not like

1. Cp. Voth I 150.

any boy in the village. She never went out with the other girls. The girls would have liked to come to her house to grind, but she did not like the girls to come. Every night, as she ground corn, the boys would look in through the window and try to talk to her. But she would not talk to them. So they would go away and not come back. The boys from the other villages would come, but she would not talk to them. Her father wanted her to marry. During the day she would embroider blankets (*shehka' pęhle*) [1] and at night she would grind corn.

There were some people living at a lake (*pokwingeh*). Those people were called Su'makoli. One of these Su'makoli boys heard that there was a nice girl living ot Kuṇluokyut'e'e. He said to his mother and father that he wanted to go and see that girl. His father and mother said it was all right to go. He got a *shehka* and dress and belt, he made a bundle and with it he went to see the girl. She was not grinding yet. So he stayed some where until she began to grind. Soon she began to grind. He went straight up to the *kwak'eibe*. The girl said, " Sit down. " She asked him what he wanted. " I have come to marry you, " said the boy. She did not know what kind of a boy he was. He was a Su'makoli boy. He wore a buckskin shirt (*puyetoh*), buckskin leggings (*puyekoh*), with strings tied on each side with little shells, olivella shells (*dididi*). He had a quiver (*sudě*). He was a good-looking boy. " Wait until I tell my father and mother, " she said. She went down and said, "Mother and Father, there is some one come to me in *kwak'eibe*. " Her father and mother came up and looked at the boy. The father thought that boy did not belong to any of those villages. He was some kind of a boy, maybe a Cloud boy. So he went down to *koye'* and got his bag of tobacco and his pipe. He blew out four times and gave the pipe to the boy. The boy said, " My old man (*Nabie seṇe*). " [2] The man said, " My child (*Nabi e'*). " The boy kept on smoking till the tobacco was out. He handed the pipe back to the man. The man said, " My child. " The boy said, " My old man. " The man said, " What did you come here for ? " — " I came to see your child. I want to marry her, " said the boy. " I am not the one to say, " the man said to the boy. " If the girl likes you, she is the one to say. " The boy went out and got his bundle of goods and put it near the girl. She went up and untied the bundle and found the marriage blanket and belt and dress. She said she liked the goods. Her father was pleased. He said, " This is what I wanted for you. I am getting old, I can not do all the work. I want a helper. I am glad you will marry this boy. " — " I will take you home in the morning, " said the boy. They went to bed, but they did not go

1. Formerly girls used to embroider, nowadays men embroider.
2. Addressing him as a chief.

to bed together, they slept separate. Early in the morning, before daylight, the father and mother dressed up the girl. The girl carried corn meal with her. They started to the east. The girl said that she was tired carrying the corn meal. The boy said he would help her. She was tired, she said, " I can not go any farther. " — The boy said, " It is a long way to my home. Stand close to me, close your eyes, do not open them until I tell you, " said the boy. The boy did something to make a rainbow[1], and the rainbow carried them to the lake. " It is all right to open your eyes, " said the boy. She found that she was at a big lake, and she was surprised. " Follow me, " said the boy. They came to a place full of grass and flowers outside of the lake. They came to a kiva. The boy called, " Father! Mother! *tixe!* I am not alone." Everyone inside said, "Come in! come in!" The boy stepped into the kiva first, the girl followed, carrying the corn meal on her back. The mother of the boy took the corn meal and the girl went and sat down on the buffalo bed (*kopah*) [rolled up for a seat]. The mother brought out some watermelon and muskmelon and some *maka'no*. They gave it to the girl and the boy to eat. They were glad their brother had brought that girl. Soon it was bedtime. The mother of the boy went into a room and fixed the bed. The mother said that she would sleep with the girl to take care of her. The girl went to sleep right away. She was very tired. Next morning she woke up and began to grind corn for them. In front of the girl they hung up a *shehka*.[2] They gave her breakfast and she began again to grind. They gave her dinner. She began to grind again until evening when the mother of the boy went in and told her to stop grinding. The girls of that house did the cooking. At bedtime, the mother slept with the girl to take care of her. Next morning she woke up and again ground corn till evening. Then the mother of the boy stopped her. She rested again. It was supper time and then bedtime. The mother of the boy went to bed with the girl. It was daylight. She woke up and started to grind. They gave her dinner. She ground again until evening. The mother of the boy stopped her. It was evening. They ate supper. At bedtime the mother of the boy went to bed with the girl. Early in the morning they began to pound yucca roots, to wash the girl's head. All the girls and women living there washed the girl's hair. When her hair was dry, the mother of the boy began to comb and cut the girl's hair like the hair of the Tewa women. She was a woman now. She began to grind corn, and for them she cooked *muwashing*. In the evening all ate their supper together. They were glad to have their

---

1. *kweñka, mąkweñkaweño*, make a rainbow.
2. That none might talk to her, or the sun shine on her. When a bride grinds, they hang up a blanket across the door into the inner room where is the corn-grinding place.

sa'i with them. In the next room men were making a *shehka* for the girl.
They worked all day. Next day they worked again. They were done in
two days, the *shehka* and belt. Bowsnake was making the *shehka*, also the
wedding belt; Runnersnake was making the *ayu'*. That day the boy had killed a deer; he killed it and made a big buckskin for her moccasins. A big man
came in, Nepokwa'i 'i, and made moccasins for her. He finished the moccasins in one day. That evening the mother of the boy said, "Well, we
will take you back to the house of *sa'i.*" The mother of the boy told
him not to be lazy there, to get the wood and water. All of them
started off. The mother of the boy went ahead of the others, carrying
a basket full of corn of different colors, next came the *sa'i*, next the
boy, next the father and sisters of the boy. All in a line, they came
out of the kiva. In a little way they told their *sa'i* to shut her eyes
until they told her to open them. They made a rainbow, and on it
they reached Kuṇluokyut'e'e. The mother of the boy said to *sa'i*, "Open
your eyes." They were near the house. They all went up the ladder
to the *koye'*. They called down. "Get this corn," said the mother
of the boy." — "Come down," said the mother and father of the
girl. The mother of the girl took the basket of corn. They were glad
that their daughter had come back. The mother and father gave them
all something to eat. When they were through eating, they said that
they were glad to have their *sa'i* work for them, " and so we bring
our child to you," they said. They all went away and left the boy
there. They went to bed. Early in the morning the girl's mother went
and told her clanswomen (*iiking*) to come to her house. They all
came to her house, and they began to wash the boy's head. He went
out to *yohoaho* (Hopi, *homuya*; i. e. to sprinkle corn meal to the sun
and pray that his life be long.)

The people of the village saw that he had married Crier chief's
daughter. Some were glad, some were angry. Some people, *ky'ugeh*,
witches, were spinning in their kiva. These *ky'ugehte'eing* (members of
witch kiva) were very, very angry. They said, " We will kill the boy as
soon as we can, and we will take his wife." — "If a man or boy kill the
man, let him take the woman," said the senior (*señochę*) in the kiva.
" So you must think this over. When you have found out what we
are to kill with, come back here tonight and we will talk it over."
They went to their houses for supper. As soon as they had eaten their
supper, they went back to the kiva. They began to talk about what
they could do to kill that man and take his wife. One said one way,
another said another way; but they did not find any special way. The
senior said they could go home and return tomorrow and talk it over
all day. Next morning that Su'makoli said to his wife, " Get ready
some lunch. I am going hunting." He went to the north, he saw a
deer. He went close up and shot him with an arrow, he killed
him. He started to take the deer on his back, but it was too heavy.

He took out his medicine and spat it on the deer, and lying there was a little animal. He carried it back and laid it on top of the *koye'*. He stepped over the deer from every direction and it became a large deer again. He went in and said he had brought a deer. She did not know what a deer was. She went out and saw a big thing lying there. She called her father. He came out and he was the only one who knew what that big thing lying there was. He took one leg, and the girl took the other leg and dragged it into the *koye'*. Next day, Su'makoli skinned it himself. He told his wife to boil all that meat and to go and tell the people to come and eat it with them. That evening Su'makoli met a boy walking about, a dirty looking boy. That was Fire-making boy.[1] The people did not like him. Fire-making boy made friends with Su'makoli and they walked together outside the village. The wife of Su'makoli went and invited all the women to come and have supper. They all came, and ate. When the women went back, they told their husbands what kind of meat they ate. " We don't like that kind of meat, " said some of the men. They were the witches. They were talking all day about how to kiil Su'makoli. Next day Su'makoli went to the west and killed an elk (*t'ah*). It was too heavy to carry, so he took his medicine and spat it on the elk, and it lay there a small animal. He carried it back and put it on the *koye'* and jumped ed over it and it was large again. Next morning he met Fire-making boy again, and they went together around the village. That Fire-making boy went with Su'makoli to the house of his wife and ate there with them. That evening even more people than before came there to eat. That night all the witches went to the kiva to talk. A young boy said, " I have found something. " — " What is it? " the witch old man (*ky'ugeh seno*) said. He (the boy) went to the fireplace and smoked four times and gave his pipe to the witch old man. " What did you find? " — " It is not very bad, but it might help us, " said the boy. " Tomorrow morning I am going after *chiko* (Hopi, *t'ebe*, greasewood). " He began to sharpen the wood. He went out again and brought in a rattlesnake (*pengyu*). He opened the rattlesnake's mouth, and there was poison in the roof of the mouth. He took out the poison[2] and rubbed it on the greasewood. " I am going to Su'makoli's wife's house and put it under the ladder, " he said, " and tomorrow morning he will step on it and he will never be able to get it out. " — " Good for you, " said the witch old man. Early in the morning before daylight he placed the stick under the ladder. The witches were watching for Su'makoli to come down. Su'makoli came down and stepped on the stick and it went through his moccasin. He

1. See pp. 77, 91, 94, 95, 99, 177.
2. Of some interest in relation to the current controversy as to whether or not the poison sac is extracted from the snake in the Snake hunt.

sat down and tried to pull it out, but he could not. The stick was broken. He did not go back to his wife, but went outside the village dragging his foot. There he laid down his rainbow and traveled back on it to the Lake. " Well, what happened? " asked his mother. " What happened? " asked his father. " I stepped on a stick, " said Su'makoli. He looked very badly, the stick was still in his foot, blood was coming out. They could not take out the stick and soon his foot was swelling up.

The wife of Su'makoli said, " Where is my husband? " She asked Fire-making boy, " Where is your chum? "[1] — " I did not see him this morning, I thought he was going out hunting. " After four days she was going to have a baby. Her belly ached. She had two boys. Her mother washed those babies herself, because it was a long way off to their father's mother. So she would take care of them herself. Those babies were nice babies. In four days they began to crawl. In four days they began to walk. In four more days they were going about, in four more days they could run and in four more days they could go a long way (i. e., in twenty days after they were born.) " Mother! " said one of them. " What? " she said. " Where is our father? " both asked. She began to cry. She did not know where their father was. They kept on asking, " Where is our father? " — " My children, " she said, " your father has gone somewhere, I don't know where. He went away and never came back. " — " We want to go and look for our father, " said both little boys (*enungeye*). " You are too young to look for your father, " said the mother. " But we want to go, " said the two little boys. " You will never find where he is, " said their mother. " But we are going, you make us some *keñshi*, " said the two little boys. That night their grandfather (*tete*) made eight prayer-sticks (*odupeh*) and eight feather-strings (*pehlichidi*) for them. When they were ready to go, their mother said, " My children, *shengitidimongbi* (goodbye) ". Their grandmother said. " My grandchildren, *shengitidimongbi*. " And then their grandfather took them down from the house and out of the village and put down *p'olu* (Hopi, *pü'tabi*)[2] for them. He said again *shengitidimongbi* to them. These little boys did not know where they were going to. They came to a place where somebody was doing something. It was Pocket gopher with his paw on his face. " Grandfather, " they said, " do you know where our father lives? " they said to Pocket gopher. He looked around at them. " My poor grandchildren, " said Pocket gopher, " you never will reach your father, he is far off and he is about to die, " said Pocket gopher. " I cannot help you, " said Pocket gopher. So they went on. They met a man, a young good-looking man. Younger brother said to El-

1. *Ivichungjiix*; Hopi, *namiantata suntsi* (Freire-Marreco, 270.)
2. Long, feathered string; a road marker.

der brother, " I think this is father. " Younger brother said, " Father
(*tada*) ! " and he ran to him and caught him by the leg, and Elder brother ran and caught his other leg. " Father! " they said. " My son, I
am indeed your father, " he said. But your [other] father is living a
long way off. You will never reach him. I am your father's brother
(*totung*), " he said, " and I am your father, too, my children (*nabi eye*)" [1]
he said, " shut your eyes and do not open them till I say. " So they
closed their eyes, still holding to his legs. " Now open your eyes, "
said the man. When they opened their eyes, they were at a big lake,
to their surprise. " Soon we will get to your father, " said the man.
The little boys ran along. They came to a kiva. " Father, " said the
man, " I am not coming alone. " — " Well, come in, " said the
people inside. He carried the little boys in. They saw a man lying
there. They ran to him. " Father! " they said, " Father! " He was
too sick to speak. His father and mother and sisters were all crying.
Then they gave the little boys something to eat. After they finished
eating, they said, " We might help our father, " said both. " We will
go out and find something to help him. " They went out to the fields
and found the stalk of a sunflower. They picked it and carried it back
to their father's house. He was just about to die. " Have you any *kuh'-
ni' tung* (a flat basket) ?" they said to their grandmother. " Yes, we have
one. " — " Bring it out, " said the two little boys. " Well, we want to
wash our heads, " they said. Then their grandmother washed Elder
brother, and their father's sister (*imbikyiyu*) washed Younger brother.
They asked for an arrow point (*chikave*). Their grandfather gave it to
them. They asked for buckskin. They got it and brought it out.
They asked for a *shehka*. They got it and brought it. After their heads
were dry, they said, "Now you go out, into another room, we will
work alone. " Everybody went out. They got the sunflower stalk
between them. Elder brother was sitting to the south, Younger
brother to the north. They cut out the inside of the stalk (*aliping*),
out of it they made humming-birds (*tangkoleh*). Elder brother made
five, Younger brother made five. They used the stalk for the beak
of the birds. Out of the flowers they made their wings and legs. Elder
brother made five feather–strings. Younger brother made five feather-
strings. They spread buckskin underneath, and put the basket on top,
and the humming-birds on top and the feather-strings, they tied
around the necks of the birds, and all this they covered with a
shehka. They had forgotten to ask for a rattle (*powiye*). Elder brother
told Younger brother to go into the south room and ask his grandfather for a rattle. — " Grandfather, have you a rattle? " He gave
him two rattles. Elder brother sat on the north side and Younger

---

1. Strictly your father's brother calls you *tunge'*. The usage in the text bears out
Freire-Marreco's observation that *tunge'* is an obsolete term.

brother on the south side and their father lay to the east with the basket at his feet. They began to sing four songs. The *shehka* began to move. After six songs there were sounds, after eight songs humming-birds came out from under the *shehka*. They began to fly around inside the room. They told the humming-birds to go and suck out the stick from their father's foot. The humming-birds began to suck and they could see the stick move. Soon the stick came out. " We are glad you have done this for our father. You have saved our father. ᵛou can go out to live forever among the flowers, " said the little buys to the humming-birds. Then the boys gave some medicine to their father. Next day their father was better. Every day he was better. In eight days he began to walk, but he dragged his foot. " Try to walk out, " they said. After twelve days they said, " Let us go to the fields. " He was still lame.

In sixteen days they went to the fields again. They left their father under the shade. Their father said, "Do not go to the south. " They were playing. In the afternoon Elder brother said to Younger brother, " Let us go to the south. " So they went to the south and they came to a forest. They heard a noise. That was a bear with pups, and the bear ran after them. He was just about to catch Younger brother when Elder brother shot at him and killed him. Then they skinned the bear. Elder brother said, " Younger brother ! what do you think about it? " Younger brother said, " Let us put some grass inside of the skin and scare our father. " They put in the grass and sewed up the slip and made a rope of yucca and tied it in the middle, and to the legs, arms, and feet. The bear went along as if it were alive. " This will scare our father, " said Elder brother, " it will make him able to run. " When they got near the field, they cried out, " Father! here is a bear chasing us, " they said. " Here is a bear chasing us! " Their father heard them. He stood up and looked. There in the field was a bear chasing his children, " My poor children, I told you not to go to the south, but you went and the bear chased you. " He began to run and the boys and bear ran after him. He called out, " Elder brother and Younger brother, come and help us! " They came out with their bows and arrows. The bear was still chasing them. Elder brother would fall down and get up again. They began to shoot. The little boys began to laugh. " It is not alive, it is a dead bear, " they said. They asked the boys, " Where did you kill it? " — " In the south, in the forest. " — " I told you not to go there, " said their father. " We did this to make our father run, " they said. After this Su'makoli got well.

There were some enemies of the Su'makoli called Pisabi [1] and as

---

1. Sabi is Tewa for Navaho, but Pisabi refers to some other tribe, a hostile tribe, but what tribe, my informant did not know.

the Su'makoli were working in the field the Pisabi killed one of them. In four days the Su'makoli all went to see where the Su'makol was killed. The two little boys went with them. An oak was growing where the Su'makol was killed. They said they would make a bow out of the oak. They cut it, they heard a sound, " That is my blood." Some bones were lying around. " Let us gather up the bones, and make him alive, " they said. They went back and asked for a *shehka* and a buckskin, and they put the bones on top of the buckskin and covered them up. Younger brother sat on the north side, and Elder brother on the south. They used four songs. The *shehka* began to move. After six songs somebody said, " *Ai!* " After eight songs there was a man come to life, he moved away the cover. But he was blind, they had forgotten his eyes. He groped out with his arms. They looked for his eyes, but they could not find them. " I think the crows ate them up. What could we make for his eyes? " they said. " Let us get gum, " said Elder brother. So they went to a piñon tree and got some gum, a round piece of gum wax, two pieces, and put them in to be his eyes, and covered him up. They sang again. After eight songs they pulled his cover off again. Su'makol could see, but not very well. They were going along, Su'makol dragging along his foot. Su'makol had his bow in his hand. Elder brother said, "I will lead him and he will follow me, " and Elder brother began to sing. When he finished singing, he called, " *Yahahai!* " Su'makol called, " *Hö! hö!* " Then he went on singing until they reached the house. At the end of each song he said, " *Yahahai!* " and Su'makol said, " *Hö! hö!* " When they reached the house of Su'makol, they said, " Well, from now on we shall all be blind, [1] and we shall be lame, [2] and when they finish their song, they shall say, ' *Yahahai!* ' and ' *Hö! hö!* ' "

16. FIRE-MAKING BOY HUNTS RABBITS :
COYOTE KILLS THE GRAND-MOTHER OF FIRE-MAKING BOY.

Far away at Kuṇluokyut'e'e they were living. There was a boy named Fire-making boy (Potekeęnu). [3] He had a grandmother, but neither mother nor father. They lived near the people at Kuṇlu-okyut'e'e. The people did not like Fire-making boy. He would go from house to house morning, afternoon and evening, and at supper time

1. At Zuñi a pregnant woman should not look at the mask of Shumaikoli lest her child be born blind, the eyes in the mask are very small. The Shumaikoli society of the Tewa cure sore eyes, subsequently initiating the patient.

2. Cp. Parsons 10 : 116.

3. See p. 250, n. 1. Potekeenu is not only a kachina, Fewkes 2 : 83, appearing in the *niman* kachina ceremony; he is also the elder of the two war-gods (*awęlę pipi*). He figures a great deal in Tewa tales as in Zuñi tales. Younger brother or *awęlę tiye* is Tobatokwenu, Echo boy. See also Voth 1 : 120.

he would go to the houses and ask for food. The people were mean to him, they did not like him, only at some of the houses would they give him a little food. He had a hard time. His grandmother said, " My grandchild, do not go around these houses, because they are angry with us." After this he did not go around. His grandmother said, "Fire-making boy, you might go and hunt rabbits for us to have rabbits to eat. " Thus spoke she to her grandchild. Fire-making boy said to his grandmother, "I don't know what kind of tracks rabbits have." — "My grandchild, go and get some sand and bring it in. "They were living in the *koyé*. He brought in some sand. His grandmother put her fingers like this. "Jack-rabbit's track is a little larger," said his grandmother. So Fire-making boy learned about the rabbit's track.[1] At night they went to bed. Next morning when they woke up, Fire-making boy went out from his *koyé* and saw a lot of snow on the ground. He went back in and said, "Grandmother, there is a lot of snow on the ground." — "Well, my grandchild, this is a good time for men to hunt rabbits. When there is a lot of snow on the ground, it is easier to kill them. " He wrapped up his feet and his legs with old cloth from his grandmother's dress, and he got a mouse skin cover (*winpuya*) and put it on his back, and his grandmother made *muwat'oko*[2] for him, and put it in a fawn skin sack. (*Koyemshi* carries one[3]). He carried it on his back. He went and looked for tracks. He did not see any until he was a long way off. Then he found the tracks of a cottontail rabbit. He followed them a long way until he came to rocks and a hole, and in there was the rabbit. He got a long stick of grease wood. He wet the stick in his mouth and put it into the hole and touched the rabbit and twisted the fur. He twisted so tight that he twisted off the fur, he pulled out the stick. He put the stick in again and twisted again. He twisted all the skin off the rabbit. He put the stick in again and twisted the rabbit out, without any skin. It was about sundown. He looked for a good place to sleep. He found a place and he began to pick up wood for a fire, to have a fire all night. He began to cook the rabbit. He heard a sound. Somebody was singing. Pretty soon he heard the sound closer, somebody was coming and singing. He knew that his grandmother was coming to look for him. He put more wood to the fire. He sat listening. She sang :

> Soyuyukana
> Soyuyukana
> Obix'kwiya seno' in mam

1. Cp. Voth 1 : 155.
2. Meal baked in corn husk.
3. So does Shulawitsi of Zuñi, a fire-making boy.

Shikain meyu
Natiwehami natiwehami
Suyuku-u

Fire-making boy was very angry. "My grandmother is coming."
He called out, "Grandmother, here I am, why do you come after me?
I am safe. Nothing will harm me." He was very angry. He called
again, "Grandmother, here I am! Grandmother, here I am!" He said
it three times. Soon she came nearer to him. He saw his grandmother
coming. He saw her. He looked at her. It was not his grandmother.
He was very much frightened. He looked. It was a big giant. "It is
Suyuku," he said. It was too late for him to run away. She stood by
him. "My poor grandchild," she said to him, "what are you doing?
I am sorry you came over here, so I came after you." He hung
his head, he said nothing. Fire-making boy was afraid of her. She
had a great big mouth and big teeth. She would eat him up. "Grandchild, is your rabbit already cooked?" He said nothing. Again she
said, "Grandchild, is your rabbit cooked? Give me the rabbit. I am
very hungry." She said again, "Give me the rabbit." He took the
rabbit and threw it to her. She picked up the rabbit and put it into
her mouth and swallowed it down whole. "Have you any more?"
said Suyuku. "No, I have no more." — "But I am still hungry.
I haven't got enough. I will eat you up. That's what I came for."
She had a long stick with shells on it (*dididi*). She put her stick around
his neck and pulled him to her. Fire-making boy lay on the ground.
She walked to Fire-making boy and caught him by the arm and
pulled him up and began to try to swallow him. But Fire-making boy
said, "Grandmother, wait! I am going to get you another rabbit."
"Wait!" he said when she was just about to swallow him. "Wait!
I have another rabbit over there." "Hurry then," said Suyuku. "I
am hungry." He started off. "Wait! First let me tie you," said
Suyuku. She tied him around the waist. He went off. He untied
himself, and he put in a piece of wood and he said to the wood,
"When Suyuku says, 'Hurry and bring me a rabbit,' you answer,
'Wait! Grandmother, wait!'" Soon Suyuku said, "Hurry, my
grandchild, hurry!" The piece of wood answered, "Wait! my grandmother, I haven't got the rabbit yet." Suyuku said, "Hurry! hurry,
my grandchild. I am so hungry." The wood said, "Wait! the rope
is so short, I haven't reached the wood yet." Three times Suyuku
spoke. When she spoke the fourth time, the wood said nothing to
Suyuku.[1] So she pulled the rope in to her and there was tied to it
the piece of wood. "Well, even if he did run away, I will follow

---

1. Having an inanimate substitute call out is a characteristic incident in the
European tales of Magic Flight.

him and get him, " said Suyuku. Fire-making boy had run a long way
off. There was somebody very busy in the ground. There was a
little creature, Pocket gopher. Fire-making boy said to him, "My
grandson (*tee* ^e), hide me!" Pocket gopher had his hand on his face
like this. Fire-making boy said again, " Hide me! "— " Poor Fire-
making boy! I have no place to hide you." — " Here is Suyuku
coming after me. " — "Well, I will try to hide you. Here is my hole.
Go into my hole. " Fire-making boy went in and Pocket gopher
after him. "In this hole I can't hide you, better go into my mouth,"
said Pocket gopher. Suyuku was following the track. When she came
to the hole, the track was lost. "Well, Fire-making boy went into
Gopher's hole, I will surely get him. " She called into the hole,
" Fire-making boy, come out! I am so tired running after you, I'm
not going to eat you up. Your grandmother is not able to follow
you. " — "Well, I can't give you Fire-making boy," said Gopher.
"Come in yourself and look for him. " She went in and looked
around and could not see Fire-making boy. " He is not here. I think
he went on." — " Go out, I have no time to talk to you, I have
toothache!" — "You have toothache !" said Suyuku. So she
hit him with her cane on the side of his mouth, and out
jumped Fire-making boy. He went on and came to a place where
there was somebody busy. It was Goat (*chivato*). "My grandchild, "
he said, "hide me. Suyuku is coming after me. " — " I haven't any
place to hide you, " said Goat. "Please hide me, " said Fire-
making boy. "I have no place to hide." — " Go in my house, and I
will kill Suyuku. " Soon there was a sound. Suyuku was saying,
"My grandchild, why did you run away from me ? I have come after
you for your grandmother. I am not going to hurt you. " Goat was
outside when she came to him. "Did you see my grandchild ?" said
Suyuku. Goat did not answer her. "Did you see my grandchild ?" —
"No, I haven't seen anybody, " said Goat. "I think you have hidden
him, " said Suyuku. "I have no place to hide him. " — "I think you
have hidden him down in your room, " said Suyuku. "If you think
he is down in my room, go in yourself and get him out. " So she
went in to his house. Then Goat jumped down on her. He wanted
a woman very much. So he kept Suyuku in there, and he said to
Fire-making boy to go out. So Goat kept Suyuku there doing that
business all day until he killed that Suyuku and Fire-making boy
was safe. He went back home the next day. His grandmother asked
him, "Why didn't you get any rabbits? " — " I thought it was you
who came when I went out hunting, but it was a Suyuku. I killed a
rabbit and cooked it, and that Suyuku came and said she was hungry
and I gave her that rabbit. And she said it was not enough, and she
would eat me up. So I ran away. " So his grandmother said, "That
Suyuku is very mean. She comes around the village and whenever

she finds a child, she carries it away, and her children eat it up. Had
you not run away, she would have eaten you up." After this Suyuku
ate no more children. She never carried any more children away
from Kuṇluokyut'e'e.

After a few more days Fire-making boy said he would go hunting
rabbits again. This time he knew the tracks. His grandmother gave
him a lunch which he carried on his back. He found a rabbit track
and followed it to a hole, he got his stick, he twisted it, he pulled
out a rabbit and killed him. He found another rabbit track, he followed it, there were lots of tracks about this hole. He put in his stick,
he twisted it, he pulled out a rabbit. He saw another rabbit, he twisted
his stick, he pulled out the rabbit and killed it. He kept on taking
out the rabbits from this same hole. It was sundown. He went under
a rock and built a big fire. He cooked one of the rabbits for his
supper. He slept there. Next day he looked for some more rabbits. He
killed a lot of rabbits. About sundown Water-drag man (i. e., Coyote)
came to him. Water-drag man said to him, " My grandchild, I am
looking for you. Your grandmother sent me to look for you. There
is a great deal of snow on the ground, you might freeze, so your
grandmother told me to look for you." — " I am all right," said
Fire-making boy. " Is that all you have killed ? " said Water-drag man.
" I have some more rabbits over there at my camp. Let's go over
there and sleep together and tomorrow let us go hunting rabbits
together." They went there and found the rabbits. " Let's eat, "
said Water-drag man. So they cooked a rabbit and ate it. "I am still
hungry," said Water-drag man. So they cooked another rabbit. "It is
a long way from your home, I am tired. Let us cook another
rabbit." So they cooked another rabbit. So Water-drag man ate four
rabbits, and he had enough. In the morning Water-drag man said,
"Your grandmother told me if I found you and you had killed seven
rabbits to bring them to her." Fire-making boy did not believe him,
but he tied up the rabbits and gave them to Water-drag man. " I will
not go back till tomorrow," said Fire-making boy. Well, Water-
drag man did not go to Fire-making boy's house, but went on to his
own house. He lived not far from Kuṇluokyut'e'e where he had a lot
of children. " Here I have lots of rabbits for you," said Water-
drag man to his children. And they ate all the rabbits up. Next morning Fire-making boy said, "Well, I have enough rabbits. I guess I
will go home." After he got home, he said to his grandmother, " Did
Water-drag man bring you those rabbits? " — " Nobody brought me
any rabbits. " — " Well, Water-drag man said you had sent him
after me to bring you back all the rabbits. I guess Water-drag man
was lying and just took the rabbits back to his children," said Fire-
making boy.

After a few days Fire-making boy told his grandmother he wanted again to go rabbit hunting. She made a lunch ready for him and he put it on his back. He found rabbits again. He killed one rabbit and then he killed another rabbit. He killed about ten rabbits. It was sundown. He went to the same place he went before. He gathered lots of wood and made a fire. He went to sleep. Next morning he ate breakfast and went after more rabbits. Soon he found a rabbit. While he was chasing it, Water-drag man came again. " My grand-child, are you hunting rabbits again ?" — " Yes, " said Fire-making boy. "The time I was here when I started off to your grandmother, I got tired and stayed two nights. This morning I reached your grandmother and she told me to go after you again and, if you have any rabbits, to take them to her". Fire-making boy believed him and made a bundle of rabbits and gave them to Water-drag man. Water-drag man took them and went on to Fire-making boy's grandmother and gave her the rabbits. She was glad to get them.

Water-drag man said, "I am so hungry. Give me one of the rab-bits. " So she did. Water-drag man said that he would sleep there that night. So grandmother went to sleep. Water-drag man got up and got a stick and killed grandmother, and Water-drag man took all the rabbits back to his children. Fire-making boy said, " I have enough rabbits, I will go home. " He called, "Grandmother, I have some rabbits for you ! " She did not answer. He went in and found his grandmother lying there. He picked her up, and she was dead. He was very sad. "What can I do?" he said. "I guess I had better go and find some other place to live." He went to Kwayege. There another grandmother was living. He said to her, " Water-drag man killed my grandmother, so I came here to live with you. " This grandmother was glad to have him live with her. So Fire-making boy lived with her, and he is living with her yet.

17. TRANSFORMING BATH : BUTTERFLY SEDUCER.

Far away there at Awatobi was living Kusawe. He had no home, no mother or father. He went from house to house, asking for something to eat, in the morning, afternoon, and evening. Some-times the women would give him something to eat, sometimes they would scold him. Only a few people liked him. He was a dirty kind of a boy. That was the way he lived. In the winter time, during the *elu* moon he went to the kivas. The men did not like him and they would chase him out. He was growing up. He had no field, so in the springtime he could not plant corn. He was very poor. He just went around bothering people and they did not like him.

He heard that there were people living at K'ochatopelpee.[1] He

1. Southwest of Walpi.

thought he had better go over there. "I might find a home there," he said, "I wonder what people are living there?" He came across here (to First Mesa) and he got there. He went up to a house. The woman went up and said, "Here is the dirtiest boy I have ever seen, I wonder who he is." Her children came out and said, "Mother, we must not let this dirty boy come in." He went to another house. The woman there came out and said, "What a dirty boy! He must not come in." He went around to all the houses. Nobody gave him anything to eat. The last house he came to, the woman was baking outside. She said to him, "Have you eaten your supper yet?" — "I have not eaten supper or dinner or breakfast," he said to her. She gave him some *muwat'oko'*. He was very glad. He thought he would lie down where she had been baking, the place was warm. Next morning he went around. Nobody gave him anything to eat. He went to Mashup'-kwishe [1]. He heard a voice, "Shö! shö!" He looked around, he saw nobody. He heard a voice saying, "My grandchild." He saw Spider Grandmother sitting by the side of her hole. "My grandchild, people have been treating you very badly, giving you nothing to eat. This is your home, here you were born." She let him into her house. Every day he went for wood for his grandmother. She had some corn to cook. She ground corn and made food for him. He lived a long time with her, he grew to be a big boy. Spider Grandmother said to her grandchild, "I am going to make you into a fine boy." So she sent him to Anápölva for water. When he came back in the evening his grandmother poured water into a big pot and made the water boil. She put her grandson into the water and spit some medicine into the water. She twisted her cross stick into his hair and twisted and twisted his hair to make it long. She passed her hand over his face and over his hands, but she forgot his feet. So his feet stayed long. She looked him over and saw his feet were still long. But the water got cold and she could do nothing more for him. "Well, my grandson, now you are a good-looking boy." She fixed a kilt (*wage'*) for him to wear. She told him to return to Awatobi. "See what the people there will say to you," she said to him. "There will be a dance there tomorrow." He left and reached Awatobi in the afternoon. All the people wondered who he was. "Who is that boy?" asked everybody. Soon a man came and said to him, "Let's go to my house and have something to eat." Another man came and said, "Come to my house and have something to eat." All the men of Awatobi took him to their house and gave him something to eat. Nobody knew who he was. He slept at the house of one of the men. Next morning all the girls went out to the fields. He went out with one of the men. They ate out at the field, — watermelon, muskmelon,

1. A place between Walpi and Awatobi.

corn. In the evening the man said, "Will you marry one of my girls ?" The man had two girls. He said that he would. The girl gave him *makáno* and *kensi*. He carried it to his grandmother. The next evening he went to Awatobi and stayed in the girl's house. The next day he brought the girl back to his grandmother. The girl saw no corn there to grind. "Tomorrow you will find some corn to grind," said Spider Grandmother. Next morning when she woke up it was in a big room with everything hanging around the walls. She had gone to sleep in a little room. She ground corn all day till the sun went down. She stopped grinding, they ate supper and they went to bed. The next day she ground corn again until evening. Then she stopped grinding, they ate supper, they went to bed. Again the next day she ground corn all day until supper-time. They ate supper and went to bed. The next morning Spider Grandmother washed the girl's head by herself, she was alone. "You are my *sa'i*," said Spider Grandmother. She made some *muwashing*. Next morning Spider Grandmother said, "I think I am going to take you home." The girl did not know that they had made for her a blanket and dress and belt and moccasins. Spider Grandmother dressed her up. Then she took her *sa'i* and her grandson to Awatobi. They got there by midnight. The girl said "Mother ! Father!" They heard her calling, they made a fire, they were happy she had come back. Next morning her mother went to her clanswomen and told them to come and wash their *soyingi*. So they all came. The boy stayed there one day. Next day he went to hunt deer. He killed two deer and brought them to his wife's mother (*ya kwiya*).[1] She went and told all the people to come and eat deer. They all came and ate meat. They were much pleased, they had never eaten meat before.

Next day he went hunting again. While he was gone a butterfly came into his wife's house. She began to chase the butterfly. It flew out of the house. She followed it out until the butterfly went to a field of flowers. She chased the butterfly until she came to a mountain with many trees. The sun was about to set. The butterfly flew away. The girl met a man. "Where is that butterfly ?" asked the girl. "I saw no butterfly." — "Well, I was chasing a butterfly, I want to have it." — "I am butterfly," said the boy. He persuaded the girl to go home with him to the top of the mountain where inside of the mountain he lived. It was dark. The boy said to the young woman (*kwiya ky'ele*), "Let us go to bed." She went to sleep in one room, and the boy in another room. The girl went to sleep right away. The boy was a mean sort of boy, he threw the girl off the side of the mountain. She died. The husband of the girl came back from hunting and waited for his wife, but she did not come.

1. See Freire-Marreco, 280.

He asked her parents where she was. They could not find her. Nobody had seen her. Next day he thought, "I better go back to my home." Her father and mother kept on looking for her. But the girl was dead. Then her mother died because she had lost her child. Thus far I know.

18. OWL-BOY.

Far away at Kunluokyut'e'e a boy named Sawingyuenu [1] was living. He had a father and mother. He was a good boy, but sometimes he was naughty. These people did lots of things in the winter time. They danced with girls and played *elu* with the women and girls in the kiva in the *elu* moon. If a woman wanted to have a game she would go to the kiva and call out, "If you want a fire, tie up a bundle of wood and put it above your fireplace and it will get dry and we will have a good fire tonight." After they had eaten their supper, all the women whose husbands belonged to that kiva or whose sons belonged went to that kiva. The women sat on the left hand side, the men on the right hand side. There was white corn husk on one side for the women, black on the other side for the men. The woman game leader dropped the corn husk. The side that was uppermost would be the side to begin. They counted the men and boys and made as many sticks as there were men and boys. The women's leader picked the sticks; as she picked up each stick, she called it off by a man's name. A woman came and got it. Then they began to play. If the women were beaten, next afternoon they would take their food down into the kiva; if the men were beaten they would get wood for the women. (The man got wood for the woman who had his stick). In this game the men were beaten. Next night they were to be the leader. They said, "We will have another game tomorrow night." That day they went for wood. Every night they played in the kiva.

This little boy went down every night. His father and mother told him he was too young to go, but he did not mind his father and mother and he would go. One night while they were playing some people called Pisabi came and killed some of the men in the kiva. Next day the Town chief (*poantohun*) told the people they would go after the Pisabi. They came to a place and made camp. Early next day they started, and went all day and stopped to camp. That night two boys went around looking for the Pisabi. The Pisabi were having a dance. The boys returned and said, "We have found them. They were a lot of people and they were dancing. "The men said, "We will go and fight them." About midnight they reached

1. Meaning unknown, 'an old Tewa word.'

the place where they were dancing. They shot at them and they killed some of them. None of them was killed. They cut pieces of skull [scalp ?] out of the Pisabi. In two days they were back home. "We will have a dance," said the Town chief. They made a big fire and they danced all night. While they were dancing this little boy's father told him not to go. But he did not mind and he went there. At daylight the people went back to their houses to sleep. They slept all day. At night the little boy said to his father, "I am going to the kiva again." — "Do not go," said his father. "I have to go." His father got a stick and hit him, hit him hard. He was crying under the ladder. There was something coming and settling over the top of the ladder and saying, "Hu hu! Hu hu!" It was an owl (*kwakye'*). He said to the little boy, "Get on my back." The little boy was afraid. "Do not be afraid of me," said Owl, "I am your father." He got on his back. Owl flew off to a canyon, to a place called T'obatseni' (cliff white). Owl brought the little boy to T'obatseni'. He came to a hole where he kept his young ones. He left the little boy inside of the hole. "This will be your home," said Owl, "I was very sorry for you because your father and mother were always scolding you, so I went for you. [1] This will be your home. These will be your brothers and sisters." He stayed there that night. At daylight the big owl said, "I am going out to hunt for you." The little boy stayed with the little owls. The little boy looked down and he saw he was on a high cliff. He was very unhappy and all day he cried, cried, cried. Owl came back in the evening with a rabbit. The little owls ate it, but the little boy could not eat it because it was not cooked. "Why didn't you eat the rabbit together with your brothers and sisters?" asked Owl. "It was not cooked." Next morning Owl flew away again. The little boy was very hungry and now he was very thirsty. In the afternoon he heard something on the edge of the cliff. It was *k'oiye* (chipmunk). "Are you hungry?" said Chipmunk. "Yes, I am hungry and thirsty," said the little boy. "Yes, that was why I came up to ask you." So Chipmunk went away and pretty soon he brought up a piñon shell, very small, it was full of water. "Do not drink it all," said Chipmunk. "It will last you for two days." So he drank, but he did not drink it all. [2] "Eat this," said Chipmunk. It was piñon nuts. "Tomorrow I will come again," said Chipmunk. In this way Chipmunk fed the little boy. Every day Owl brought a rabbit which the little owls ate, but the little boy could not eat. The little boy was getting very homesick for his father and mother. The morning after he had been carried off his father and mother were

1. Cp. "Voth 1 : 167-9."
2. For the self-replenishing cup in Keresan tales, see Dumarest, 232; Boas 1. See also Voth 1 : 163. For a self-filling sack of meal, see Stevenson 2 : 606, n. *a*.

looking for him. All day they were looking for him. Then Chipmunk said to himself, "I think I had better take down that boy." Chipmunk planted a piñon nut under the foot of the cliff. He sang two songs and the pine (*chele*) came up. He sang two more songs and it was that high (four inches). He kept on singing and the pine kept on growing. The pine came up and Chipmunk pulled it with his teeth to make it grow faster. It was up to the side of the hole. "Come on; climb down on this pine," said Chipmunk to the little boy. "It may not be strong enough," said the boy. "It is strong enough," said Chipmunk. So he climbed down on the pine, down to the foot of the cliff. Then he cut down the pine so Owl would not know how the little boy had come down.

"I will take you to your grandmother," said Chipmunk. He took him to Spider Grandmother. She was living in the *koye'*. "Grandmother!" called Chipmunk. "Grandmother!" he called again. "I have brought you your grandchild." — "Come down," said Spider. They went down. Spider gave them something to eat. "I am glad you brought me my grandchild," said Spider. "You will stay and live here with me," said grandmother. He stayed a long time. He grew up and was old enough to hunt for his grandmother. "Have you any bow and arrow?" he said to grandmother. "Yes," and she got a bow and arrows out of another room. "I want to go and hunt rabbits for you," he said to grandmother. "All right, but don't go very far, come back early." He went off to look for rabbits. He found a rabbit and killed it. He went to look for another rabbit. He found one and killed it. He came back home and grandmother was very glad to have the rabbits. Every day he went rabbit hunting. Owl was looking for the boy. He asked the little ones, but they did not know. He went to the foot of the cliff but could not see what became of the boy. The boy went hunting every day for his grandmother. He grew to be a big boy. Grandmother told him, "You go to your uncle (*meme*)." — "Where is my uncle?" asked the boy. "Go to the north and then you will find your uncle." He started to the north, he went a long way and there was somebody sitting on a rock. He said to him, "My nephew, where are you going?" It was Hawk (*seping*). "I am going to my uncle," said the boy. "Well, I am your uncle," said Hawk. "I guess you are coming to me, I know what you have come for," said Hawk. "I am going to get you a head. Stay here until I come back." He stayed all day. Hawk returned with a head he had got from the Pisabi, a head tied with feathers. "Tomorrow come back here at the same time," said Hawk. He went back to his grandmother and told her all his uncle had done, and grandmother was glad. Next morning he went straight to his uncle. He said, "Uncle, I have come back again." — "You stay here all day." In the evening Hawk flew back and brought him a quiver he

got from the Pisabi. "Tomorrow come back here at the same time,"
said Hawk. He went back to his grandmother and told her what
Hawk had done. Next morning he went back to Hawk. He waited
for his uncle all day until he came in the evening and brought
anchobe (moccasins with leggings to the knees). He went back to his
grandmother. Grandmother said, "I think you have enough. You
better go back to your mother and father. It has been a long time,
and your father and mother are very homesick for you," said
grandmother. "Go hunt more rabbits tomorrow," said grandmother.
He went rabbit hunting and found lots of them. He brought
them back to grandmother and she skinned them and cooked them
for him. "Hunt tomorrow," said grandmother. Next day he went
hunting and found many rabbits and brought them back. "I think
you have enough," said grandmother, "Go home tomorrow." Soon
they heard a sound. It was Owl on top of the house saying, "Hu
hu! hu hu!" Owl came into the koye'. "What do you want?" said
grandmother. "Is this my son?, "asked Owl. Grandmother said, "Yes,
this is your son." — "I have been looking for him for a long
time, but I could not find him, but Chipmunk told me today that
he brought him down and took him home." — "Well, you can't
have him, for tomorrow he is going home to his father and mother?" — "That is why I have come," said Owl. "His father and
mother are lying very homesick, they can't eat, they are almost
dead." — "Well, you can carry him home. We will go tomorrow
night," said grandmother. So she cooked the rabbits and fixed them
on a k'yalekon (ladder, rabbits stretched between rungs). Next morning grandmother washed the boy's hair and combed it. In the
evening she put on that head and his buckskin shirt and his high
moccasins. "You look all right," said grandmother to the boy.
"Your father and mother will be happy over you." In the evening
there was a sound on top of the house. Owl came. He flew into
the koye'. "Are you ready?" asked Owl. "Yes." — "All right,
you can go," grandmother said to the boy. She got the k'yalekon.
"You can get on my back," said Owl. And the boy got on his back
and carried the k'yalekon on his own back. They flew all night and
came to a place a little way from Kunluokyut'e'e. "Stay here until afternoon," said Owl, "then you can go to your house. When you get to
your father and mother tell them to put you in a room without
window or door, and do you stay there four days. Then they are to
take you out and you will be their son. But if they look in after two
days or three days, then you will come back to my house." In the
afternoon he started with his k'yalekon. The people saw him coming,
but they did not know him. He reached his home, he called, "Mother! Father!" Nobody answered him. He called, "Mother! Father!"
Nobody answered him. He went down into the koye'. And there

was his father lying and his mother lying. He went to his father and said, "Father!" He went to his mother and said, "Mother!" His mother got up. "Who are you?" asked his mother. "Who are you?" asked his father. "I am your son," said the boy. "Once you hit me and Owl came and carried me away." Then they knew it was their son. "My son, we have been very homesick for you. We are about dead." That night they ate the rabbits. Next morning he told his father and mother that Owl told him that they were to put him in a room and leave him there four days, and not look in. "If you look in after two or three days, I will go back to Owl. If you do not look in, in five days, early in the morning, I will come out and live with you." Early the next morning they put him in *kwak'eibi*. They shut the windows and doors. There he stayed all day and all the next day. On the fourth day his mother made some *mowakoxke* (Hopi, *pigami*) and some *tohsęhle* (boiled meat). His mother and father were happy. The next day they were to take out the boy. His mother was very anxious to see the boy. She watched the sun. The sun went down. "The time is up," she said. She went up and looked in through a crack in the door (the door was of cottonwood), and saw her boy sitting there. She came down and they ate supper, and she said, "We had better go to bed so we can get up early in the morning." At midnight (*nop'no*) there was a noise up in *kwak'eibi*. They could not sleep, it was such a loud noise. The boy's father said, "Did you go up and look at our boy?" — "Yes, I went up and looked in through a crack." — "You did wrong," said her husband. "He has become an owl up there." Next morning he went up to *kwak'eibi*, and there in the center of the room was a big owl. "Poor boy!" said the man, "Your mother was a bad woman, she came up and looked through the crack in the door. Stay here until I come back." He was crying about it and he went down and made five feather-strings. Then he went back up to *kwak'eibi*, he and his wife. There was a big owl sitting there. "Sit still," said the man. The mother was crying, crying. The boy's father tied two feather-strings around each leg and one around his neck. "Now you may go back to your people. You are no longer our son. You are an owl. If an enemy approaches, come and tell the people." [1] He (Owl) shook his head like this (nodding). "If sickness is coming, you can tell the people." [2] He shook his head (nodding). He went around the house four times and then he flew away. That is the way the boy became an owl. This is the reason that men and women must not whip their children

1. Cp. Zuñi; Stevenson 2 : 138 fr. *a* ; Taos, Parsons 2.
2. When an owl comes to the top of a house and hoots, people believe sickness is coming. This is a sign. (Tewa, *piyepo'* ; Hopi, *töauta*.)

outdoors because Owl will come and take their children away. [1]
This is all I know.

19. DEER BOY.

Far away there at Öchapłöbełpe (old Walpi) there was a girl living.
She was a good-looking girl, but she always stayed at home. When
the people did anything she never went to see. She was the daughter
of the Crier chief. In January and February when the girls danced,
she never joined them. She stayed at her house all day, grinding and
blanket embroidering. One day when she was embroidering in *kwa-
k'eibi*, a boy came up and talked to her for a while and then went
down. Next day at the same time he came again. Four times he came
up, the fourth time he had intercourse with her. He never came back to
her again. She did not know who he was. He was the son of Gyigya. [2]
At the end of February moon (*k'aut'opoye*), they called out that there
would be a hunt, and that the girls would go with the men. " My child, "
said the girl's father to her, " You had better go with the girls and be happy. You never go out, and it would make you happy to go. " This time
the girl wanted to go. Next morning she began to cook some *mowa-
chigi* (meal cooked in corn husk tied in two places.) By that time the
people were ready to go. They went to the west. One of the girls
came along, it was the daughter of the Town chief, and she went up
to the girl, she said, " Would you like to go with me ? " — " Yes, "
said the girl. So they went together. They went below and the men
had started. Whenever a man killed a rabbit, a girl ran up to him and
got the rabbit. The girls went to a place called Kwakwiobi, [3] and then
the girl's belly pained and she could go no farther. The daughter of the
Town chief left her there. Her belly ached very badly and pretty soon
something came out of it and there was a baby. She did not know
what to do with it. So she threw it into some grass and left it there
and went on after the hunters. The girls were getting rabbits. She did
not get any rabbit until they got back to the foot of the mesa and
then she got one. When she came back she was unhappy. " Why
are you unhappy? " asked her father and mother. "I am tired, " she
said. " Tomorrow you will be all right, " they said to her. All night
she was unhappy, thinking of that baby.

That night Coyote old man came along, looking for his food, and
he heard a sound. " I wonder if there is a baby somewhere here? "
Then he found the baby in the grass. " Well, I have my food, " said

1. Mothers threaten children with Owl. They say that Owl will come and carry
the child away.
2. The mother or sister of the Town chief (Hopi, gigmongwi).
3. In Tewa, Tamukyogye. It is west of Walpi, in the sand hills at the foot of the
mesa.

Coyote old man. Then the baby cried again. He was just about to bite it, when it cried again and he thought, " Well, I had better not eat him but carry him to my grandmother, " said Coyote. So he looked at the baby again and saw it was a boy baby. So he picked it up with his mouth and carried it to the north near a place called Wökukoha (Hopi in Tewa, P'oso', a spring north of Walpi). He said to himself, " I think I had better leave it and go and tell my grandmother. " He left the child there, tired carrying it, and went on to his grandmother. At that place lived a woman who was a deer, and she found the child and took him to her house. There was high grass growing there and that was her door. She took away the grass and there was a hole in the ground to her kiva. This deer woman (*ťoṇkwiya'*) had lots of milk. She washed the baby's head and she said to herself, " I have to lie beside this baby for twenty days. "[1] So she was lying there by the baby. Meanwhile Coyote reached his grandmother. " Grandmother, " he said, " I found a baby. " — " What did you do with it ? " — " I left it in the grass and came over here to you. Let us go now after the baby. If you say that we should kill it, we will kill it, or, if you say keep it, we will keep it. " So both went after the baby. They got to the place where he left the baby, they did not find it. There was no track. His grandmother said, " You ought not to have left it here, you should know better than that. " — " Well, I was tired and so I left it. What has become of it ? " — " I think that woman who lives here has taken it into her home. " — " Well, let's go, " said his grandmother. So they went.

This Deer woman stayed in her house twenty days, and then another Deer woman washed the child's head. After this the child began to grow very fast. As he was playing around, she said to him, " You play with those other boys. " She had two little deer children. So he played with them and got stronger and stronger. Soon he was grown up. " You run a race with the other boys, " she said to him. Soon he could keep up with the deer boys and then he could overtake them. He was a good runner. Deer woman dressed him up and gave him a bow and arrow. " Go out with these deer boys (*ťoṇeṇu'*), your brothers, go to the west, and make a track around there. " Next day he went out again. On the third day there was a man hunting and he found a track which he did not know. (Before this the deer had always stayed below underground.) He said when he got home, " I found a track, to the north, and I did not know it. " The next day two other men went with him and they found tracks, and then they saw the two deer and a boy with them. They went home and called out, " Tomorrow we go hunting rabbits and deer. Girls and men will go. " The next morning the girls began to cook their lunch. The girl who

---

1. The confinement period of a Hopi mother.

had had the baby wanted to go, too. That night Deer woman said to the boy, " Tomorrow the people are going to hunt, and they are going to catch you. About evening they are going to find your brothers and then they are going to run after you. If anybody catches you, it will be your father. Your mother is coming too. If your father does not catch you, run to your mother and say, ' My mother '. The boy with your mother will be your father. " That morning they went hunting and in the evening they tracked the deer and killed them. Then they saw the boy and began to chase him. All were surprised to see a boy with the deer and they wanted very much to catch him. Soon the boy saw his mother coming with his father. Then he ran to her and put his arm around her neck and said, " My mother! " and he turned to his father and put his arm around his neck and said, " My father ! " Everybody was surprised, but the woman said, " Surely this is my child. " So she took him. " This is your grandchild, " she said to her mother and to her father. " This is my mother, " said the boy. " Long ago I was born down below in the grass and my mother left me there and then Coyote man came along and carried me with him, but he got tired carrying me and went on to his grandmother. Then Deer woman came and took me to her house, and I grew up there and now she has sent me back to you, " said the boy. " So now I come back to live with you. But my deer mother told me that you should put me in a room without window or door where nobody can look in, " said the boy. " If anyone looks in before four days, I will go back to my mother, " said the boy. " It is all right, " said his grandmother. So that night they put him in a room without window or door where nobody could look in. There he was one day, and they counted that day and he was there another day and they counted that day and they counted the next day. On the fourth day about sundown the mother of the boy said, " It is time for me to look in where my son is. " She looked in through a crack in the door. There the boy was sitting. She was very glad to see him and she was happy to think of taking him out next morning. About midnight there was a big noise up the ladder. Grandmother said, " There is a big noise. Did anyone of you look into the room ? " — " Yes, " said the mother of the boy. " I looked in through a crack. It was sundown, and I thought we could look. " — " It was not yet time, " said Grandmother, " We had not counted the day yet. " So next morning the grandfather went up and there in the middle of the floor stood a big deer. He went down and began to make feather-strings for him. Everybody knew that the boy had turned back into a deer and everybody was sorry about it. So everybody made feather-strings for him. Somebody called out for the people to come. So they all came with feather-strings and meal. Grandfather went up and opened the door. The deer began to run. " Grandchild, do not run. I am going to tie something on your horn. " Then the grandfather led him by the horn and the people came up and tied their feather-strings to both horns. They said to him, " We were very anxious to see you, but your mother did not know enough not to look in. " Everybody tied their feather-strings. They turned him loose. He ran. Everybody watched him. He ran north. He came to where his deer mother and his deer brothers were standing waiting for him. Then all of them went to the mountains. " Hereafter we shall live among the mountains, " said Deer woman. So they went west to Comp'ing. [1] And thereafter they lived there in the mountains.

20. WITCH RABBIT : COYOTE TEACHES WITCHCRAFT. [2]

Once upon a time the people were living at Sa'apa. Other people were living at Mitstuxki. Most of the people were living at Sa'apa and Mitstuxki was a small village. They were living there and sometimes one village had some kind of a dance or a game to enjoy themselves. There was a girl named Yellow corn girl. She had a mother and a father and she had a brother, and they called him Yellow boy (Sikiatateyu). They were brother and sister, but he did not want his sister to go with the other girls. He wanted her to stay in her own house all the time instead of going around with the other girls. She was a fine looking girl and he was a fine looking boy. The boys tried to marry the girl. All the boys of the village tried it, but he did not want to have any of the boys marry his sister, and she thought the same. He did not want to marry any of the girls of the village. Both were the same. They did not want to get married at all. Once in the winter when there was a little snow the boy went out and saw that it was snowing. He came back and told his sister to fix some lunch for him to take along. He said, " It is snowing. I want to go and hunt rabbits tomorrow morning, so I want my lunch fixed tonight and ready for me to start early in the morning. " She did it. She baked some kind of sweet corn meal and she cooked different kinds of food for him for his lunch to take along. Daylight came and he woke up early in the morning and he just took his lunch and went out. He went to the south. He was going away to the other side to Tcepa. That was a good place to hunt rabbits and so he was going away down there. Before he got there, just as the sun was coming up he saw a track, a jack-rabbit track. He followed the track. He went along and the jack-rabbit jumped out of the bush and he began to chase the jack rabbit. He ran and ran after that jack-rabbit. After a while the jack-rabbit began to get tired. He was just about to take the jack-rabbit when the jack-

1. Snow Mountain (*p'om*, snow, *p'ing*, mountain) i. e. San Francisco Mountain.
2. Recorded by Ruth Bunzel.

rabbit jumped into a hole in the cliff. He was running and he slipped down into the hole, the boy. He did not know it was a big hole because the snow covered it up. He fell down. He reached the bottom of the hole. He was badly hurt. Soon he knew that his leg was broken. He looked around. There was some one sitting way back in the hole. He was looking at him. He just wore a rabbit ear. He put his head down and looked at him. He was the jack-rabbit but had gone in there and changed into a person. The boy suffered. He had broken his leg. He was wondering how he would get out, but he could not get out because his leg was broken. Finally a badger came along. He was from Wona-napokwape. He was going along looking for the track of a rabbit. By and by he saw the track going along, where some one had been chasing a jack-rabbit. He stood there looking at the track and thought, " I wonder who is the fellow who has been chasing this rabbit this early. I thought I was early, but some one came earlier. I wonder who the boy is, " he said. He looked around and followed the track. Soon he saw the track of the jack-rabbit running. He followed that track. Soon he got to the place where the jack-rabbit jumped in. He looked right down and stepped in a little way and saw a person's track, but the track just went down into the hole. He looked there at the track. " I wonder who has fallen down, " he said to himself. Then he looked down into the hole where the person had fallen down. He saw someone lying down in the hole suffering. Then he looked down wondering who the person was. Then he heard that he was suffering. Then he said, " Poor fellow, " he said. " My poor grandson, I wonder how you fell down in there, " he said. Then he crawled right down into the hole. Soon he reached the boy. Then he put his hand on this man's body and said, " Poor grandson, how did you get down here? " He knew that he was still alive. He said, " I fell down. I was chasing a rabbit and slipped at the edge of this cliff and fell right down. I never knew I would fall down. My leg is broken and I cannot stand up, " he said. " The rabbit ran down into this hole and there was a person sitting way back in the hole. He just put his head down and never looked at me. He was wearing rabbit ears, " he said, " and whitewash all over his body. " — " Where is he now ? " he said. " I was watching this person and a little later there was a little fly that went out of this hole. That person turned himself into a fly and flew out. " Then Badger asked the boy, " Do you know who is the person?" — " Yes, " he said, " I know who he is. He is from the same village that I am from. He is from the Corn clan and he has a sister. He wanted me to marry his sister, but I did not want the girl for my wife. That is the reason why he wanted to kill me. " The Badger said, " Yes, that is true. I heard about it. The girl wanted to marry you, but you did not want to marry the girl and that is the reason he wanted to kill you. I know all about it. Now you just

stay here, " he said. " I am going out to look for something. " He
went out of the hole which was a crack in the cliff and he crawled
out and went up on top of the rock and looked around to see if there
was no one around there. He could not see anyone there and then he
said to himself, " I guess I am alone. I had better go right down and
take the boy out. " He went down there and told the boy, " Just get
on my back and I will carry you on my back. I will go up on top. "
He did so. " Just take hold of my neck and hold tight so that you
won't fall off. " He did so. He went out and went up on top of the
mesa. He left the boy at a place where it was dry on top of the rock.
" You stay right here and lie still. I am going to look for some medicine, " he said. He did and he went out and looked around in the
snow and soon he found some kind of roots for medicine. " Well, I
had better go back home and get my outfit, " he said, " my medicine
and everything I use. " He went on and went to his home at Wona-
napokwape. He went there. He had a wife and he hurried in and his
wife was very surprised. " What has happened? Something surely
happened! " She looked at him and said, " What is the matter, what
has happened? " she said again, but he never answered for a long time.
But after a long time he answered and said, " It is Sikiatateyu. He has
fallen down and broken his leg. I was hunting and saw his track and
followed it and found him way down in a hole. I took him out and
his leg is broken, so I am going to give him medicine. " Both of them
felt sorry for him. He took his outfit and hurried back. He got there
to the boy. Then he put his hand on his leg and sang some kind of a
song that would cure the pain. He sang the song once, then he stopped
and spread some kind of medicine on the leg. Bye and bye the
bones began to join together. After the fourth song he sang, it began
to be cured. Bye and bye the pain stopped. Then Badger asked the
boy, "Does it still hurt? " — "No, it doesn't pain now. " — " Let me
see you stand. " The boy stood up but he was afraid he might break
it again. He stood up and sat right down. " Does it hurt? "
said Badger. " No, " said the boy. " Well, stand up again and take one
or two steps and see if it hurts. " He stood up and took one step and
then another and it did not hurt. Then he was well. His leg was fixed
all right. He said, " I am well. " — " Now you must sit right here
and let me hunt some rabbits, " said the Badger. He did so and he
waited. When the Badger saw a jack-rabbit he chased him and when
he went into a hole, he dug the hole and dug the rabbit out. That
is the way he killed rabbits. He killed a lot of them. Then he said,
" Well, I think this is enough. I think this is about as many as you
could kill in a day. You just go right home now. "

About that time a Coyote came along. He was looking for his
meal. He saw a track where some one had been chasing rabbits and
wondered who had been chasing rabbits. He looked around and saw

two persons sitting. He walked over to them and got there. It was
Sikiatateyu sitting with Badger. As soon as he came to them, " My
grandson, " he said, " my friend, I have been hunting rabbits and I
killed lots of them and I left them over yonder. I put them up in a
cedar tree. I saw your tracks and followed them to see who was here.
It was you, my friends, " he said to Badger, and he called Sikiatateyu his grandson. Sikiatateyu told Coyote, " I have had my leg
broken. "— " Why, how did you have your leg broken? " he said. "I fell
down into a hole, " he said. " Shall I go and tell your father and
mother and sister ? " he said. " Yes, you had better go and tell them,
and have my father come and help me carry these rabbits, " he said.
He took his lunch and Coyote went on. He went to the house of
the boy. His sister was grinding corn. She heard some one and she
looked and saw that a stranger was coming. She looked out and saw
it was Coyote. Then Coyote said, " Where is your father? " — " He
went to get wood. " — " And where is your mother ? " — " She
went to get water, " she said. " Well, your brother killed many rabbits and he can't carry them all because they are so heavy. He wanted
me to come and tell you he had killed rabbits and could not carry
them all, and he wanted me to tell your father to go and help him
carry them. " She believed Coyote. Then Coyote said, " Your brother told me he wanted you to marry me. " — " I don't believe my
brother told you that. " — " Yes, he told me to marry you. " Then
the girl believed Coyote and Coyote stayed there and married the
girl instead of going back. The girl married him, and while they
were lying down together her mother came in. She saw she was
not grinding corn and she went to look for her and saw her
lying there with some one. Then she looked and saw it was Coyote,
and she took a stick and hit Coyote. Coyote ran away and the people
ran after him. Coyote went back to the boy. Then the boy started
to come back home. He came home in the evening. He had lots of
rabbits. His sister was sad. She was not happy to see her brother. As
soon as her brother came in he said to her, " Sister, what is the matter that you are not happy? " She said, " Mother has been scolding me. " — " What has she been scolding you for ? " said the boy
to his sister. Then his mother told him what the girl had done. Then
the girl said, " You told Coyote to come and marry me. I trust you
and I did what you told me. He told me truly and said you had sent
him to me. If he had not said you had sent him, I would not have
married him. I want to do just what you tell me, " said the girl.
" Well, never mind, " said the boy, " let it go. " His mother kept
on being angry about it.

Next day when the sun came up the girl got up and dressed herself
and went away from home. She went off to the south. As she went
along she met some one. " Where are you going ? " he said. " I am

18

going away. I don't know where I am going. I am going for my life. " —
" Well, do you know me ? " said Coyote. " No, " she said. " Well,
I am the one who married you yesterday. You are going to my house.
I made you come this way, and now you are going to my home, "
he said. " All right, " she said, and he took the girl to his home. He
lived on the other side of Tcepa. When they came to Coyote's house
he lived in a hole. Coyote was very proud that he had married the
girl. " Everyone wanted to marry that girl and she did not want to
marry anybody, but now she has married Coyote. " He was very proud
of it. Then he said, " Now let us do something. Let us both of us be
alike. " — " How can I be like you? " said the girl. " I will show you, "
he said and went into the back room and brought out something,
some kind of wheel like a big ring. He talked to it. He watched the
ring. He laid it on the ground and he went in again and brought out
some kind of a bundle. He laid it down by the ring. Then he put up
the ring. " Now you just jump right over (through?) this ring, " said
Coyote. " Do this way. Just watch me. " He put his head down by
the ring and just turned himself over the ring. There was an owl sitting on the other side. He had turned himself into an owl. Then he
jumped back. Then he said to the girl, " You do the same. " She did
it and there was a big wolf sitting there. " That is not how to do
it, you must be like me. Turn yourself into a coyote. " Then she did
it again and she was a coyote. " Now you are like me ! I will teach
you what to do. " He was a witch coyote and he taught the girl how
to turn a person into a coyote or anything else; and how to make a
person sick and how to kill a person. He taught the girl to do these
things and she learned them.

Then he said, " Now you go back to your home. When you get
to your home you turn yourself into a coyote. " Then he gave her a
little sharp spindle. He gave it to the girl and said, " When you go to
the house, you go to where your mother is sleeping and just spin
this over her heart and take out her heart. Then go to your brother
and do the same thing. When you have their hearts you bring them
here, " he said to the girl. She did it. She turned herself into a coyote
and went there. She came to the village and turned herself into a fly.
She flew into the house where her mother and brother were sleeping.
Late at night she went there and stood in the door and thought what
she should do to her mother. She loved her mother very much but
she was angry because of what she had done to her. She went to her
mother and spun the spindle over her heart and took out the heart of
her mother. Then she went to her brother and spun it and took out
his heart too. That was the way she took them. Then she went back
to the coyote. " Did you bring them? " — " Yes, " she said.
" Well, now let us see them. " Then he took them and he
took arrows and they both shot and they killed their hearts. That is

the way the girl killed her mother and brother. Next day her mother and brother died. That is the way she killed them.

After this she was living with Coyote. Each day her husband went out to hunt. She stayed there the rest of the day. He went to hunt rabbits for their food. That is the way they lived. They lived on rabbit meat. One day when the coyote went to hunt rabbits the people living at Sa'apa were going to hunt rabbits. While they were hunting rabbits they saw a coyote. When they got to the place they wanted to hunt they went one by one around in a circle. Some went in one direction and some went in the other direction and they met. Some of the men followed one hunter and the rest followed the other and they met and formed a big circle and lots of rabbits were in the circle. The coyote was in the circle. They saw the coyote and shot it with arrows and soon they killed the coyote. They killed him, and in the night the coyote did not come home from the hunt. The girl was looking for him, but he did not come. Late at night he still did not come. She was very sorry that her husband did not come. " I wonder why he does not come, " she said. She sat there all night and he did not come. At daybreak she dressed as a coyote and went out to look for her husband. She looked for him all day. Soon she saw tracks where people had been hunting. She saw tracks of many people. She looked around the tracks and soon she saw a Coyote lying on the ground. It was her husband. She was very sorry for her husband. She picked up her husband and put him on her back and carried him home. She went with the dead coyote on her back. She put him down and tried to make him alive, but he never came alive. Then she went home. At night she came into the house. Then a boy came in. He saw some one in the house. It was the girl. Then he said, " Your mother and brother have died. Where have you been? " — " I have been away. " — " Where have you been? " — " I have been visiting at Tcepa. " Then the boy said, " I want to marry you. " She said, " All right. " Then they were married and next day all the people knew that the girl and boy were married. Soon they had a baby boy. After about two or three days the baby began to crawl and soon, in about ten days, he began to stand. In fifteen days he began to walk. In twenty days he was strong enough to go out and go around. His mother taught him how to make a person sick and how to kill a person and how to turn himself into any kind of animal. This boy was taught witchcraft. After this there were witches. There were never witches before that, but the girl married a coyote and from that time there have been witches. That is the reason why people are witches now. They have been taught by Coyote.

21. RACE AGAINST WITCHES: FALSE MESSAGE.

Far away at Kuṇluokyut'e'e the E̠we̠le (Hopi, (*pühokonhoya*) were living. They had no mother or father, only a grandmother. They did nothing but play stick ball (*tenghuṇtamehleo*), even in the evening when they stayed in the *koyé*. In the daytime they went to a place called Naṃpiliṇmulĕ, a slope where they played upward. Their grand-mother told them to go get wood for her. But they wanted only to play. The people at Kuṇluokyut'e'e had races every day with the round ball (*kwawing*) during the *elu* moon. The people of the witch kiva always beat the people of the other kiva. The people thought that they would like to beat the witch kiva. They asked the kiva old man, *t'e'e seṇotse*, how they could beat the witches. " I will try to see how we can beat them. " He made four feather-strings and four prayer-sticks and he made two sticks (*kwetiing*) and two balls (*huṇtamehle*) and took them to the house of the E̠we̠le. [1] These E̠we̠le were still playing ball. Grandmother saw grandfather old man (*tete seṇotse*) and asked him to sit down by the fire. The E̠we̠le never knew that anybody had come in. She hit them on the head with a stick, so they stopped play-ing ball. So they sat down by the fireplace. " Did you want some thing ? " said Grandmother. " Yes, " said kiva old man. " I came to ask these boys to help us in the races tomorrow. " — " Did you bring anything for them ? " asked Grandmother. " Yes, here is the bundle for them. " Grandmother opened it and found the feather-strings, the prayer-sticks, the sticks and balls. She divided the things, putting two feather-strings on one side, two feather-strings on the other side, two prayer-sticks on one side, two prayer-sticks on the other side, one ball on one side and one ball on the other side, one stick on one side and one stick on the other side. She called to her grandchildren, " Come over here, " said Grandmother to them. " This is for you and this for you, " said Grandmother. " Tomorrow we are going to have a race. These witch kiva people we have never beaten, so I am to ask you to help beat them. " — " We will come and help you beat them, " said the E̠we̠le. So he went back to his kiva, and all the men were there. He filled his pipe with tobacco and smoked and passed it around. " What did they say? " they asked the old man. " Those E̠we̠le were glad to get what I brought them and they said that they would help us, " said the old man. Next morning another man went to each house and said they were going to race in the afternoon. They began to paint themselves. With white paint they made designs on their body (*tiwitaang*). " Those who lose

---

1. Gaming implements in imitation are offered to the war gods at Zuñi, and in a Sia war god shrine I have seen the corn-cob dart of the dart-and-ball game.

this race we will cut off their heads, " said the leader of the race. He took out a big knife and an old man took it to the other side of the mesa. The leader of the race (*kwahi toyo,* race chief) was of the witch kiva. The others were sad. They started off in the race. The witches were way a head. The Ęwęle were hidden somewhere with their ball. They kicked it on and overtook the witches. There was a line they always raced to. The Ęwęle got there first. " Well, we will cut your head off, " said the old man. " All right, "said the witches, " we said so, we must do it. " So they cut the heads off of all the witches. They used the knife of Ęwęle. The women had come down to this line, all but a witch woman who had a baby and did not go down. They cut off the heads of all the men and then of all the women. They thought they had killed all the witches, but there was one witch woman left, the woman with the baby. (So there are still witches left.)[1]

There was a Suyuku who came to this village and every day she would carry off in her basket (*yamele*) all the children who went down to the foot of the mesa. They had a hard time. Down at the foot of the mesa there lived a turkey. He would go out to gather piñon nuts. One day while he was looking for something to eat, there came the Suyuku. Suyuku said to Turkey, " What are you doing ? — "Looking for something to eat. " — " Well, if you want something I will put you in my basket and take you to my house. " — " I know where your house is and I can go there. " — "I will eat you up, " said Suyuku. " All right, " said Turkey, " but wait, I know where your home is, I will take this knife and when I get to your husband he can cut my head off at your home instead of in this place. " — " All right, " said Suyuku, " take this knife and go to my house. If my husband is not there, wait until he comes. " When Turkey got to Sukuyu's house, he said to the husband of Suyuku. " Your wife sent me here, " said Turkey. " Why ? " said the husband of Suyuku. " She said that you were to kill one of these Suyuku girls and give her to me, " said Turkey. " She gave me this knife and said that with it you were to cut off the head of the biggest girl. " So the husband of Suyuku took the knife and called for his children, " My children, come over here," said the Suyuku man. "Why did you call us? " asked the Suyuku children. " Your mother said to Turkey that I was to cut off your head. " So he took the oldest girl — there were four girls and two boys — and cut off her head and put it in the place where Suyuku used to put the children. Then Turkey flew away. As soon as the Suyuku woman came home, she said to her husband, " Did you cook the turkey? " — "I cooked no turkey. " — " What did you cook for me? "

asked Suyuku woman. " Turkey told me that you said I was to kill
our oldest daughter with the knife you gave him and cook her for
you. " Suyuku woman began to cry for her daughter. Then they went
off to the forest to look for Turkey, but they did not find him. Next
day Suyuku went to Kunluokyut'e'e and caught two more children. She
caught a child of Town chief and carried him off. When evening came
the child of Town chief did not come back from his play and Town
chief went to ask for his child. He looked through all the houses, but
could not find the child. He was very unhappy. Next morning he went
down at the foot of the hill and found the track of Suyuku who had carried them off. He went back to his house and told his wife how Suyuku
had carried them off. At midnight the Town chief made six prayer-
sticks and six feather-strings and two *huntaṃ̇hle* and two sticks, and then
he went to the *koye'* of the Ẹwẹle. They were asleep. He went in and
called, " Ẹwẹle, are you asleep?" The grandmother of the Ẹwẹle said yes.
She got up and made a fire and standing there was Town chief. " Sit
down there, " she said. He put tobacco in his pipe and smoked four
times and handed it to Grandmother. She smoked it out, and handed
it back to Town chief, and then she woke up her grandchildren. Grandmother said, " Ẹwẹle, move over here, Town chief has come here. "
So they moved over to their grandmother. Town chief handed
his bundle to Grandmother, and she opened it and found the six feather-strings, the six prayer-sticks, the two balls and the two sticks.
She divided the things, putting the two feather-strings on one
side, two on the other side, two prayer-sticks on one side, two on
the other side, one ball in one place, one in another place,
one stick in one place, one in the other, and two feather-strings
and two prayer-sticks for herself. Grandmother was glad to have them.
" What did you come for? " said Grandmother. " Yesterday Suyuku
took my child, " said Town chief. " My child was a boy. He can no
longer be alive. He must be already cooked. " — " I know it and I
am sorry, " said Grandmother. " So I came down here to ask Ẹwẹle
to go and kill that Suyuku, " said Town chief. It was almost daylight.
So they said they would go at once, for Suyuku went early in the
morning to steal the children. They went out, playing ball as they
went. Just before sunrise they got to the house of Suyuku, and there
they were playing ball. Suyuku had not yet killed the child of Town
chief or any other child. She had many other children to kill and
eat. Suyuku started off to go to Kunluokyut'e'e. Then she came to
where the Ẹwẹle were playing. " Here are some children playing. I
will get them and take them home and then go after some other children... Come on here, " said Suyuku to the Ẹwẹle. " Get into my
basket. " They just laughed at her. She caught them with her long
cane (*tape*) and put them into her basket and took them to her house.
When she got there, she said, " I had better cook these children first, "

said Suyuku, so she put them into the oven (*tehmele*).[1] Then the Ewęle spit out some medicine into the oven, and it got cold. Suyuku put more fire into the oven, but the Ewęle did not get burned. Next morning Suyuku took the lid off the oven and they jumped out alive. "Why didn't you cook?" said Suyuku. "Because you did not put on enough wood," said Ewęle. So she put them back into the oven for the next day. Then at night the Ewęle came out and caught two little Suyuku and put them into the oven and put a stone on top of them and put a big fire on top of them. They went into the house of Suyuku and there was a big jar (*pomele*). One said to the other, " Let us go and get into that jar. " They got into the jar and stayed there all night. Next morning Suyuku got up and went to the oven. " They are cooked enough to eat them this time, " said Suyuku. She put them into a bowl to eat. When they were about to eat, two children were missing. They looked close at the food and there were two little Suyuku. From within the jar the Ewęle called out, "Suyuku, here we are! " — " Come down, this time I will kill you, " said Suyuku. When she took out her knife they shot at Suyuku. They cut open her chest with their knife and took out her heart. She had a shell (*eyi*, abalone) for a heart[2]. They took everything out from inside of Suyuku and they brought back all the children, and Town chief was glad to get back his child. After this the children of Kuŋluokyut'e'e were safe from Suyuku, and Town chief was grateful to Ewęle for having killed that Suyuku[3].

22. KILLING THE QUILT.

Far away there at P'owitsei[4] there were living two Ewęle. They had a grandmother. They played ball (*huŋtamęhle*) all the time. They played all day and after they ate their supper they played inside of the *koye'*. Their grandmother told them to stop and go to bed. Sometimes Elder brother would hurt Younger brother and only then would they stop playing. Coyote old man was living at Avaiyu chikyai (water-snake, sticking out).[5] He had a grandmother, too. He would go out every day to find something to eat. Sometimes he would find something, sometimes nothing. In the evening he would go back to his grandmother. Thus he lived. Well, these Ewęle were playing ball and once their grandmother made a quilt (*poya*) of rabbit skins. She finished the quilt and told her grand-

1. A hole in the ground, plastered and lidded and hooded, placed at the corner of the house, outside.
2. See pp. 13, 86.
3. Cp. Voth 1: 86-88.
4. A spring to the north east of Tewa.
5. A hill of Tewa.

children to take it down below and bury it in the sand. " After it is buried awhile, then you can roll it down the hill and you can hit it with the stick as many times as you want. That way you can kill the quilt, "¹ said their grandmother. They took it down, they buried it in the sand, they kept it in there for a little while and then they took it out. Just then up came Coyote old man and he said to them, " *Yaki, yaki pee.* What are you doing? " asked Coyote old man. " Our grandmother died and we brought her down here to bury her. We buried her, but we took her out again, and are going to roll her down this slope. It is a fine thing to roll her down. " Then Elder brother took it on his back and took it up the hill and rolled it down and they began to hit it with their stick as if it were a rabbit running. " Are you sure that is your grandmother? " asked Coyote old man. " Sure, it is a fine thing to play with. " — " Well, I have a grandmother, too, " said Coyote old man. " I will get her and kill her and bring her over here and roll her down too. " So he ran to his grandmother's house. She was sitting outside in the sun. As soon as he got to her, he took a stick and hit her on the head and killed her. He wrapped her up in his quilt and carried her along. Soon there was coming Coyote old man with a load on his back. " Well, did you bring your grandmother ? " asked the Ewẹle. " Yes, " said Coyote old man. " All right, we will all go up on top and then we will roll together, "said Ewẹle. They carried their loads up together and hit them with their stick. They had a great time rolling down their quilts. " Well, we are going now, " said Ewẹle. Then they untied their quilt and there was nothing inside of it, and Coyote old man untied his quilt and there was his grandmother inside of it. " Well, you believed us too quickly, " said Ewẹle. " We just brought this quilt and there was nothing inside of it, " said Ewẹle to Coyote old man. Then they ran away and Coyote old man tried to catch them, but Coyote old man never caught those Ewẹle. One ran one way and the other ran the other. First he tried to catch one, and then the other, but he caught neither of them. This is the way Coyote old man lost his grandmother.

23. COYOTE PRETENDS TO BE MA'SEWA KACHINA. ²

Bear was living on the west side of First Mesa at the spring Ana'-pöba. He was using that water to cook with. He was living alone. Every day he went out hunting for his family. One day he went out to Nöfatökyaobe' (San Francisco mountain.) He killed a deer, and so

1. Formerly, when a quilt was finished, in the evening, boys and girls would bury it in the sand, and then roll it down, and hit it with a stick, thereby killing the rabbits in the quilt, so it would not be dangerous for them to use the quilt.
2. The narrator knew this was a Hopi story.

he was carrying the deer on his back. Not far from his home Coyote old man (*iswux'taka*) was coming. He was going home from his hunting, too. He had been looking for food all day, too, but he could find nothing. Then he met Bear. As soon as he met Bear, he said, " My friend, where are you going? " Bear stood there and looked at Coyote old man. "I am coming back from my hunt. " — " Where were you hunting ? " — " At San Francisco Mountain. " — " That is a fine deer that you have killed. Let us be friends. " — " All right. Go to my house tomorrow. " Coyote was living at Wökukuba, " Big spring, " on the north side of First Mesa. (In fact, it is a little bit of a spring.) So Coyote went home and got there in the evening. Bear went to his house and he skinned the deer. It was a fine fat deer. He cooked some of it, for his supper. Next morning just about sunrise Coyote said, " I guess I better go and see my friend. " He went and got there. He made a noise on the house top. " Come in, my friend, " said Bear, sitting by the fire. So Coyote sat down on the other side of the fire. They talked about their hunting. Bear told Coyote where he had killed the deer. In the afternoon Bear said, " My friend, it is time for us to have our dinner. " He went into the back room and got out a piece of meat. He cooked it and they ate. Coyote was very hungry, he ate very quickly. Bear watched him. The sweat came out on Coyote's face, he was very hungry. The meat was gone. Bear went and got another piece of meat, cooked it, and passed it to his friend. He ate it all, but still he had not enough. Bear got another piece and cooked it and gave it to Coyote. Then he had enough. " Thank you, my friend. I wish I had this kind of dinner all the time. " — " Well, if you go out to San Francisco Mountain and kill a deer, you will have this kind of meat all the time. I am thinking we must be doing something, " said Bear. " Do what ? " said Coyote. " What can we do? " — "Let's play something. " — " What kind of play ? " — " I will go out and dress myself. I will come in and if you don't scare, you will be a brave man. But if you scare, I will be the brave man. " — " All right. " Bear went out and went to the spring and got some red clay, he put it on a stone and poured water on it, and put it on his ears and on his hands. He said to himself, " Poor Coyote! I am sure I am going to scare him! He won't be a brave man. " He swung along like a mad bear to his house. Coyote heard. He peeped out, and there his friend was coming, scratching on the earth, and holding up his arms as if he were going to jump on Coyote. " I won't be scared, " said Coyote, but he peeped out as if he was scared. Pretty soon Bear comes up closer, opening his mouth and showing his teeth. Coyote pretended that he was afraid of him. Bear came to the door and stood up again, and jumped into the house to catch Coyote. Coyote was sitting by the fire. " Well, my friend, " said Coyote, " I was not scared, " he said, " I am a man. I am never scared, no matter what big thing comes at

me. " Then Bear said, " Do you do something and scare me. " —
" Well, I have nothing to scare you with, " he said. " I have paws
like you, but they are little paws. I have little teeth, little ears, nothing
to scare you with, " said Coyote. " Yes, but go and see if you can't
scare me. " Coyote laughed. " All right. I will see how I can scare
you. " He went out, thinking, and going to the mesa. First he went
to the shrine (*pahoki*). He got a big bunch of willows from the shrine. He
knew there was an empty house where there were hanging an old dance
belt and dance kilt. " I must see if they are still hanging there. " So
he went in, and they were still hanging there, and he got them down
and brought them to where he had left his prayer-sticks. Then he said
to himself, " There is one thing I wonder where I could get it —
an old rabbit quilt. " In a corral he had seen one. He went to the
corral and found it. " I want some bones, " he said. He picked up a
sheep head and some bones and tied them together. " I have enough, "
he said. Then he put the quilt on for his dress, and tied it with the
belt, then he put the dance kilt on his head and he stuck the prayer-
sticks into it. The bones he put over his belt, and some bones for his
beads around his neck. He saw his shadow. " Poor friend! " he said,
" I am sure I am going to scare him, " he said. " I am sure I am going
to drive him off, " he said. (The people used to say Bear was afraid of
Másewa kachina, that is why he made that.) [1] " Wa-a! Wa-a! " he
said again and again, jumping along. Then he started off to his friend's
house, keeping on saying " Wa-a! Wa-a! " His friend heard something. He laughed and said, " Poor friend! Coyote will not scare
me, " he said. Then he heard the voice plainly, and he peeked out
from his house. He saw it coming closer, he never thought it was his
friend. Bear kept watching, it was coming closer. Then he just jumped out of his house and ran, he was so frightened by that Másewa
kachina, he never thought it was Coyote. He ran and Másewa kachina
ran after him. He looked back and saw Másewa kachina. He kept on
going, kept on going till he got to Colorado River (Payö'). He turned around again, and his friend said, " My friend, I am your
friend, " he said. " Don't jump into the river, I am your
friend. " Then he pulled off the kilt, " I am your friend. " Bear was
still looking at him. He pulled off his belt. " I am your friend, don't
jump into the river. " But Bear would not believe it and jumped into
the river. Coyote took off everything. By that time Bear was on the
other side of the river. Coyote called, " I am your friend, there is
nothing to scare you. Come back! " he said. " Let's go back to your
house. " But Bear was still looking at him. " No, I guess I wont go

[1]. The mask of the Ma'sewa kachina is spotted different colors, with prayer-sticks
attached, the kilt is around the neck. The impersonator wears a rabbit quilt and a
necklace of bones.

back to you. I have crossed this river, I won't go back. You are a bad Coyote, you scared me and drove me from my house. You go back to my house. I am going to these mountains. Hopi people are afraid of me and are not friendly to me, so you go and live in my house, and I will go and live in these mountains, " said Bear. That's the reason there are no bear living close to Walpi.

24. THE BIRDS TAKE BACK THEIR FEATHERS.

Far away at Tamolutide[1] there lived the birds called *koli'*.[2] They grew *tamu*. They were happy to have it, so they said to one another, " We better have a dance for it, " they said. They sang :

isawö	isawö
coyote	coyote
selömuki	selömuki
homesick	homesick
selömuki	selömuki
homesick	homesick
akyamihemi	
drop down	
umi hemi	ach' !
up down	(their call)

Then they all flew up, circling way up in the air. Then they all sang again :

isawö	isawö
coyote	coyote
selömuki	selömuki
homesick	homesick
selömuki	selömuki
homesick	homesick
akyamihemi	
drop down	
umi hemi	ach' !
up down	

Then they all flew down back. All day they sang. Soon Coyote old

1. *ta*>*tamu*, a grasslike wheat, *kwahwi* in Hopi; *molutide*, hill.
2. A little brown bird with yellow neck and little black horns (crest ?)

man came up to one and said, " *Yaki yaki pee*, what are you doing? " —
" We are having a dance. We raised lots of *tamu* and we are so happy.
That is the reason we are having a dance. " — " Let me see you do it
again. " So they sang:

isawö	isawö
coyote	coyote
selömuki	selömuki
homesick	homesick
selömuki	selömuki
homesick	homesick
akyamihemi	
drop down	
umi hemi	ach'!
up down	

Coyote old man was watching them. They sang up in the air :

isawö	isawö
coyote	coyote
selömuki	selömuki
homesick	homesick
selömuki	selömuki
homesick	homesick
akyamihemi	
drop down	
umi hemi	ach'!
up down	

They flew down to the ground. " What a fine dance you have, "
said Coyote old man. "Could I join with you?" — " It would be a
fine thing for you to dance with us. We will give our feathers to you. "
So each one pulled a feather out and gave it to Coyote. So he had
enough feathers to fly with. So he flew up with the *koli'*, and they
sang:

isawö	isawö
coyote	coyote
selömuki	selömuki
homesick	homesick
selömuki	selömuki
homesick	homesick

akyamihemi
drop down

umi hemi   ach'!
up down

Then the *koli'* chief said, " Well, you know your feathers; we will go to him and take back our feathers. " They danced again.

isawö   isawö
coyote   coyote

selömuki   selömuki
homesick   homesick

selömuki   selömuki
homesick   homesick

akyamihemi
drop down

umi hemi   ach'!
up down

And then each one went and said, " This is my feather. " — " This is my wing feather. " — " This is my tail feather. " And each pulled his own feather out of Coyote's body. " Let us fly away, " said their chief, and they flew away in every direction. Then Coyote old man began to fall down. He fell down and down on the ground and broke into pieces and that is the way they killed Coyote old man.

25. INSIDE ELK: THROWING DOWN ELK'S BACKBONE.

Far away there on a river Coyote woman (*paiena kwiya*) was living. She had some children. Porcupine (*song*) lived down close to Coyote woman. One day Coyote woman said she was going to find something for them to eat. So as she went along the river she met Porcupine. He was doing something. Coyote woman said, " My friend, what are you doing? " — " I am taking my rest. What are you doing around here? " — " I am looking for something to eat, " said Coyote woman to Porcupine. " I am looking for my food, too. Let us go together." Porcupine could not run fast, but Coyote woman could run very fast. So Porcupine said to Coyote woman, " If we find a rabbit, you chase it, and when it goes into the hole, I will get it. " So pretty soon they found a rabbit sitting under a cottonwood tree, and Coyote chased the rabbit. Rabbit ran into a hole in a log. Coyote woman told Porcupine to go in after it. So Porcupine went right into the hole to get out the rabbit. Soon she struck out the rabbit. Soon Coyote said, " My friend,

you are too small to carry the rabbit. " — " Indeed, " said Porcupine, " I am too small to carry it. " — " I am strong enough to carry
the rabbit, " said Coyote woman. They went on and chased another
rabbit. It ran into a log. Coyote woman told Porcupine to go in and
get out the rabbit. Porcupine struck it out. "My friend, " said Coyote
woman, " you are all right in getting the rabbit out, but you are
too small to carry it. " So Coyote woman took it on her back. They
went on and found another rabbit. Coyote chased it into a hole in the
log. " My friend, go in and take out the rabbit. " Porcupine took out
the rabbit. Porcupine looked in again and saw another rabbit. Porcupine said, " There is another rabbit in the hole. You better go in and
take it out. " Then Coyote said to herself, " I better shut in Porcupine in this hole. " So Coyote found a stone and shut up the hole.
Then she found another stone and put it against the other.
" Poor Porcupine ! " said Coyote. She will never come out again. "I
better go home to my children. " Then she picked up the four rabbits
and she started off. She was very happy. In the evening she reached
home. Her little children were very glad to see her. " My little children, I have a load on my back, " she said. Then she took
the rabbits off her back, and she began to cook them. By that
time Porcupine had got the rabbit in the hole and started to come out,
and came to the stone closing up the hole. " Poor me, " said Porcupine, " There is no way to get out, I am sure to die. " She went far
back where she had taken out the rabbit, and there at the other end
there was a little light and a hole there. She came out. " My friend is
mean, " said Porcupine, " she thought she would kill me, but she
could not kill me. Wherever I meet her, I will kill her. " She went
to the home where she lived alone. She skinned the rabbit and she
cooked it and ate it.

Next morning she started out. She came to a river and she waited
to go across, but the water was so high that she could not cross. As
she sat by the edge of the river, an elk came by. " Could you
kindly take me across the river ? " said Porcupine to Elk. "I could
take you across the river, but you have too many points over
your body, they would hurt me, " said Elk. " Well, I could put them
inside of my body, " said Porcupine. Elk said to Porcupine, " I could
not take you on my back, but if you want me to take you across the
river, climb up on my horn. " — " No, I could not climb up on your
horn, for I might fall down in the river and drown. " — " Well, how
could I take you across the river ? " — " Take me inside your body, "
said Porcupine. " No, it might hurt me, " said Elk. " Just feel me. "
She was soft. " Well, go into my body. " She went inside of Elk from
behind. " Did I hurt you ? " said Porcupine. " No, " said Elk. Porcupine moved a little further. " Did I hurt you ? " — " No, " said Elk.
She moved a little further. " Did I hurt you ? " — " No. " She moved

a little further until she got right up to Elk's heart. "Did I hurt you?" — "No," said Elk. "Well, I had better go across the river." — "Wait until I ask you some questions," said Porcupine. "What is this jumping inside your body?" asked Porcupine. "That is my heart," said Elk. "What is that?" asked Porcupine. "That is what makes me live," said Elk. Then Porcupine said, "Did I hurt you when I touched your heart?" — "Just a little bit," said Elk. "Don't touch it hard, I might die," said Elk. "Let me touch it a little more," said Porcupine. "I might die," said Elk. Then Porcupine shook herself and touched the heart. Then Elk fell down dead. "Did I hurt you?" asked Porcupine. Elk never answered. "Did I hurt you?" asked Porcupine. Elk never answered. Then she came out of Elk. There Elk was lying dead. "What shall I do?" said Porcupine, "I guess I better go to the river to get an arrow point to skin Elk." She went. She got an arrow point and skinned Elk. Just before she finished skinning, there was Coyote coming. "My friend," said Coyote, did you kill this elk yourself?" — "No," said Porcupine, "I did not kill it myself, I guess it just died here." — "Let's skin it." said Coyote. "I have almost finished skinning it." She was very angry with Coyote. Well, they finished skinning it. "My friend," said Coyote, "you take this piece of meat and go to the river and wash it, there is too much blood on it," said Coyote. So Porcupine took the meat and went to the river and washed the meat. She was very hungry. She had not eaten anything, so she began to eat the meat. Then she came back. "What did you do with that meat?" — "The river was too strong, it carried it away from me," said Porcupine. There was another piece of meat, "Take that piece and wash it, too much blood on it," said Coyote. Porcupine took it and washed it and ate it. Then she came back. "What did you do with the meat?" asked Coyote. "I dropped it down in the river," said Porcupine. "That river is not so strong, I guess you have eaten it up. Let me see your teeth." So Coyote made Porcupine open her mouth and there was a piece of meat in her teeth. "You are bad," said Coyote. "You ate up those two pieces of meat." So she took a stick and knocked Porcupine on the head and killed her. "Well, I guess I better go back to my children," said Coyote. She ran as fast as she could. She had not eaten anything yet. She said to herself, "I better not eat until I get my children and we eat all together." As soon as Coyote left, Porcupine opened her eyes and saw Coyote run off. There was a big cottonwood by the elk. "I guess I better take up this meat to the top of this tree," said Porcupine. So she took up the meat piece by piece, she took it all up, even the skin. Coyote reached her children. She was in a hurry. They were surprised she was in such a hurry. The sweat was running from her body. The little coyotes asked their mother, "What has happened that the sweat is running off you?" — I killed a big elk by the river, " said Coyote and I came after you so we could all eat the meat together. " So they started. As they went some lizards ran by them and they began to chase the lizards, but Coyote said not to chase the lizards, there was plenty of meat there by the river. So they went on. Coyote was carrying her quilt on her back, because they were going to stay several days until they ate up the meat. "Here is the place, " said Coyote, " you children stay here under this tree. " So she left the quilt there. She went to the place where she left the meat, and there was no meat there. " Porcupine must have come to life, " said Coyote. " She can't run very fast, I will follow her track. " Her track ran back and forth, so it was broad, and she followed it to the cottonwood tree. She looked up and there was Porcupine up in the tree eating the meat. " My friend, how did you get up there ? " said Coyote. " I came up easily, " said Porcupine. " Come up and we will eat together, " said Porcupine to Coyote. " I am not alone, " said Coyote, " my children are away over yonder, " said Coyote to Porcupine. " Well, you go and get your children and come up here and we will eat up here, " said Porcupine to Coyote. So Coyote went and got her children and her quilt, and Porcupine told them to come up. But it was hard for them to go up. " We never climbed a tree, " said Coyote. " Well, you stay down there all in a line, " said Porcupine. " You lie down and cover yourselves up with that quilt, " said Porcupine, " and don't look up, and I will throw a piece of meat down. " So they covered themselves with the quilt, and the last one, the smallest coyote, was not covered with the quilt and she was looking up with one eye. " Are you ready ? " asked Porcupine. "Yes, " said Coyote. " All right, " said Porcupine, " I will throw down the meat. " Then she took the backbone, it was long, and she threw it down on Coyote and her family. But the last little coyote saw the backbone falling down, and she jumped out and was safe. Well, Porcupine went down from that tree and she said to that little coyote, " Let us go back up on the tree and eat up there. Your mother and brothers and sisters are all dead. I will carry you up. " So Little Coyote climbed up on the back of Porcupine, and they went up to the very top of the tree where the meat was. And they began to eat the meat, and they ate and ate. And Porcupine said, " I think I had better kill Little Coyote and then no coyote will be left. " She asked Little Coyote, "Have you had enough ? " — " Yes, I have had enough. I am full, " said Little Coyote. " Well, I think you had better move a little back. " She moved back. " Now, back! " said Porcupine. She kept on moving back until she came to a little branch and the branch broke and Little Coyote fell down and was killed. And Porcupine was glad that she had killed all those coyotes. Hereafter Porcupine lived alone by the river and there were no more of her friends, the coyotes.

That is all I know.

(*Variant.*)[1]

Coyote old woman lived at Homolabi (near Winslow). She had seven children. They were living on the east side of Homolabi. Her little babies would play around outside while their mother went out to look for food for them. One day Coyote old woman was going on her way to the northwest (*mönyauĕ'*). Porcupine (*möuyauo'*) was living way north of Homolabi. One morning he was on the bank of the river looking for food. A big deer came to him and asked him, " What are you doing, my friend ? " — " Well, I am just watching this river. I want to cross it, but my legs are short, I can't cross. That is what I am thinking about, " said Porcupine. Then Deer asked Porcupine, " Where are you living? " — " Yes, my friend, I live on the south side of that big mountain. " — " And how did you cross this river? " — " Yes, I crossed about four months ago. A friend came here. He looked just like you. Maybe you are he. " — " No, I was not here. " — " Well, my friend, I think you are the one, he looked like you. " — " No, I am not the one. Well, how, did he carry you? " — " I went inside of his body. " — " How did you get in? " — " I went in by the anus. " — " You have hard feathers. " — " Well, I changed myself and became a soft man, " he said. " Let me see you do it, " said Deer. Then Porcupine made his quills go inside of his body and he was a small fellow. " Let me try and get in. " — " All right. " So Deer lay down. And he went inside of Deer, to the stomach. " Did I hurt you ? " — " No, no, you did not hurt me. " — " All right, let's go across. " Then Deer went into the river. When he crossed the river Porcupine went out. " My friend, " said Porcupine, " I forgot my quilt. I left it on the other side of the river. Will you go and get it for me ? " — " No, I can't get it. Go and get it yourself. " — " How could I get it? Will you take me across? " — " All right. " Then he went inside Deer. As they were crossing, Porcupine said, " What is this thing in here? " — " That is my stomach, " said the Deer, " where my food goes. " — " And up here, what is this jumping, moving too much. " — " That is my heart, when it is jumping like that it keeps me alive. " — " All right, " said Porcupine. Then he put out his quills and shot them into the heart and killed Deer. The heart stopped. " What is this? " he asked again. Deer did not answer. Porcupine went out and there the big deer was lying. " What can I skin him with ? I have no knife. I guess I will go over to Homolabi and look for an arrow point (*yuisi-*

---

1. Recorded four years after the time of recording the preceding tale, from the same informant.

ba), " said Porcupine. So he went to look for an arrow point. While he was gone, Coyote old woman came to where the deer was lying. She was very surprised. " It is fine that I find a dead deer. I must go and get my children " Just then up came Porcupine. Coyote said, " What a fine thing that I found this deer? " — " That's mine. I killed it this morning. Let's skin it, " said Porcupine. " I have two knives, " said Coyote. They began to skin it, and take out the insides. " I will go and wash these parts, " said Porcupine. He did not want to eat with Coyote. He was stingy and did not want to give Coyote anything. So he took the meat to the river, but instead of washing it, he ate it. When Porcupine came back, Coyote asked him, " What did you do with the piece of meat you took? " — " The river took it away from me, " he said. Coyote said to herself, " I must kill this Porcupine, so I can have all this meat to myself. " So she picked up a big stick and killed Porcupine. Then she ran to her home and her baby coyotes were playing outside. She said, " I have killed a deer, but it is too heavy to bring home, we will all go and eat it where it is. " So she took all her babies along. Then they got to the place where the meat was. But after Coyote ran off Porcupine came alive again, and cut all the meat and took it all up on top of a cottonwood tree and began to eat up there. About that time Coyote came with all her children. She saw no meat, she was very mad. She looked around and saw the track of Porcupine and followed it to where Porcupine was up on top of the tree with all the meat. " My friend, " she said. " How did you get all the meat up there. " — " I just carried it up on my back. " — " Well, throw a piece down for our dinner. " — " No, I can't throw it down. Come up here. " But they could not climb the tree. They were just looking up at him. " Lie down all in a line so I can throw a piece down on you and it wont get dirty, " said Porcupine. " Cover yourselves up with the quilt. " So Coyote old woman lay down and all the children lay down in a line and they covered themselves with the rabbit skin quilt. The last baby coyote could hardly cover herself, so she was watching with one eye, looking at Porcupine. Then he took the deer's backbone and threw it down. As soon as he started to throw, that baby coyote jumped out and was saved. All the others were killed. Porcupine said, " My grandson, I will bring you up here and you can eat all you want. " He carried him up on his back and gave meat. Pretty soon he was full, could hardly breathe. " Lie down on that branch, " said Porcupine. Then he shook the branch, and shook off the baby coyote and killed him. That is the way he killed the coyotes. After he ate all the meat he had up there, he went away.

26. COYOTE WOMAN CAN NOT REVIVE HER CHILDREN.

Far away there at Ochehlenangye [1] there lived a bird named Sąlioṇ. [2]
She had some little ones. They were just hatched out, so they were
very small. Sąlioṇ was very kind to her children. In the morning
she said to her children, "My children, I am going to look ·for food
for you. You must stay here and not go down, so no harm will
come to you." Coyote woman was living at K'elanpo·gye (Badger
spring). She had children there. Every morning she would tell her
children not to go outdoors and play, but stay inside so nothing
would hurt them. Then she would go hunting for them. Sometimes
she got nothing for them, sometimes she killed something for them
to eat. In this way Coyote woman looked after her children. Sąlioṇ
was hunting for her children and when she came back their wings
were coming out. So Sąlioṇ thought they had better learn to fly.
She said to them, "My children, you had better fly a little way."
She would take one by the wing and say, "*Pipi sa'löki*,"[3] and let him
fly. One morning Coyote woman was coming along and Sąlioṇ said
to her children, "My children, there is Coyote woman coming
along." Sąlioṇ would put some bones in a basket and throw them
out and say, "*Pipi sa'löki*," and the birds would fly out. Coyote
woman was watching her and she said, "My friend, what are you
doing?" — "I have been killing my children and then I throw out
their bones and they come alive again." — "How do you do it?" —
"I get a stick and kill all my children and eat them up. Then I gather up their bones in a basket and throw them out and say, '*pipi
sa'löki*,' and they come to life again." — "Well, I must go and get
my children and kill them and eat them and throw out their bones
and see if they come to life again." So she went off. Soon she reached
her house and then she said to her children, "My children," said
Coyote woman, "I have come after you." — "Why?" asked her
children. "I went to my friend's and there I saw something good for
you all to eat." So they went with her. They went to Sąlioṇ's
house, and then they began to play with Sąlioṇ's children. Then
said Sąlioṇ, "My children, come to me," and she took a stick and
hit them and then she cooked them; but it was a rabbit she cooked
and ate. But Coyote woman did not know this. Then Coyote
woman went out, and called her children and took a stick and killed
them and cooked them. Then they ate together, and Sąlioṇ gathered up the bones and threw them out and said, "*Pipi sa'löki*."

1. On the north side of First Mesa.
2. Little brown bird, living in the rocks.
3. Meaningless words.

They all flew up to their mother. "My children, there is Coyote woman, she has killed her children and cooked them and eaten them ; but they will not come to life, so we had better fly away." Then Coyote woman gathered up the bones and threw them out of the basket and called out "*pipi sa'lōki,*" but they did not come to life. Three times she called out "*pipi sa'lōki!*" The fourth time all the birds flew away. Sąlioṇ said to her, "You are always credulous, you thought I had killed my children, but I did not kill them. Then you killed your children and they will never come back to life." Coyote woman began to chase them, but they all flew away, and Coyote woman cried about her children ; but they never came back to life.

(*Variant.*)[1]

Once upon a time there was a bird called Tëëtciwa living at the north side of Walpi. She lived in a hole in the cliff. She had some young birds. She went out for food for her children every morning. She went out and looked for food, and sometimes she came back in the afternoon with a worm in her bill. The children were glad and ran to meet their mother to get their food. That is the way she fed her children. One day when she came back from her work looking for food, a coyote came along. Coyote saw the bird, and Coyote stopped right there at the foot of the cliff where she lived. Coyote looked up and said, "Friend, what are you doing up there ?" — "We are living up here," said the bird. "How can I come up and have a visit with you," said Coyote. "Up the ladder," said the bird, "I have a ladder up here." — "All right," said Coyote. She hung down the ladder. And Coyote climbed up the ladder. She got up there. There was a room up there. She was very glad she had found her friend. "I am glad I have found you," she said. (It was a woman coyote.)

In the afternoon they were talking about the way they looked for food for their children. "Well, let us have dinner," said the bird. Then she went into the room and brought out some kind of meat. Then she said, "Let us eat." The little children had gone into the back room. The mother bird and Coyote ate by themselves. While they were eating, the bird told Coyote, "Do not break the bones," said the bird mother. "Please do not break the bones," she said. Coyote did not break the bones. She just ate the flesh off. After they had finished, the bird picked up all the bones they had eaten the meat from and put them in a basket and threw it out

---

1. Recorded by Ruth Bunzel, four years after the preceding tale was recorded, from the same informant.

of the door and said, "Come back, my children," said the bird
mother, and threw out the bones. Then her children came flying out
of the basket. Coyote was very surprised that the bones came to life
again. The mother said, "The meat that we ate was my children's
flesh. I just kill my children when I want to eat. I just kill my
children and cook the meat and eat, and as soon as I eat the meat I
throw out the bones and they come back to life again. That is the
way I eat my meals," she said. Then the Coyote woman said, "My
friend," she said, "tomorrow afternoon you come to my house. I
live north from here at Hiya'o. I will wait for you before noon. Be
sure and come," said Coyote. Next morning the birds got up and the
mother of the birds said, "We shall all go, my children." So before
noon they went. They came to Coyote's house. Coyote had children,
too. There were about a dozen of them. The children went outside
the door and played together. They were good friends, so all the
children played together outdoors and the mothers sat inside and
talked about hunting and the other kinds of things women talk about.
In the afternoon the mother coyote called for her children to come
in. The coyote children came in and went inside into the back room.
She got a stick and went in there and killed all her little children and
cooked their meat. When dinner was ready she said, "Let us have
our dinner," and they sat down at their places. The mother bird and
her children all sat down and they had their dinner with Coyote.
While they were eating the coyote mother said, "Please do not
break the bones, but just eat the meat off the bones," she said. Then
she said again, "Please do not break the bones, but just eat the meat."
The mother of the birds just broke the bones without knowing
that she was breaking the bones. After they had finished their dinner,
then the mother coyote picked up the bones and put them in a
basket the same way as the mother of the birds had done the day
before. She put them into the basket and went to the door. The
birds just flew out, the mother bird and the children. The mother
coyote said, "Come back, my children," and threw out the basket,
but they never came back alive. The birds all flew away. She picked
up the bones and threw them again and said, "Come back, my
children," but they never came back alive. Then she went chasing
the birds but she never caught them. They went back to their hole.
Not all the bird children went into the same hole they had been
living in. One went with her mother, but the rest flew into other
holes in the rocks. That is why all the birds do not live in the same
hole, but as soon as they are big enough to fly they go to their own
holes.

27. FATAL IMITATION.

Hawk (*kwa·yo'*) was living on the other side of the Gap. Every morning he sat up on his house top, he had a hole for his house. He sat on top of it watching for his food, and sometimes in the evening he sat there. Coyote man was living at Östekabi (at Five Houses) and every day he would go out to look for his food. One day he went towards the Gap and early in the morning he saw Hawk sitting on the mesa. He went up close, standing at the foot of the cliff. "My friend, what are you doing up there?" — "I am just looking around." — "Is that a fine place up there?" — "Yes." — "Can I go up there?" — "Yes, come up! We will sit together." Coyote went up and was looking at Hawk. He saw he had only one leg. "What a fine place up here!" — "Yes, I got a fine place." — "I live way down and can hardly see anything. Well, friend," said Coyote, "what makes you have only one leg? Who cut off your other leg?" — "Well, I was born like this, with only one leg," said Hawk. "But you look so nice," said Coyote. "How can I have one leg like you, and we can sit together looking alike?" — "Well, you get a knife and cut off your other legs and you will have only one leg and we can sit together and look alike." — "I haven't any knife," said Coyote. "Well, I will get you one," said Hawk, and he flew down in his hole and brought up a knife. "Now you just cut off your legs," said Hawk. Then Coyote asked him again, "Why have you only one leg?" — "Well, I just grew like this. A fellow with two legs never catches anything, any rabbit or deer, I have only one leg and that is why I kill rabbits and jack-rabbits and deer. Two legs bother a man. That is too much," he said. "That is why, you, my friend, are always hungry, you have four legs, that's too much. They bother you, you can't catch rabbits. If you had only one leg, you could catch rabbits quickly and never starve," he said. "All right, my friend, you just chop off one leg and one arm, and then I will be like you." — "I can not chop, you chop!" So Coyote held out his leg. "Ai!" he said. "Ai!" he said again. "I think it will hurt me!" — "No, it wont hurt you. I have only one leg, it does not hurt." Then he held out his leg again. "Ai!" he said, "It will hurt me." — "Don't look at it. Shut your eyes and chop it off. It wont hurt you," said his friend. At last he shut his eyes and just chopped off his leg. "Now your other hand before you open your eyes," he said. As soon as he chopped it, his friend showed that he had two legs. "Poor Coyote! you will never live again. You always believe everything. How could I go with only one leg?" Poor Coyote, he could not stand up and he died right there. Coyote always believes anything. [1]

---

1. "You are Coyote man, you believe so quickly," they may say to a credulous fellow.

28. FORGETTING THE SONG.

Far away at Sopoik'omulo [1], there at the wash, Kọmpuyon (like a
fly, but bigger) was living alone. He had no grandmother or mother
or father. In the daytime he would look about for something to eat.
One morning there was a bad windstorm and he said to himself. "It
is a very bad day to look for food and I must stay at home all day."
He had breakfast, and he thought he would do something to enjoy
himself. "I think it would be a good time to have a dance." So he
dressed himself up. He put on his buckskin shirt and his buckskin
leggings and on his back he put his quiver. He held his bow in his
left hand. He went to a place in the wash, where there was a terrace
(*kowaki*), a place where there was no wind. He said to himself, "I
think this is the best place." He started to sing,

Amanitee' amanitee'
pa·teki [2] *su·diki* [3] *me e*
aa mite mite heo heo

He danced with this song. He sang again.

Amanitee' amanitee'
pa·teki su·diki me e
aa mite mite heo heo

He danced twice. There was a coyote around there, looking for
food, hunting rabbits. She was going along on the south side of
the wash. As she went she heard something saying or singing something. She stopped and cocked her ear in one direction. Certainly it
was a song. She held her ear to every direction. The song sounded
close by, so she said to herself, "I must look for somebody nearby
singing." She heard it again.

Amanitee' amanitee'
pa·teki su·diki me e
Aa mite mite heo heo

"Surely some dancing is going on," she said. "I must look for
him." She turned her ear. She heard the sound to the north. She

1. *Sopoi*, beard, *k'omulo*, curve (in wash). Wash east of First Mesa. Somebody
with a beard had a field there.
2. An old word for the first dance.
3. *su·de*, quiver. Quiver dance.

walked north to the edge of the wash. She turned her ear to every direction. She heard again,

> *Amanitee' amanitee'*
> *pa·teki su·diki me e*
> *Aa mite mite heo heo*

"Well, it must be right under me," said Coyote woman. She looked down and there was a terrace where somebody was doing something. She looked for a long time. The song began again.

> *Amanitee' amanitee'*
> *pa·teki su·diki me e*
> *Aa mite mite mite heo heo*

From up in the top of the wash where Coyote old woman was she said to him, "*Yaki yaki yaki pee',*" said Coyote woman to him. "What are you doing?" — "I was happy this morning, so I thought I'd have a dance here. The wind was blowing too hard, so I could not go hunting." — "Sing it again," said Coyote woman. "Why do you want me to sing again?" — "You are singing a very pretty song. I like to hear it." So he sang again,

> *Amanitee' amanitee'*
> *pa·teki su·diki me e*
> *Aa mite mite heo heo*

"What a pretty song!" said Coyote woman, "I would like to learn it. I have some children, I would like to sing it to them." — "You can't learn it if you stand up there." — "You want me to come down, but how can I come?" — "Well, jump down right here," said Kompuyon. So she tried to jump, but could not jump. "Jump right down," said Kompuyon. "If I jump, I might fall this side of the wash," said Coyote woman. "Well, if you fall, I will catch you." So she jumped down and Kompuyon caught her. "Now, sing again. I will listen close to you, so I can get the song and sing it to my children," said Coyote. "Well, listen closely," said Kompuyon. "I will sing it again. He sang,

> *Amanitee' amanitee'*
> *pa·teki su·diki me e*
> *Aa mite mite heo heo*

"Sing it again," said Coyote old woman. "It is a very pretty song." So he sang again,

> *Amanitee' amanitee'*
> *pa·teki su·diki me e*
> *Aa mite mite heo heo*

"Did you learn it?" said Kǫmpuyon to Coyote woman. "Yes, I think I have learned it," said Coyote woman. "I must go back to my children to sing it to them." — "Well, I will give you my wings so you can fly down and not get hurt." So Kǫmpuyon pulled out his right wing and stuck it in Coyote woman's arm, and then pulled out his other wing and stuck it in Coyote's other arm. "Now, you have wings," said Kǫmpuyon. "As soon as you fly down, run to your children and when you get to them sing to them." So Coyote woman flew down and ran a little way from the wash, she stumbled on a stick, and right there she forgot the song. She could say only *amanitee amanitee,* so she said to herself, "I must go back and ask him to sing again." So she ran back to Kǫmpuyon to the edge of the wash. "*Pee',* sing it again. I fell down and lost my song." So he sang again. As soon as Kǫmpuyon stopped singing, Coyote woman turned and ran, she ran as fast as she could go. Just before she reached her house, she put her foot in a prairie dog hole, and she forgot her song. She shook herself and said, "*amanitee amanitee!*" again and again. "I must go back and ask my friend to sing it to me," said Coyote woman. She ran back to the wash and Kǫmpuyon was just starting to sing again,

Amanitee' amanitee'
pa·teki su·diki me e
Aa mite mite heo heo

Coyote woman turned and ran; just as she was about to reach her house she fell down again. She got up and shook herself and she said a... a... That was all she could remember. "I guess I better run back to my friend. He is so kind, he will sing again." She ran back. Kǫmpuyon was still dancing, "My friend, again I fell down and lost my song. Sing it again so I can take it to my children." Kǫmpuyon sang again,

Amanitee' amanitee'
pa·teki su·diki me e
aa mite mite heo heo

Coyote woman turned and hurried back home. Inside of her house she fell down again and she got up and said *amani, amani.* She got up and said to her children, "I heard a pretty song and I want to learn it, so when you cry I will have something to sing to you." She went back. Her friend was still singing. "Well, sing it again. I fell down inside my house." — "Well, I can't sing it to you again, my throat is so tired, but come down close and I will sing it to you many times." So Coyote woman jumped right down, and Kǫmpuyon caught Coyote woman, so she did not fall down over the wash. "Listen very closely this time, so you wont forget it."

> *Amanitee' amanitee'*
> *pa˙teki su˙diki me e*
> *Aa mite mite heo heo*

"Listen very closely now. I will sing it again," said Kọmpuyon to herself, "and then I will fly away." She sang,

> *Amanitee' amanitee'*
> *pa˙teki su˙diki me e*
> *Aa mete mite heo heo*

Then she flew away. Coyote jumped at Kọmpuyon, she jumped and she fell into the wash and broke her neck and never went back to her children. Thus far I know.

29. RABBIT'S SONG.

Far away there at K'ocheyiti[1] there lived a rabbit with some little ones. Every morning when they got up, she told the children they were to stay indoors, not to open the door while she went for food for them. She took her basket (*yame'le*) on her back, she went south to T'ayeholuge where there was a lot of cactus fruit. When she got to T'ayeholuge she gathered the cactus fruit and put it in her basket and came back home. She sang,

> nạwe' nawee kwe' kwe'[2]
> here   here
> nạwe' nawee kwe' kwe'
> here   here
> sabatutu'[3] pinelehkyu'
> glutton
> ehyan pingsanp'e ko[4]
> children cactus fruit eat

As soon as she sang *sanp'e ko* she reached her door and threw the cactus fruit in, and the little rabbits ran to it and began to eat. They were happy when their mother came. At night she told them, "Well, my children, your eyes are open now, but you must not go

1. *K'o*, rock, *ch'eye*, yellow, *ti*, there, locative. The yellow rocks just below Tewa to the southeast.
2. Archaic. " Perhaps means coming. "
3. Archaic. Current term for glutton is *kwemele.*
4. Archaic. Current term for eat is *wiya.*

out, for the little boys from Peṇmochae'de [1] might see you and catch you and kill you." She would tell them this every night and early every morning. She would go out. She went down to T'aye-holuge and there picked cactus fruit and then went back home with a big load and sang,

nąwe' nawee kwe' kwe'
here   here
nąwe' nawee kwe' kwe'
here   here
sabatutu' pinelehkyu'
glutton
ehyan pingsanp'e ko
children cactus fruit eat

She always sang this song on her return. Soon her children were big enough to run out. Early in the morning she left, then the little rabbits said, "Well, let us run out. If enemies come, we can run back." Soon some big boys were hunting about there and saw the little rabbits. One boy said to the others, "There are some rabbits down here." They ran up to him, and he told the boys on which side to go, one on every side. So they scattered and drew in on the little rabbits. The little rabbits began to run, but they could not run very fast and they all were caught. In the evening the rabbit mother came home and began to sing,

nąwe' nawee kwe' kwe'
here   here

nąwe' nawee kwe' kwe'
here   here

sabatutu' pinelehkyu'
glutton

ehyan pingsanp'e ko
children cactus fruit eat

She threw the cactus fruit in, but nobody ran to it. "I wonder where they are gone," she said to herself. She went in and found no rabbits. She looked for tracks and saw the boys tracks. Then she cried and cried for her children. She said to herself, "I must go away from here and live out in the plain. If I live in here, I will never have any children." So she started out into the plain. So whenever she was going to have children, she would make a hole under grass or bush, and she would always cover it with sand.

1. A little ruin east of K'ocheyiti.

30. COYOTE'S FALSE TAIL.

Far away there at Pohe'ligye [1] there Avaiyun (Horned water serpent) was living. Once in a while he would visit his friend at Kosanwep'oa (a spring at Keam's canyon). He would go in the morning and return in the evening and his friend there also would visit Avaiyun. Once on his way Avaiyun met Coyote old man. He said to him, " *Yaki yaki pee.*" — "Where are you going?" Coyote said to Avaiyun. "I am going to visit my friend." — "Where is your friend?" — "He is living at Kosanwep'oa." — "Do you think I may visit you in your house?" — "Tomorrow is the best time to visit me." Coyote old man went back home to Paiena'ping (Coyote Mt.),[2] and was keeping his friend in mind. Next morning he started for Pohe'ligye. Avaiyun was outside of his house. "Well, my friend, did you come?" — "Yes." — "Well, come in." Then he opened the door of the spring and he went in first. His friend, Coyote old man, walked behind him. He had a buffalo skin for a seat and he put it out for his friend. Avaiyun asked Coyote old man, "How are you getting along? What work do you do?" — "I go hunting every day. I kill lots of rabbits each day. In summer I raise corn and watermelons, muskmelons, squash". — "Well, we do the same kind of work," said Avaiyun. "I, too, raise corn and melons. We do the same," said Avaiyun. It was about dinner-time, so Avaiyun went into the other room and brought out watermelons and muskmelons. They ate together and then they smoked together. Avaiyun blew out four times and handed it to Coyote. Coyote blew out four times and handed it to him and said, "My friend (*nabi k'eme*)." Coyote kept on smoking until the pipe was out. He handed it back. He smoked so much it had made him sick. "Time to go home," said Coyote. He went out, shaking all over. (He had never smoked before). That night he slept. The next morning, he said, "I think I better go visit my friend." He went to Pohe'ligye. "My friend, did you come?" — "Yes." — "Come in." They talked together of what they were doing. Avaiyun brought out watermelons and muskmelons. They ate together. Avaiyun put tobacco in the pipe, he blew out four times, he handed the pipe to Coyote. Coyote said, "My friend," to him. He smoked it all out, he handed it back. He was used to it now, it was not so hard on him this time. In the evening, "I had better go home," he said. "Come back tomorrow." — "All right." He returned the next day. Avaiyun brought out melons. They ate, they smoked. Avaiyun smoked four times, he handed the pipe to Coyote. Coyote said, "My friend."

---

1. Hopi, *ispa*, Coyote spring, a little below Tewa.
2. Southeast of Walpi.

He smoked out the pipe, he handed it back. It was time to go home.
" Well, my friend, you visit me tomorrow, " said Coyote. " All
right, I will. " When Coyote reached home, he thought what he
would give his friend next day. "I guess I will go over to P'oëtschei
(Hopi, Sikyiatki). Some time ago I saw lots of watermelons there in
a house." When he came to P'oëtschei he looked in the house and
the watermelons were still there. He went in and picked up the
largest watermelon and carried it back to his house. Next morning
Avaiyun got up and went to his friend's house. Coyote was sitting
outside his house. "Well, my friend, have you come ?" — "Yes."
— "Well, come in." Coyote went in, and Avaiyun started after him,
but he was too big to get in. "I can't go in there, there is not enough
room. I can talk to you from outside." So Coyote was inside and
talked to Avaiyun outside. In the afternoon Coyote went and got
watermelons and gave to Avaiyun. He had no tobacco. "I have no
tobacco, I never smoke," he said. "All right, we don't need to smoke.
Come to my house tomorrow," said Avaiyun. "All right," said
Coyote. Then he began to think how he could make himself into a
large man, so he could not go into the house of Avaiyun. So he
went to a cedar tree and stripped off the bark and brought back long
pieces of bark and then put the pieces together and out of it made a
great long tail. He worked at it all night, he had no sleep that night.
Next morning he tied it very tight to his tail and walked into his
room and coiled it around and it filled up his house. "Well, when
I get to Avaiyun, I will not be able to get into his house." So he
went along to his friend's house, laughing as he went. When he got
there, Avaiyun was sitting outside. "Well, did you come?" — "Yes."
— "Well, come in." Avaiyun saw that his friend had a big long
tail. He laughed at him. "You have a long tail." — "Yes," said
Coyote. So Avaiyun went in, and Coyote followed him and coiled
around his long tail, but it did not fill up Avaiyun's big room. They
talked, then Avaiyun went in and brought out watermelons and
muskmelons. He brought out his pipe. He smoked it four times and
handed it to Coyote. When Coyote was through he said, "I think
it is time for me to go back home." Said Coyote, "Tomorrow you
come to my house and visit me." "All right," said Avaiyun. As
Coyote was going out, Avaiyun made a fire on the end of Coyote's
tail, and Avaiyun looked and saw fire following Coyote. Coyote
looked back and saw the fire behind him. He looked back again, he
saw fire following him. Then he began to run, the fire was near to him.
He ran, ran, he looked back, he saw that his tail was on fire, he
ran, ran, to the west. The fire overtook him and began to burn his
fur. Soon his fur was all burned up and Coyote lay there in the
grass and there he died. This is the way Coyote was killed.

LIST OF REFERENCES

Boas. Franz Boas. Keresan Texts. Publications, American Ethnological Society, vol. VIII, 1927.

Cushing. 1. Frank Hamilton Cushing. Zuñi Folk-Tales. 1901.
2. Origin Myth from Oraibi. Journal American Folk-Lore, 36 : 163-170. 1923.

De Huff. Elizabeth Willis De Huff. Taytay's Tales. N. Y. 1922.

Dorsey. George A. Dorsey. The Cheyenne. Field Columbian Museum, Pub. 99, Anthrop. Series, vol. IX, no. 1. 1905.

Dumarest. Noël Dumarest. Notes on Cochiti, New Mexico. Memoirs, American Anthropological Assn., vol. VI, no. 3. 1919.

Fewkes. 1. J. W. Fewkes. The New Fire Ceremony at Walpi. American Anthropologist, N. S. 2 : 80-138. 1900.
2. Hopi Katcinas. XXI (1899-1900) Annual Report Bureau American Ethnology.
3. Tusayan Migration Traditions. XIX (1897-8) Annual Report Bureau American Ethnology.

Fewkes and Stephen. J. W. Fewkes and A. N. Stephen. The Nā-ác-nai-ya : A Tusayan Ceremony. Journal American Folk-Lore, 5 : 189-221. 1892.

Freire-Marreco. Barbara Freire-Marreco. Tewa Kinship Terms from the Pueblo of Hano, Arizona. American Anthropologist, N. S. 16 : 269-287. 1914.

Goddard. P. E. Goddard. San Carlos Apache Texts. Anthropological Papers, American Museum Natural History, vol. XXIV, Pt. I, 1918.

Handy. E. S. Handy. Zuñi Tales. Journal American Folk-Lore, 31 : 451-471. 1918.

Harrington. John Peabody Harrington. The Ethnogeography of the Tewa Indians. XXIX (1916) Annual Report Bureau American Ethnology.

Henderson and Harrington. J. Henderson and J. P. Harrington. Ethnozoology of the Tewa Indians. Bulletin 56, Bureau of American Ethnology. 1914.

Mason. J. Alden Mason. Myths of the Uintah Utes. Journal American Folk-Lore, 23 : 299-363. 1910.

Matthews. Washington Matthews. Navaho Legends. Memoirs, American Folk-Lore Society, V, 1897.

Parsons.   1. E. C. Parsons. Die Flucht auf den Baum. Zeitschrift für Ethnologie, 1922, pp. 1-29.

2. Taos (in ms.).

3. Pueblo Indian Folk-Tales, Probably of Spanish Provenience. Journal American Folk-Lore, 31 : 216-255. 1918.

4. Folk-Lore from the Cape Verde Islands. Memoirs, American Folk-Lore Society, XV. 1923.

5. Nativity Myth at Laguna and Zuñi. Journal American Folk-Lore, 31 : 256-263. 1918.

6. A Pueblo Indian Journal. Memoirs, American Anthropological Association, 32, 1925.

7. The Origin Myth of Zuñi. Journal American Folk-Lore, 36 : 135-162. 1923.

8. Notes on Zuñi, Memoirs American Anthropological Association, IV. Pts. 3, 4. 1917.

9. Zuñi Folk-Tales (in ms.).

10. Notes on Ceremonialism at Laguna. Anthropological Papers, American Museum Natural History, XIX, Pt. IV. 1920.

11. The Hopi Buffalo Dance. Man, XXIII, 21-26. 1923.

12. Laguna Genealogies. Anthropological Papers, American Museum Natural History, XIX, Pt. V. 1923.

13. Winter and Summer Dance Series in Zuñi in 1918. University of California Publications in American Archaeology and Ethnology, vol. 17, no. 3. 1922.

14. A Zuñi Detective. Man, XVI, 168-170. 1916.

Parsons   E. C. Parsons and Franz Boas. Spanish Tales from Laguna
and Boas.   and Zuñi, N. Mex. Journal American Folk-Lore, 33 : 47-72. 1920.

Robbins,   W. W. Robbins, J. P. Harrington, B. Freire-Marreco.
Harrington, Ethnobotany of the Tewa Indians. Bulletin 55, Bureau
Freire-Marreco. American Ethnology. 1916.

Russell.   Frank Russel. The Pima Indians. XXVI (1905) Annual Report Bureau American Ethnology.

Stevenson.   1. M. C. Stevenson. The Sia. XI (1889-90) Annual Report Bureau American Ethnology.

2. The Zuñi Indians. XXIII (1901-2) Annual Report Bureau American Ethnology.

Voth. 1. H. R. Voth. The Traditions of the Hopi. Field Columbian Museum Publication 96, Anthropologial Series VIII. 1905.

2. The Oraibi Soyal Ceremony. Field Columbian Museum Publication 55, Anthropological Series III, no. 1. 1901.

3. The Oraibi Powamu Ceremony. Field Columbian Museum Publication 61, Anthropological Series III, no. 2. 1901.